1000 Turn-of-the-Century Houses

With Illustrations and Floor Plans

Herbert C. Chivers

Dover Publications, Inc., Mineola, New York

Bibliographical Note

This Dover edition, first published in 2007, is a very slightly abridged republication of the work originally published as *Artistic Homes* by Herbert C. Chivers, St. Louis, Missouri, in 1910. Most of the original front matter (except the Foreword) and the back matter (except the Index) has been eliminated for space considerations. The house plans have been enlarged and arranged four to a page for this reprint.

International Standard Book Number-13: 978-0-486-45596-9
International Standard Book Number-10: 0-486-45596-3

Manufactured in the United States of America
Dover Publications, Inc., 31 East 2nd Street, Mineola, N.Y. 11501

FOREWORD

"Knowledge is power." It has been said that there are two kinds of knowledge, the one to know facts and the other to know where to find facts. The object of this publication is to enable the prospective home builder to find facts which are equivalent in this case to knowing facts; to put in the hands of the intending builder the power of knowledge – knowledge of what constitutes good plans, design and construction, and a satisfactory whole in a modern home.

The knowledge contained between the two covers of this book represents an outlay of thousands upon thousands of dollars in time and money and embodies the best thoughts and ideas obtainable in the matter of modern home building.

Books and pamphlets along this general line have been published from time to time by theorists, publishers and cheap-plan concerns but it has been the pleasure of the compiler of this work to place in the hands of the public for the first time a practical and understandable work containing the finished ideas of a practicing architect of high rank in his profession.

Osceola design 51014, story heights 10 ft 6. Large spacious rooms, width over all 55 ft. Plans $55.

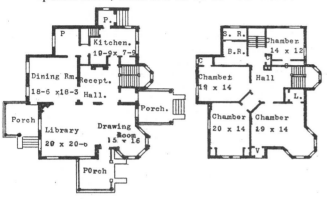

·PREPAREDNESS·HAS BEEN MY SUCCESS

HERBERT C. CHIVERS

ORDER BLANK.
Please fill out the enclosed order and question blank in back of book as near as you can, and I will immediately proceed with the preliminary plans. These plans may probably require changing several times, in order to suit you exactly, and I shall expect prompt replies, so that I can give the matter attention while it is fresh in mind. You possibly have a view of a house which comes near suiting you, or a partly executed plan, which you can send rough tracing of

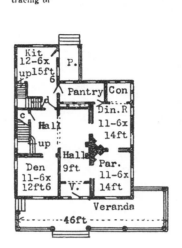

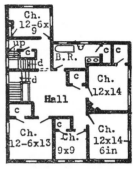

Quannah Design 510 story heights 10 ft. Plans $15.

STYLE IN ARCHITECTURE. —

STYLE in architecture is that original beauty which establishes a standard of excellence in each individual building and gives a sense of indefinable completeness.

Style in architecture is a product of the fancy of the architect which can be simple and economical and still beautiful, or common-place and yet quite expensive.

Style in architecture is something about a building in the way of improvement of outline or detail which makes it attractive and desirable to the casual observer.

Style in architecture is an innovation of the architect who has dared to be original and individual and who can produce a building which will, at the same time, appeal to popular favor.

HOME MAKING

HOME is the word of broadest, deepest and tenderest significance in the English language. The home is the culmination of domestic love and the training school for future generations. The young married couple has no more sacred duty than the building a home which shall reflect their thought and embody their life together.

There are four important factors to be considered in the making of a home, the bank account, the wife, the husband and the architect. These must harmonize or there will be a failure where so much depends upon success.

If there is only a few thousand dollars to be invested there must be no reaching out after the unattainable. The fact must be squarely faced.

It is by the preparation of designs and the making of accurate estimates on the sum named as the limit that I make friends of my clients.

An alliance of this kind becomes something more than a mere business proposition, hence I enter sympathetically into the plans of the home-makers and when they take possession of the house it is with the happy consciousness of having what they wanted, frequently at less outlay than they at first anticipated.

The whims, fancies and idiosyncrasies of home-makers are innumerable. Where it is impossible or ill-advised to gratify them I rarely fail, by the employment of reason and the exercise of tact, to direct the thoughts of my clients into more rational channels. I have never assumed the office of dictator preferring to be looked upon as helper, an expert assistant, whose judgment carries the weight of practical experience.

I do not take the easiest means to please a client until I have first submitted my ideas and it is therefore sometimes necessary to antagonize frankly and fairly the wishes of a client, and not infrequently I have been amused at the trick of memory by which the home maker assumes responsibility for the feature to which he strenuously objected in the very formation of the plans.

Home-makers, as a rule are earnest, honest men and women who, if their confidence is gained will trust implicitly to the wisdom of the architect they employ. I have never given a client cause to consider his trust in my ability as misplaced.

WAUSON COTTAGE.—Design 58M; cost, $3,590 to $3,998; plans, $30. Special features; Cement floor to veranda, attractive library with panelled ceiling and nook and very attractive exterior appearance. See page 65.

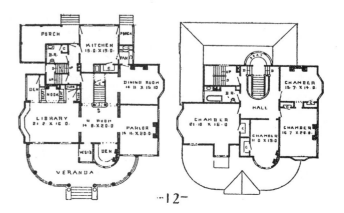

Yakima design 51013, story heights 9 ft 6, width 26 ft.
width over all 40 ft. Plans $15.

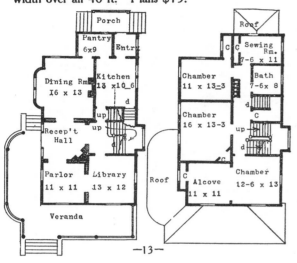

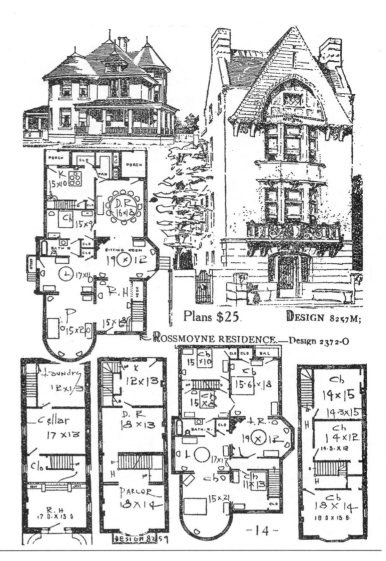

Plans $25. DESIGN 8247M;

ROSSMOYNE RESIDENCE.—Design 2372-O

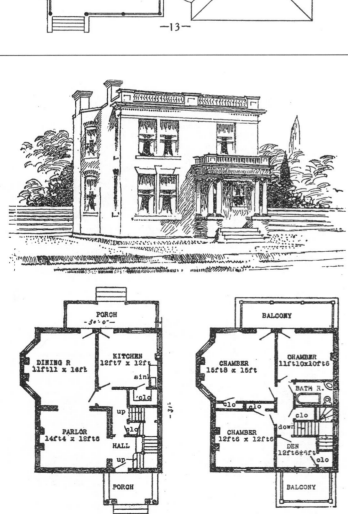

DIXMONT RESIDENCE.—Design 2015-O; cost in frame.
$1,280 to $1,395; in brick, $2,290 to $2,380; plans, $20.

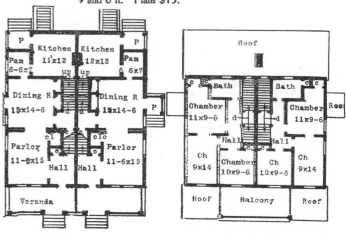

Northbrae design 5016, width 21 ft. story heights
9 and 8 ft. Plans $15.

Double House design 5017, width 34-ft 6, width over all 51-ft. Story heights 9-ft 6 and 8-ft 4. Plans $15. Commodious dining room.

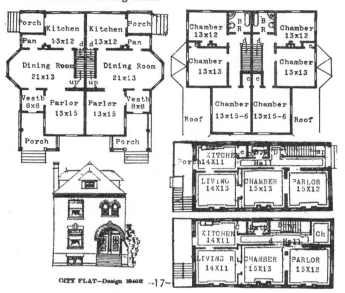

DeForest design 5018, width over all 25 ft, story heights 9-ft 6. Very compact. Plans $15

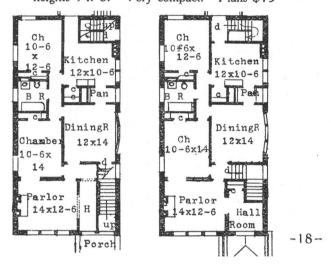

—18—

—17—

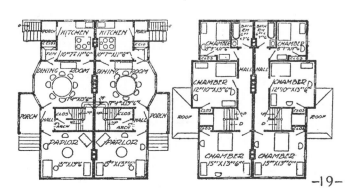

FELDON RESIDENCE.—Hacker Design 100,060-M; size 32x47; cost $1,998 to $2,149; plans, $15.
FELDON RESIDENCE No. 2 Woodington Design, same as above; with 11.6x12 ft. parlor; 13.6x12 ft. dining room and 12x9 kitchen. See page 65.

—19—

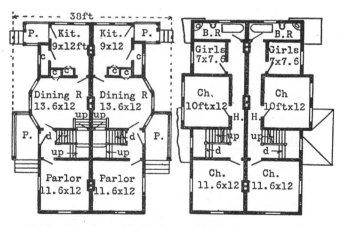

Feldon Residence No. 2 design 5020-A. See page 19 for exterior. Story heights 9-ft. 3 and 9. Plans $15.

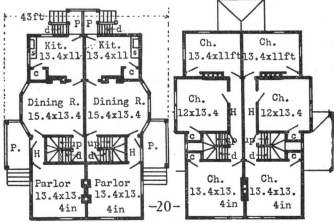

—20—

Feldon Residence No. 3 design 5020-B. See page 19 for exterior. Story heights 9-ft 3 and 9. Plans $15.

San Andreas design 5021, width 29-ft, extreme width 36-ft, story heights 10 and 9-ft 6. Plans $15.

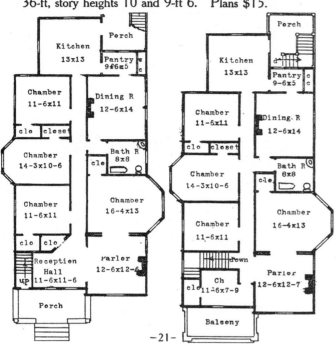

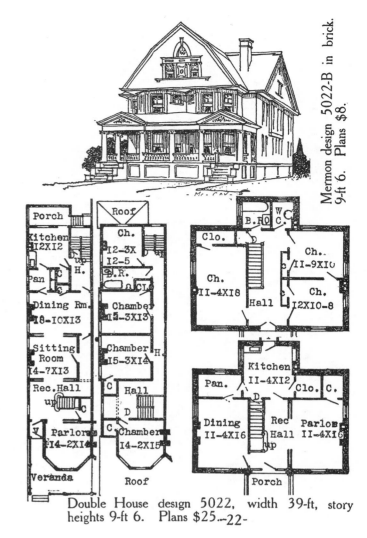

Mermon design 5022-B in brick. 9-ft 6. Plans $8.

Double House design 5022, width 39-ft, story heights 9-ft 6. Plans $25.

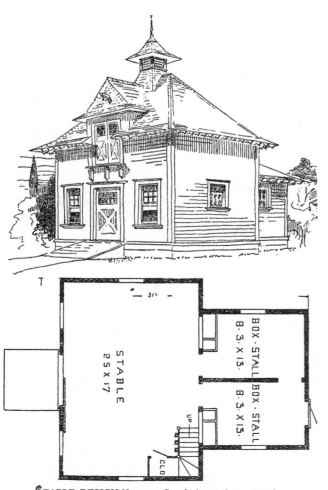

STABLE DESIGN No. 10.—Cost in frame, $250; plans $5.

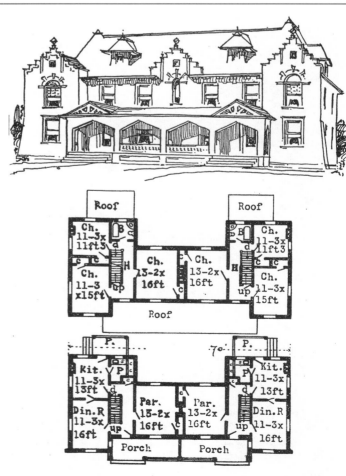

Double House design 5024, story heights 9 and 8-ft 6. Plans $20.

Double House design 5025, story heights 9-ft 6 and 9 ft cut to 5 ft at side walls.   Plans $15.

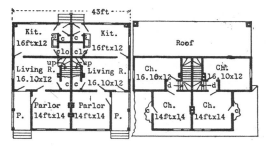

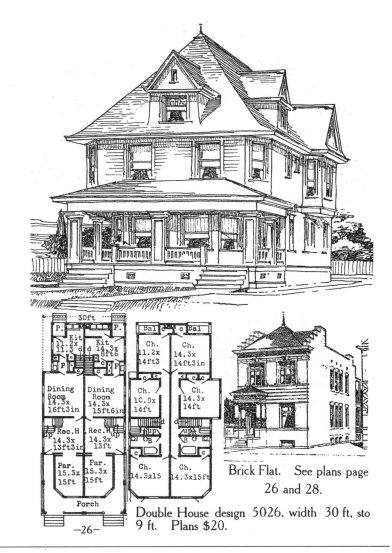

Brick Flat.   See plans page 26 and 28.

Double House design 5026. width 30 ft, sto 9 ft.   Plans $20.

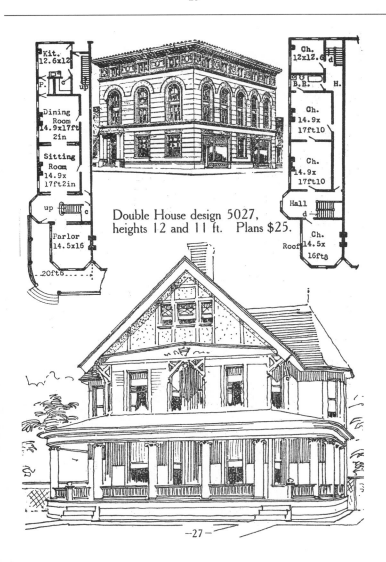

Double House design 5027, heights 12 and 11 ft.   Plans $25.

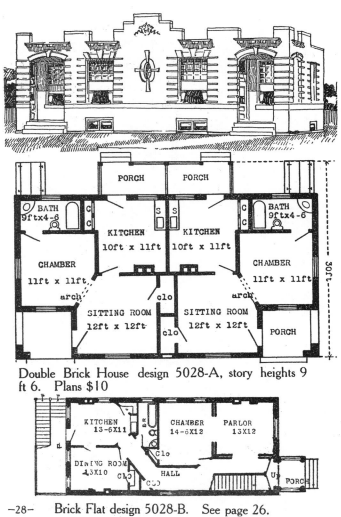

Double Brick House design 5028-A, story heights 9 ft 6. Plans $10

Brick Flat design 5028-B.   See page 26.

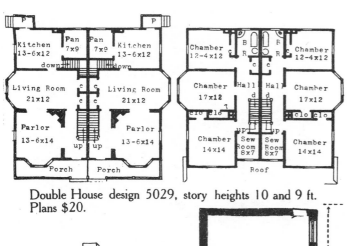

Double House design 5029, story heights 10 and 9 ft.
Plans $20.

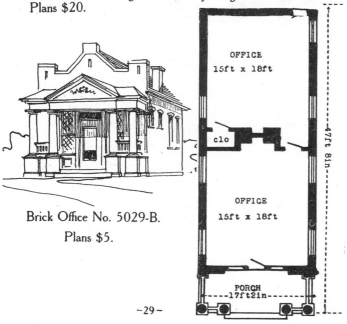

OFFICE
15ft x 18ft

clo

OFFICE
15ft x 18ft

47ft 8in

PORCH
17ft 2in

Brick Office No. 5029-B.

Plans $5.

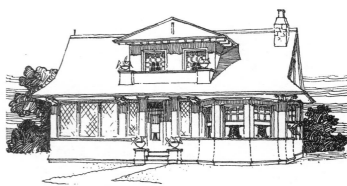

Santa Clara design 5030, width over all 28 ft, story heights 9 ft, cut down at side walls on the second.
Plans $15

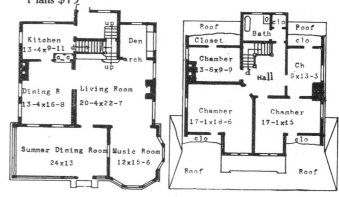

TO THE CONTRACTOR

The contractor who works to my plans finds that they redound to his credit as well as mine. Wise contractors know what it means to have attributed to them a structure attractive in design, complete in every detail and perfectly adapted to the uses for which it is intended. This is possible only when the services of a thoroughly competent architect are secured. It is as much to my interest as to the contractors, that I should work in perfect harmony with him. I receive credit for the design and he for the execution. If either is faulty then both of us are blamed, and we fall together. If both are good then we divide honors, and when the questions are asked, "who planned that building?" and "who constructed that building?" we may well be proud to be named together.

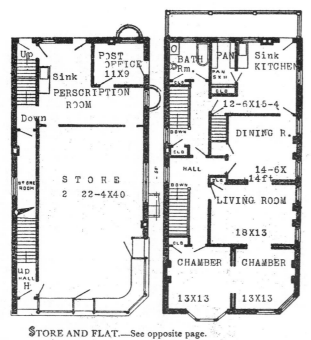

STORE AND FLAT.—See opposite page.

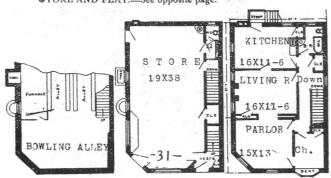

STORE AND FLAT.—Design 1786-O; cost in brick, $5 590; plans, $35. See opposite page.

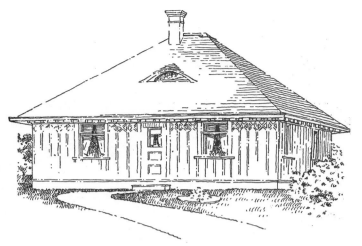

Boulder Creek design 5033, story heights 8-ft. Plans $5.

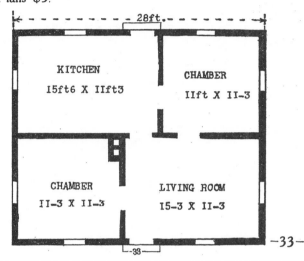

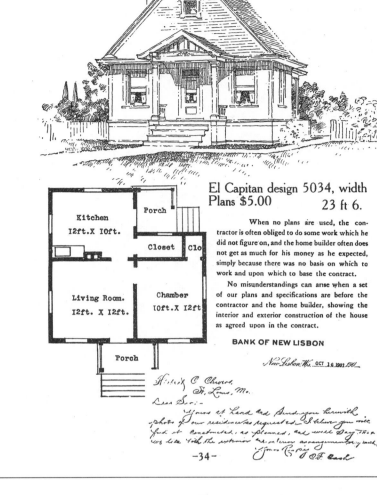

El Capitan design 5034, width 23 ft 6. Plans $5.00

Story 9 ft. 6.

When no plans are used, the contractor is often obliged to do some work which he did not figure on, and the home builder often does not get as much for his money as he expected, simply because there was no basis on which to work and upon which to base the contract.

No misunderstandings can arise when a set of our plans and specifications are before the contractor and the home builder, showing the interior and exterior construction of the house as agreed upon in the contract.

BANK OF NEW LISBON

—33—

—34—

CLARKSDALE COTTAGE.—Design 1796M; in frame, $175 to $200; plans, $5.

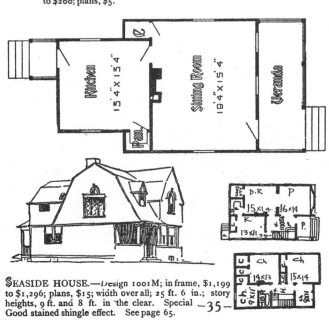

SEASIDE HOUSE.—Design 1001M; in frame, $1,199 to $1,296; plans, $15; width over all; 25 ft. 6 in.; story heights, 9 ft. and 8 ft. in the clear. Special Good stained shingle effect. See page 65.

—35—

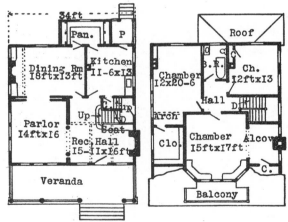

Plans $10.

—How to Send Money—

Remittances can be made by-Post Office Money Order- Express Money Order-Bank Draft-

FAIRVIEW COTTAGE.—Design 1131-O; in frame, $1,292 to $1,498; plans, $10; width over all, 34 ft. 4 in.; story heights, 9 ft. and 8 ft. (full story). Special features: Quaint exposed chimneys at sides; stained shingle design.

—36—

BUFFALO COTTAGE.—Design 1760-N; in frame, $550 to $698; plans, $5; width, 27 ft. by 28 ft. 8 in.; story heights, 8 ft.; neat, clean-cut mouldings and porch ornaments.

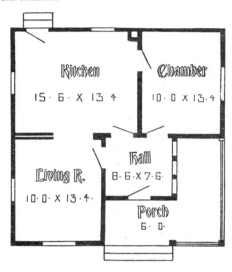

Kitchen
15·6 X 13·4

Chamber
10·0 X 13·4

Living R.
10·0 · 13·4

Hall
8·6 X 7·6

Porch
6·0

—37—

AMBRIDGE COTTAGE.—Design 1968-N; cost in frame, $699 to $798; plans, $7; story heights, 10 ft. Special features: Compact plan arrangement; alcove for bed, allowing front chamber to be used as parlor, with curtain between; clean-cut exterior.

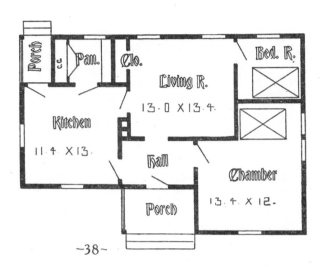

Porch
Pan.
Clo.
Bed. R.

Living R.
13·0 X 13·4

Kitchen
11·4 X 13

Hall

Chamber
13·4 x 12·

Porch

—38—

Orville No. 2 design 5039, story heights 10 and 9-ft. Plans $10.

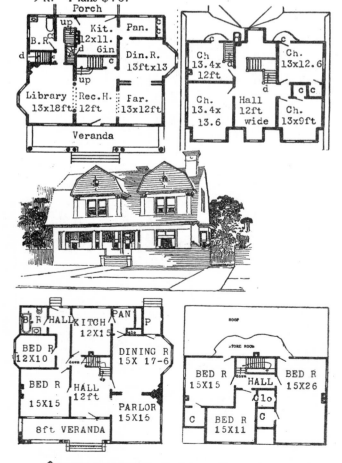

Porch

B.R.
up
Kit.
12x11.
6in
Pan.

Din. R.
13ftx13

up

Library
13x18ft
Rec. H.
12ft
Par.
13x12ft

Veranda

Ch.
13.4x
12ft
Ch.
13x12.6

Ch.
13.4x
13.6
Hall
12ft
wide
Ch.
13x9ft

B. R.
HALL
KITCH
12X15
PAN
P

BED R
12X10

DINING R
15X 17-6

BED R
15X15
HALL
12ft
PARLOR
15X15

8ft VERANDA

ROOF
STORE ROOM

BED R
15X15
HALL
Clo

BED R
15X26

C
BED R
15X11
C

—39— **ORRVILLE COTTAGE.**—Design 1930M, cost in frame $1,492 to $1,580. plans $10. See page 65.

←——— 58ft-6in ———→

Store
Pan.
Kitchen
12x12
P.
B. R.
Clo.
Hall
Roof

Dining R.
17-2x14ft
Hall
Chamber
17-2x14
Chamber
17ftx13
Chamber

Parlor
14x14
Rec.
Hall
12x19
Chamber
14x15ft
Chamber
25-6x12-6

Veranda

Roof

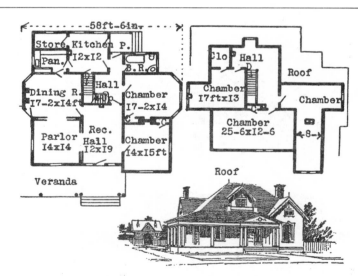

DONNELL COTTAGE.—Design 2356M; $1,298 to $1,499; plans, $10. See page 65.

C
P.
K
11x11
D·R·
12x15
Ch·
L·R·
15x16
H·

C
B R
C
Ch.
11x14
Ch
11x15

Ch.
15x15

—40— **RANDOLPH RESIDENCE.**—Design 1554 M; in frame, $1199 to $1399; plans, $10; width, 28 ft. 6 in. x 29 ft. 6 in.; story heights, 9 ft. in the clear. Special features—Very com-

Temescal design 5041, story heights 10 ft. Plans $10.

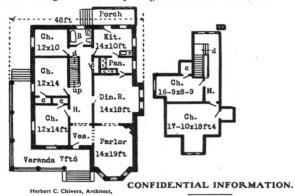

Elmhurst design 5042, story heights 9-ft 6 and 8.
Plans $12.

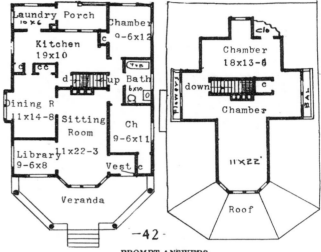

PROMPT ANSWERS.
To insure prompt answers to questions always give design number, page number and name of book and put questions on a separate sheet containing your full address, date, etc., and leaving ample space below each question to plainly write answers. Always use our return envelopes when sent.

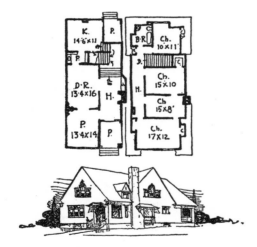

JOSLIN RESIDENCE.—Design 909M: in frame; $1,199 to $1,308; plans $15; width 22 ft. 6 in.; story heights; 9 ft. and 8 ft., cut down by roof to 6 ft. at walls. Special features. Rustic chimney; bay window and seat in hall; combination stairs. See page 65.

WAVERLY RESIDENCE.—Design 1560-O; in frame, $1,198 to $1,389; plans, $15; width, 24 ft. 8 in. by 32 ft., story heights, 9 ft. 6 in. and 8 ft. 6 in. Special Features; Plain neat exterior. See page 65

Woodville design 5044, story heights 10-ft, width 32-ft. Plans $10.

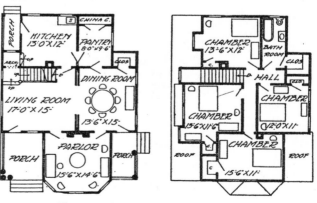

WOODVILLE RESIDENCE.

The plans received from you are perfect in every way. In fact I do not see how you can sell them so cheap Shall call on you for others soon.
Charles Wurt, South Norwalk, Conn.

McWILLIAMS RESIDENCE.—Design 9982-O; in frame, $1,290 to $1,488; plans, $10; width, 31 ft. 4 in. by 34 ft.; story heights, 9 ft.; special features: Semi-circular porch; attractive dormer windows; unique reception hall. Modifications: See index Baraboo plan. We have $10 plan with larger rooms and pier foundation. Modification No. 2, Whitmore design, with porch like this but stairs like Baraboo Cottage and central hall. Modification No. 3, Clark design with fire-place in hall; vestibule; bay in dining-room and exterior and front porch like Baraboo design. (See index).

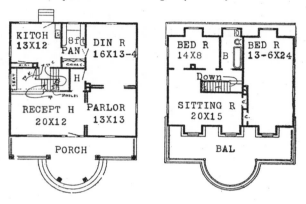

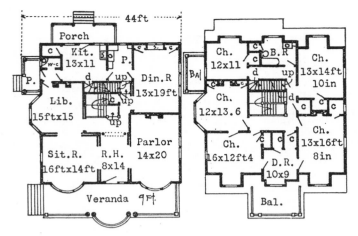

McWilliams Residence No. 4 design 5046, story heights. 9-ft 6, cut down slightly on second floor. Design similar to page 45 and 49. Plans $10.

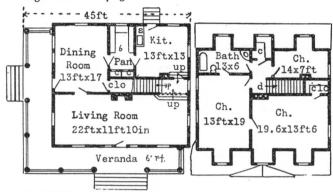

McWilliams Residence No. 5 design 5046, story heights 9-ft and 9-ft cut to 6 at side walls. Exterior similar to page 45. Plans $10.

BARABOO DESIGN NO. 3-O— Southern construction—— Design 192,840-O; in frame, $1,290 to $1,499; (pier foundation); plans, $10; width, 38 ft. 6 in. by 31 ft. 4 in.; story heights, 11 ft., cut down to 8 ft. by roof, forming cove around room. Special features: Large rooms; simple roof treatment. Modifications: See index for other Baraboo cottages. See page 65.

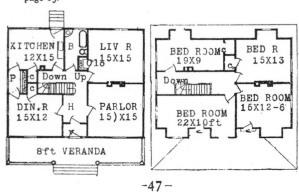

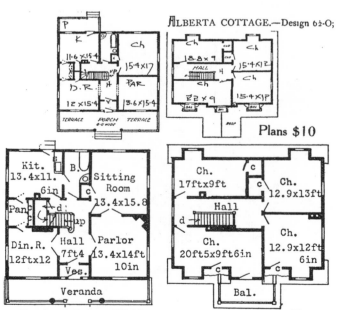

ALBERTA COTTAGE.—Design 62-O;

Plans $10

Baraboo design 5048, exterior similar to page 47. Plans $10.

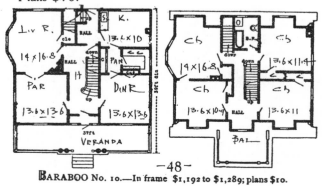

BARABOO No. 10.—In frame $1,192 to $1,289; plans $10.

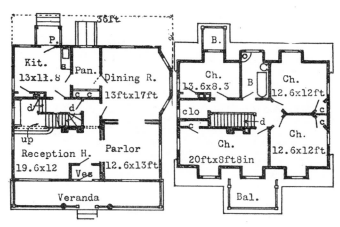

BARABOO COTTAGE. – Design 1639-N; cost in frame, $1,494 to $1,688; plans, $10; width, 34 ft. by 31 ft. 4 in., story heights, 10 ft. and 9 ft. 6 in. Side walls cut down by roof to 8 ft.; cellar, 7 ft. Special features: Economical second story construction. Modifications: Dining-room could be used for sitting-room, with pantry where bath is. Can furnish these plans in stock as shown, or reversed, with the following changes at $10. Baraboo Residence No. 3, Edwards design, full 10 and 8 ft. 4 in. stories; dining-room, 12x15 ft. 4 in.; sitting-room, 15 ft. 4 in. by 17 ft. A very fine plan.

Baraboo design 5050-A, story heights 9-ft 6 and 9. Exterior similar to McWilliams design page 45. Plans $10.

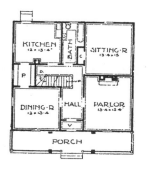

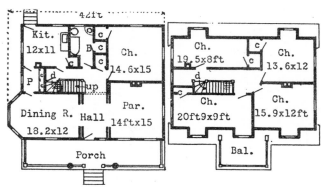

Baraboo design 5050-B, story hts 9-ft and 9-ft cut to 4-ft 6 at side walls. Exterior similar to page 49. Plans $10.

WACO COTTAGE.—Design 2169-O; in frame, $390 to $497; plans, $5; width, 29 ft. 10 in. by 24 ft. 2 in.; width over all, 31 ft. 10 in.; story heights, 10 ft. Can furnish this plan in stock with kitchen addition in rear of living room. Waco No. 2. Spangler design, same as Waco, with 15x13 parlor, 13x14 living room, with rear stairs going up from living room, with space for two rooms above. Waco No. 3. Lohr design; same as Waco, with 10 ft. 6x10 one-story kitchen addition. See page 65.

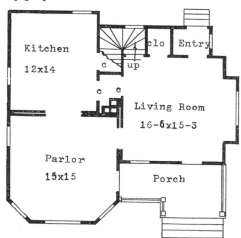

Waco design 5052-A, 10-ft story. See opposite page. Plans $5.

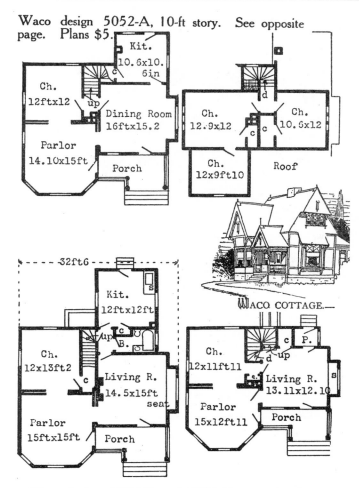

DO US A FAVOR
By showing this catalogue to your neighbors contemplating building and when they order of us, we will send you a suitable and appropriate remembrance of your friendly efforts in our behalf.

Waco design 5052-B and 5052-C, story heights 10-ft, cut to 8-ft 6 in story. Plans $5.

Strang Design 9080-O; cost $1090; full story heights, 9 and 8 ft.; plans $5.

Harthorn Design 9082M; cost in frame, $692 to $840; plans $15.

~Insurance~

Immediately upon receipt of information from you that your house has been destroyed by fire, either totally or partially, we will forward you, free of cost, a duplicate set of plans and specifications,

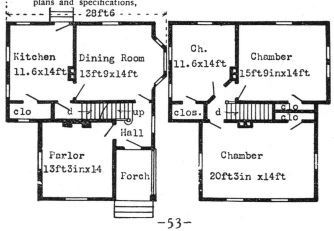

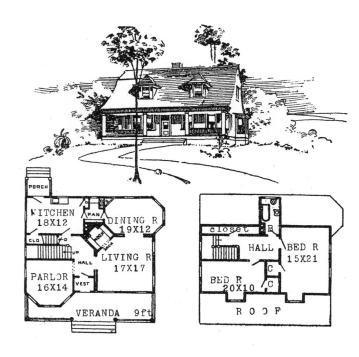

HORNSBORO COTTAGE.—Design 2421M; cost in frame $1,492 to $1,560; plans $15. See page 65.

I consider I have the best arranged house in this county, and it is so pronounced by every one that visits me. I am more than pleased with the construction of same. and your courteous and prompt method of doing business has met with my general approval. Yours with respect,

J. KESSLER, General Merchandise.

DERBY RESIDENCE.—Design 1536M; in frame, $1252 to $1480: plans, $10; width, 24.6 x 41 ft.; story heights, 9 ft, 6 in. (full story). Special features: Pleasing side-gable effect; parlor well ventilated; reception hall, 19 x 15 ft., with fireplace. See page 65.

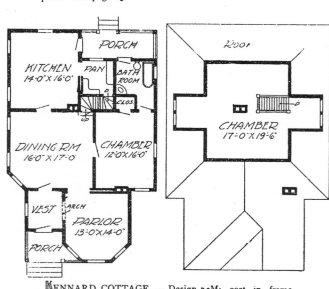

KENNARD COTTAGE. — Design 73M; cost in frame, $1,092 to $1,180; plans, $10

ALBEMARLE COTTAGE.— Design 9067-O; in frame, $1,200 fo $1,499; plans, $5; story heights, 10 ft. See index for Kennard and Garber plans. See page 65.

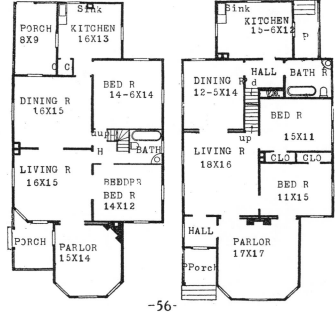

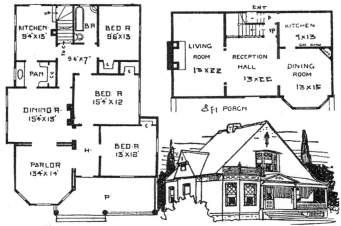

NEW LONDON COTTAGE.—Design 1408-O; in frame, $1,200 to $1,498; plans, $10; width, 34 ft. 10 in. by 41 ft. 6 in.; story heights, 10 and 9 ft., cut down at walls to 8 ft. Special features: Broad attractive front. See page 65.

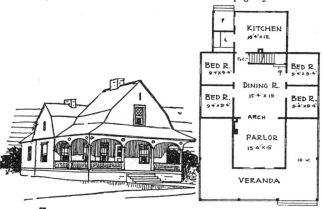

TARRYTOWN COTTAGE.—Design 2145-O; in frame, $850 to $950; plans, $10; width over all, 36 ft.; story heights, 10 ft. and 8 ft. attic. Special features: Large central space 34 ft. long. See page 65. —57—

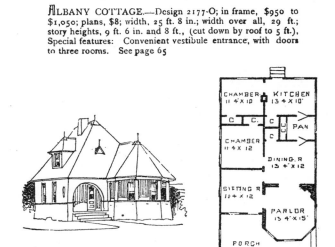

ALBANY COTTAGE.—Design 2177-O; in frame, $950 to $1,050; plans, $8; width, 25 ft. 8 in.; width over all, 29 ft.; story heights, 9 ft. 6 in. and 8 ft., (cut down by roof to 5 ft.), Special features: Convenient vestibule entrance, with doors to three rooms. See page 65

—58—

BALTIMORE COTTAGE.—Rumble design 2234-O; in frame, $750 to $850; plans, $5; width, 25 ft. 8 in. by 36 ft. 4 in.; story heights, 9 ft. 6 in. Special features:

A special feature of my buildings is; they are not disappointing when built, but pleasing in general appearance. This is due to starting right with the important preliminary plans

If interested in the erection of a building, for either private or public use, you can secure as good or better services of this office than elsewhere, and at no more cost for plans

HANOVER COTTAGE.—Design 7M; in frame, $400 to $498; plans, $7; story heights, 9 ft. 6 in. and 8 ft. Special features: Neat roof arrangement. See page 65

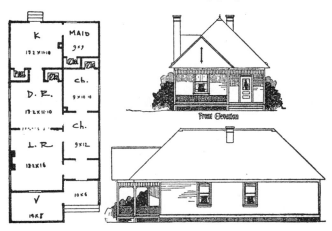

HARTVILLE COTTAGE.—Design 6029-O; in frame, $500 to $696; plans, $5; width over all, 24 ft.; story heights, 10 ft. Special features: Plain, neat exterior and large veranda. See page 65.

—59—

Many have little or no conception of the value of a competent architect's services and are content with merely the scale plans, without the vitally-important detail drawings

When you build, make it attractive, obviate that everlasting sameness in style. Consult an architect of ability, large practice, modern methods and ideas. It is money well-spent

CADMUS COTTAGE.—Design 2391M, cost in frame, $1,092 to $1,348; plans, $15. See page 65.

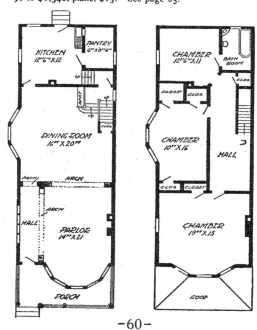

—60—

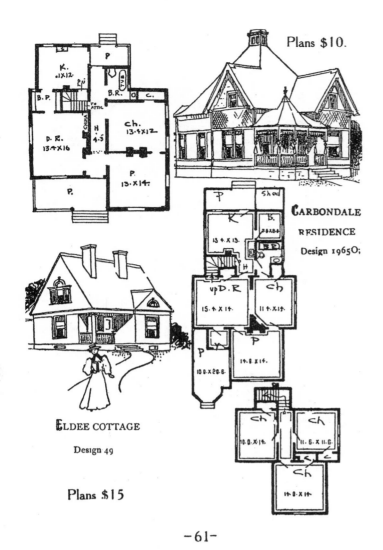

Plans $10.

CARBONDALE
RESIDENCE

Design 19650;

ELDEE COTTAGE

Design 49

Plans $15

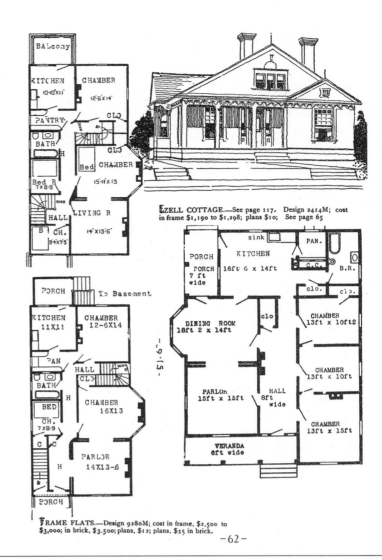

EZELL COTTAGE.—See page 117. Design 2414M; cost in frame $1,190 to $1,298; plans $10; See page 65

FRAME FLATS.—Design 9280M; cost in frame, $2,500 to $3,000; in brick, $3,500; plans, $12; plans, $35 in brick.

SPOKANE COTTAGE.—Design 1058-O; in frame, $898 to $994; plans, $7; width over all, 29ft.; story heights, 10 ft. See page 65.

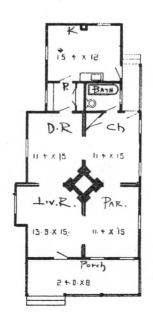

DOES AN ARCHITECT PAY?

An architect's plans are the greatest economy in a building operation, and the cheaper the building the greater is the importance of plans.

For instance take it on a $1,000 basis, for cheap but convenient illustration, what is $35 or 3½ per cent for accurately-drawn plans, and details of construction and carefully-worded specifications, when in the first place the style and dignity which an architect-planned house gives is 500 per cent greater than that of the commonplace amateur-planned house.

WALCOTT RESIDENCE.—Design 100,012M; cost $1935 to $2128; plans, $20; size 24.6x36; special features: nook in hall, large front room, side entrance.

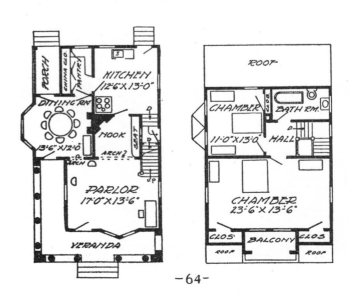

MODERATE COST HOUSES.

PLANS which refer back to this page have 18-inch stone or 13-inch brick foundation walls, as desired, with cellar under the main portion of house where cellar stairs are shown and flue for furnace where practical, with general good finish throughout. Plumbing is included where shown. Story heights average 10 feet.

All rooms are plastered and finished with yellow pine, or native wood, in natural finish. All mouldings are detailed in stock patterns, and details of porches, cornices, etc., are very simple in construction. It is important to have the entire construction of a building clearly shown by large scale or full-size drawings. It assists the workmen on the building, for they do not then have to ponder over problems of construction. The plans are all neatly and accurately drawn, and above all, carefully figured, giving dimensions of glass, location and size of doors, windows, etc., and all information necessary for the successful guidance of the builder.

It costs no more to put style into a house than it does to have it commonplace and as long as discretion is used in the conomical and practical selection of mouldings, ornaments, etc., there is no danger of running up the cost of construction.

Carefully-drawn plans, details and specifications should be prepared for structures of all kinds. Where you have complete plans, you then know that all contractors are figuring on the same basis, and when you do get a reasonably low bid you are assured it is not for inferior work. The difference in estimates here given are supposed to cover the total costs in different localities, giving the lowest and highest probable costs, and we therefore give no absolute guarantees as to the actual cost, for prices are regulated more or less by the amount of competition there is among builders. All estimates are based on the schedule of prices in front pages If you have plans you can always get reasonably fair bids. At the prices given for stock-plans, no changes or modifications are included, but we will furnish plans reversed, if desired, or will change any floor plan for $2.75 extra and any elevation or exterior view for $2.50, or will make special plans for 2 percent. on cost of building, or $25.00 for houses of less than $1,250 in cost.

GURNEE RESIDENCE.—Design 2269M;

Plans $25.

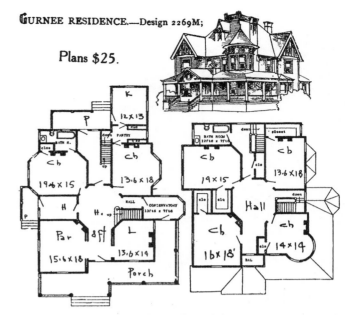

THE COMPETITIVE IDEA.

Many presume that an architect should be expected to enter into work in competition. This is wrong. An architect should no more be expected to "give samples of his work as you might say, than a lawyer, a physician, or any other professional man. This is unjust for the reason that important ideas are given in the preliminary plans, and no architect will care to give his best ideas or spend the time and study in competitive work as he will when he knows he will be paid for his services, if satisfactory. Furthermore the competitive architect usually takes the easiest means to please, which does not always mean the best thing for the client.

I would much rather take work at half price and have a positive order, than take any chance of losing an order; as an architect does when he enters into work competitively. I take all work on condition, that I give entire satisfaction in the preliminary or pencil plans, before making the completed work, or no pay. Where architectural work is done on this arrangement, it facilitates matters all around. The client saves time by concentrating his time with one architect, and the architect, does likewise in return,

---

RICHMOND COTTAGE.—Design 1766-O; in frame, $798 to $892; plans, $5; width, 24 ft. 2 in.; story heights, 9 ft. 6 in. (cut down by roof to 4 ft. at walls.) Special features: Economical flue connections, and 11 ft. verandas. See page 65.

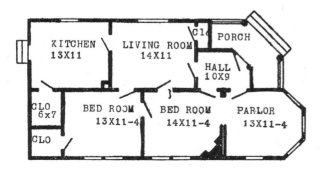

The plans received of you this summer, gave entire satisfaction. I have no photo of house yet, but will mail you one later.
H. STAKMER, Owattonna, Minn.

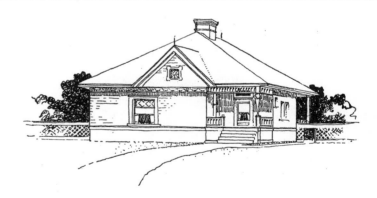

LAUREL COTTAGE.—Design 1942M; in frame. $569 to $650; plans, $10; width over all, 24 ft. 6 in.; story heights, 10 ft. Special features: Compact plan, good flue connections. See page 65.

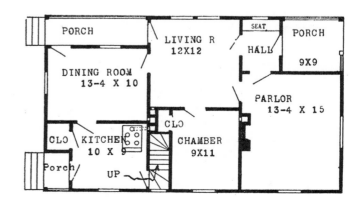

I must say; you put convenience and style into a plan.
CHARLES R. ROBB. Powhattan Point, Mo.

KENNETH RESIDENCE.—Design 100,613M; plans, $15; cost, $1556 to $1698; size, 24,6 x 36.6; special features; conservatory back of dining-room, semi-circular balcony in front. See page 65.

"My house, my house, tho thou art small,
Thou art to me the Escurial."

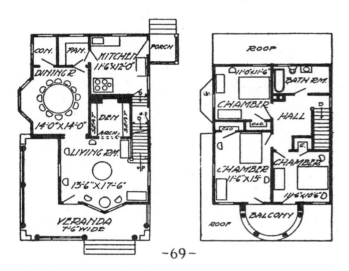

-69-

In dealing with this office, DISTANCE is no barrier to conscientious dealings. I can not afford to advise you unrelibaly. My office is just as close to you as your nearest mail-box.

JUNEAU COTTAGE.—Design 1964M; in frame, $1299 to $1480; plans, $10; width, 30 ft. 8 in. by 48 ft. 9 in.; story heights, 9 ft.; with second story walls cut down by roof to 5 ft. See page 65.

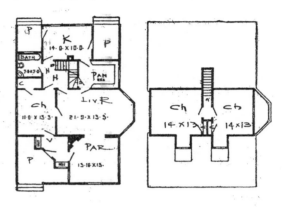

-70-

CHAGRIN FALLS COTTAGE.—Design 1776-O: in frame. $380 to $450; plans, $5. See page 65.

Chagrin Falls No. 2 design 5071, story heights 10-ft. Plans $5. Neat attractive exterior.

-71-

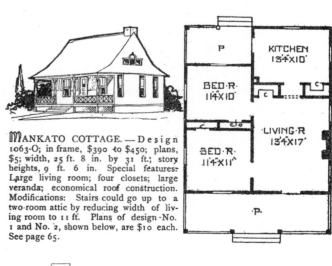

MANKATO COTTAGE.—Design 1063-O; in frame, $390 to $450; plans, $5; width, 25 ft. 8 in. by 31 ft.; story heights, 9 ft. 6 in. Special features: Large living room; four closets; large veranda; economical roof construction. Modifications: Stairs could go up to a two-room attic by reducing width of living room to 11 ft. Plans of design No. 1 and No. 2, shown below, are $10 each. See page 65.

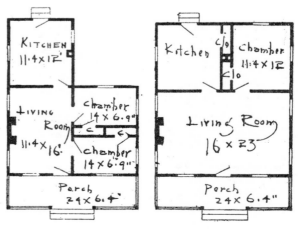

-72-

BATMER COTTAGE.—Design 100189O; in frame, $450 to $550 plans, $7; width, 21 ft. 2 in by 42 ft. 8 in.; story heights, 10 ft. Style: Plain exterior; ordinary plaining-mill design. We have this with parlor 16x16 ft. 6 in.; sitting-room 13x15 ft.; chamber 10x15 ft.; dining-room 13x16 ft 2 in., kitchen 11x13 ft.; story heights, 10 ft. See page 65.

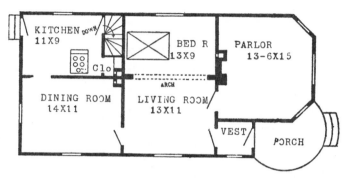

The plans and specifications furnished specially for my residence were said to be very complete. The building is now complete.
REV. W. D. STEVENS, Scio, Iowa.

CLIFFORD COTTAGE. — Design 100,203M; in frame, $675 to $790; plans, $7; width over all, 39 ft. 8 in.; story heights, 10 ft. Style: Ordinary plaining-mill design and ornamentation. Will make stylish exterior for $10 additional. See page 65.

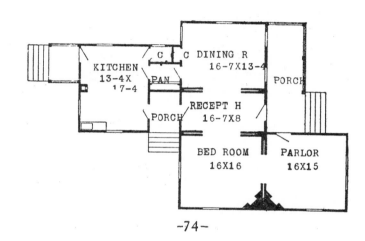

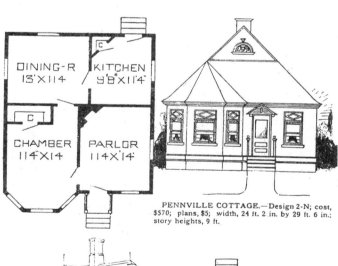

PENNVILLE COTTAGE.—Design 2-N; cost, $570; plans, $5; width, 24 ft. 2 in. by 29 ft. 6 in.; story heights, 9 ft.

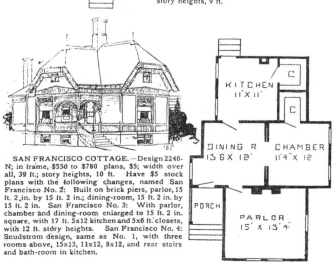

SAN FRANCISCO COTTAGE.—Design 2240-N; in frame, $550 to $780 plans, $5; width over all, 39 ft.; story heights, 10 ft. Have $5 stock plans with the following changes, named San Francisco No. 2: Built on brick piers, parlor, 15 ft. 2 in. by 15 ft. 2 in.; dining-room, 15 ft. 2 in. by 15 ft. 2 in. San Francisco No. 3: With parlor, chamber and dining-room enlarged to 15 ft. 2 in. square, with 17 ft. 5x12 kitchen and 5x6 ft. closets, with 12 ft. story heights. San Francisco No. 4: Snudstrom design, same as No. 1, with three rooms above, 15x13, 11x12, 8x12, and rear stairs and bath-room in kitchen.

MUSKEGON COTTAGE.—Design 2056-N; in frame, $450 to $550; plans, $5; width, 24 ft. 2 in. by 29 ft. 6 in.; story heights, 10 ft. Special features: Neat exterior, the details of this cottage are very complete and insure an attractive building.

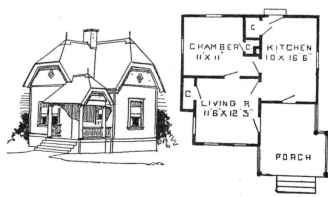

ROSSDALE COTTAGE.—Design 1982-N; in frame, $480 to $690; plans, $10.

I found much pleasure in looking over your "Artistic Homes."
MRS. C. R. TIDINGS, Ocala, Fla.

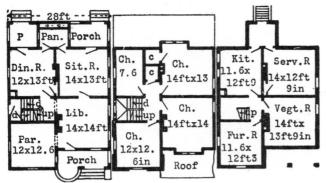

Jamestown Cottage No. 2, design 5077. See design page 78, width 28, story heights 9 and 9-ft. Plans $10.

J AMESTOWN COTTAGE.—Design 9076-N; cost in frame, $1,124 to $1,298; plans, $10; width, 26 ft. 2 in.; story heights, 9 ft. 6 in. Special features: Attractive stained shingle effect; plain simple and easy to construct. A good corner-lot design.

HERBERT C. CHIVERS - ARCHITECT

Plans $15.

ELMIRA COTTAGE.—Design 1558-O; in frame, $1276 to $1479; width 29ft. 4 in.; story heights, 9 ft. 6 in. (full second story). Special features: den or conservatory to dining-room Porte—cochere; side entrance; in expensive tower. See page 05.

House came out all right as per plans furnished by you. Am pleasantly surprised, with general appearance.—D. M. Spicer, Tiffany, Wis.

—77—

—78—

It costs no more to embody style, convenience and economy in plan arrangement than when it is commonplace. Make a wise selection of your architect and depend on results

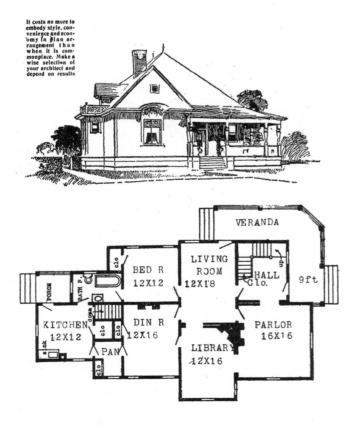

PINO COTTAGE.—Design 2402M; cost in frame $1,292 to $1,380; plans $10. See page 65.

—79—

My ideas are not cheap ideas and therefore I cannot usually enter into work competitively, as many do, at a possible loss, but will guarantee entire satisfaction in plan arrangement

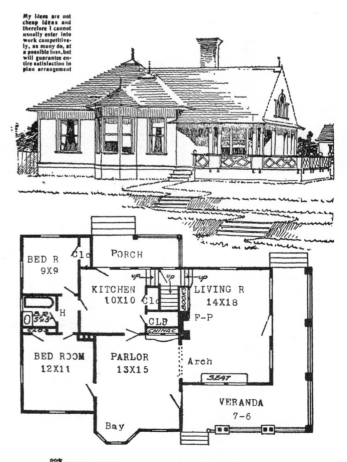

MARCO COTTAGE.—Design 2349M; cost, $998 to $1,098; plans, $10; special features: Convenient bath-room arrangement; pleasant out-look from main rooms. See page 65.

—80—

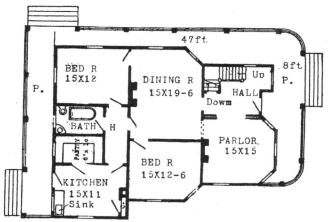

KERSHAW COTTAGE.— Design 2407-O; cost in frame $1,492 to $1,560; plans $10. See page 65.

I am in possession of one of your books to-wit: "Artistic Homes," and am well pleased with the book.—P. M. Beam, Poteau, Ark.

—81—

PENFIELD COTTAGE.—Design 100,035-N; cost, $1,592 to $1,642; width, 42 ft.; story heights, 1st 10 ft.; cellar, 7 ft. under rear of house. Special features: Large rooms and bath; pleasant outlook to front chamber; plenty of closets; large attractive porch.

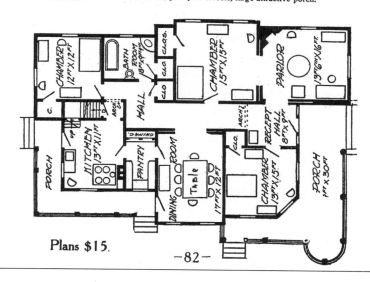

Plans $15.

—82—

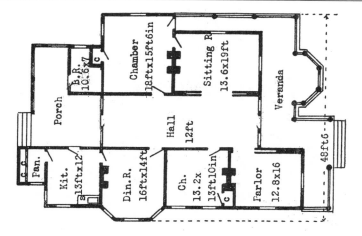

Corapolis Cottage No. 2 design 5083-A, story 12 ft. See design page 84. Plans $15.

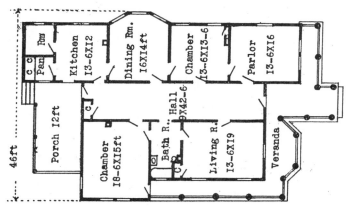

Corapolis Cottage No. 3 design 5083-B story 10 ft, see design page 84. Plans $15.

—83—

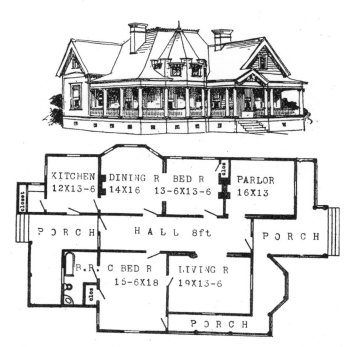

CORAPOLIS COTTAGE.—Design 2248M; cost in frame, $1,292 to $1,380; plans, $15. See page 65.

My residence is considered the handsomest in the city, and the local papers have commented on it favorably. The house shows up even better than the original perspective view which you sent.

A. F. BAUER, Ft. Madison, Iowa.

We are very much pleased with the house and wish to thank you for the interest taken by you while we were building same. Your plans and specifications were perfectly satisfactory.

FRANK A. LEAVENS, (Paper Makers' Supplies), Neenah, Wis.

—84—

CLINTON COTTAGE.—Design 1767-O; in frame, $998 to
$1,098; plans, $10; width over all, 31 ft. 4 in.; story heights,
11 ft. Special features: Convenient bath-room. See page 65.

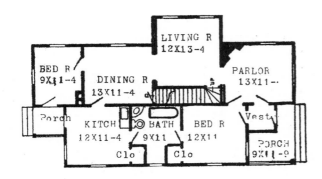

After having plans furnished by you for my house I feel it due you and your
work to make some statement relative to same. I found plans and specifications absolutely correct in every respect. I could have paid twice what I did
for plans and then found them a great saving of time, material and money.
It isn't worth while, though, for me to state that I am well pleased with your
work, for you will find enclosed check and order for a second plan which will
demonstrate the fact. REV. F. H. QUINN, Fayette, Mo.

BLYVILLE COTTAGE.—Design 100,034-O; size 34x51;
cost, $1,000 to $1,200; story heights, 10 ft. Special features:
Pleasant outlook to chambers, and spacious porch; space for
one large room above. See page 65.

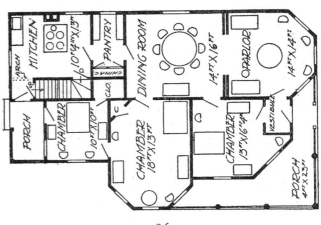

PACOLET COTTAGE.—Design 2427M; cost in frame
$1,190 to $1,285; plans $10. See page 65.

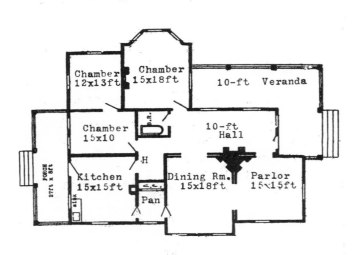

GAYLORD COTTAGE.—Design 847M; in frame, $1,798
to $1,809; plans, $15; width, 30 ft.; story heights, 9 ft. 6 in.
and 8 ft. 6 in. (full story at tower one room above). Special
features: Simple but attractive exterior, Tower would look
well of stained shingles, with corner windows and white
trimmings. It has a swell appearance. The seat in reception hall looks well. See page 65.

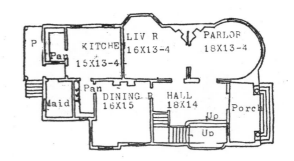

WINSTON COTTAGE.—Design 2398-N; cost in frame, $1,390 to $1,482; plans, $10. Special features: Large rooms; attractive dormer windows on roof; side entrance to dining-room; neat square vestibule; large rear porch.

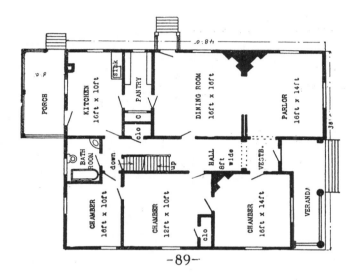

RUTHERFORD COTTAGE.—Design 2406M: cost in frame $1,180 to $1,292; plans $10. See page 65.

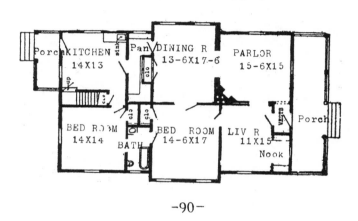

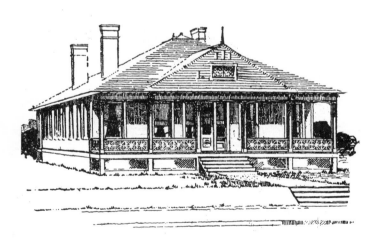

DYSON COTTAGE.—Design 2413M; cost in frame $1,180 to $1,240; plans $15. See page 65.

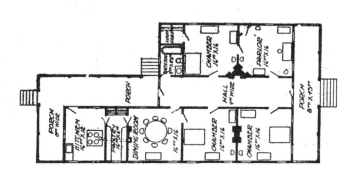

Having a special department for the planning of low-cost houses it is reasonable to presume that you can secure better and quicker services of this office than can be had elsewhere

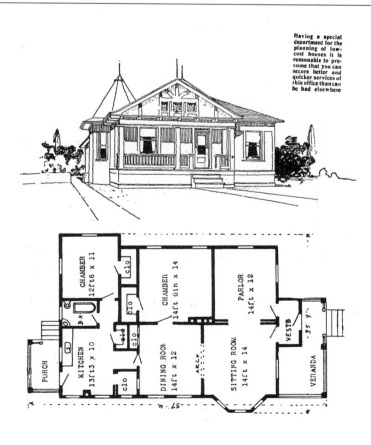

RAYWOOD COTTAGE.—Design 2404-N; cost in frame, $1,030 to $1,240; plans, $10; neat, clean-cut exterior.

SARATOGA COTTAGE.—Design 1998-O; in frame, $990 to $1,000; plans, $8; width, 33 ft. 8 in. by 28 ft.; story heights, 9 ft. 6 in. and 8 ft. Special features: Bay in parlor. See index for Saratoga plan revised. See page 65.

FORETHOUGHT IN BUILDING

Man is king of all out-doors,
Fields and factories, and stores...
Woman has her realm inside,
Where she reigns with dainty pride.

Build of marble, brick or wood,
But build woman's kingdom good.
Let her Royal Highness choose
Which of Chivers' plans to use.

Have them changed to suit her taste,
Everything necessary, yet nothing waste
Treat your wife as if you were
Kingly consort unto her.

I have completed my house from the plans purchased from you last spring. They worked out very nicely. Every one who sees my house thinks it the most convenient one they were ever in. I thank you for your kind attention in the past and wish you future success.   Park F. Yengling, Salem, O. (Second unsolicited testimonial.)

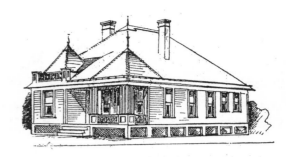

ROGERVILLE COTTAGE.—Design 7441-O; in frame, $1,098 to $1,189; plans, $5; width, 41 ft. by 57 ft.; story heights, 11 ft.; brick pier foundation. Special features: Wide central hall, large rear porch. See page 65.

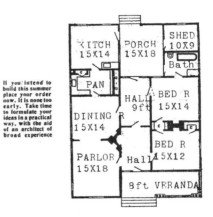

If you intend to build this summer place your order now, it is none too early. Take time to formulate your ideas in a practical way, with the aid of an architect of broad experience

I am satisfied with my house. I had it built according to plans and I believe that I have the nicest, best arranged and most convenient house in our city.   W. M. STIGALL, Stewartsville, Mo.

CORWIN COTTAGE.—Design 100,032-O; size 29x56; cost $1,099 to $1,296; story heights, 1st 10 ft., cellar 6 ft. 6 in. Special features: Well-ventilated parlor, pleasant outlook, convenient bath-room, large closets. See page 65.

Plans $10.

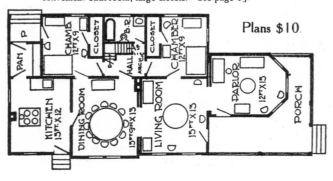

DELVEY COTTAGE.—Design 1789-N; cost in frame, $1,392 to $1,440; plans, $10.

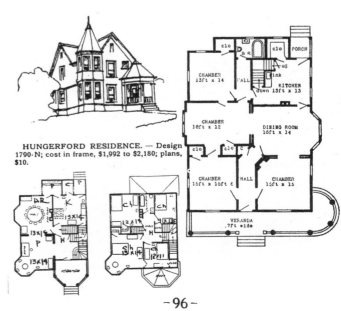

HUNGERFORD RESIDENCE. — Design 1790-N; cost in frame, $1,992 to $2,180; plans, $10.

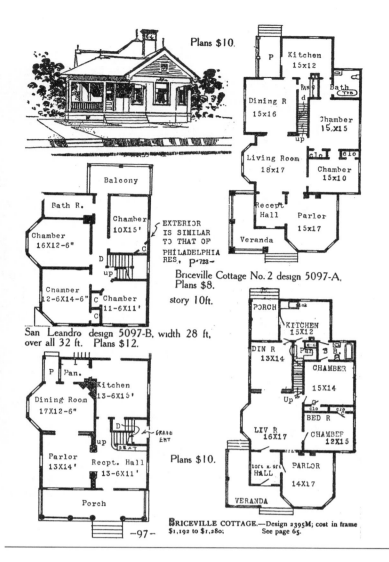

Plans $10.

Kitchen 15x12

Dining R 15x16

Pan d

Bath TUB

Chamber 15.X15

up

Living Room 18x17

Chamber 15x10

Balcony

Bath R.

Chamber 10X15'

Chamber 16X12-6"

EXTERIOR IS SIMILAR TO THAT OF PHILADELPHIA RES. P·723·

C

D up

Chamber 12-6X14-6"

C Chamber 11-6X11'

C

Briceville Cottage No. 2 design 5097-A. Plans $8.

story 10ft.

San Leandro design 5097-B, width 28 ft. over all 32 ft. Plans $12.

Recept Hall

Parlor 15x17

Veranda

PORCH

KITCHEN 15X12

P Pan.

Kitchen 13-6X15'

DIN R 13X14

Pan 3 B.

Dining Room 17X12-6"

CHAMBER 15X14

D up GRADE ENT

Up

clo clo

BED R

Parlor 13X14'

Recpt. Hall 13-6X11'

Plans $10.

LIV R 16X17

CHAMBER 12X15

10ft x 9ft HALL

PARLOR 14X17

Porch

VERANDA

BRICEVILLE COTTAGE.—Design 2395M; cost in frame $1,192 to $1,280; See page 65.

-97-

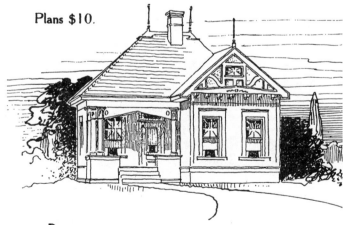

KITCHEN 15ft6 x 11ft6in

BATH ROOM

down

CHAMBER 13ft6 x 10

up

CHAMBER 13ft6 x 9

clo

PANTRY

PORCH

DINING ROOM 15ft x 12

SITTING ROOM 14ft x 13ft

PARLOR 17ft x 13

PORCH

Plans $10.

WELLSBORO COTTAGE.—Design 1785-N; cost in frame, $1,090 to $1,240; plans, $10; story heights, 10 ft. 6 in. Special features: Large bay-shaped parlor; chambers convenient to sitting-room. Bath-room could be shortened and linen closet placed in end.

-98-

I must say; you put convenience and style into a plan.
CHARLES R. ROBB, Powhatan Point, Ohio.

Purchasers of 1024-page book will require no other, as it is the largest published. Indispensable to any one intending to build.

Plans $10.

CANTON COTTAGE.—Design 1768-O; in frame, $498 to $697; plans; $10 width, 30 ft. 6 in. by 39 ft. 4 in.; story heights. 10 ft. Special features: Compact combination of rooms; large parlor. The working plans are very neat and attractive in design. See page 65.

CLO.

BED ROOM 12-4X13

KITCHEN 12 X 14

PARLOR 13 X 17

LIVING R 12-4X16

PORCH PAN

VEST PORCH 8X8

-99

Plans $10.

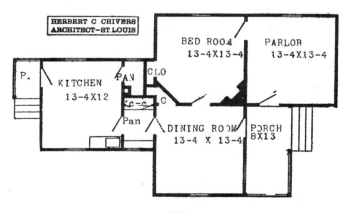

DUNBAR COTTAGE.—Design 100191-O; in frame, $550 to $680; plans, $10 width, 28 ft. 2 in.; story heights, 10 ft. See page 65.

HERBERT C CHIVERS ARCHITECT-ST LOUIS

BED ROOM 13-4X13-4

PARLOR 13-4X13-4

P.

KITCHEN 13-4X12

PAN

CLO

C

c-c C

Pan

DINING ROOM 13-4 X 13-4

PORCH 8X13

-100-

Plans were all right and am well pleased. HARRY A BROOKS, Oto, Ia.

Plans $5.

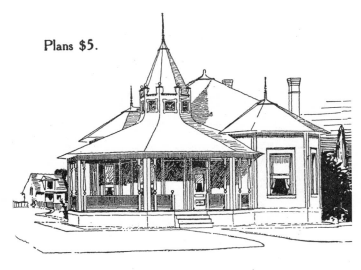

DE SOTO COTTAGE.—Design 72-N; cost, $798 to $899; size, 35 ft. by 52 ft. Very attractive design; plans, $5. Special features: Attractive, octagonal porch; bay-shaped parlor and chamber.

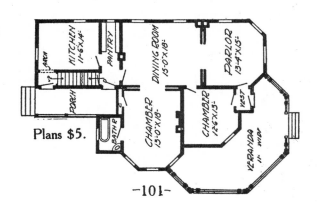

Plans $5.

—101—

DeSoto Cottage No. 2 design 5102-A. See page 101. Story heights 10 ft. Plans $5.

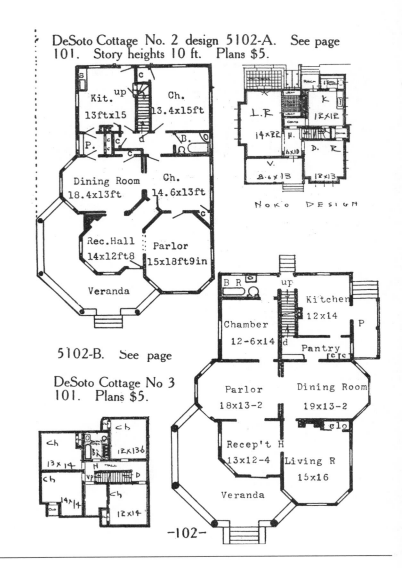

5102-B. See page

DeSoto Cottage No 3
101. Plans $5.

—102—

PAPINSVILLE COTTAGE.—Design 7142-N; in frame, $1,492 to $1785; plans, $15; width, 27 ft. 4 in.; story heights, 9 ft. 6 in. and 8 ft. 6 in. Special features: Attractive design. Plan No. 2, same as above, but reversed, with sitting-room 13.4x13 ft.; parlor 13 ft. 6x15 ft. 6 in.; bath-room connects also with kitchen, with 4x6 ft. kitchen closet back of bath-room and stairs to attic from dining-room and stairs to basement.

Plans $15.

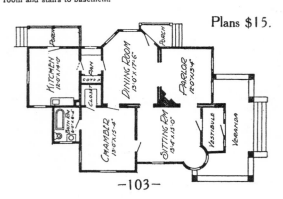

—103—

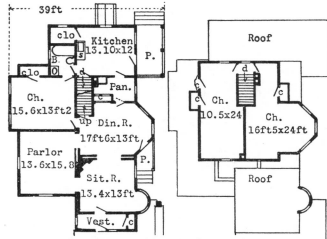

Papinsville Cottage No. 2 design 5104, story heights 10 and 8 ft cut to 5 ft 6 side walls above. Plans $15.

Plans $15.

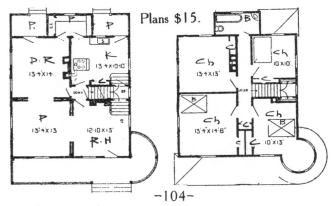

—104—

RICHVILLE RESIDENCE.—Design 9149 M; in frame, $1490 to $1596; plans, $15; width, 28 ft. 2 in. x 29 ft. width

ROCHESTER COTTAGE.—Design 1742-O; in frame, $879 so $998; plans $10; width, 34 ft. 6 in. by 39 ft.; width over all, 46 ft.; two rooms, 15 ft. 8 in. by 18 ft. and 15 ft. 8 in. by 12 ft., above.; story heights, 9 ft. 4 in.; 9 ft. in the clear. Special features; Stone work in front comes up to window sill, all is corbelled-out for oriel window, giving a substantial effect. See page 65.

Plans $20.

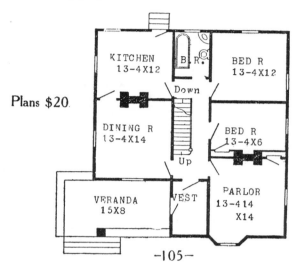

KITCHEN 13-4X12
B.R.
BED R 13-4X12
Down
DINING R 13-4X14
BED R 13-4X6
Up
VERANDA 15X8
VEST
PARLOR 13-414 X14

SUNFIELD COTTAGE.—Design 1780-N; cost in frame, $1,392 to $1,480; plans, $10. Special features: Large attractive sitting-room, with book-case on the side. Attractive, yet inexpensive exterior. Good clean cut architectural design.

Plans $10

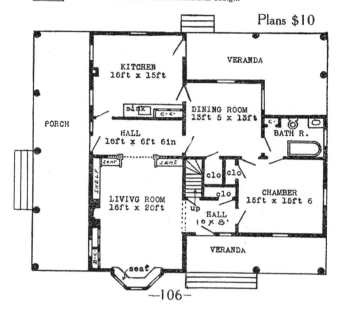

KITCHEN 16ft x 15ft
VERANDA
sink c-c
DINING ROOM 13ft 5 x 13ft
c
BATH R.
PORCH
HALL 16ft x 6ft 6in
SHELF
seat
seat
clo clo
clo
LIVIVG ROOM 16ft x 20ft
CHAMBER 15ft x 15ft 6
up
HALL 10 X 8'
VERANDA
seat

ARKVILLE COTTAGE.—Design 9490-O; in frame, $898 to $1,099; plans, $10; story heights, 10 ft. Special features: Side entrance makes it serviceable as a physician's residence. See page 65.

Plans $10.

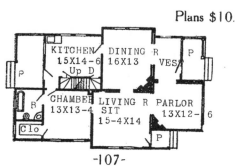

KITCHEN 15X14-6
DINING R 16X13
P
VEST
Up D
CHAMBER 13X13-4
LIVING R SIT 15-4X14
PARLOR 13X12-6
P
B
Clo
P

Plans $10.

CASSVILLE COTTAGE.—Design 9742-N; in frame, $650 to $799; plans, $10. Special features: Compact plan; attractive and novel exterior.

Plans $5

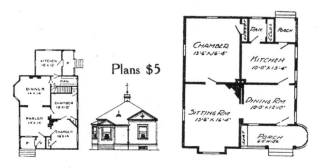

CHAMBER 13'6"X16'4"
PAN CLO PORCH
KITCHEN 10'-0"X13'4"
DINING RM 10'-0"X12'10"
SITTING RM 13'6"X16'4"
PORCH

KITCHEN 18 x 12
PAN
DINING R 14 x 14
CHAMBER 12 X18
PARLOR 14 x 14
CHAMBER 13 x 14
P

CARR COTTAGE.—Design 4201-N; in frame, $750 to $789; plans, $5; story height, 10 ft.

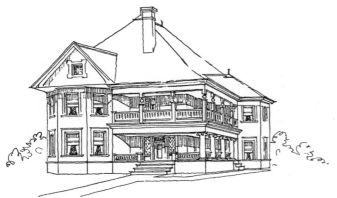

Fairfax design 5109, width over all 39 ft 6. Story heights 11 and 10 ft 6. Plans $15.

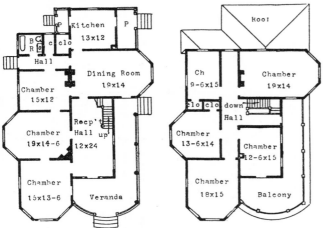

Pinole design 5110, width over all 30 ft, story heights 9 and 8 ft. Plans $15. Very compact plan

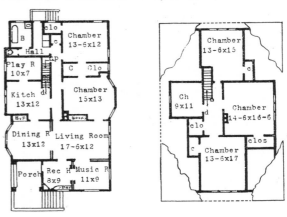

THE NECESSITY OF PRELIMINARY PLANS.

It is seldom that one gets a suitable arrangement the very first time, therefore it is necessary to first send the plans in sketch form so as to make them handy for approval, or disapproval of certain parts as you see fit. Our greatest difficulty is in getting a client's first ideas. And this is sometimes more tedious than making the plans. We have never yet failed to please any one where they have treated us with due consideration.

If you have any printed designs from which you wish to adopt certain ornamental features, we can embody them in your designs and endeavor to still improve on any suggestions offered.

Plans $15.

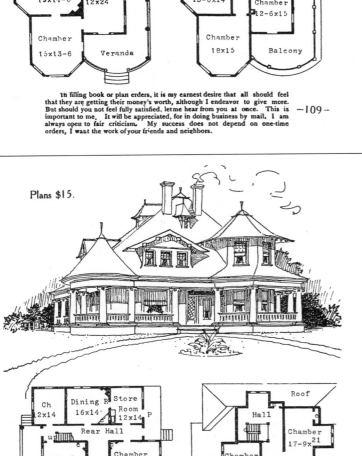

Avisadero design 5111, width over all 51 ft, story heights 9 and 8 ft. Suitable for southern climate. Plans $15.

Lumber Bill

We do not furnish a lumber bill. We state this here particularly, as some people have an idea that a lumber bill should accompany each set of plans and specifications.

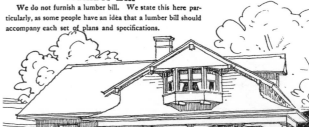

Redding design 5112, width over all 48 ft, story heights 9 ft, cut down slightly above by roof. Plans $15.

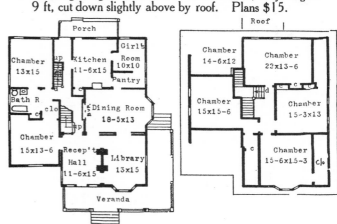

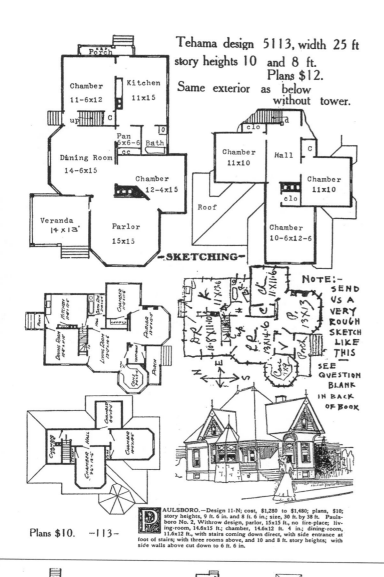

Tehama design 5113, width 25 ft story heights 10 and 8 ft. Plans $12. Same exterior as below without tower.

Porch

Chamber 11-6x12 | Kitchen 11x15

Pan 6x6-6 | Bath

Dining Room 14-6x15

Chamber 12-4x15

Veranda 14x13' | Parlor 15x15

clo

Chamber 11x10 | Hall

Roof | Chamber 11x10

clo

Chamber 10-6x12-6

—SKETCHING—

NOTE:— SEND US A VERY ROUGH SKETCH LIKE THIS — SEE QUESTION BLANK IN BACK OF BOOK

PAULSBORO.—Design 11-N; cost, $1,280 to $1,480; plans, $10; story heights, 9 ft. 6 in. and 8 ft. 6 in.; size, 30 ft. by 38 ft. Paulsboro No. 2, Withrow design, parlor, 15x15 ft., no fire-place; living-room, 14.6x15 ft.; chamber, 14.6x12.4 in.; dining-room, 11.6x12 ft., with stairs coming down direct, with side entrance at foot of stairs; with three rooms above, and 10 and 8 ft. story heights; with side walls above cut down to 6 ft. 6 in.

Plans $10. —113—

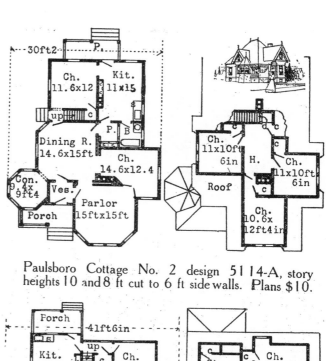

—30ft2— P.

Ch. 11.6x12 | Kit. 11x15

up | c

Dining R. 14.6x15ft | P. B

Con. 4x 9ft4 | Ves.

Porch | Parlor 15ftx15ft

Ch. 14.6x12.4

Ch. 11x10ft 6in | H. | Ch. 11x10ft 6in

Roof

Ch. 10.6x 12ft4in

Paulsboro Cottage No. 2 design 5114-A, story heights 10 and 8 ft cut to 6 ft side walls. Plans $10.

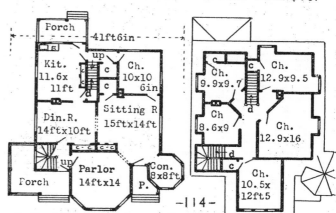

Porch | —41ft6in—

Kit. 11.6x 11ft | up | Ch. 10x10 6in

Din.R. 14ftx10ft | Sitting R 15ftx14ft

Porch | Parlor 14ftx14 | Con. 8x8ft | P.

Ch. 9.9x9.7 | Ch. 12.9x9.5

Ch. 8.6x9 | Ch. 12.9x16

Ch. 10.5x 12ft5

—114—

Paulsboro No. 3 design 5111-B. story heights 9-ft 6 and 8-ft 6 cut to 6-ft 6 side walls. Plans $10.

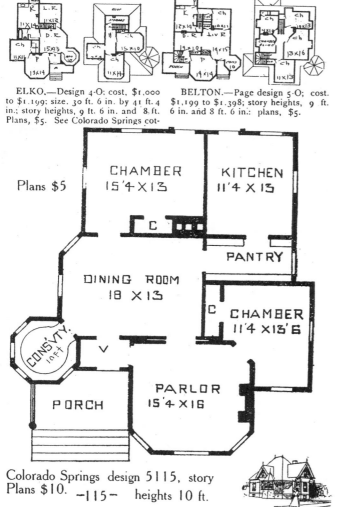

ELKO.—Design 4-O: cost, $1,000 to $1,199: size, 30 ft. 6 in. by 41 ft. 4 in.; story heights, 9 ft. 6 in. and 8 ft. Plans, $5. See Colorado Springs cot-

BELTON.—Page design 5-O; cost $1,199 to $1,398; story heights, 9 ft. 6 in. and 8 ft. 6 in.; plans, $5.

Plans $5

CHAMBER 15'4X13 | KITCHEN 11'4 X 13

C

PANTRY

DINING ROOM 18 X 13

C | CHAMBER 11'4 X 13'6

CONS'V'TY. 10ft | V

PORCH | PARLOR 15'4X16

Colorado Springs design 5115, story heights 10 ft. Plans $10. —115—

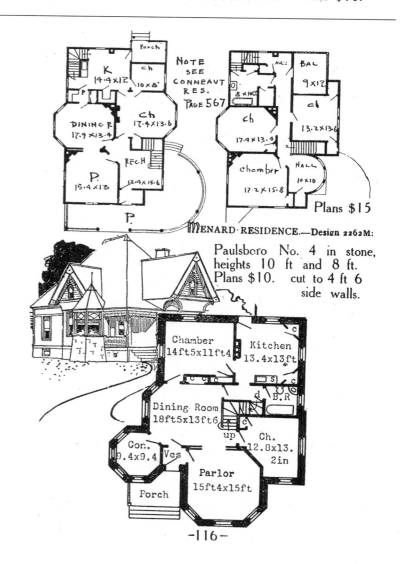

Porch

K 14.4x12 | ch | 10x8'

Dining R 17.9x13.4 | ch 17.4x13.6

P. 15.4x13 | 12.9x15.6

RECH

P.

NOTE SEE CONNEAUT RES. PAGE 567

HALL | BAL 9x12

8x10 | cb | cb 13.2x13.6

ch 17.4x13.4

chamber 17.2x15.8 | HALL 10x10

Plans $15

MENARD RESIDENCE.—Design 2262M:

Paulsboro No. 4 in stone, heights 10 ft and 8 ft. Plans $10. cut to 4 ft 6 side walls.

Chamber 14ft5x11ft4 | Kitchen 13.4x13ft

B.R

Dining Room 18ft5x13ft6 | up | Ch. 12.8x13. 2in

Con. 9.4x9.4 | Ves | Parlor 15ft4x15ft

Porch

—116—

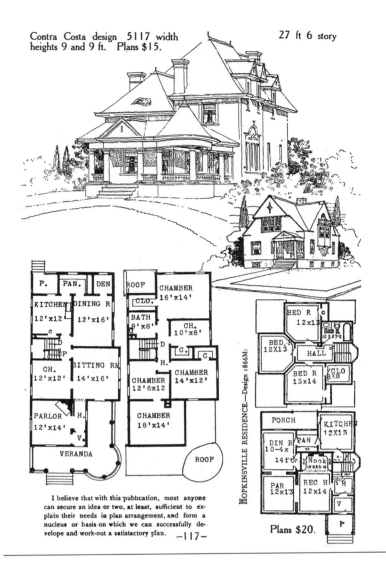

Contra Costa design 5117 width 27 ft 6 story
heights 9 and 9 ft. Plans $15.

P.	PAN.	DEN	ROOF	CHAMBER 16'x14'
KITCHEN 12'x12	DINING R 12'x16'		CLO.	
			BATH 0'x8'	CH. 10'x8'
CH. 12'x12	SITTING RM 14'x16'		CHAMBER 12'6x12	CHAMBER 14'x12'
PARLOR 12'x14'	H.		CHAMBER 18'x14'	
VERANDA				ROOF

HOPKINSVILLE RESIDENCE.—Design 1866M:

BED R 12x13	
BED R 12x13	HALL
BED R 13x14	CLO 8x8
PORCH	KITCHEN 12X13
DIN R 10-4x 14ft	PAN Nook
PAR 12x13	REC H 12x14
	V P

Plans $20.

I believe that with this publication, most anyone can secure an idea or two, at least, sufficient to explain their needs in plan arrangement, and form a nucleus or basis on which we can successfully develope and work-out a satisfactory plan. —117—

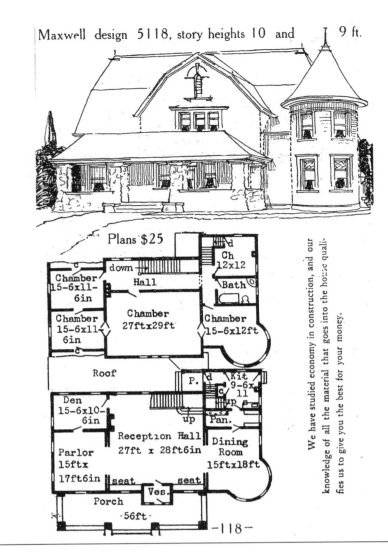

Maxwell design 5118, story heights 10 and 9 ft.

Plans $25

	Ch 12x12
Chamber 15-6x11-6in	down Hall
	Bath
Chamber 15-6x11-6in	Chamber 27ftx29ft	Chamber 15-6x12ft
Roof		Kit 9-6x 11
Den 15-6x10-6in	up	P. up Pan.
Parlor 15ftx 17ft6in	Reception Hall 27ft x 28ft6in	Dining Room 15ftx18ft
	seat Ves. seat	
Porch -56ft		

—118—

We have studied economy in construction, and our knowledge of all the material that goes into the house qualifies us to give you the best for your money.

Tamarack design 5119, width over all 45 ft, story heights 10 and 8-ft 6. Plans $10.

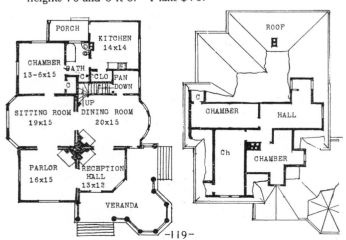

PORCH	KITCHEN 14x14	ROOF
CHAMBER 13-6x15	BATH CLO PAN DOWN	
SITTING ROOM 19x15	DINING ROOM 20x15	CHAMBER HALL
PARLOR 16x15	RECEPTION HALL 13x12	CHAMBER
VERANDA		

—119—

Riovista design 5120, story heights 10 and 8 ft 6.
Plans $10.

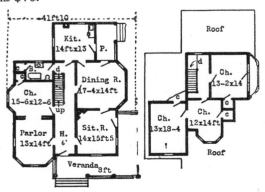

	Kit. 14ftx13	P.	Roof
Ch 15-6x12-6	Dining R. 17-4x14ft	Ch. 13-2x14
Parlor 13x14ft	Sit.R. 14x15ft5	Ch. 13x18-4 Ch. 12x14ft
Veranda 3ft		Roof

41ft10

—120—

Dunsmuir design 5121, story heights 9 ft 6 and 8, width 31 ft. Plans $10.

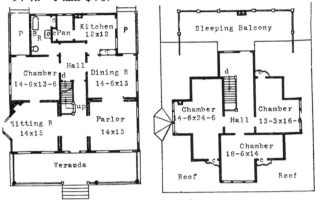

| P | B R | o | c | Pan | Kitchen 12x12 | P |

Sleeping Balcony

Hall

Chamber 14-6x13-6

Dining R 14-6x13

Sitting R 14x15

Parlor 14x15

Veranda

Chamber 14-6x24-6

Hall

Chamber 13-3x16

Chamber 18-6x14

Roof   Roof

PROSPECTIVE CLIENTS.

Prospective clients at a distance should be very emphatic if they mean business. I get so many idle inquiries, to which I can pay no attention and it will pay you to be frank in your dealings with this office, as I take great interest in appreciative clients, who have ambition enough to have my plans carried out right when they get them, as it means satisfaction all around, and leads to other work.

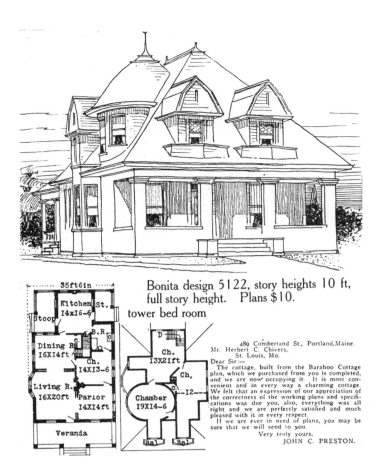

Bonita design 5122, story heights 10 ft, full story height. Plans $10.

tower bed room

35ft6in

Kitchen 14x16-6

St.

Stoop

Dining R 16X14ft

B.R

Ch. 14X13-6

Ch. 13X21ft

Living R. 16X20ft

Parlor 14X14ft

Chamber 19X14-6

Ch.

12

Veranda

Bal   Bal

489 Cumberland St., Portland, Maine.
Mr. Herbert C. Chivers,
St. Louis, Mo.

Dear Sir:—

The cottage, built from the Baraboo Cottage plan, which we purchased from you is completed, and we are now occupying it. It is most convenient and in every way a charming cottage. We felt that an expression of our appreciation of the correctness of the working plans and specifications was due you, also, everything was all right and we are perfectly satisfied and much pleased with it in every respect.

If we are ever in need of plans, you may be sure that we will send to you.

Very truly yours,
JOHN C. PRESTON.

There is no comparison between the excellent work turned out at this office and the work of the carpenter-architect, or the "sketch-em and catch-em" architect, who offers free sketches, or publishing and plaining-mill companies. Architecture is a distinct profession, and is above all of this. It is my distinct occupation to prepare plans, in the best possible manner, and at the least possible cost, and in doing a larger business than any four concerns combined in the country, it is quite reasonable to presume that "practice makes perfect," or nearly so.

Porch

Kitchen 12-6x10

Pan

Nook

Chamber 12x10-6

Dining Room 15-6x10-6

up

Living Room 32x15-6

Reading Room

Veranda

Roof

Chamber 11x13-6

Chamber 13-6x8

Hall

Ch 12x12

Roof   Roof

Donna Anna design 5123, width 29 over all 39 ft, story heights 8 ft 6. Large living room. Plans $10.

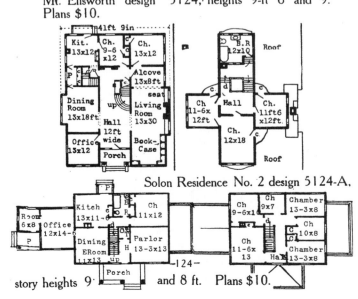

Mt. Ellsworth design 5124, heights 9-ft 6 and 9. Plans $10.

41ft 9in

Kit. 13x12

Ch. 9-6 x12

Ch. 13x12

Alcove 13x8ft

seat

Dining Room 13x18ft

Hall 12ft wide

Living Room 13x30

Office 13x12

Book-Case

Porch

B.R 12x10

Roof

Ch 11-6x 12ft

Hall

Ch. 11ft6 x12ft.

Ch. 12x18

Roof

Solon Residence No. 2 design 5124-A.

Room 6x8

Office 12x14

Kiteh 13x11

Ch 11x12

Dining E Room 11x13

Parlor 13-3x13

up

Porch

Ch 9-6x10

Ch 11-6x 13

Chamber 13-3x8

Ch 10x8

Chamber 13-3x8

story heights 9   and 8 ft. Plans $10.

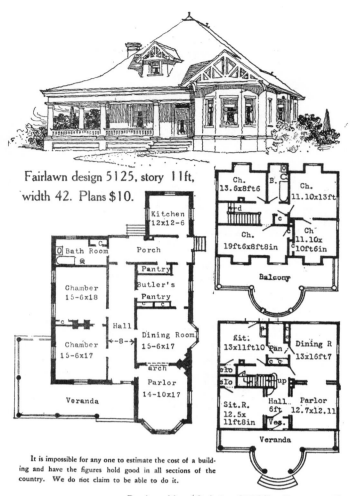

Fairlawn design 5125, story 11ft, width 42. Plans $10.

Floor plan labels (upper):
Kitchen 12x12-6
Bath Room
Porch
Chamber 15-6x18
Pantry
Butler's Pantry
Hall 8
Chamber 15-6x17
Dining Room 15-6x17
arch
Parlor 14-10x17
Veranda

Second floor:
Ch. 13.6x8ft6
B.
Ch. 11.10x13ft
Ch. 19ft6x8ft8in
Ch. 11.10x 10ft6in
Balcony

Right plan:
Kit. 13x11ft10
Pan
Dining R 13x16ft7
clo
clo
Sit.R. 12.5x 11ft8in
Hall 6ft
Parlor 12.7x12.11
Ves.
Veranda
up

It is impossible for any one to estimate the cost of a building and have the figures hold good in all sections of the country. We do not claim to be able to do it.

—125—

Baraboo No. 12 design 5-125-B. See page 45 for exterior. Story heights 9 and 9. Plans $10.

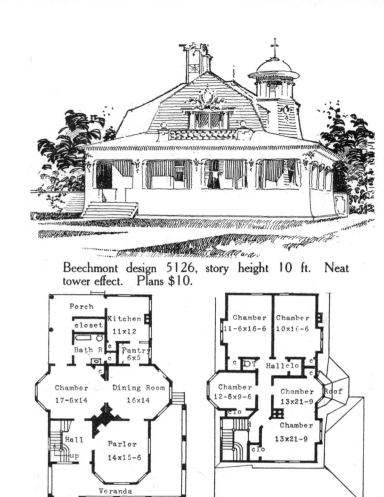

Beechmont design 5126, story height 10 ft. Neat tower effect. Plans $10.

Floor plan labels:
Porch
closet
Kitchen 11x12
Bath R
Pantry 6x5
Chamber 17-6x14
Dining Room 16x14
Hall up
Parlor 14x15-6
Veranda

Second floor:
Chamber 11-6x16-6
Chamber 10x16-6
Hall clo
Chamber 12-5x9-6
clo
Roof
Chamber 13x21-9
Chamber 13x21-9
clo

—126—

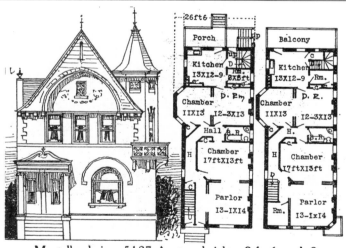

Floor plan labels:
26ft6
Porch
Balcony
Kitchen 13X12-9
Kitchen 13X12-9
D. Rm
Rm.
D. R.
Chamber 11X13
12-3X13
Chamber 11X13
12-3X13
Hall
B.R.
H.
B.R.
Chamber 17ftX13ft
Chamber 17ftX13ft
Parlor 13-1X14
Parlor 13-1X14
Rm.

Mantelle design 5127-A, story heights 9-ft 6 and 9. Plans $15.

Rio Blanco design 5127-B, story heights 9-ft 6. Plans $15.

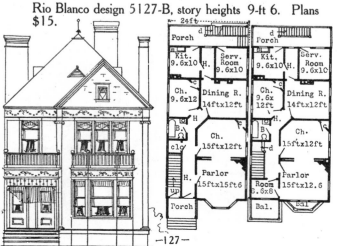

Floor plan labels:
24ft
Porch
Porch
Kit. 9.6x10
Serv. Room 9.6x10
Kit. 9.6x10
Serv. Room 9.6x10
H.
H.
Ch. 9.6x12
Dining R. 14ftx12ft
Ch. 9.6x 12ft
Dining R. 14ftx12ft
B.
B.
Ch. 15ftx12ft
clo
Ch. 15ftx12ft
clo
Parlor 15ftx15ft6
Parlor 15ftx12.6
Room 6.6x8
Porch
Bal.
Bal.

—127—

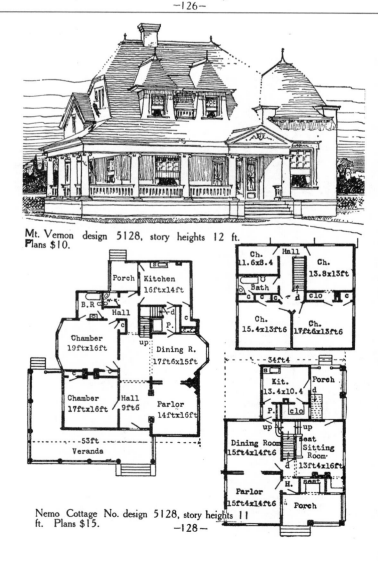

Mt. Vernon design 5128, story heights 12 ft. Plans $10.

Floor plan labels:
Porch
Kitchen 16ftx14ft
B.R.
Hall
Chamber 19ftx16ft
up
Dining R. 17ft6x15ft
Chamber 17ftx16ft
Hall 9ft6
Parlor 14ftx16ft
Veranda 53ft

Second floor:
Ch. 11.6x8.4
Hall
Ch. 13.8x13ft
Bath
Ch. 15.4x13ft6
Ch. 17ft6x13ft6
clo

Lower right plan:
34ft4
Kit. 13.4x10.4
Porch
P.
clo
up
Dining Room 15ft4x14ft6
Seat Sitting Room 13ft4x16ft
seat
Parlor 15ft4x14ft6
Porch
H.

Nemo Cottage No. design 5128, story heights 11 ft. Plans $15.

—128—

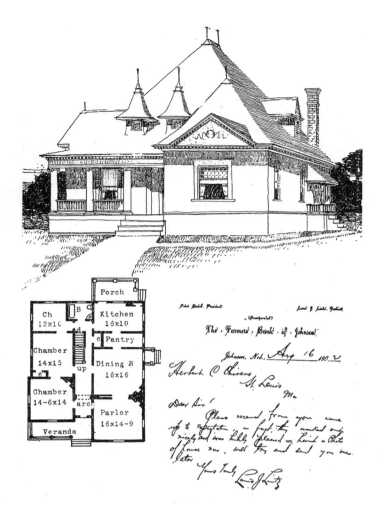

Ch 12x10 B | Porch | Kitchen 16x10
Chamber 14x15 | Pantry
up | Dining R 16x16
Chamber 14-6x14 | arch
Parlor 16x14-9
Veranda

(handwritten letter)

The Farmers Bank of Johnson

Johnson, Neb. Aug 16 1902

Herbert C Chivers
St Louis
Mo

Dear Sir'

Plans received from you are up to expectation in fact they worked very nicely and was highly pleased — Send a Photo of house now, will try and send you one later.

Yours truly
Louis J Lirtz

Port Angeles design 5129, story heights 10-ft, width 37 ft. Plans $5.

—129—

Ch 10-6x8 | Kitchen 10-6x11 | Porch
Bath | Hall | Pantry clo
Chamber 13-6x11 | Dining R 15-6x13-3
c | c
Chamber 15-2x13-9 | arch **Parlor** 17-6x13-9
Porch

Fayman design 5130, story heights 10 ft, Very compact plan. Plans $10.

width 33-ft 8.

Emporia, Kansas, May 24, 19

Mr. Herbert C. Chivers,

Dear Sir:—
Permit me to say a word concerning our satisfaction with the plans which you have prepared of our church and the appreciation of your methods of doing business.
Sincerely yours,
W. A. PARKER,
Minister of the First Christian Church.

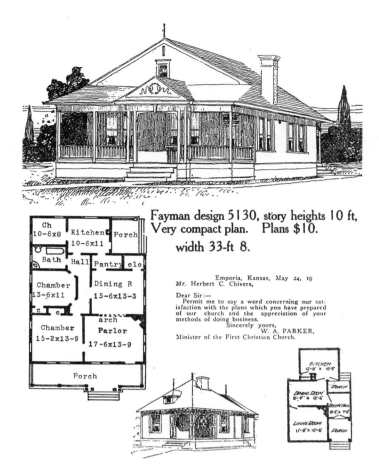

MEMPHIS COTTAGE.—Design 1063-O; in frame, $425 to $490; plans, $5; width, 25 ft. 4 in. by 24 ft.; width over all, 28 ft.; story heights, 9 ft. 6 in. Special features: Unique and inexpensive porch and general grouping of gables. Modifications: Chamber could be used for dining-room; kitchen for sitting-room; and a kitchen addition built on back of chamber. See page 65.

—130—

Leslie design 5131, story heights 9-ft 6 and 9. Plans $10.

Porch | Bath Room 16x5 | Porch
Kitchen 13-6x10-4 | Chamber 14x12
up
Dining Room 17x17-6 | Parlor 13-6x13-6
Veranda

Chamber 21-4x18-3
Hall | down
Chamber 21-4x18-3

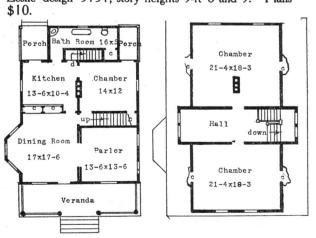

Yours of recent date to hand. Would say that we have a very good house in process of construction, built from your plans, and have just got it plastered. If I was to build another house should get my plans the same way. Will send you a photograph as soon as we have one taken.
DANIEL COLT, Winsted, Conn.

—131—

Loredo design 5132, story heights 9 and 8. Plans $10.

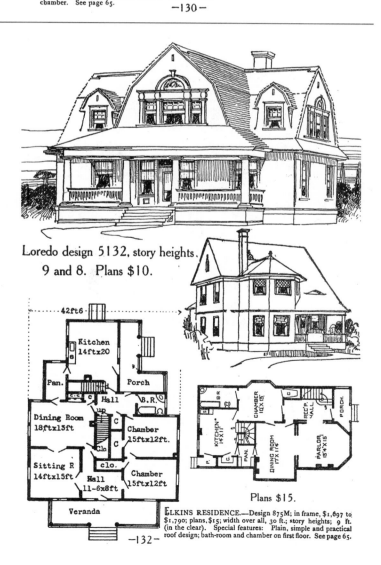

42ft6

Kitchen 14ftx20
Pan. | Porch
Hall | B.R.
Dining Room 18ftx15ft | Chamber 15ftx12ft.
up | clo.
Sitting R 14ftx15ft | clo. | Chamber 15ftx12ft.
Hall 11-6x8ft
Veranda

Kitchen 14x11 | B R | Chamber 10x15
| RECP. HALL | PORCH
Dining Room 17x14 | Parlor 13"x15

Plans $15.

ELKINS RESIDENCE.—Design 875M; in frame, $1,697 to $1,790; plans, $15; width over all, 30 ft.; story heights; 9 ft. (in the clear). Special features: Plain, simple and practical roof design; bath-room and chamber on first floor. See page 65.

—132—

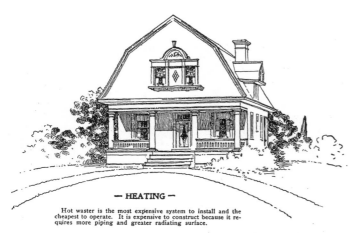

— HEATING —

Hot waster is the most expensive system to install and the
cheapest to operate. It is expensive to construct because it requires more piping and greater radiating surface.

Los Banos design 5133, story heights 9 and 9 ft. Very
compact. Plans $10.

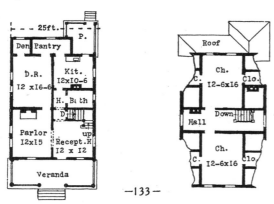

—133—

The house you enquire for is near the seashore, a long distance off, and a
photo would cost quite a sum. The building is very satisfactory.
THOMAS WILMARTH. Saundersville. Mass.

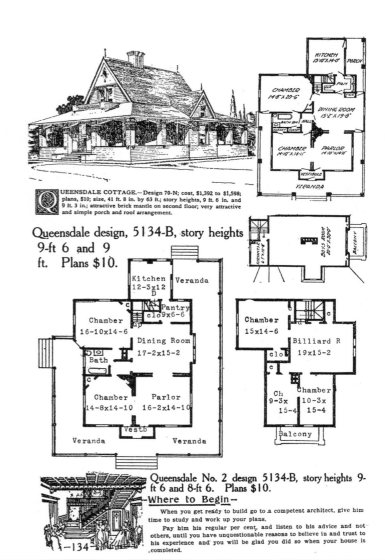

QUEENSDALE COTTAGE.—Design 70-N; cost, $1,392 to $1,598;
plans, $10; size, 41 ft. 8 in. by 63 ft.; story heights, 9 ft. 6 in. and
9 ft. 3 in.; attractive brick mantle on second floor; very attractive
and simple porch and roof arrangement.

Queensdale design, 5134-B, story heights
9-ft 6 and 9
ft. Plans $10.

Queensdale No. 2 design 5134-B, story heights 9-
ft 6 and 8-ft 6. Plans $10.

Where to Begin—

When you get ready to build go to a competent architect, give him
time to study and work up your plans.

Pay him his regular per cent, and listen to his advice and not
others, until you have unquestionable reasons to believe in and trust to
his experience and you will be glad you did so when your house is
completed.

—134—

Berendo design 5135, story heights 11-ft 6. Plans $10:

—135— CITY RESIDENCE.—Design 8256M.

Berkshire design 5137, in brick, story heights 10 ft.
Plans $10.

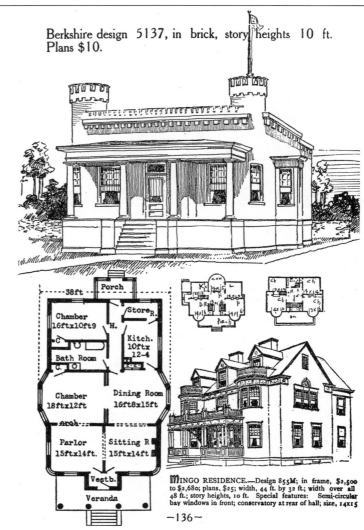

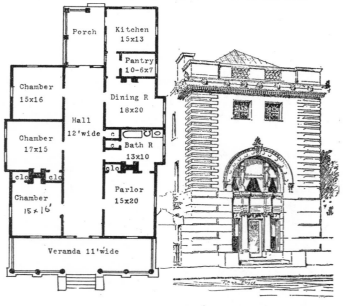

MINGO RESIDENCE.—Design 855M; in frame, $2,500
to $2,680; plans, $25; width, 44 ft. by 32 ft.; width over all
48 ft.; story heights, 10 ft. Special features: Semi-circular
bay windows in front; conservatory at rear of hall; size, 14x15

—136—

Berthera stone design 5137, story heights 10 and 8-ft 6.
Plans $15.

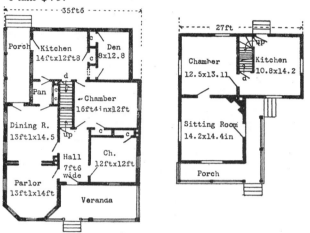

OLIVIA COTTAGE.—Design 100,206-O; in frame, $359
to $495; plans, $5. Special features: Wide overhanging
eaves, beautiful home-like exterior. See page 33. AND 138

-137-

Benona design 5138, story heights 10 ft. Attic space,
above. Plans $5.

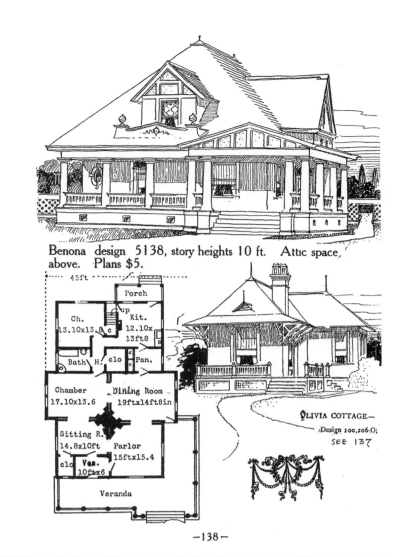

OLIVIA COTTAGE—
Design 100,206-O;
SEE 137

-138-

Belvidere design 5139, story heights 10 ft. Plans $5.

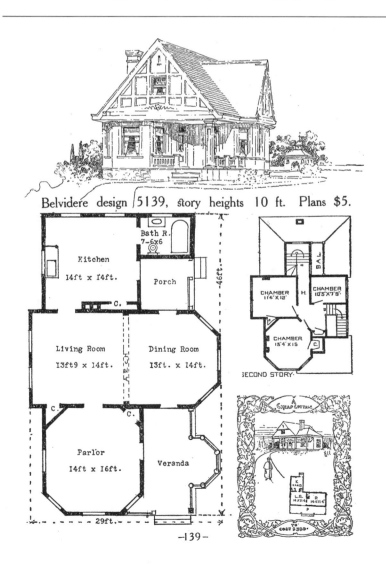

-139-

Iolanthe design 5140, story heights 12 ft. Plans $5.

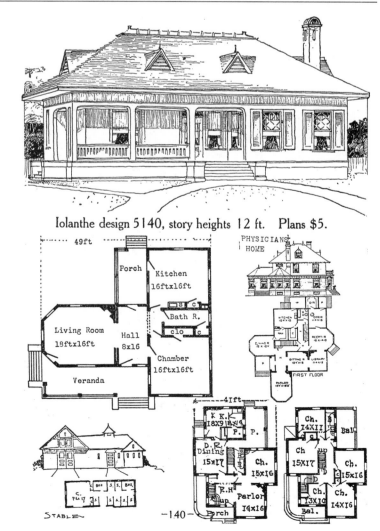

-140-

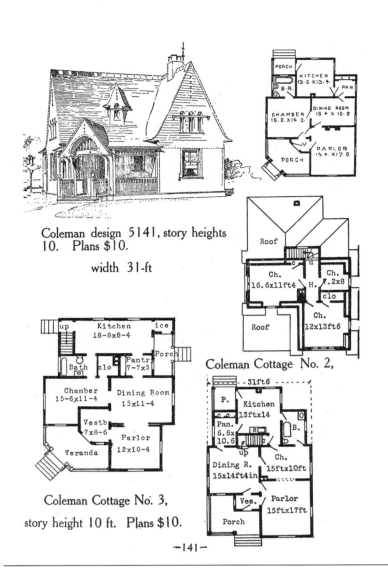

Coleman design 5141, story heights 10. Plans $10.

width 31-ft

Coleman Cottage No. 2,

Coleman Cottage No. 3, story height 10 ft. Plans $10.

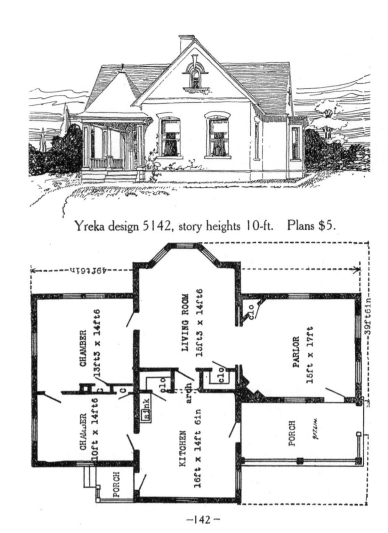

Yreka design 5142, story heights 10-ft. Plans $5.

Cloverdale Cottage No. 4, design 5143, story heights 9-ft 6 and 9. Plans $10.

Remember in building a home that the best is none too good and is the cheapest in the end.

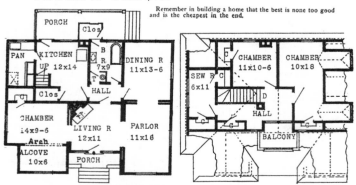

When it is considered that nearly every page of this book contains very expensive plate-matter, for which drawings and cuts must first be made, some idea of its cost of production can be imagined, therefore, it is hoped, in the interest of better house plans, that purchasers will loan this work freely as an incentive to ones neighbors to improve attractively, and thus enhance the value of large residential districts.

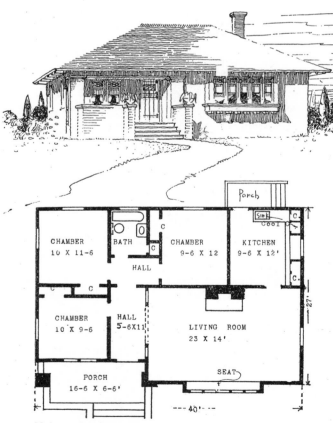

Kalama design 5144, 9-ft story. Large attractive living rooms. Plans $10.

Mrs. House and myself are highly pleased with our home and do not hesitate to recommend your work to any one intending to build a home.
Dr. J. C. HOUSE, Port Townsend, Wash.

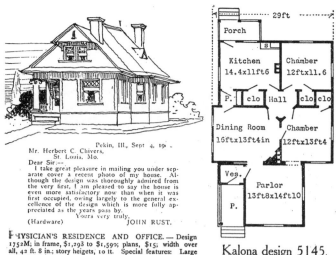

PHYSICIAN'S RESIDENCE AND OFFICE.— Design
1752M; in frame, $1,293 to $1,590; plans, $15; width over
all, 42 ft. 8 in.; story heights, 10 ft. Special features: Large
central sitting-room which is available for office or residence.
Compact fire-place arrangement, neat simple exterior. (See
index for other physicians' houses.) See page 65.

Kalona design 5145.
Plans $5.

Plans $15.

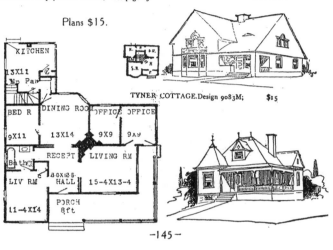

TYNER COTTAGE. Design 9083M; $15

—145—

Denvers design 5146, story 9-ft.   Plans $10.

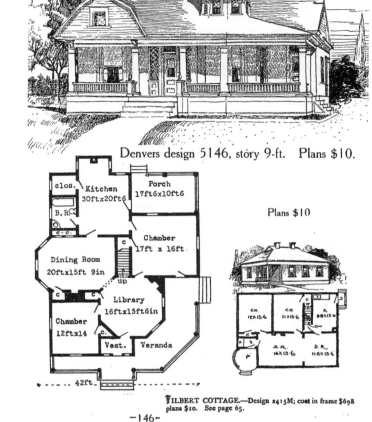

Plans $10

FILBERT COTTAGE.—Design 2415M; cost in frame $698
plans $10. See page 65.

—146—

Plans $10.

REDONIA COTTAGE.—Design 9946-N; cost in frame, $1,144 to
$1,349; plans, $10; width, 25 ft. by 56 ft.; story height, 10 ft.
Special features: Unique circular-top porch; attractive design;
convenient bath-room; large vestibule.

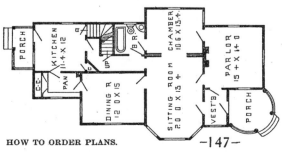

HOW TO ORDER PLANS.

—147—

Plans $20

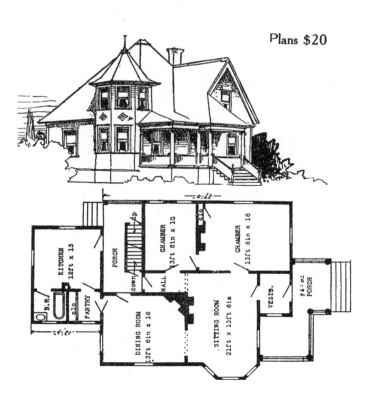

DAWKINS COTTAGE.—Design 2410M; cost in frame $1,-
290 to $1,340; plans $20. See page 65.

—148—

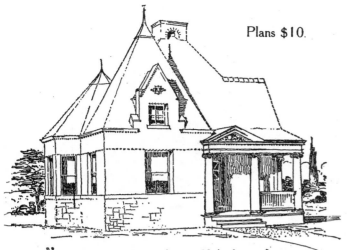

VIKING COTTAGE.—Design 9142M; in frame, $599 to
$690; plans, $10; width over all, 30 ft. 4 in.; story heights,
10 ft. Special features: Compact plan, pleasing roof lines.
See page 65.

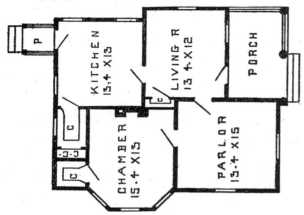

CARLISLE COTTAGE.—Design 100192-O; in frame, $450
to $598; plans, $10; width, 27 ft. 10 in.; story heights, 10 ft.
Special features: Plain, neat exterior. See page 65.

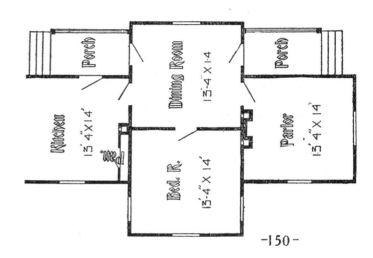

Dulzura design 5151, story heights 10 ft, width 34-ft.
Plans $5.

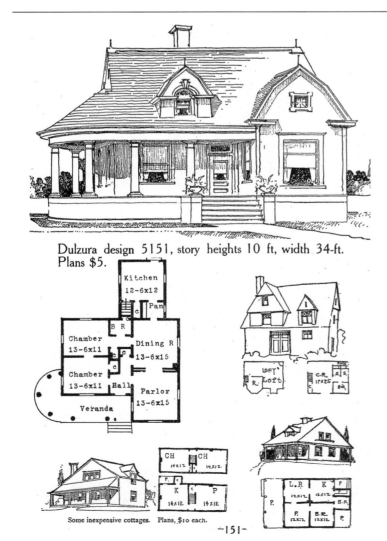

Some inexpensive cottages. Plans, $10 each.

East Gaines design 5152, story 10 ft, width 34 ft.
Plans $5.

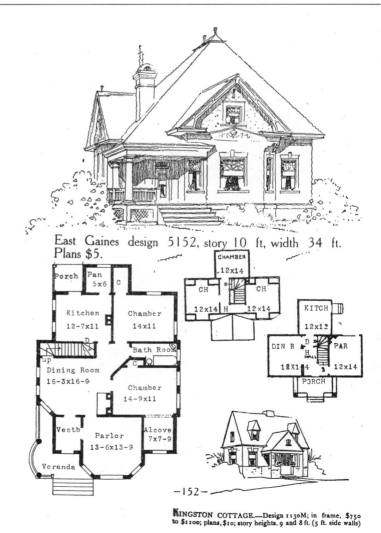

KINGSTON COTTAGE.—Design 1130M; in frame, $750
to $1100; plans, $10; story heights, 9 and 8 ft. (5 ft. side walls).

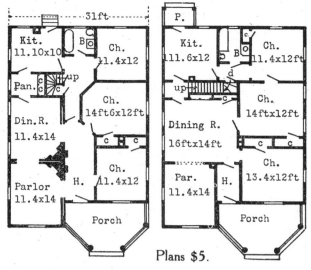

Plans $5.

Mobile Cottage.—Design 1743-O; in frame, $890 to $1,098; plans, $5; width, 31 ft. 2 in. by 39 ft. 8 in.; story heights, 9 ft. 6 in. Special features: Neat, compact plan, convenient bath-room, good fire-place arrangement. See page 65.

I built Dr. Green's house for which you prepared plans, and know the value of working plans and have worked after some good architects. You certainly have novel ideas.
JOHN DOYLE, Builder, Wilmington, O.

Plans $10.

Harrisburg Cottage.—Design 1941-O; in frame, $940 to $1,029; plans, $ width, 30 ft. by 50 ft.; width over all, 35 ft.; story heights, 10 ft. The working plans show bay window to bed room as indicated on plan. We have $8 plan with dining-room and bed-room connected, leaving out central hall, and fire-place in parlor. See page 65.

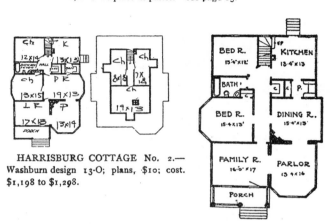

HARRISBURG COTTAGE No. 2.—Washburn design 13-O; plans, $10; cost. $1,198 to $1,298.

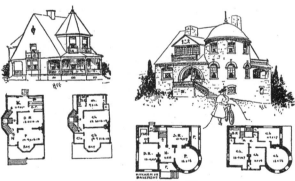

VINTON COTTAGE.—Design 4528 M; in frame, $1399 to $1369; plans, $5; story heights, 9 ft. and 8 ft. 6 in. See page 65·

Plans $25.

A SUBURBAN HOUSE.

Plans $5.

DU PUE COTTAGE.—Design 1, 029M; cost $1390 to $1492; size, 46 x 29; extreme width, 56 ft.; special features; plain, practical roof, home-like exterior. Plans, $15. See page 65

Plans $15.

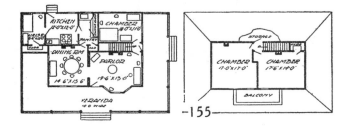

Plans $10

PANDORA COTTAGE.—Design 1207M; size, 39x44 ft. 6 in.; story height, 10 ft. Special features: Bath-room close to bed rooms; compact plan. Cost, $1,045 to $1,199; plans $10. See page 65.

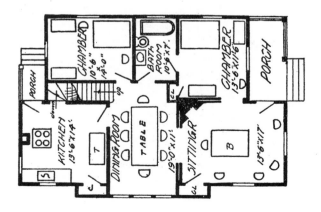

We moved into our new home in Oct. We are well pleased. A great many people admire our home and think it artistic and beautiful.
JOHN S. MORRIS, Westport, Ind.

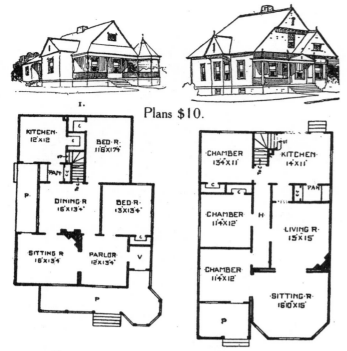

Plans $10.

ADIRONDACK COTTAGE.—Design 2208-O; in frame,
$898 to $990;   width, 29 ft. 6 in. by 45 ft. 4 in.;
width over all, 39 ft.; story heights, 10 and 8 ft. attic. Special
features: Plain, simple roof treatment; large rooms; side
No. 1. porch to dining-room. Have $8 stock plans with the follow-
ing changes, named (Edmonds plan), with bay 13x13 ft. 4 in.
to bed room, making this room 17 ft. long; rear chamber, 11
ft. 6 in. by 12 ft., with bath-room between the two; with fire-
place in large bed room and parlor. See page 65.

—157—

HARTFORD COTTAGE.—Design 2136-O; in frame, $1,-
099 to $1,198; plans, $ width, 29 ft. 8 in. by 47 ft. 2 in.;
No.   story heights, 10 and 8 ft. attic. Special features: Large
sitting-room; space for one 15x35 ft. room on second floor.
See page 65.

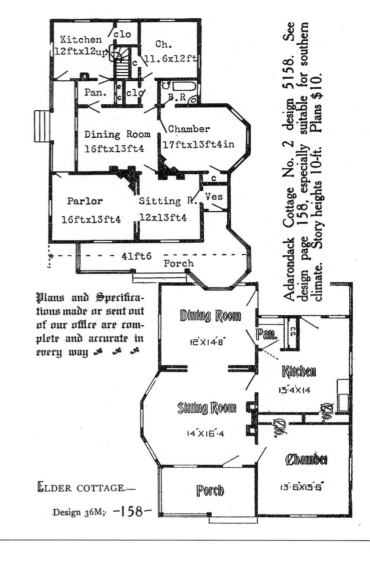

Plans and Specifica-
tions made or sent out
of our office are com-
plete and accurate in
every way

Adarondack Cottage No. 2 design 5158. See
design page 158, especially suitable for southern
climate. Story heights 10-ft. Plans $10.

ELDER COTTAGE.—

Design 36M; —158—

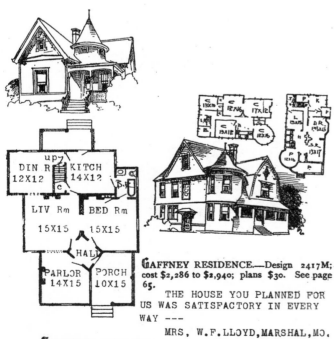

GAFFNEY RESIDENCE.—Design 2417M;
cost $2,286 to $2,940; plans $30. See page
65.

THE HOUSE YOU PLANNED FOR
US WAS SATISFACTORY IN EVERY
WAY ---
                    MRS, W.F.LLOYD,MARSHAL,MO.

FREDONIA COTTAGE.—Design 2416M; cost in frame
$1,080 to $1,190; plans $15. See page 65.

ARTISTIC HOMES—

IN many cases our plans will produce houses of better construction, more convenient arrangement, more complete
as to details, more artistic in appearance, and yet, owing to
our superior designs, at actually lower cost than a house less
skillfully planned.

Elklawn design 5160, width over all 38 ft. Large
dining room, commodious veranda. Story heights
9-ft 6. Plans $15.

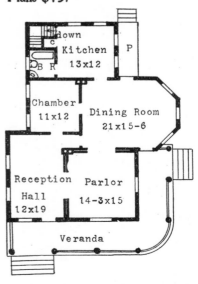

The house plans came to hand promptly and appear to be all right, at least
my builder pronounced them so.   PARK F. YENGLING, Salem, O.

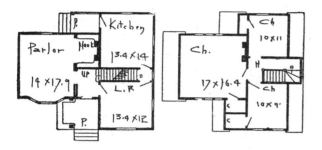

ST. CHARLES COTTAGE.—Design 1769 M; in frame, $988 to $1092; plans, $10; width, 34 ft. 8 in. by 31 ft.: story heights, 9 ft. (second story walls cut down to 5 ft. by roof). See page 65.

In behalf of the Board of Education of the City of Bloomfield, I will say that we are more than well pleased with your work on plans and specifications for our new high school. They are a credit to any architect.
RALPH WAMMOCK, (Pres. Board of Education), Bloomfield, Mo.

Plans $10.

PORT UNION RESIDENCE.—Design 2327-O; cost, $1490 to $1,567; plans, $10; space for four good-size rooms above; special features: Large, wide verandas. See page 65.

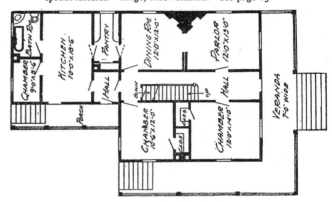

Oxonia, Ind., Jan. 29, 19 7.
Mr. H. C. Chivers,
St. Louis, Mo.
Dear Sir:—
  In regard to plans for my house, would say we are well pleased in every respect. A remark made by one of my friends covers all I could say: "Could not add or take anything away to add to its beauty."
Yours truly,
(Merchant) CLARENCE DENNIS

Plans $20.

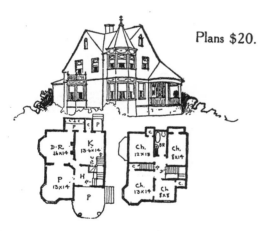

CHAMPAIGN RESIDENCE.—Design 901-O; in frame, $1,292 to $1,414; plans, $20; width, 28 ft.; story heights, 9 ft. 6 in. Modifications: Can furnish this with octagon porch. See page 65.

Plans $15.

BUSHFIELD RESIDENCE.—Design 1527-O; in frame, $1,298 to $1,498, plans $15; width over all, 23 ft. 6 in. story heights, 9 ft. 6 in. See page 65.

Plans $20.

PERRYVILLE RESIDENCE.—Design 7101-O; in frame, $2,280 to $2,399; cost of plans, No. 1 or No. 2, $20, width of plan, No. 1, 41 ft. 10 in. by 50 ft. 2 in.; of plan No. 2, 42 ft. by 50 ft. 2 in.; story heights, plan No. 1, 9 ft. and 8 ft. 6 in.; plan No. 2, 10 ft. and 9 ft.; special features: Balcony first floor; bath; isolated kitchen. See page 65.

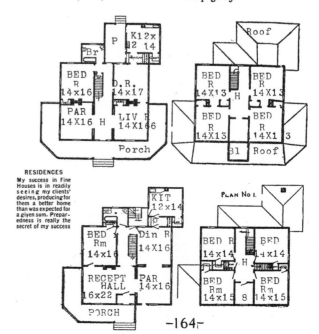

RESIDENCES
My success in Fine Houses is in readily seeing my clients' desires, producing for them a better home than was expected for a given sum. Preparedness is really the secret of my success

HELWEGSDALE COTTAGE.—Design 9077M; in frame, $1,199 to $1,380; plans, $10; width over all, 31 ft. 6 in.; story heights, 9 ft. 6 in. See page 65.

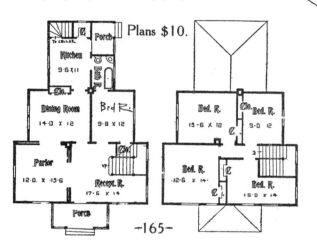

Plans $10.

-165-

LOWELL COTTAGE.—Design 1523-O; in frame, $1298 to $1490; plans, $10; width, 25 ft. 8 in. x 34 ft. 4 in.; story heights, 10 ft. and 9 ft. (full story). Special features—Simple and attractive roof. See page 65.

LOWELL Plan No. 2, Staubber residence, with 12 x 12 Reception Hall, 14 x 16 Parlor, 14 x 12 Dining-room, with 7 x 7 rear porch, 12 x 9 Kitchen and 10 x 7 Storage-room or Servants room opening into kitchen with three good size chambers above: 9 ft. story heights: cut down to 6 ft. front and rear.

Plans $10.

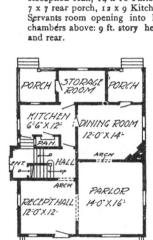
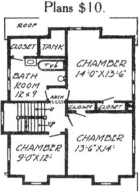

Every man should be proficient in his profession or trade. An architect who is practical and efficient in design has all he can attend to without attaching "Builder" to his name; and the same rule applies to practical builders.

-166-

KONA COTTAGE.—Design 1135M; in frame; $1298 to $1449; plans, $20; width, 36 ft. by 31 ft.; story heights, 9 ft. 6 in. and 8 ft. 6 in. (full story). Special features: Large reception hall, combination stairs, simple roof treatment; stairs do not cut up front rooms. Modifications: The working plans show a very attractive exterior. See page 65.

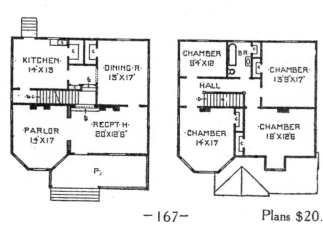

-167- Plans $20.

Plans $10.

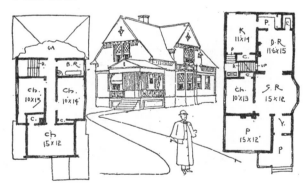

JERICO COTTAGE.—Design 1533M; in frame, $1,398 to $1498; plans, $10; width, 24 ft. 6 in. x 42; width over all, 26 ft. 6 in.; story heights, 9 ft. 6 in. and 9 ft. See page 65.

Plans $15.

LEBOS COTTAGE.—Design 1533M; in frame, $1490 to $1598; plans, $15; width, 24; width over all, 26 ft. in.; story heights, 9 ft. 6 in. and 8 ft.; All chambers full story. Front design in working plans very neat and attractive. See page 65.

-168-

EMMETSBURG COTTAGE.—Design 1974-O; in frame, $550 to $656; plans, $5; width, 26 ft. 4 in.; story heights, 9 ft. Special features: Compact chimney arrangement; economical roof to build. See page 65.

Plans $5

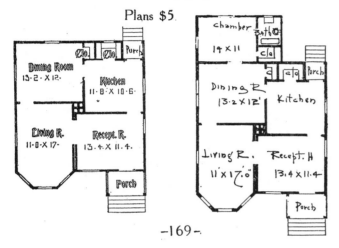

BENZONIA RESIDENCE.—Design 9044-O; in frame, $1,890 to $2,180; plans, $10; (with two rooms above); width, 63 ft. 4 in. by 38 ft.; story heights, 10 ft. and 9 ft. Special features: Heavy shingle-post porch, with built-up bent beams of natural oak; with rough stone treatment below. See page 65.

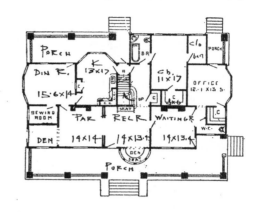

Your work is indeed beautiful, and I shall recommend you to my friends.
J. W. BUTLER, (Banker), Clinton, Tex.

The house plans arrived "O. K." and I thank you for your promptness. It is a pleasure to deal with you. CHAS. BROWNING, Sacramento, Cal.

Plans $5

NASHVILLE COTTAGE.—Design 2223-O; cost in frame, $850 to $998; plans, $5; width over all, 41 ft.; story heights, 10 ft. See page 65.

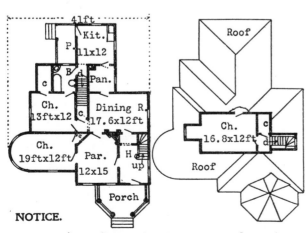

NOTICE.

As our clients are located in nearly every State and Territory we can likely give, as special references, the names of those in your community who have used our plans.

We like our house very much as planned by you, and should we ever build again, will certainly favor you with another order.
MRS. FRANK LANE, Boise, Idaho.

Plans $20.

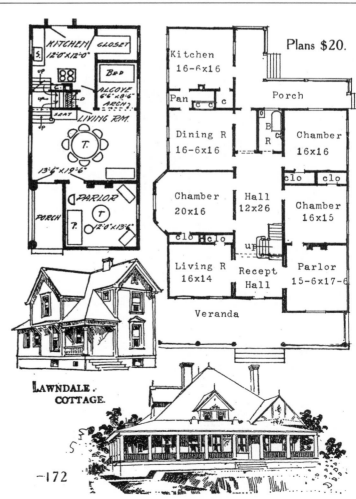

LAWNDALE COTTAGE.

RONDA COTTAGE.—Design 2405 M; cost in frame $1,892 to $1,980; plans $20. A good Southern cottage. See page 65.

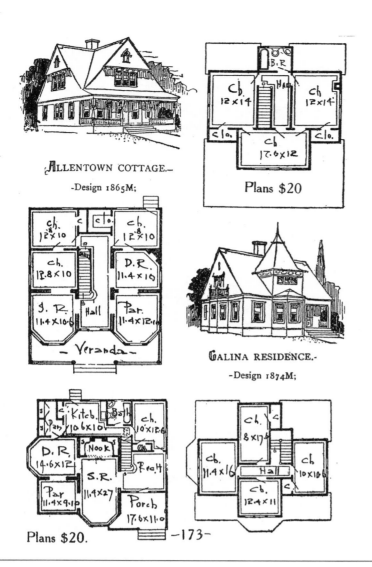

ALLENTOWN COTTAGE.—

-Design 1865M;

Plans $20

Ch 12 x 14 — B.R — HALL — Ch 12 x 14

Cb 17·6 x 12 — clo. — clo.

ch. 12 x 10 — c — clo. — ch. 12 x 10

ch. 17·8 x 10 — D.R. 11·4 x 10

S.R. 11·4 x 10·6 — Hall — Par. 11·4 x 12·11

— Veranda —

GALINA RESIDENCE.—

-Design 1874M;

Kitch. 10·6 x 10 — Bath — ch. 10 x 12·6

Pan.

D.R. 14·6 x 12 — Nook — Porch

S.R. 11·4 x 27

Par. 11·4 x 9·10 — Porch 17·6 x 11·0

ch. 8 x 17·6

Cb 11·4 x 16 — Hall — ch 10 x 10·6

Cb 12·4 x 11 — c

Plans $20.

-173-

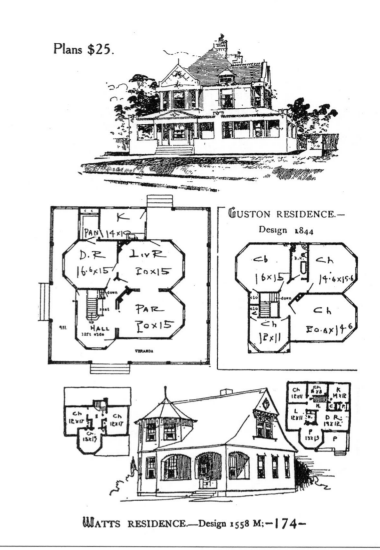

GUSTON RESIDENCE.—

Design 1844

c c — K

PAN 14 x 16

D.R 16·6 x 15 — Liv R 10 x 15

down — coat

PAR 20 x 15

HALL 12 ft wide

VERANDA

Cb 16 x 15 — B.R. — ch 14·6 x 15·6

clo — down

clo

ch 12 x 11 — Ch 20·6 x 14·6

ch 12 x 11 — ch 12 x 17

ch 13 x 17 — Ch 12 x 17

K 14 x 12 — ch 12 x 11

L 12 x 11 — D.R. 19 x 12

13 x 13 — P

WATTS RESIDENCE.—Design 1558 M; -174-

Plans $15.

FOLKSVILLE COTTAGE.—Design 8222-O; in frame, $590 to $698; plans, $15; story heights, 10 ft. Special features: Large living-room, corner porch, a good corner-lot house. See page 65.

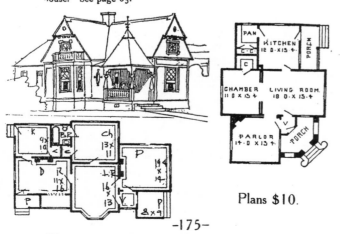

PAN — KITCHEN 12·0 x 15·4 — PORCH

c c — c

CHAMBER 11·0 x 15·4 — LIVING ROOM. 18·0 x 15·4

PARLOR 14·0 x 13·4 — PORCH

Plans $10.

k 9 x 10 — B.R. — ch 13 x 11 — P 19·4 x 14

D.R. 11 x — L.R. 16 x 14 — P

P — V — P 8 x 9

-175-

MADISON COTTAGE.—Design 1970-O; in frame, plan

MONTANA COTTAGE.—Design 5-O; in frame, $450 to $550; plans, $5; width, 21 ft. 6 in. by 33 ft. 2 in.; story heights, 9 ft. 6 in. Special features: Compact arrangement could be used as two-family house.; good flue connections; economical porch construction. See page 65.

Plans $5

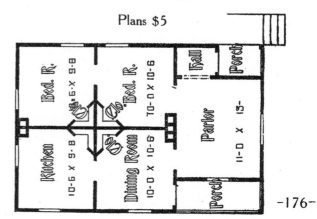

Bed. R. 9·6 x 9·8 — Bed. R. 10·0 x 10·6 — Hall — Porch

Kitchen 10·6 x 9·8 — Dining Room 10·0 x 10·6 — Parlor 11·0 x 13·

Porch — Porch

-176-

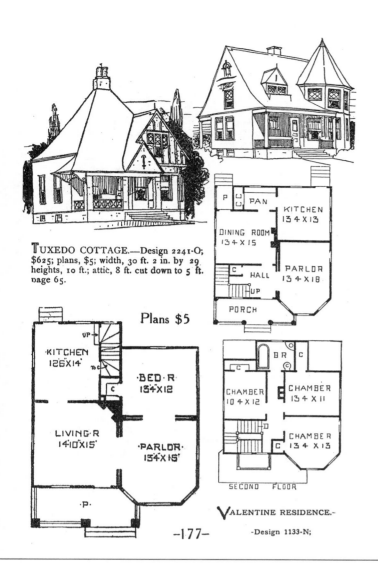

TUXEDO COTTAGE.—Design 2241-O; $625; plans, $5; width, 30 ft. 2 in. by 29 heights, 10 ft.; attic, 8 ft. cut down to 5 ft. page 65.

Plans $5

P CC PAN

KITCHEN 13·4 X 13

DINING ROOM 13·4 X 15

PARLOR 13·4 X 18

C HALL UP

PORCH

KITCHEN 12·6 X 14

·BED·R· 13·4 X 12

LIVING·R· 14·10 X 15·

·PARLOR· 13·4 X 15·

·P·

BR C

CHAMBER 10·4 X 12

CHAMBER 13·4 X 11

CHAMBER 13·4 X 13

SECOND FLOOR

VALENTINE RESIDENCE.—

—Design 1133-N;

—177—

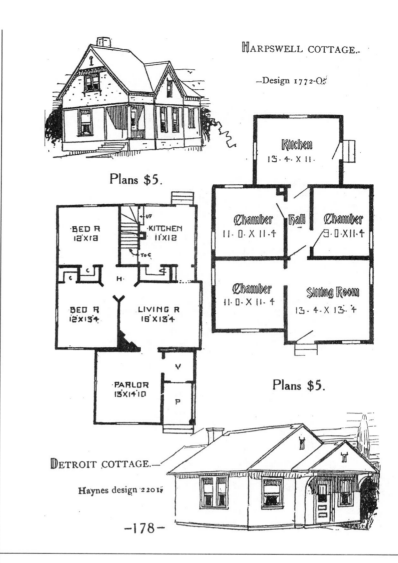

Plans $5.

Kitchen 13·4 X 11·

Chamber 11·0 X 11·4

Hall

Chamber 9·0 X 11·4

Chamber 11·0 X 11·4

Sitting Room 13·4 X 13·4

BED R 12 X 12

KITCHEN 11 X 12

C UP ToC

C H

BED R 12 X 13·4

LIVING R 16 X 13·4

PARLOR 13 X 14·10

V P

Plans $5.

DETROIT COTTAGE.—

Haynes design 2201?

—178—

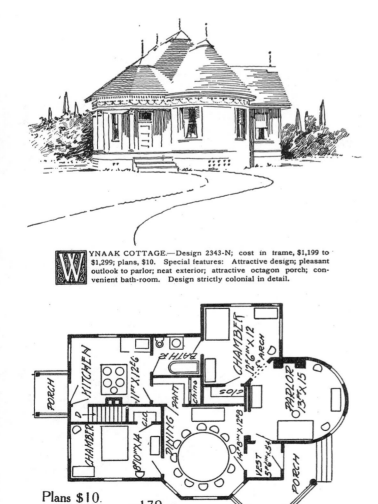

WYNAAK COTTAGE.—Design 2343-N; cost in frame, $1,199 to $1,299; plans, $10. Special features: Attractive design; pleasant outlook to parlor; neat exterior; attractive octagon porch; convenient bath-room. Design strictly colonial in detail.

PORCH

KITCHEN

11'X12·6

BATH

CHAMBER 12·6 X 12

PORCH

CHAMBER 13·10 X 14

DINING 14·8 X 12·8

PANT CHINA CLOS

PARLOR 13 X 15

VEST 5·6 X 5·6

PORCH

Plans $10.   —179—

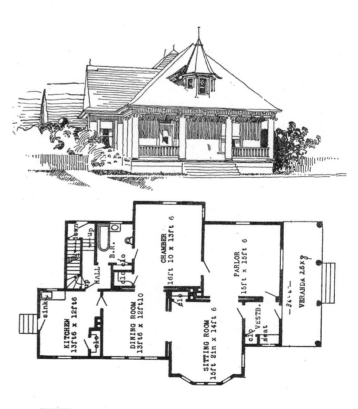

PROCTOR COTTAGE.—Design 2303-N; cost in frame, $1,240 to $1,390; plans, $10. Special features: Quaint dormer window on roof; combination inside and outside cellar stairs; large rooms; large attractive vestibule; a very attractive cottage.

down up

BR

sink

KITCHEN 13ft6 x 12ft6

HALL

CHAMBER 13ft 10 x 13ft 6

DINING ROOM 13ft6 x 12ft10

PARLOR 15ft x 15ft 6

SITTING ROOM 16ft 2in x 14ft 6

VESTB.
seat

VERANDA 26X8

Plans $10.   —180—

OCONOMOWOC COTTAGE.—Design 1649-O; in frame, $550 to $700; plans, $5; width, 21 ft. 4 in. by 23 ft.; width over all, 35 ft.; story heights, 9 ft. 4 in. and 8 ft. Special features: Attractive stained shingle seashore house. Modifications: An extra room could be placed where porch now is. See page 33.

BROOKSVILLE COTTAGE.—Design 8200-N; in frame, $1,192 to $1,390; plans, $10; story heights, 9 ft. and 8 ft. 6 in.; floored attic with space for two good sized rooms. Special features: Practical and attractive design; well-ventilated rooms.

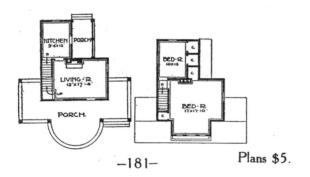

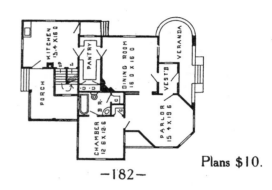

-181-   Plans $5.

-182-   Plans $10.

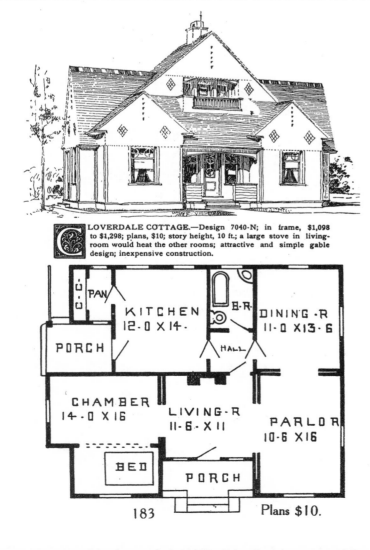

LOVERDALE COTTAGE.—Design 7040-N; in frame, $1,098 to $1,298; plans, $10; story height, 10 ft.; a large stove in living-room would heat the other rooms; attractive and simple gable design; inexpensive construction.

183   Plans $10.

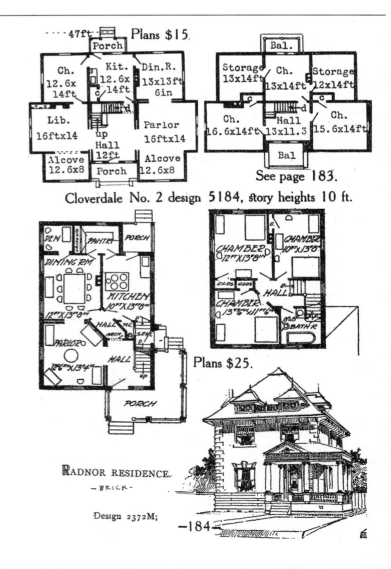

Plans $15.

Cloverdale No. 2 design 5184, story heights 10 ft.

See page 183.

Plans $25.

RADNOR RESIDENCE.
—BRICK—

Design 2372M;

-184-

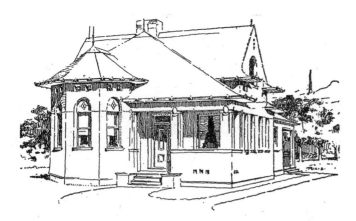

CYNTHIANA COTTAGE.—Design 81-O; cost $692 to $749; plans, $10. Also modified plan No 2, Banker design, with 9x9 ft kitchen back of rear chamber, with pantry, with fire-place to front chamber only, with present back chamber used as 13x14 ft dining-room, with present parlor and dining-room used as chambers, with extra 9x10 ft. chamber back of this, with large closets in two back chambers; plans, $10. Also modified plan No. 3, Boucher design, same as No. 2, except it has rear stairs and bath in place of rear chamber, with 9x12 ft. kitchen; also (Raben) Cynthiana No. 4, with 7x12 bath in place of pantry, with fire-place omitted in rear chamber and dining-room, with door and stoop to dining-room. See page 65.

Plans $10.

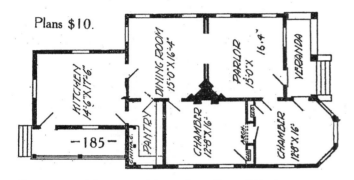

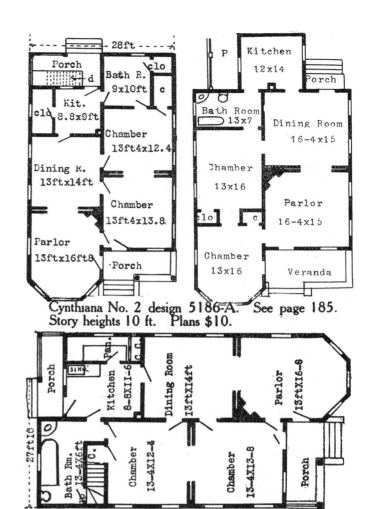

Cynthiana No. 2 design 5186-A. See page 185.
Story heights 10 ft. Plans $10.

Cynthiana No. 3 design 5186-B. See page 185.
Story heights 10 ft. Plans $10. —186—

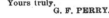

Albany, Mo.
Mr. Herbert C. Chivers, St. Louis, Mo.
Dear Sir: I have neglected to write until now, but will say that my house gives me entire satisfaction. It is just what I wanted. It is. roomy, well lighted and ventilated. It is admired by everybody for its inside comfort. Your plans were a success and were followed in every particular.
Yours truly,
G. F. PERRY.

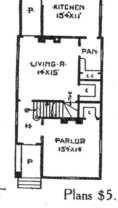

Plans $5.

ALBERT LEA COTTAGE.—Design 2213-O; in frame, $380 to $450; plans, $5; width, 21 ft. 6 in. by 44 ft.; story heights, 10 ft. Special features: Large living room, pantry and closets; convenient stairs; very economical to build.

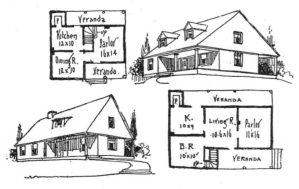

CHEAP COTTAGES.—Plans $5 each. Plans $5.

CLAREMONT COTTAGE.—Design 1971; in frame, $575 to $680; plans, $5.; width, 31 ft. x 22 ft. 6 in.; story heights, 9 ft. 6 in. and 8 ft. 6 in. Special features; large living room. See page 65.

Plans $5.

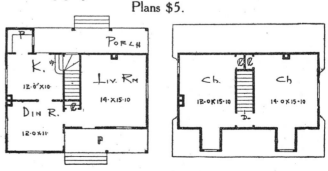

The plans which you drew for my house have not yet been used, owing to lateness of season, but builders state that plans are finely executed.
L. GALLAGHER, Allegheny, Pa.

My summer house will cost a little more than I expected to put into it, but I am so well pleased with the arrangement, that I have decided to make no changes.
A. LOEB, Philadelphia, Pa.

NAPLES COTTAGE.—Design 1782-N; cost in frame, $1,592 to $1,780; plans, $10. Plain, neat exterior; large parlor; compact arrangement.

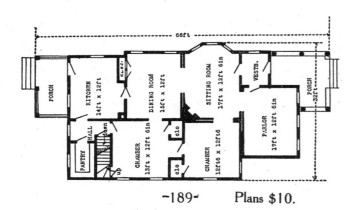

-189-   Plans $10.

LAVADA COTTAGE.—Design 82M; cost, $590 to $698; story heights, 9 ft and 8 ft. Plans, $10. See page 65.

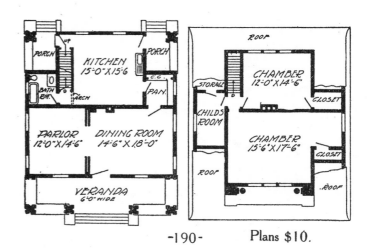

-190-   Plans $10.

RACINE COTTAGE.—Design 1764-O; in frame, $789 to $998; plans, $10; width over all, 26 ft. 2 in.; story heights, 10 ft. Special features: Compact plan, attractive tower-like bay, bath-room ventilated through slat window to attic stairs and lighted by ceiling panel of ground glass. See page 65.

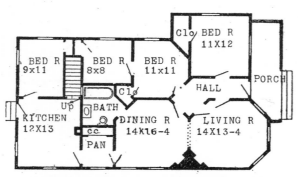

The plans you sent were correct in every respect and the work on them something to be admired.   IRA LAUT. Wenona, Ill.

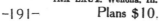

-191-   Plans $10.

ADKIN COTTAGE.—Design 2399-N; cost in brick with 9-inch wall, $2,580 to $3,000; plans, $15. Special features: Attractive porch; large sitting-room; well-ventilated kitchen; large bathroom; very suitable as a corner-lot design; circular portion of porch works-up attractively in design.

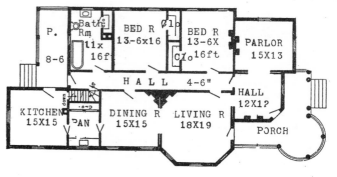

Plans $15.   -192-

ITASCA RESIDENCE.—Design 2255-O; cost in frame $1,492 to $1,580; plans $10. See page 65.

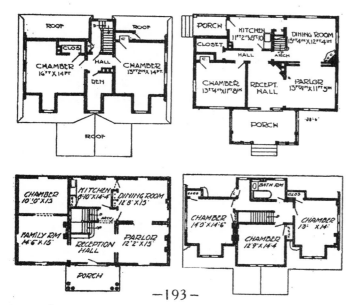

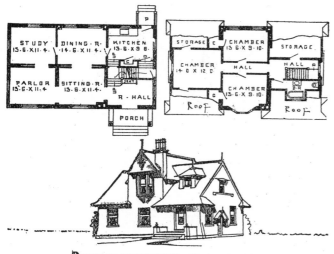

—193—

ITASCA RESIDENCE No. 2.

ALGONA RESIDENCE.—Design 100,040-O; width, 47 ft.; cost, in brick, $2,340 to $2,498; plans, $15; story heights, 1st 10 ft. 6 in., 2d 9 ft. cut down to 5 ft. See page 65.

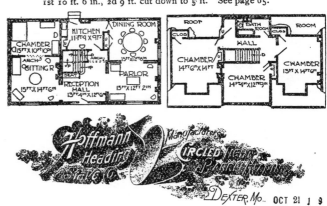

HERBERT C. CHIVERS, ESQ.,
ST. LOUIS, MO.

DEAR SIR:—

PLANS MADE BY YOU HAVE PROVED SATISFACTORY. THE DESIGN OF THE HOUSE IS NEAT IN APPEARANCE AND COSY. I AM WELL PLEASED.
YOURS TRULY,

—194—

DWIGHT RESIDENCE.—Design 9742-O; $422 to $527; plans, $7.50; width over all, 16 ft.; story heights, 9 ft. cut down to 5 ft. walls. Special features: Stained shingle

H. C. Chivers,
St. Louis, Mo.

Dear Sir:—
The plans and specifications furnished me by you about a year ago were satisfactory in every respect and I take pleasure in stating to you that I am well pleased with the house in every detail.

Yours respectfully,

L. E. Tyler.

—195—

CHATTANOOGA RESIDENCE.—Design 1869 M; in frame, $960 to $1090; plans, $10; width, 36 ft. 2 in. by 29 ft. 6 in.; width over all. 40 ft.; story heights, 9 ft. 6 in. and 9 ft.

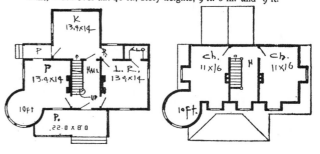

GEO. W. BARKER.
Attorney and Counselor at Law.
509 MONADNOCK BLD.
CHICAGO. ILL.

June 27th 19

Herbert C. Chivers, Esq.,
St. Louis, Mo.

Dear Sir:—

My house built from your plans is the envy and admiration of the whole village and redounded greatly to the credit of the architect.

Respectfully,

Geo. W. Barker.

—196—

DAYTON COTTAGE.—
Design 1638-O;

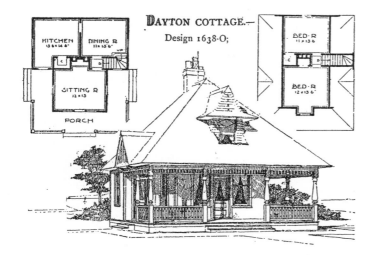

Mr. Herbert C. Chivers,
    St. Louis, Mo.
Dear Sir:-

    The house for which you prepared plans,
suits me exactly. I could not be better pleased.
I consider distance no barrier when dealing with
an architect of your ability, as you seem to know
intuitively what pleases one.

        Yours very truly,

—197—

JAMAICA RESIDENCE.—Design 1599-O; in frame, $1,-
285 to $1490; plans, $10; width, 27 x 39 ft.; story heights, 9 ft.
6 in. and 9 ft.; special features; bath room on first floor. See
page 65.

GALLATIN RESIDENCE.—Design 1530-O; in frame, $1,-
190 to $1260; in 9 in. brick, $1399 to $1480; plans, $10 in
frame or brick; width over all, 20 ft. 6 in.; story heights, 9.6
and 9 ft.; special features; large living-room, with fire-place;
chamber convenient to living-room; a very picturesque house
when built; modifications; Can furnish plans, with cellar entrance at grade, connecting with the regular cellar stairs by a
swinging door See page 65.

—198—

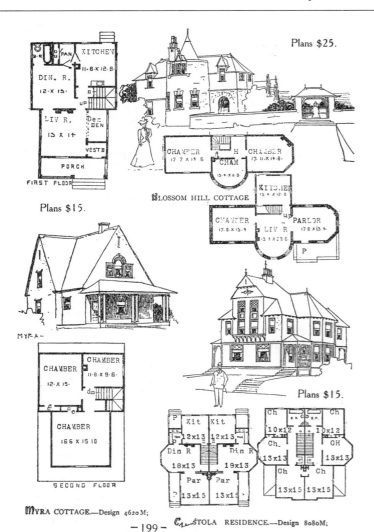

Plans $25.

Plans $15.

BLOSSOM HILL COTTAGE.

MYRA—

Plans $15.

MYRA COTTAGE.—Design 4620 M;

CRESTOLA RESIDENCE.—Design 8080M;

—199—

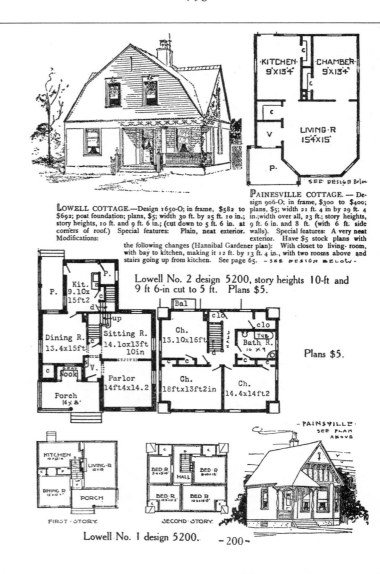

LOWELL COTTAGE.—Design 1650-O; in frame, $582 to
$692; post foundation; plans, $5; width 30 ft. by 25 ft. 10 in.;
story heights, 10 ft. and 9 ft. 6 in.; (cut down to 5 ft. 6 in. at
corners of roof.) Special features: Plain, neat exterior.
Modifications:

PAINESVILLE COTTAGE. — Design 906-O; in frame, $300 to $400;
plans, $5; width 21 ft. 4 in by 29 ft. 4
in.;width over all, 23 ft.; story heights,
9 ft. 6 in. and 8 ft. (with 6 ft. side
walls). Special features: A very neat
exterior. Have $5 stock plans with
the following changes (Hannibal Gardener plan): With closet to living-room,
with bay to kitchen, making it 12 ft. by 13 ft. 4 in., with two rooms above and
stairs going up from kitchen. See page 65. —SEE DESIGN BELOW—

Lowell No. 2 design 5200, story heights 10-ft and
9 ft 6-in cut to 5 ft. Plans $5.

Plans $5.

Lowell No. 1 design 5200.

—200—

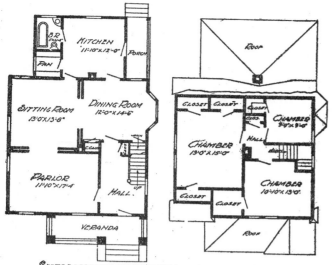

SHELLMOUND RESIDENCE. — Hutton design 19-O; cost, $940 to $1,090; story heights, 9 ft. Plans, $10. See page 65.

Shellmound No. 2, Shervell design, same as above; with 12x12 ft. kitchen; with three rooms above and large attractive bath-room and with light attractive gables and porch.

Shellmound No. 3, Welen design, same as Shellmound, with bay and kitchen porch on opposite side of house; with bath omitted and door out onto porch in its place; with stairs to basement on opposite side and extra kitchen closet.

Lindsborg, Kansas, June 28; 19
Herbert C. Chivers, Architect.
St. Louis, Mo.
My Dear Sir:—
The plans for my house are all in the contractor's hands. Were very much pleased with them, and will send you snap shot picture of the structure as soon as completed. We are trying to follow your suggestions as closely as possible, and will certainly be glad to speak a good word for you to others who are contemplating to build houses in the near future.
Truly yours,
SAMUEL THORSTENBURG.

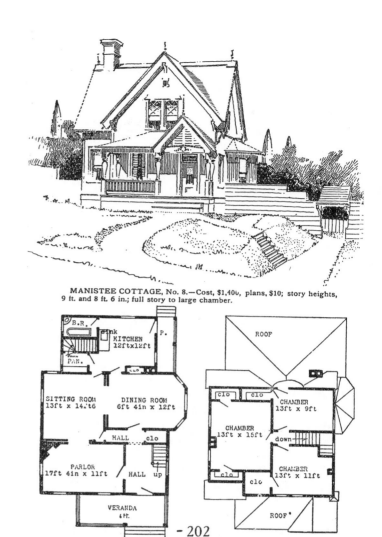

MANISTEE COTTAGE, No. 8.—Cost, $1,400, plans, $10; story heights, 9 ft. and 8 ft. 6 in.; full story to large chamber.

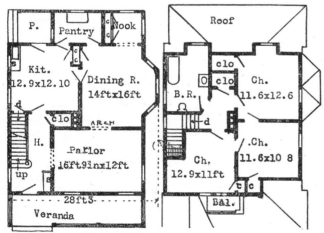

Manistee No. 13 design 5203-A, story heights 9 and 9 ft cut to 6 ft. See pages 201-2-4-5-6 and 208. Plans $10.

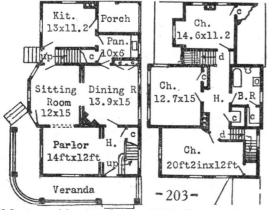

Manistee No. 14 design 5203-B, story heights 9 ft 6. See pages 201-2-4-5-6 and 208. Plans $10.

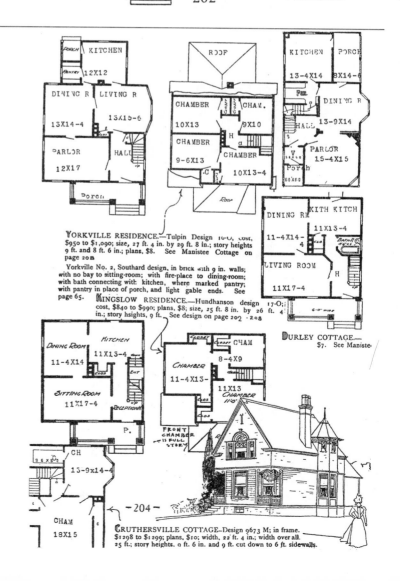

YORKVILLE RESIDENCE.—Tulpin Design 16-O, cost, $950 to $1,090; size, 27 ft. 4 in. by 29 ft. 8 in.; story heights 9 ft. and 8 ft. 6 in.; plans, $8. See Manistee Cottage on page 208.

Yorkville No. 2, Southard design, in brick with 9 in. walls; with no bay to sitting-room; with fire-place to dining-room; with bath connecting with kitchen, where marked pantry; with pantry in place of porch, and light gable ends. See page 65.

KINGSLOW RESIDENCE.—Hundhanson design 17-O; cost, $840 to $990; plans, $8; size, 25 ft. 8 in. by 26 ft. 4 in.; story heights, 9 ft. See design on page 202 -208

DURLEY COTTAGE.— $7. See Manistee

CRUTHERSVILLE COTTAGE-Design 9673 M; in frame. $1298 to $1299; plans, $10; width, 22 ft. 4 in.; width over all. 25 ft.; story heights, 9 ft. 6 in. and 9 ft. cut down to 6 ft. sidewalls.

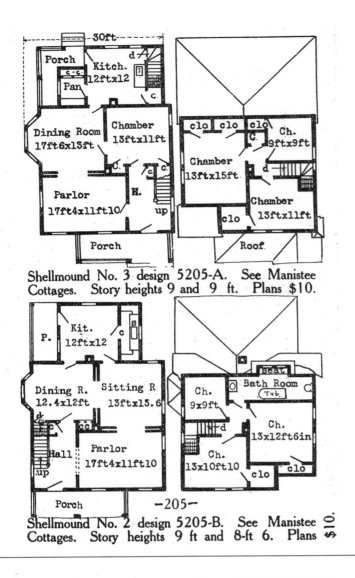

Shellmound No. 3 design 5205-A. See Manistee Cottages. Story heights 9 and 9 ft. Plans $10.

Shellmound No. 2 design 5205-B. See Manistee Cottages. Story heights 9 ft and 8-ft 6. Plans $10.

—205—

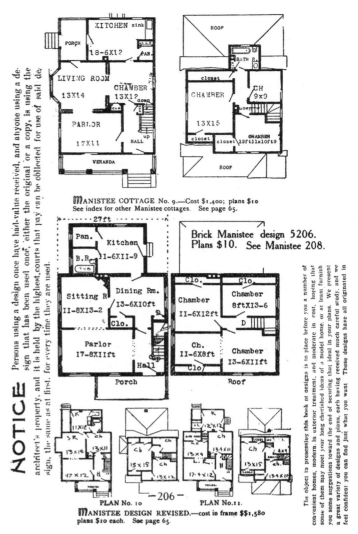

MANISTEE COTTAGE No. 9.—Cost $1,400; plans $10 See index for other Manistee cottages. See page 65.

Brick Manistee design 5206. Plans $10. See Manistee 208.

PLAN No. 10   PLAN No. 11

MANISTEE DESIGN REVISED.—cost in frame $$1,580 plans $10 each. See page 65.

—206—

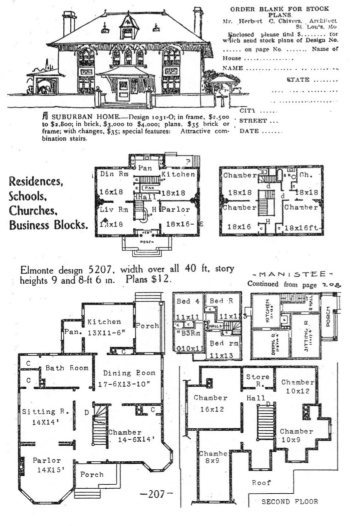

ORDER BLANK FOR STOCK PLANS.
Mr. Herbert C. Chivers, Architect, St. Louis, Mo.
Enclosed please find $.......... for which send stock plans of Design No. .... on page No. .... Name of House ....
NAME ....
STATE ....
CITY .....
STREET ...
DATE ....

A SUBURBAN HOME.—Design 1031-O; in frame, $2,500 to $2,800; in brick, $3,000 to $4,000; plans $35 brick or frame; with changes, $35; special features: Attractive combination stairs.

Residences, Schools, Churches, Business Blocks.

Elmonte design 5207, width over all 40 ft, story heights 9 and 8-ft 6 in. Plans $12.

—MANISTEE—
Continued from page 208

SECOND FLOOR

—207—

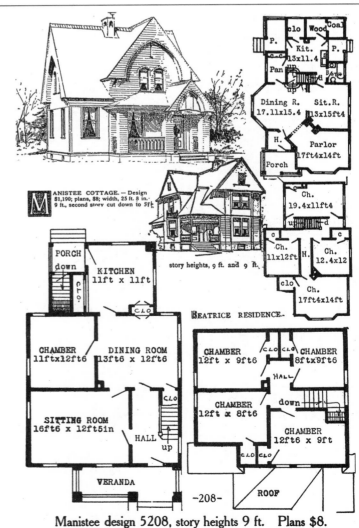

MANISTEE COTTAGE.—Design $1,190; plans, $8; width, 25 ft. 8 in. 9 ft, second story cut down to 5 ft.

story heights, 9 ft. and 9 ft.

BEATRICE RESIDENCE.

Manistee design 5208, story heights 9 ft. Plans $8.

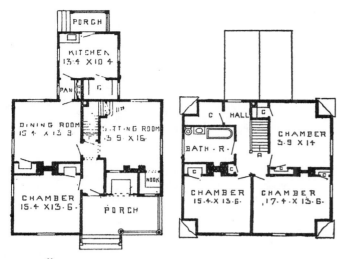

NEMO RESIDENCE. — Design 49-Q; cost, $1,089 to $1,198; size, 33 ft. 8 in. by 46 ft.; story heights, 11 ft. Suitable for the south, design similar to Lowell Cottage on page 399. See Winchester des. on page 336. See page 65.

Nemo Res. No. 2, Smith design, (reversed) with 13 in. brick walls to first story, with kitchen, porch on dining-room side; with kitchen stairs to basement.

Nemo No. 3, Brand des., same as above, with exterior like Winchester des, with sliding door at dining-room in place of fire-place, with porch back of sitting-room and extra 12x9 chamber above. See page 65.

COLONIAL RESIDENCE. — Design 888M; in frame, $3,590 to $4,980; plans, $40. See page 65.

-209-

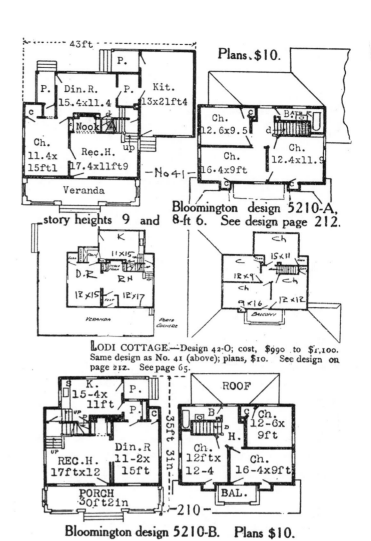

Plans, $10.

story heights 9 and 8-ft 6. See design page 212.

Bloomington design 5210-A.

LODI COTTAGE. — Design 42-O; cost, $990 to $1,100. Same design as No. 41 (above); plans, $10. See design on page 212. See page 65.

Bloomington design 5210-B. Plans $10.

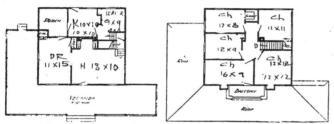

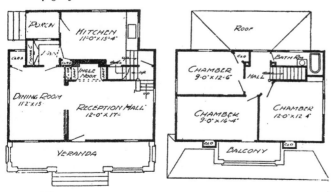

AVILLA COTTAGE. — Sparey design 41-O; cost, $896 to $995; size, 29 ft. 8 in. by 29 ft.; story heights, 9 ft. and 8 ft. 6 in. in the clear. See general design on page 21 but porch has posts, and veranda is extremely wide; plans, $10 See page 65.

MURRAY COTTAGE. — Design 40-O; cost, $699 to $889; story heights, 9 ft. and 8 ft. in the clear; plans, $7. Also have modified plan No. 4, (Rupe design) with kitchen and dining-room; with 5x5 serving pantry where sink is; and with 13x24 kitchen extension at right hand side. Modification No. 5, Coryell design; the only change being corner-fire-place in reception room in place of wide angle-nook fire-place.

Plans were very complete and it will make a fine building when complete. R. C. McWilliams, Boscobel, Wis

-211-

BLOOMINGTON. — Design 1627-N; in frame, $1,199 to $1,298; plans, $10; width, 29 ft. 8 in. by 27 ft.; story heights, 9 ft. and 8 ft. 6 in.; cut down by roof in front and rear to 6 ft. 9 in. Special features: Large living room; unique porch arrangement. I have this plan with several other modifications.

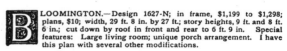

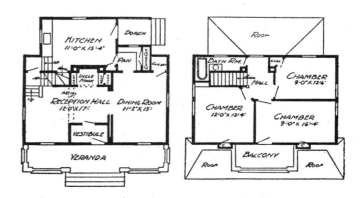

-212-

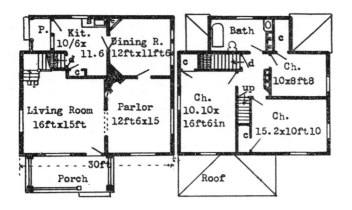

Bloomington design 5213-A, story heights 9 and 9-ft 3. See similar design page 211. Plans $10.

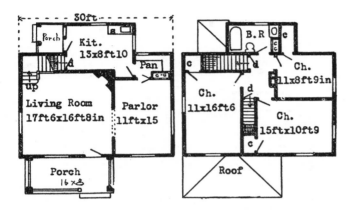

Bloomington design 5213-B, story heights 9 and 9-ft 3. See page 212. Plans $10.

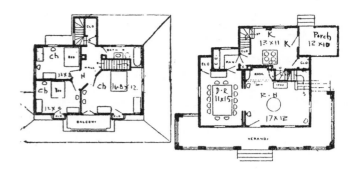

Hagerstown-Bloomington design 5214-A. See design page 212. Story heights 9 ft and 8 ft 6. Plans $10.

Bloomington design 5214-B, story heights 9 and 8-ft 6. Plans $10.

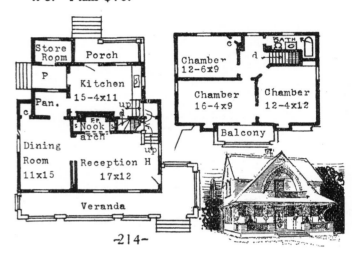

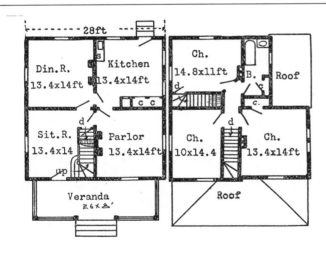

GALVESTON COTTAGE.—Design 1747-O; in frame; $590 to $648; plans, $10; width 26 ft. 6 in. by 19 ft.; story heights, 9 ft. 6 in. and 8 ft. 6 in. (full story in large chamber). Special features: Compact plan; wide front; a large appearing building for the money; 6 ft. porch across front. See page 65.

My Plans are well made. Everything is carefully laid out and figured. Experience in construction is a great teacher.

RED OAK COTTAGE.—Design 899M; in frame, $695 to $789; plans, $10; width, 26 ft. 10 in. by 25 ft. 3 in.; story heights, 9 ft. cut down by roof to 5 ft. 6 in. inside walls. See page 65.

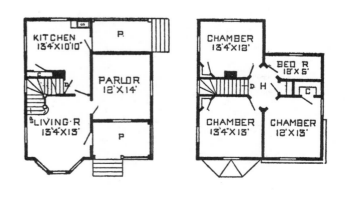

ENGLISH COTTAGE.—Design 1620-O; in frame, $422 to $528; plans, $7; width over all, 23 ft.; story heights, 9 ft. and 8 ft., (cut down by roof to 5 ft.). Special features: Quaint English gable; large dining-room. Modifications: Stairs could go up from living-room; bath-room could be placed in second-story hall. See page 65.

Edgerton O., October 10, 1899.
I like your plans better than any others I have seen.
MISS R. KATE GARDINER, Amsterdam, N. Y.

—Books—

Small books of plans have been published heretofore by so-called plan associations, and publishing companies, but nothing has yet been produced by a regular practicing architect on this stupendious scale, and devoted entirely to moderate-cost houses.

BUCKINGHAM COTTAGE.—Design 1954M; in frame, $690 to $799; plans, $10; width, 37 ft. by 24 ft.; story heights, 9 ft. and 9 ft. cut down by roof to 7 ft. Special features: Attractive window at stairs. See page 65.

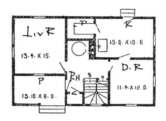
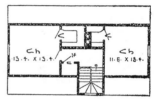

The plans and specifications you furnished for my cottage at Webster Groves were very satisfactory. I feel well assured that I have the best planned house in St. Louis County. W. A. WILSON. (Pacific Express Co.), St. Louis.

 BOSTON COTTAGE.—Design 1646-N; in frame, $1,288 to $1,410; plans, $10; width over all, 37 ft. 6 in.; story heights, 9 ft. 6 in. and 9 ft. in the clear. Special features: Open terrace in front; unique stained shingle exterior; good skylines; simple to construct.

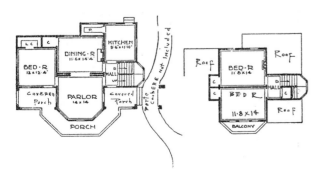

I want to congratulate you on your plans, as they certainly contain many desirable features which commend themselves to the prospective builder.—J. N. P. Colwell, Stapleton, S. I.

GLENDALE COTTAGE.—Design 1626-N; in frame, $764 to $890; plans, $5; width, 27 ft. 4 in. by 20 ft. 4 in.; story heights, 9 ft. 6 in. and 9 ft. in the clear. Special features: Plain, simple, stained shingle exterior; large sitting-room; compact arrangement.

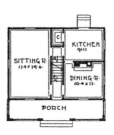
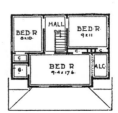

I have thought frequently that I would write and let you know how well pleased we were with our home, which was built from your plans. The house is as pretty, convenient and comfortable as I could wish. I am indeed, well pleased with your services, and would not think of building again without first seeing you. MRS. DAVID HAY, Fulton, Ky.

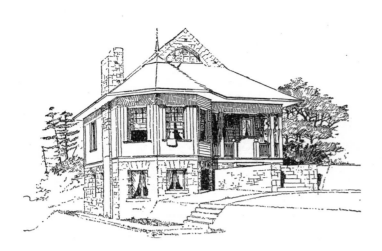

 LD ORCHARD COTTAGE.—Design 1635-N; in frame, $665 to $800; plans, $5; width, 25 ft. by 28 ft. 4 in.; story heights, 9 ft. 6 in.; suitable for a sloping lot. Modifications: Furnace can be put in storeroom. A good hill-side design. SEE PAGE 222.

FIRST STORY

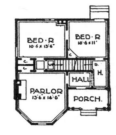

SECOND STORY

—221—

I have just completed a house from one of yours plans. The house in question is neat and tasty and of very satisfactory design.
FRANK C. PATTEN, (Manufacturer), Sycamore, Ill.

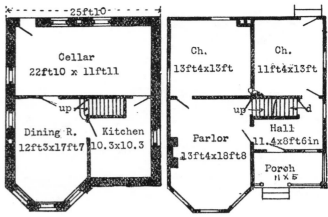

Old Orchard Cottage No. 2 design 5222-A. See design page 221. Story heights 9 and 8 ft. Plans $5.

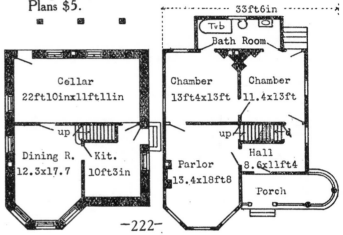

—222—

Old Orchard Cottage No. 3 design 5222-B, story heights 9 and 8 ft. See design page 221. Plans $5.

 AUKESHAW COTTAGE.—Design 1624-N; cost in frame, $650 to $750 plans, $5. See modified $5 plans in Conkey's Home Journal (Chicago, 10c.,) for December, Special features: Very compact plan; combination inside and outside cellar stairs.

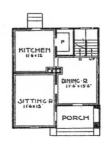

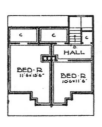

—223—

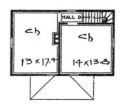

GENEVA LAKE COTTAGE.—Design 1634-N; in frame, $775 to $966; plans, $5; width, 18 ft. by 26 ft. 4 in.; story heights, 8 ft. 6 in. and 8 ft. Special features: Ornamental gable and porch design. Modifications: Dining-room can be enlarged by building one-story kitchen behind. Geneva Lake No. 2, Smith design, with 14.6x10 ft. dining-room; 14.6x9 ft. 6 in. kitchen; with three rooms above, sizes, 14x16 ft., 10.6x9 ft., and 14.6x9 ft. 4 in., with closets to each room; story heights, 9 ft. cut down to 6 ft. at four corners of building.

—224—

OMAHA COTTAGE.—Design 1626-N; in frame, $815 to $900; plans, $8; width, 24 ft. 6 in. by 28 ft. 10 in.; story heights, 9 ft. 6 in. and 9 ft. Special features: Front rooms unobstructed by stairs. Have $10 stock plans with the following changes named: Worthen plan, with corner fire place to parlor, with sitting-room 13.4x11 ft., with sliding doors between main rooms, with 14x14 ft. 6 in. kitchen, with bath-room above and 11.4x14 ft. room over kitchen, with closet, also closet in hall.

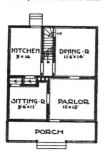 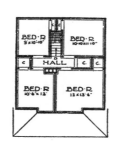

LEADVILLE COTTAGE.—Design 900 M; in frame and stone, $900 to $1,000; plans, $10; story heights, 9 ft. and 8 ft. (cut down to 5 ft. at walls.) Special features; Attractive combination of stained shingles and stone; a plain, neat design, free from unnecessary ornamentation. See page 65.

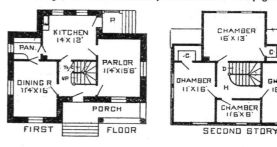

FIRST FLOOR   SECOND STORY

(From a builder).—Your books came to hand Sunday. Would say in reply it was not for myself but for a neighbor. I was telling him it would have paid him better to have procured plans of you showing all details of construction and giving a better idea of how things went together. I am a carpenter myself and know whereof I speak.—Geo. Bennett, Festus, Mo.

OAKWOOD.—Design 2350-N; cost in frame, $550 to $650; plans, $10. Special features: Attractive parlor; combination inside and outside cellar entrance; wide veranda. A good lake or sea-side cottage in stained shingles

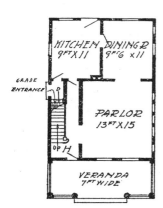 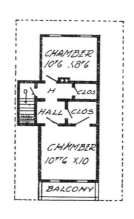

NEWARK COTTAGE.—Design 1636-N; in frame, $568 to $670; plans, $5; width, 25 ft. 8 in. by 23 ft. 8 in.; story heights, 9 ft. and 8 ft. 6 in., (side walls, 6 ft. 6 in. high). Simple shingle exterior; simple detail work; easy to construct; very little mill work.

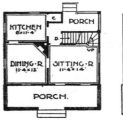 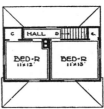

We not only have a handsome house, but a very convenient and practical floor plan. You saved me the price of plans many times over in the novel arrangement of floor plans alone.
LUTHER ARMSTRONG, Champaign, Ill.

 INCINNATI COTTAGE.—Design 1620-N; in frame, $644 to $790; plans, $5; width, 25 ft. 8 in. by 28 ft.; story heights, 9 ft. and 8 ft. 6 in. Special features: Unique porch and gable ends; economical flue connections. Modifications: Inside stairs to cellar can go down below rear stairs.

 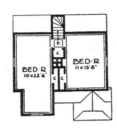

The secret of the Realty and the Power of Art lies in the fact that it is the culmination and summing up of the processes of observation, experience, and feeling; it is the deposit of whatever is richest and most enduring in the life of a Man or a Race.—Mabie

KANKAKEE COTTAGE.—Design 2361-M; plans $10; cost $650. See page 65.

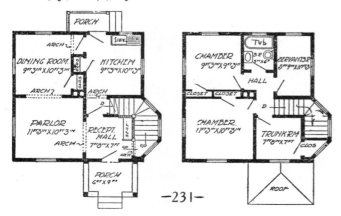

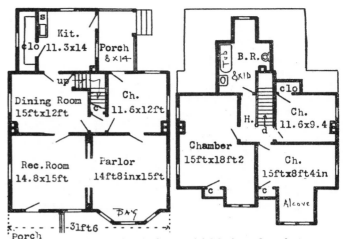

Cincinnati No. 2 design 5230-A. See design page 229. Story heights 9 and 8 ft. Plans $5.

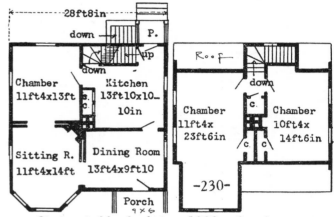

Cincinnati No. 3 design 5230. See design page 229, story heights 9 and 8 ft. Plans $5.

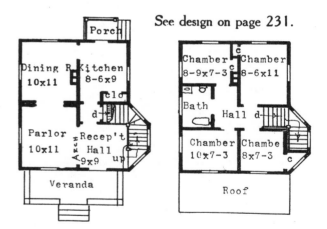

See design on page 231.

Kankakee No. 3 design 5232-B, story heights 9 ft and 8 ft 6. Plans $5.

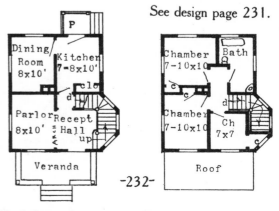

See design page 231.

Kankakee No. 2 design 5232. story heights 9 ft. 6 and 8 ft 6. Plans $5.

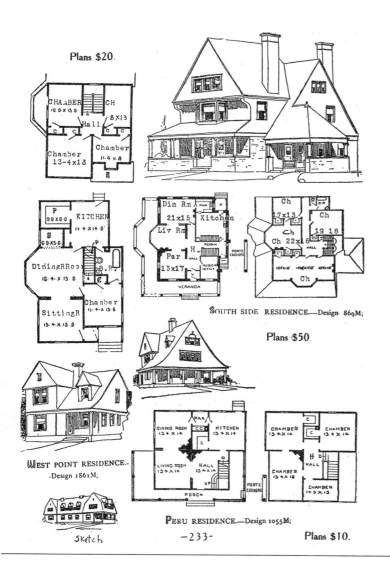

Plans $20.

SOUTH SIDE RESIDENCE.—Design 869M;

Plans $50.

WEST POINT RESIDENCE.—Design 1861M;

PERU RESIDENCE.—Design 1055M;

Sketch

—233—

Plans $10.

ALLENDALE COTTAGE.—Design 5091M; in frame, $550 to $650; plans, $5; width, 34 ft. by 22 ft. See page 65.

—234—

ADEN COTTAGE.—Design 4200M; in frame, $350 to $450; plans, $5; width, 27 ft. 4 in. by 23 ft. 8 in.; story heights, 9 ft. 8 in. and 8 ft., (side walls cut down to 6 ft.) See page 65.

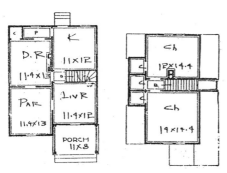

FOND DU LAC COTTAGE.—Design 1637-O; in frame, $640 to $770; plans, $5. Modifications: Bath-room could be placed in rear of sitting-room, using dining-room as a bed room with kitchen as dining-room and with one-story kitchen. See page 65.

—235—

LAKE GEORGE COTTAGE.—Design 1630-N; in frame, $499 to $546; plans, $5; width, 25 ft. 4 in. by 20 ft. 6 in.; width over all, 28 ft.; story heights, 9 ft. 6 in. and 8 ft.; side walls cut down to 5 ft. Special features: Neat exterior, attractive window to hall.

Art is one of the two organs of human progress. By words man interchanges thoughts; by the forms of art he interchanges feelings; and this with all men, not only of the present time but also of the past and of the future.—Tolstoy

—236—

OSHKOSH COTTAGE.—Design 1625-O; in frame, $375 to $475; plans, $5; width, 17 ft. 6 in. by 22 ft. 6 in.; story heights, 9 ft. 6 in. and 9 ft. Special features: Compact plan. Have $5 stock-plans with the following changes, named (Oshkosh No. 2,) with gable ends. full story and 18 ft. 4 in. by 24 ft. in size. A very attractive exterior. See page 65. & 240

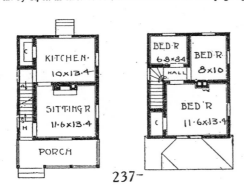

237-

GREEN PARK COTTAGE.—Design 1633-O; in frame, $744 to $899; plans, $8; width, 22 ft. by 34 ft.; width over all, 30 ft.; story heights, 9 ft. 6 in. and 9 ft. Special features: Wide open veranda on three sides of house, balcony in front. Modifications: Stairs could go up from kitchen or dining-room; the rear porch space used as pantry; the hall space enlarged by bay. See page 65.

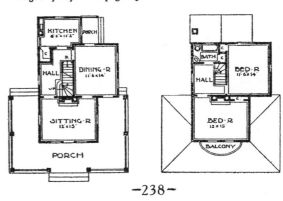

-238-

ROBROY COTTAGE.—Design 1966 M; in frame. $561 to $690; plans, $10; width 25 ft. 6 in. x 34 ft. 10 in.; story heights, 9 ft. 6 in. and 9 ft. (cut down to 4 ft. at sides.) Special features. Water closet and basin on fiirst floor. See page 65.

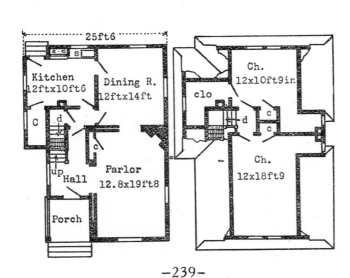

-239-

A careful comparison of the fifty plans herein with a like number in any other book will convince you that for originality, completeness, convenience, practicability, beauty of outline and general merit, these are not only unexceled but unequalled by anv other collection

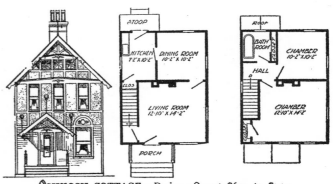

Oshkosh Cottage No. 3, story heights 9 ft and 8ft. Plans $5.

OSHKOSH COTTAGE.—Design 2-O; cost, $650 to $750; plans, $5. A very compact house. See page 65. AND 237

-240-

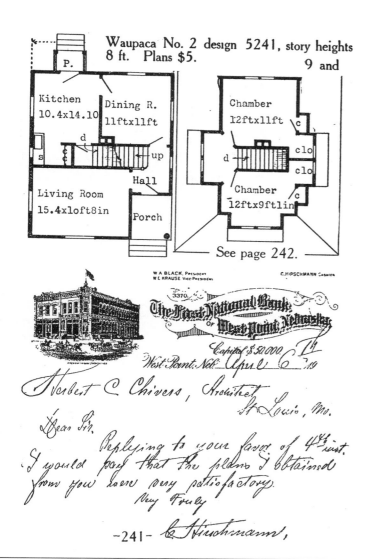

Waupaca No. 2 design 5241, story heights 8 ft. Plans $5.

9 and

Kitchen
10.4x14.10

Dining R.
11ftx11ft

Living Room
15.4x1oft8in

Hall

Porch

up

Chamber
12ftx11ft

clo

clo

Chamber
12ftx9ftl in

See page 242.

WAUPACA COTTAGE.—

KITCHEN
9x11

DINING R
11x11

LIVING R
10x14

HALL

PORCH

BED R
11x12

BED R
10x12

For Waupaca design No. 2 see page 241.

3772.

The Ohio National Bank

J.C. THOMPSON, President
Dr. F. EWING, Vice President
L.H. KIBBY, Cashier
C.H. EAST, Asst Cashier

Lima, O.

June 30th 1 9.

Herbert C. Chivers, Esq.,
St. Louis. Mo.

Dear Sir;

Your postal to hand some days since.
The plans I received from you were all right
and satisfactory and makes a very neat and
pretty house. The house was built on my farm
some ways in the country. When I think of it,
will take Kodak with me and take some pictures
of the house. It presents a very pretty exterior.
Yours etc.,

J.C. Thompson

-242-

BURTVILLE COTTAGE.—Design 9292 M; in frame; $798
to $8,049; plans, $10; width over all, 20 ft. 10 in.; story
heights, 9 ft. and 8 ft. full story. Special features; Compact
roof arrangement, covering front and rear porch. See page 65

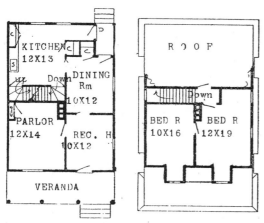

KITCHEN
12X13

DINING Rm
10X12

PARLOR
12X14

REC. H
10X12

Down

VERANDA

ROOF

Down

BED R
10X16

BED R
12X19

The plans which you prepared for my house are in every way satisfactory.
Indeed, it gives me great pleasure to recommend you to any one who desires a
first-class architect as well as honest and prompt treatment.
MRS. S. W. SPITLER, Wellington, Kan.

-243-

TAMPA COTTAGE.—Design 1746M; in frame, $350 to
$498; plans, $7.50; width, 16 ft. 6 in. by 28 ft. 2 in.; story
heights, 9 ft. and 8 ft. in the clear. Special features: Simple
stained shingle gables on side. Clean, neat detail work,
practical out-of-the-way stairs. See page 33.

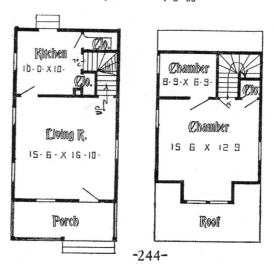

Kitchen
10·0·X 10·

Living R.
15·6·X 16·10·

Porch

Chamber
8·9·X 6·9·

Chamber
15·6·X 12·9·

Roof

-244-

ENERO.—Design 2351-N: cost in frame, $550 to $650; plans, $10. Special features: Combination inside and outside cellar entrance; full second story; attractive gable end and dormer window at side; neat, plain construction.

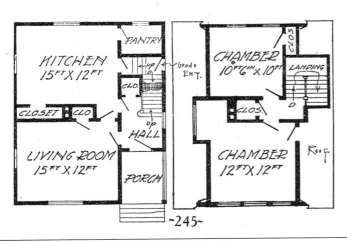

KITCHEN 15 FT X 12 FT
PANTRY
CLO
CLOSET CLO
up
grade ENT.
HALL
LIVING ROOM 15 FT X 12 FT
PORCH

CHAMBER 10 FT 6 IN X 10 FT
CLOS
LANDING
CLOS
D
CHAMBER 12 FT X 12 FT
Roof

—245—

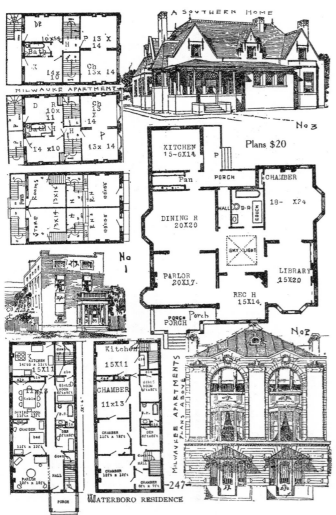

MILWAUKE APARTMENT

A SOUTHERN HOME

No 3

Plans $20

KITCHEN 15-6 X 14
P
Pan
PORCH
CHAMBER 18- X24
HALL
B-R COUCH
DINING R 20X20
SKY LIGHT
PARLOR 20X17.
LIBRARY 15X20
REC H 15X14
PORCH
PORCH

No 1

No 2

Kitchen 15X11
CHAMBER 11x13

MILWAUKEE APARTMENTS PLANS ABOVE

WATERBORO RESIDENCE

—247—

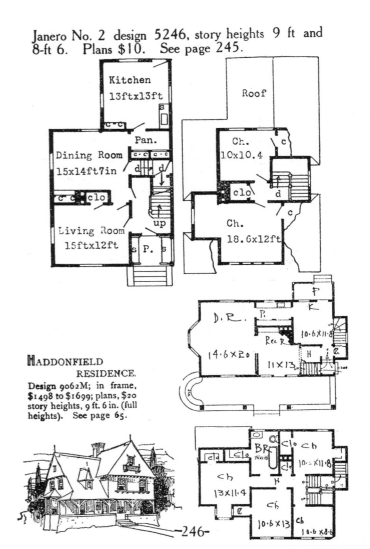

Janero No. 2 design 5246, story heights 9 ft and 8-ft 6. Plans $10. See page 245.

Kitchen 13ftx13ft
Roof
Pan.
Dining Room 15x14ft7in
Ch. 10x10.4
clo
Living Room 15ftx12ft
up
Ch. 18.6x12ft

HADDONFIELD RESIDENCE.
Design 9062M; in frame, $1498 to $1699; plans, $20 story heights, 9 ft. 6 in. (full heights). See page 65.

D. R. 14.6X20
Rec R
10.6X11.8
H
11X13

BR
clo ch 10.6X11.8
clo
ch 13X11.4
ch 10.6 X13
ch 10.6 X8.6

—246—

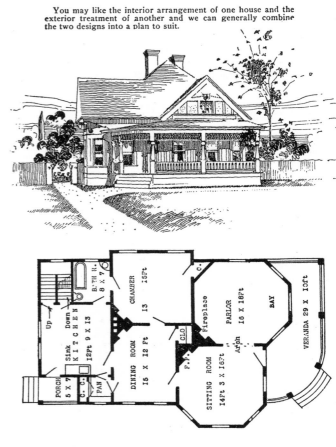

You may like the interior arrangement of one house and the exterior treatment of another and we can generally combine the two designs into a plan to suit.

Up
Down
B'TH R. 8 X 7
CHAMBER 13 X 15 Ft.
C.
Sink KITCHEN 12Ft 9 X 13
DINING ROOM 15 X 12 Ft.
CLO
Fireplace
PARLOR 16 X 16Ft
BAY
F.P.
PAN
PORCH 5 X 7
Arch
SITTING ROOM 14Ft 3 X 16Ft
VERANDA 29 X 10ft

YERGER COTTAGE.—Design 2400-N; cost in frame, $1,180 to $1,390; plans, $10; story height, 10 ft. Space for four rooms above. Special features: Attractive bay-shaped rooms; convenient bath-room; attractive porch; planing-mill ornamentation.

—248—

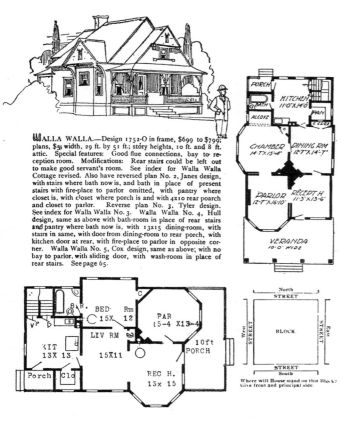

WALLA WALLA.—Design 1752-O in frame, $699 to $799; plans, $5; width, 29 ft. by 51 ft.; story heights, 10 ft. and 8 ft. attic. Special features: Good flue connections, bay to reception room. Modifications: Rear stairs could be left out to make good servant's room. See index for Walla Walla Cottage revised. Also have reversed plan No. 2, Janes design, with stairs where bath now is, and bath in place of present stairs with fire-place to parlor omitted, with pantry where closet is, with closet where porch is and with 4x10 rear poarch and closet to parlor. Reverse plan No. 3, Tyler design. See index for Walla Walla No. 3. Walla Walla No. 4, Hull design, same as above with bath-room in place of rear stairs and pantry where bath now is, with 13x15 dining-room, with stairs in same, with door from dining-room to rear porch, with kitchen door at rear, with fire-place to parlor in opposite corner. Walla Walla No. 5, Cox design, same as above; with no bay to parlor, with sliding door, with wash-room in place of rear stairs. See page 65.

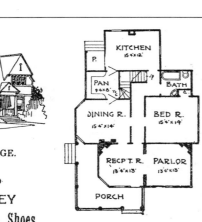

—249—

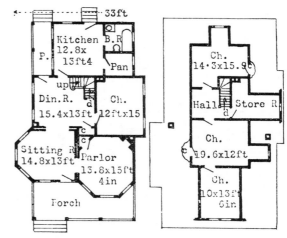

Walla Walla Cottage No. 4 design 5250-A. See Hull design and description page 249. Story heights 9 ft 8 and 8. Plans $5.

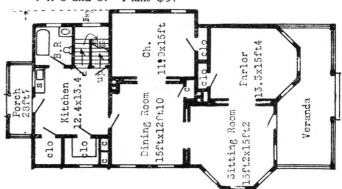

Walla Walla Cottage No. 2 design 5250-B, See Jones description and exterior page 249. Story heights 10 ft. Plans $5. --250 –

EVANSTON COTTAGE.

Design 2242-O

H. A. COREY

Dry Goods, Notions, Shoes

Lehigh, Iowa. June 30, 19

Mr. Herbert C. Chivers,
St. Louis, Mo.

Dear Sir:-

The plans we got from you proved about as good an investment as we ever made and the building far exceeds my expectations. Hundreds have told me that we have the best arranged residence in Fort Dodge. It is a grand looking building and looks to cost considerably more money than it really did, and is different from anything ever built there.

We have never had one person find fault with it, simply, because there is no chance to do so. Get plans from a good architect, save money, and get something to suit you, is my advise to anyone building. Thanking you for your prompt and pleasing ways of doing business, I am yours

Very respectfully,
H. A. Corey

—251—

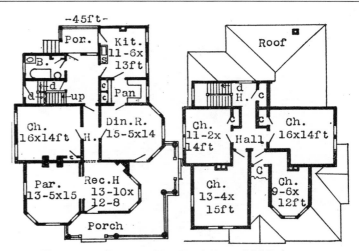

Evanston Cottage No. 3 design 5252-A, story heights 10 and 9 ft, width 45 ft. Plans $10.

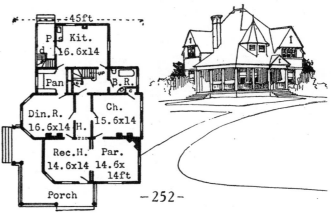

—252—

Evanston Cottage design 5252-B, story heights 11 ft and 8 ft cut down to 5 ft side walls. Plans $10.

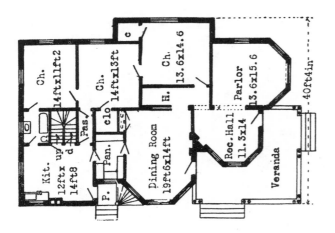

Alleghany Cottage No. 3 design 5253-A, story heights 10 See page 254. Plans $10.

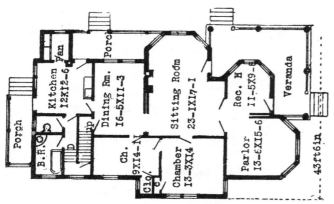

Alleghany Cottage design 5253-B, story heights 10 heights 10 ft and 8 ft 6 cut to 4 ft 6. Plans $10.

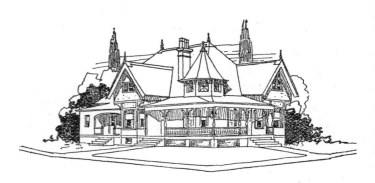

ALLEGHANY COTTAGE.—Design 1975-N; in frame, $1,989 to $2,200; plans, $10; width over all, 44 ft. 10 in.; story height, 10 ft. and 8 ft. attic. Special features: Well-ventilated rooms; large pantry; unique reception-room; wide porch. Modified plan No. 2; plans, $10; same exterior with rear stairs and bath located where pantry now is, size 13x15 ft.; also modified plan No. 3; price, $10; McIntyre plan No. 3, with fire-place in reception-room and living-room only, with rear chamber enlarge to 13x14 ft. extending to kitchen, with large closet, with 15x12 ft. kitchen extending into present pantry space with an extra chamber where bath-room now is, with bath and rear stairs between chamber and kitchen, estimated to cost $3,500. For modified plan No. 4. see Thurman design.

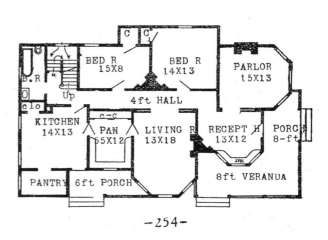

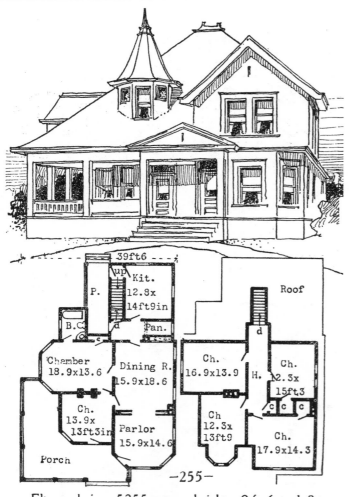

Eltoro design 5255, story heights 9-ft 6 and 8. Plans $15.

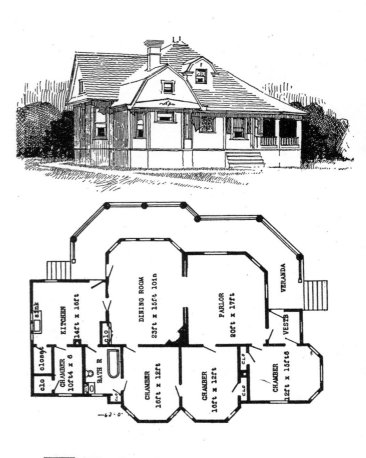

RUGGVILLE COTTAGE.—Design 1781-N; cost, $1,292 to $1,342; plans, $10. Special features: Large dining-room; bay-shaped rooms give good ventilation; servants' room convenient; large 8-foot veranda; attractive gambril roof gable.

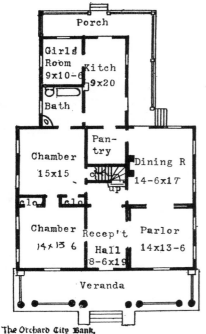

Porch

Girls Room 9x10-6 | Kitch 9x20

Bath

Chamber 15x15 | Pan-try | Dining R 14-6x17

Chamber 14x13 6 | Recep't Hall 8-6x19 | Parlor 14x13-6

up

Veranda

Clifton Springs Cottage design 5257. See opposite page 258. Story heights 11 ft. Plans $10.

The Orchard City Bank,
Xenia, Illinois.

JOSEPH H. TULLY, PRESIDENT.
ASHER R. COX, VICE PRES'T
GEO. W. COX, CASHIER

Oct. 20th 9.

Herbert C. Chivers, Architect,
St. Louis, Mo.
Dear Sir:-
    Replying to your letter of recent date, would say that the plans which you made for the two business blocks and one residence, were entirely satisfactory. I am especially pleased with the exteriors, and consider them the most attractive buildings in this part of the State.
    Should I do any building in the future, I will certainly consult with you in regard to the matter.
        Yours truly,
            Asher R. Cox

-257-

I like your plans very much.   L. L. MORSE, Digby, N. J.

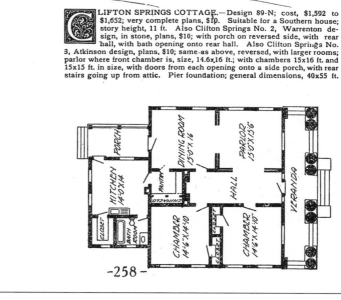

CLIFTON SPRINGS COTTAGE.—Design 89-N; cost, $1,592 to $1,652; very complete plans, $10. Suitable for a Southern house; story height, 11 ft. Also Clifton Springs No. 2, Warrenton design, in stone, plans, $10; with porch on reversed side, with rear hall, with bath opening onto rear hall. Also Clifton Springs No. 3, Atkinson design, plans, $10; same as above, reversed, with larger rooms; parlor where front chamber is, size, 14.6x16 ft.; with chambers 15x16 ft. and 15x15 ft. in size, with doors from each opening onto a side porch, with rear stairs going up from attic. Pier foundation; general dimensions, 40x55 ft.

PORCH

KITCHEN 14'x14 | PANTRY | DINING ROOM 15'x16

CLOSET | BATH ROOM | CHAMBER 14'6"x14'10 | CLOSET | CHAMBER 14'6"x14'10

HALL | PARLOR 15'0"x15'6

VERANDA

-258-

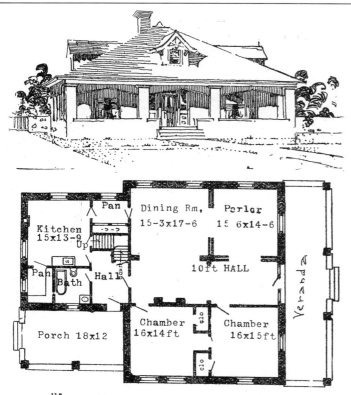

Pan

Kitchen 15x13-9 | Dining Rm. 15-3x17-6 | Parlor 15 6x14-6

Up

Pan | Bath | Hall

10ft HALL

Veranda

Porch 18x12 | Chamber 16x14ft | Chamber 16x15ft

WARRENTOWN COTTAGE.—Design 2394M; cost in stone $2,500 to $3,290; plans $25. See Clifton Springs cot.

DAVENPORT IOWA.

Mr Herbert C Chivers
Saint Louis.
        I wrote you this morning saying your Plans we sent for had not arrived, they came in this afternoons mail, they are very satisfactory

-259-   Jno D Cantwell

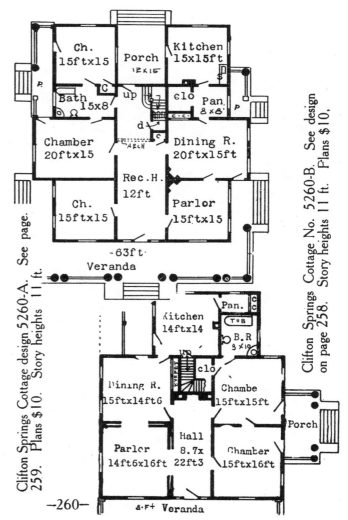

Ch. 15ftx15 | Porch 12x15 | Kitchen 15x15ft

Bath 15x8 | up | clo | Pan. 8x8

Chamber 20ftx15 | Dining R. 20ftx15ft

ARCH

Rec.H. 12ft

Ch. 15ftx15 | Parlor 15ftx15

-63ft-

Veranda

Clifton Springs Cottage design 5260-A. See page. Story heights 11 ft.

Pan.

Kitchen 14ftx14 | B.R 8x10 | TUB

clo

Dining R. 15ftx14ft6 | Chambe 15ftx15ft

Parlor 14ft6x16ft | Hall 8.7x 22ft3 | Chamber 15ftx16ft

Porch

·S·F· Veranda

-260-

Clifton Springs Cottage design 259. Plans $10. Story heights 11 ft.

Clifton Springs Cottage No. 5260-B. See design on page 258. Story heights 11 ft. Plans $10.

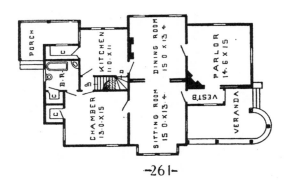

GROVE LAKE COTTAGE.—Design 9789-N; in frame, $1,198 to $1,298; plans, $10; story heights, 9 ft. 6 in. and 8 ft. 6 in. attic. Special features: Wide porch; convenient bath-room; attractive shingle design. Grove Lake No. 2, Brainard design, parlor, 16 ft. 6 in. by 14 ft. 10 in.; dining-room, 17 ft. 2 in. by 13 ft. 4 in.; sitting-room, 18 ft. 2 in. by 13 ft. 4 in.; kitchen, 14 ft. 6 in. by 11 ft.; chamber, 16 ft. by 11 ft. 6 in.; with rear porch.

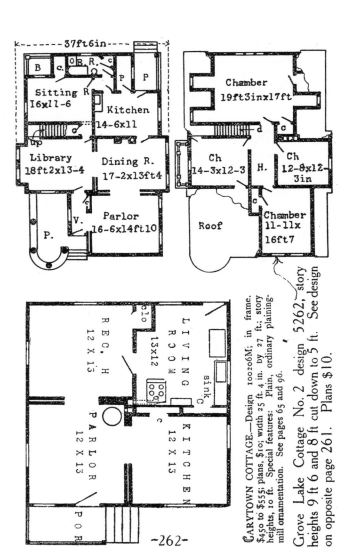

CARYTOWN COTTAGE.—Design 100206M; in frame. $450 to $555; plans, $10; width 25 ft. 4 in. by 27 ft.; story heights, 10 ft. Special features: Plain, ordinary plaining-mill ornamentation. See pages 65 and 96.

Grove Lake Cottage No. 2 design 5262, story heights 9 ft 6 and 8 ft cut down to 5 ft. See design on opposite page 261. Plans $10.

LEWISBURG COTTAGE.—Design 2396M; cost in frame $1,892 to $2,290; plans $20. See page 65.

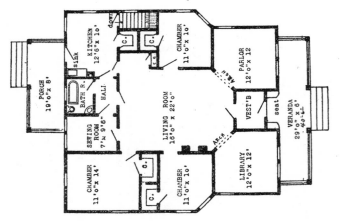

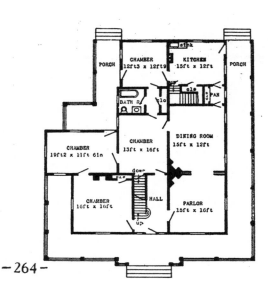

SHANNON COTTAGE.—Design 2407-N; cost in frame, $1,792 to $1,800; plans, $10. Special features: Large veranda; large rooms; convenient bath-room; attractive exterior; economical porch roof. A good Southern cottage.

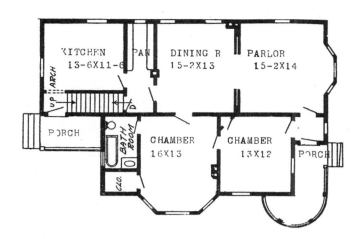

KITCHEN
13-6X11-6
PAN
DINING R
15-2X13
PARLOR
15-2X14

UP PORCH

PORCH

BATH ROOM

CLO.

CHAMBER
16X13

CHAMBER
13X12

PORCH

$AGOLA COTTAGE.—Design 2256M; cost in frame $1,292 to $1,398; plans $10. See page 65.

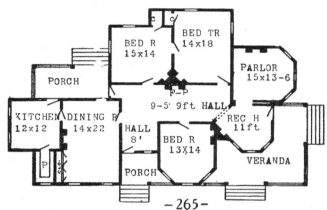

BED R
15x14

BED TR
14x18

PARLOR
15x13-6

PORCH

F-P

9-5 9ft HALL

REC H
11ft

KITCHEN
12x12

DINING R
14x22

HALL
8'

BED R
13X14

VERANDA

PORCH

P

CLO.

—265—

MARINETTE RESIDENCE.—Design 2257-O; cost in frame $1,692 to $1,780; plans $10. See Allegheny Cottage.

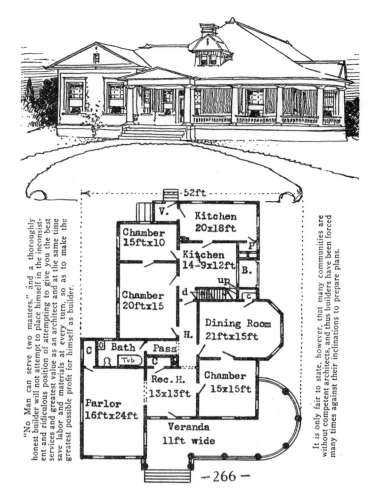

52ft

V.
Kitchen
20x18ft

Chamber
15ftx10

Kitchen
14-9x12ft

up

B.

Chamber
20ftx15

d

Dining Room
21ftx15ft

H.

C

Bath

Pass.

C

Tub

Rec. H.
13x13ft

Chamber
15x15ft

Parlor
16ftx24ft

Veranda
11ft wide

—266—

"No Man can serve two masters," and a thoroughly honest builder will not attempt to place himself in the inconsistent and ridiculous position of attempting to give you the best services and greatest value as an architect and at the same time save labor and materials at every turn, so as to make the greatest possible profit for himself as builder.

It is only fair to state, however, that many communities are without competent architects, and thus builders have been forced many times against their inclinations to prepare plans.

Hesperus design 5266, story heights 9-ft 6. A southern cottage. Plans $10.

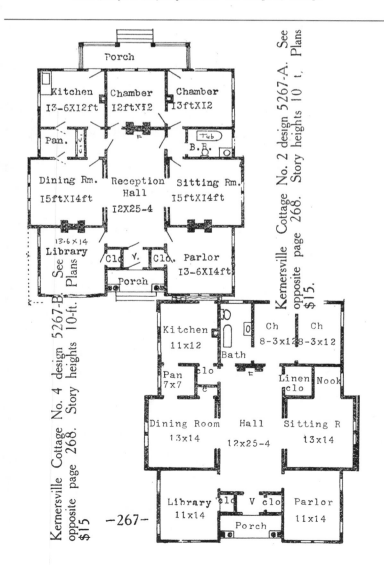

Porch

Kitchen
13-6X12ft

Chamber
12ftX12

Chamber
13ftX12

Pan.

Tub

B. R.

Dining Rm.
15ftX14ft

Reception
Hall
12X25-4

Sitting Rm.
15ftX14ft

13-6x14
Library

Clo

V.

Clo.

Parlor
13-6X14ft

Porch

Kernersville Cottage No. 4 design 5267-B. Story heights 10-ft.

Kernersville Cottage No. 2 design 5267-A. See Plans opposite page 268. Story heights 10 t. Plans $15.

Kitchen
11x12

Bath

Ch
8-3x12

Ch
8-3x12

Pan
7x7

clo

Linen
clo

Nook

Dining Room
13x14

Hall
12x25-4

Sitting R
13x14

Library
11x14

Clo

V clo

Parlor
11x14

Porch

Kernersville Cottage No. 4 design 5267-B. Story heights 10-ft. opposite page 268. Plans $15.

—267—

KERNERSVILLE COTTAGE.—Design 9298-N; in frame, $1,098 to $1,280; plans, $15; story height, 10 ft. Special features: Large central hall; attractive cut-shingle exterior. Kernersville No. 2, Violet design, parlor and library 13.6x14 ft.; kitchen and chamber 13.6x12 ft.; sliding door between reception hall, sitting-room and dining-room; fire-place for rear chamber; porch across rear; pier foundation. Kernersville Plan No. 3, Waerner design, stone house, 13x28 ft. central hall; library and parlor, 12.6x15 ft.; dining-room and chamber, 15x14 ft.; three rear rooms, 12x12 ft.; no fire-places in parlor and library; 11 ft. 6 in. story heights.

The COTTAGE

Have you figured out the blessings
Of a home that's all your own,
Of a cozy little cottage
That belongs to you alone?
Don't you feel a trifle shiftless
As the rent days go and come,
That your little ones—your loved ones
Have no really, truly home?
→Saxton

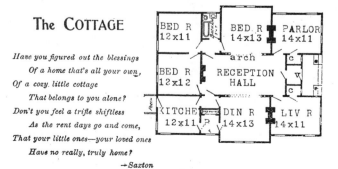

BED R
12x11

BED R
14x13

PARLOR
14x11

arch

BED R
12x12

RECEPTION
HALL

C

V

C

KITCHEN
12x11

DIN R
14x13

LIV R
14x11

P

—268—

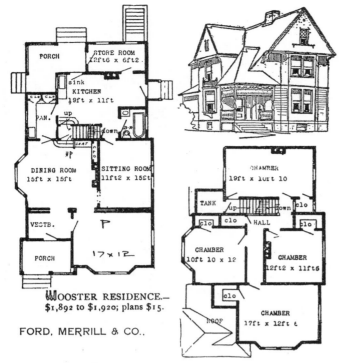

WOOSTER RESIDENCE.—
$1,892 to $1,920; plans $15.

FORD, MERRILL & CO.,

Herbert C. Chivers, Esq.,

St. Louis, Mo.

Salena, Kan., Sept. 22, 1 9.

Dear Sir:-

    I have just completed my residence, constructed under your plans No. 1810. We are proud to own the handsomest and most complet home of its size in Kansas and cheerfully attest to your genious as n Architect. It pays to have a competent architect.

        Yours truly,

-269-

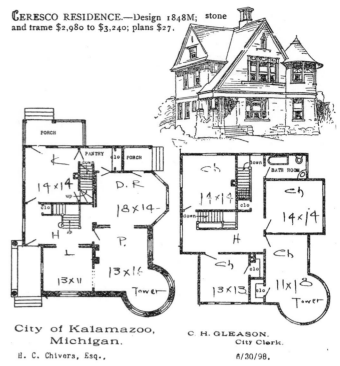

CERESCO RESIDENCE.—Design 1848M; stone and frame $2,980 to $3,240; plans $27.

City of Kalamazoo, Michigan.

C. H. GLEASON. City Clerk.

H. C. Chivers, Esq.,

6/30/98.

St. Louis, Mo.

Dear Sir:-

    Your letter is just at hand. Have not built from the plans secured of you yet. I know of no reason why they should not work all right. I would not think of building without having plans to work from. I have no fault to find with your plans, or methods of doing business; which are honest, prompt and business-like.

        Respectfully,

-270-

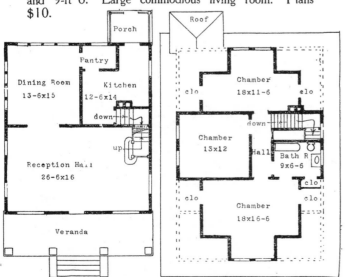

Erlanger design, 5271, width 27 ft 6, story heights 10 and 9-ft 6. Large commodious living room. Plans $10.

USELESS ORNAMENTATION.

    We do not litter up the exteriors of our buildings by useless ornamentation. Most of our cuts are pure simple outline sketches, which can be elaborated on, more or less, as desired. When we have a client who fancies cheap light grille-work ornamentation we supply it, but not by preference. We pay more for draughtsman's time who can base the beauty of a design on simple and striking features rather than on so-called "ginger-bread" ornamentation.

-271-

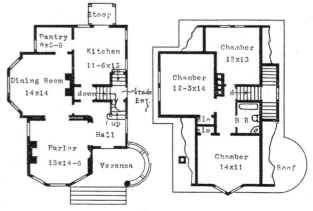

Erata design 5272, width over all 31 ft, story heights 9 and 8-ft 6. Plans $10.

UNPREJUDICED ADVICE.

    In preparing to build, the main object is to have a suitable arrangement of floor plan and this is where you will need the assistance of some one who is totally unprejudiced, regardless of any selfish interests which he may have in finally figuring on the contract to erect the house.

    Our interests lie altogether in having you well pleased and in putting up a house which will be a comfort to you as well as a credit to us. We could not afford to give you anything but the most conscientious advice on all points. If given your work we shall feel fully responsible for its ultimate success as to practicability and design.

-272-

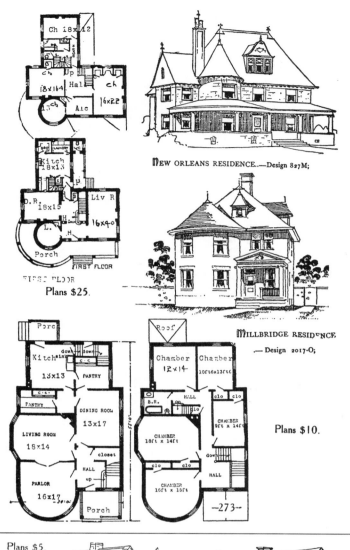

Ch 18x12

Up

18x16-4 Hall ch

16x22

Alc

Kitch 18x13

D.R. 18x15 Liv R 16x4-0

L.

H

Porch

FIRST FLOOR

Plans $25.

NEW ORLEANS RESIDENCE.—Design 827M;

MILLBRIDGE RESIDENCE
— Design 2017-O;

Porch

Kitchen 13x13 PANTRY

PANTRY

DINING ROOM 13x17

LIVING ROOM 18x14

closet

PARLOR 16x17

HALL

up

Porch

Roof

Chamber 12x14 Chamber 10ft 6 x13 ft 6

HALL

B.R. clo clo

CHAMBER 9ft x 14ft

CHAMBER 18ft x 14ft

clo clo

CHAMBER 16ft x 15ft

Plans $10.

—273—

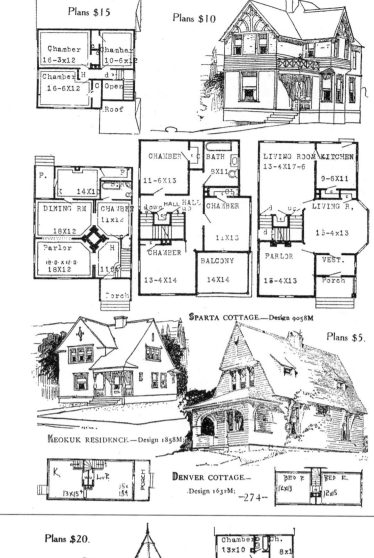

Plans $15 Plans $10

Chamber 16-3x12 Chamber 10-6x12

Chamber 16-6x12 Open

Roof

P. K 14x1

DINING RM 18x12 CHAMBER 11x12

Parlor 18-0 x12-0 H

CHAMBER 11-6X13 BATH 8X11

HALL HALL up

CHAMBER 11X13

CHAMBER 13-4X14 BALCONY 14X14

LIVING ROOM 13-4X17-6 KITCHEN 9-6X11

LIVING R. 15-4x13

PARLOR 15-4x13 VEST.

Porch

SPARTA COTTAGE.—Design 9058M

Plans $5.

KEOKUK RESIDENCE.—Design 1858M;

K 13X15 LIV R 15x 15-4 PORCH

DENVER COTTAGE.— Design 1631M;

BED R 12x13 BED R 12x15

—274—

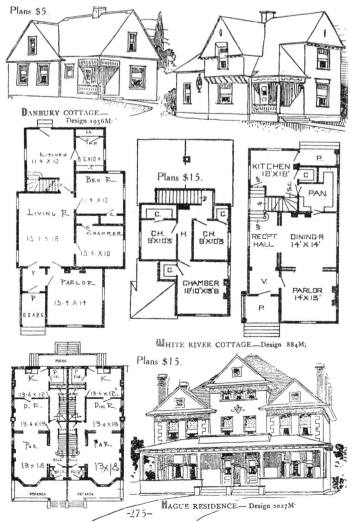

Plans $5.

DANBURY COTTAGE.— Design 1956M;

Kitchen 11-4 X 12 8-6X10-4

BED R. 11-4 X 10

LIVING R. 13-4 X 18

CHAMBER 13-4 X 10

PARLOR 13-4 X 14

Plans $15.

CH. 9X10-3 H CH. 9X10-3

CHAMBER 18-10 X 13-8

KITCHEN 12'X18' P. C

PAN.

RECPT. HALL DINING-R 14' X 14'

V.

PARLOR 14'X15'

P.

WHITE RIVER COTTAGE.—Design 884M;

Plans $15.

K 13-6 X 12 K 13-6 X 12

D. R. 13-6 X 13 DIN R 13-6 X 13

PAR PAR

13 X18 13 X18

HALL HALL

VERANDA VERANDA

HAGUE RESIDENCE.— Design 2027M·

—275—

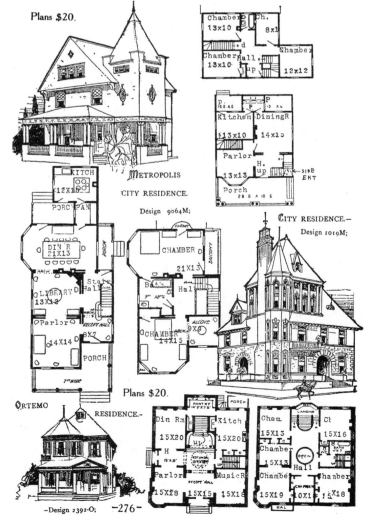

Plans $20.

KITCH 12X15

PORCH PAN

DIN R 21X13

LIBRARY 13X12

Parlor 14X14 PORCH

METROPOLIS CITY RESIDENCE.

Design 9064M;

CHAMBER 21X13

Bath Hall

ALCOVE

CHAMBER 14X15

Chamber 13x10 Ch. 8x1

Chamber 13x10 Hall up Chamber 12x12

Kitchen 13x10 Dining R 14x15

Parlor

13x13 up SIDE ENT.

Porch 28-6 X 10-6

CITY RESIDENCE.— Design 1019M;

Plans $20.

ORTEMO RESIDENCE.—Design 2392-O;

Din Rm 15X20 Kitch 15X20 Cham 15X13 Ch 15X16

Chamber 15X13

Hall

Parlor 15X18 Music R 15X18 Chamb 15X19

—276—

Adora design 5277, story heights 9 ft, width over all 40 ft. An attractive shingle and rough stone design. Plans $10.

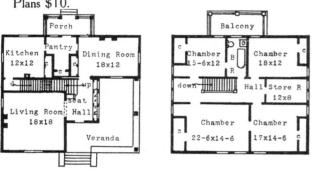

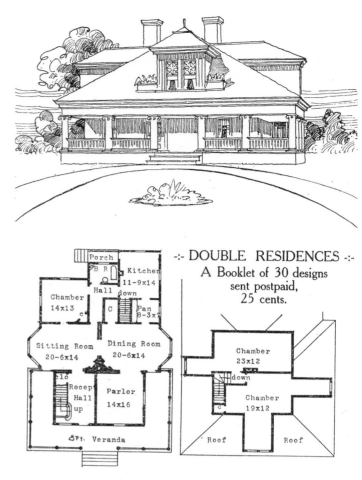

-:- DOUBLE RESIDENCES -:-
A Booklet of 30 designs sent postpaid, 25 cents.

Tasmania design 5278, width over all 42 ft, story heights 9 and 8 ft. Clean-cut simple front. Plans $10.

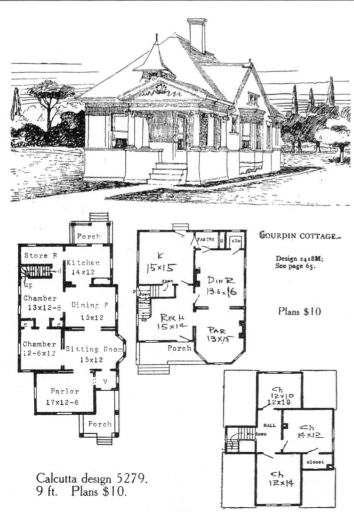

GOURDIN COTTAGE.

Design 2418M; See page 65.

Plans $10

Calcutta design 5279. 9 ft. Plans $10.

GOURDIN COTTAGE.—Design 2418M; cost in frame $1 90 to $1,280; plans $15. See page 65.

In the Bungalow, if properly designed, is combined grace, beauty and comfort—at a minimum cost.

Baffin design 5280, width over all 49 ft. Suitable for a corner lot cottage. Very roomy. Story heights 10 ft. Plans $10.

NEW ORLEANS COTTAGE.—Design 1824-O; in frame, $1,200 to $1,395; plans, $10; width, 29 ft. by 50 ft. 4 in.; story heights, 9 ft. 6 in. Special features: Compact plan; convenient bath-room; large veranda. See index for New Orleans cottage revised. See Crevi design

New Orleans plan No. 4, Welsh design, same as plan No. 2, with pantry left out; with kitchen, 13x16; with dining-room porch extending to rear; with 13x16 parlor; 8x19 hall; 13.4x13.4 front chamber; with corner fire-place; with 13.4x16 ft. dining-room; 14x9 ft. 8 in. rear chamber and two rooms above.

New Orleans plan No. 5, Barrett design, same as No. plan, with rear door and 4x5 porch to dining-room; with 17.6x13 ft. kitchen; 12x13 rear bed room, arranged for furnace; with flues at kitchen only; with turned posts to porch.

Continued on page No 282

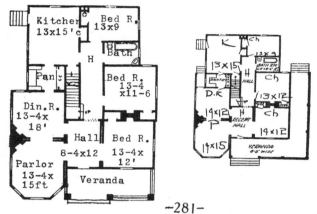

-281-

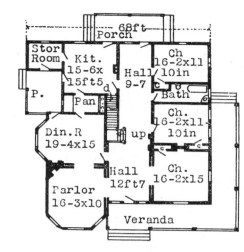

New Orleans Cottage No. 6 design 5282, story heights 10 ft. See opposite page 281 Plans $10

New Orleans Plan No. 6, Norton design, same as No. 2, with larger rooms; parlor, 18x16; dining-room, 19x15, with bay; hall 12 ft. wide, extending to rear, with large fire-place; front chamber, 16x15; central chamber, 16x12; rear chamber, 16x12; kitchen, 15x16; wide 10x12 porch at side of kitchen; 10x8 store room. Plans, $10. Story heights, 10 ft.

J. S. Byrom,
Planter and Merchant.

R. R. Points,
MONTEZUMA and PINEHURST, GA.

Byromville, Ga, Oct, 23 19

Mr. Herbert C. Chivers
St. Louis, Mo

Dear Sir—
Plans have been duly Red, and they are very complete and perfectly satisfactory.
-282-
Yours
S B Byrom

Crevi No. 52-0 design 5283, story height 9 ft. Description below. Plans $10.

-283-

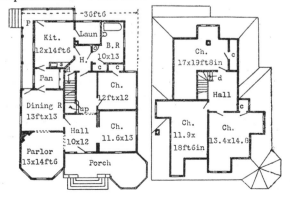

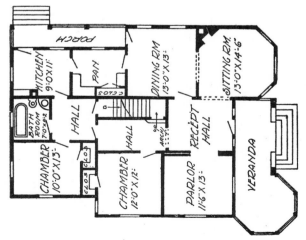

CORNER-LOT COTTAGE.—Design 1058-O; in frame, $950 to $1,198, plans, $10; story heights, 10 ft. See page 65.

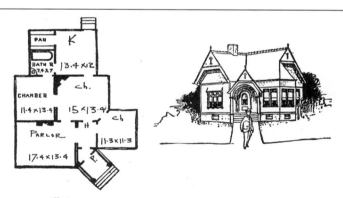

CREVI.—Design 52-O; cost, $1,290 to $1,380; size, 35 ft. 6 in. by 52 ft.; story heights, 9 ft. 2 in. Plans, $10. Design similar to New Orleans Cottage on page 168. See page 65.

Crevi No. 2, Latham design, same arrangement as above, except 10x13 rear chamber is used for bath, Continued on page 283

-284-

Cumberland design 5285, story heights 10 and 9 ft. This design has Marleboro design roof. See pages 333 and 334. Plans $10.

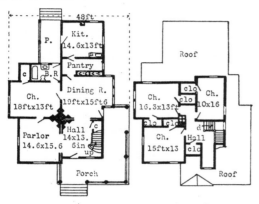

Am well pleased with plans bought of you.—W. J. Edwards, Union City, Tenn.

Penrhyn design 5286 (See Norman Cottage), 12 ft story. Plans $10.

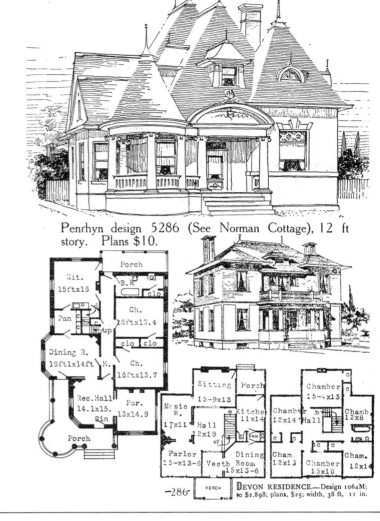

DEVON RESIDENCE.—Design 1064M; to $2,898; plans, $25; width, 38 ft, 11 in.

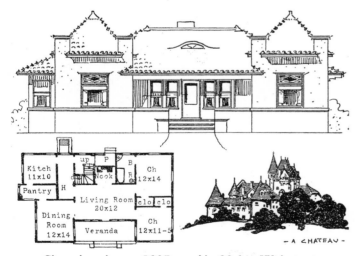

— A CHATEAU —

Clarendon design 5287, width 30 ft. Wide, inviting front, story heights 8 ft. Plans $5

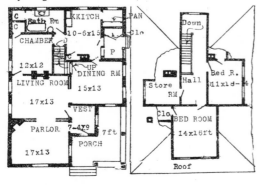

Silver Lake Cottage No. 4 design 5287-A, 9 ft story. See 332.

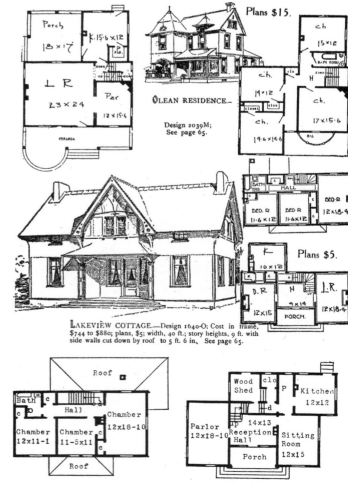

Plans $15.

OLEAN RESIDENCE.— Design 2039M; See page 65.

Plans $5.

LAKEVIEW COTTAGE.—Design 1640-O; Cost in frame, $744 to $880; plans, $5; width, 40 ft.; story heights, 9 ft. with side walls cut down by roof to 5 ft. 6 in. See page 65.

Lakeview Cottage No. 2, design 5288, wide, clean-cut front. Plans $5.

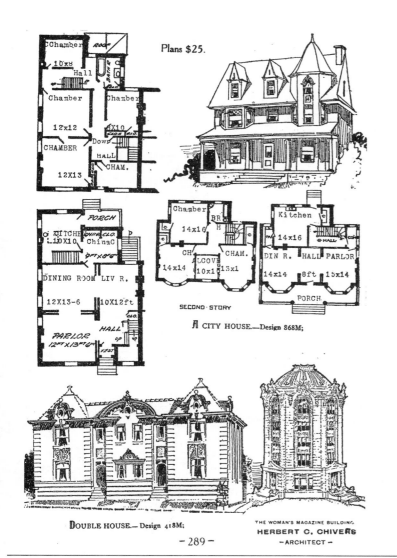

Plans $25.

Chamber 10x8

Hall

Chamber 12x12   Chamber 8X10

CHAMBER 12x13   HALL   CHAM.

PORCH

KITCHEN 10X10   ChinaC

DINING ROOM 12X13-6   LIV R. 10X12ft

PARLOR 12ft X 13ft 6in   HALL

Chamber 14x16   BR

CH 14x14   ALCOVE 10x1   CHAM. 13x1

SECOND STORY

A CITY HOUSE.—Design 868M;

Kitchen 14x16   HALL

DIN R. 14x14   HALL 8ft   PARLOR 15x14

PORCH

DOUBLE HOUSE.— Design 418M;

THE WOMAN'S MAGAZINE BUILDING.
HERBERT C. CHIVERS
—ARCHITECT—

— 289 —

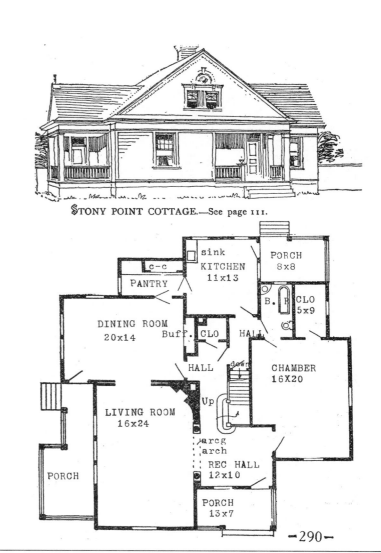

STONY POINT COTTAGE.—See page 111.

sink KITCHEN 11x13   PORCH 8x8

c—c

PANTRY   B. R. CLO 5x9

DINING ROOM 20x14   Buff. CLO   HALL

HALL   down   CHAMBER 16X20

Up

LIVING ROOM 16x24   arcg arch

PORCH   REC HALL 12x10

PORCH 13x7

— 290 —

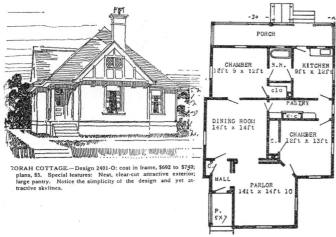

ZORAH COTTAGE.—Design 2401-O: cost in frame, $692 to $750; plans, $5. Special features: Neat, clear-cut attractive exterior; large pantry. Notice the simplicity of the design and yet attractive skylines.

PORCH

CHAMBER 12ft 9 x 12ft   S.H.   KITCHEN 9ft x 12ft

clo

PANTRY

DINING ROOM 14ft x 14ft   c—c

CHAMBER 12ft x 13ft

c.

HALL   PARLOR 14ft x 14ft 10

P. 5X7

Zorah Cottage No. 1 design 5291-A, story height 9-ft 6. Plans $5.

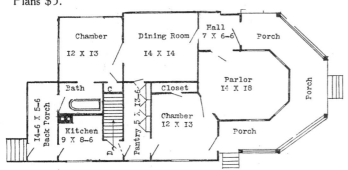

Chamber 12 X 13   Dining Room 14 X 14   Hall 7 X 6-6   Porch

Bath   Closet   Parlor 14 X 18   Porch

Back Porch 14-6 X 5-6   Pantry 5 X 13-6   Chamber 12 X 13   Porch

Kitchen 9 X 8-6

Zorah Cottage No. 2 design 5291-B, story height 9-ft 6, width 29 ft. Large, well-lighted bay-shaped parlor. Plans $5.

— 291 —

Austin design 5294, story 9-ft 6, width over all 42 ft. Neat, attractive stained shingle effect. Plans $10.

Kitchen 15-6x11   Pan   Veranda

Chamber 13-6x11-3

Dining Room 15-6x13-6   Bath R

Parlor 15x16-4   Hall   Chamber 13-6x11-3

Veranda

—PUBLIC BUILDINGS—
I have designed churches, schools, libraries, theatres, stores, hotels, banks, etc., all over the U. S., and have a special department for the planning of residences.

clo   clo

Chamber 13x14   Chamber 12-2x14

Sewing Rpom 15x9

Balco

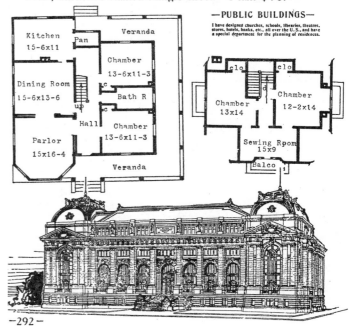

— 292 —

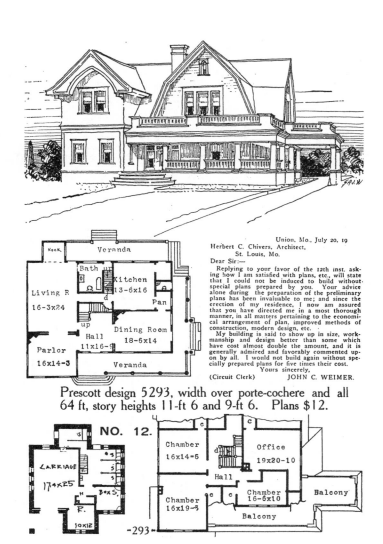

Union, Mo., July 20, 19

Herbert C. Chivers, Architect,
St. Louis, Mo.

Dear Sir:—

Replying to your favor of the 12th inst. asking how I am satisfied with plans, etc., will state that I could not be induced to build without special plans prepared by you. Your advice alone during the preparation of the preliminary plans has been invaluable to me; and since the erection of my residence, I now am assured that you have directed me in a most thorough manner, in all matters pertaining to the economical arrangement of plan, improved methods of construction, modern design, etc.

My building is said to show up in size, workmanship and design better than some which have cost almost double the amount, and it is generally admired and favorably commented upon by all. I would not build again without specially prepared plans for five times their cost.

Yours sincerely,

(Circuit Clerk)   JOHN C. WEIMER.

Prescott design 5293, width over porte-cochere and all 64 ft, story heights 11-ft 6 and 9-ft 6.   Plans $12.

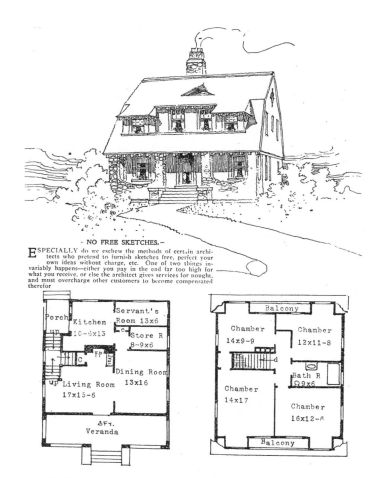

ESPECIALLY do we eschew the methods of certain architects who pretend to furnish sketches free, perfect your own ideas without charge, etc. One of two things invariably happens—either you pay in the end far too high for what you receive, or else the architect gives services for nought, and must overcharge other customers to become compensated therefor

Tulon design 5294, width 43 ft, story heights 9 and 8 ft.   Large commodious living room, with wide fireplace.   Large front chamber.   Combination front and rear stairs.   Large porch.   Plans $10.

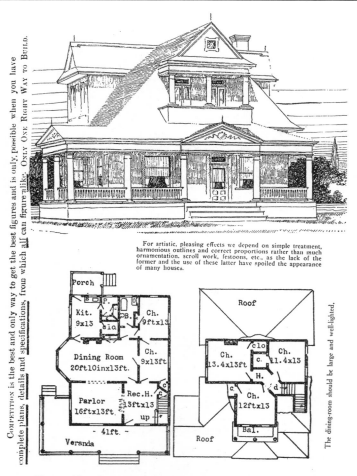

Competition is the best and only way to get the best figures and is only possible when you have complete plans, details and specifications, from which all can figure alike. Only One Right Way to Build.

For artistic, pleasing effects we depend on simple treatment, harmonious outlines and correct proportions rather than much ornamentation, scroll work, festoons, etc., as the lack of the former and the use of these latter have spoiled the appearance of many houses.

The dining-room should be large and well-lighted.

Chemuckla design 5295, story 10 ft.   Large dining room.   Two chambers and bath on first floor, neat, attractive front.   Plans $10.

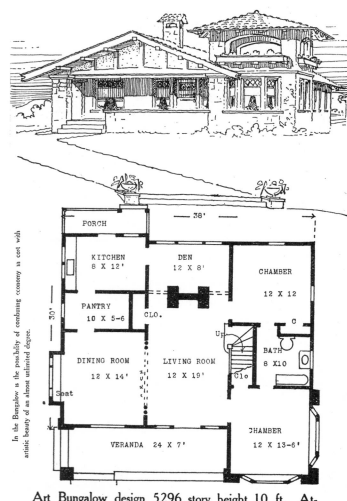

In the Bungalow is the possibility of combining economy in cost with artistic beauty of an almost unlimited degree.

Art Bungalow design 5296, story height 10 ft.   Attractive sleeping balcony.   Plans $10.

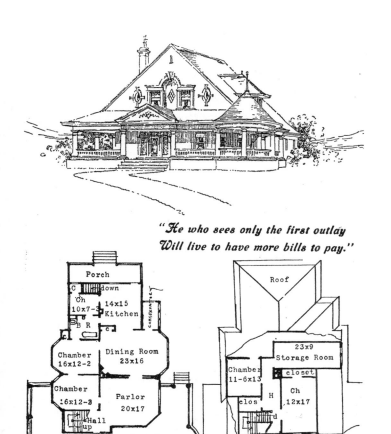

*"He who sees only the first outlay
Will live to have more bills to pay."*

Summerland design 5297, width over all 48 ft. Two chambers and bath on first floor, story heights 10 and 9-ft 6. Plans $10.

—297—

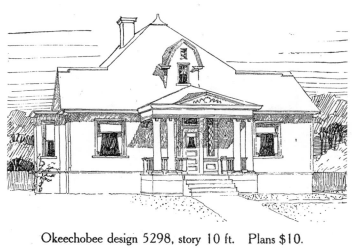

Okeechobee design 5298, story 10 ft. Plans $10.

Plans $10.

—298—

Carbon plan. See exterior page 313.

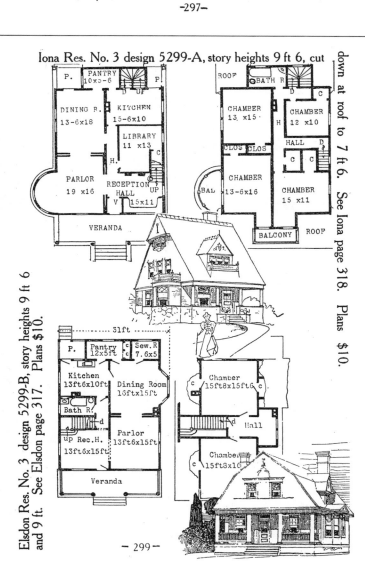

Iona Res. No. 3 design 5299-A, story heights 9 ft 6, cut down at roof to 7 ft 6. See Iona page 318. Plans $10.

Elsdon Res. No. 3 design 5299-B, story heights 9 ft 6 and 9 ft. See Elsdon page 317. Plans $10.

—299—

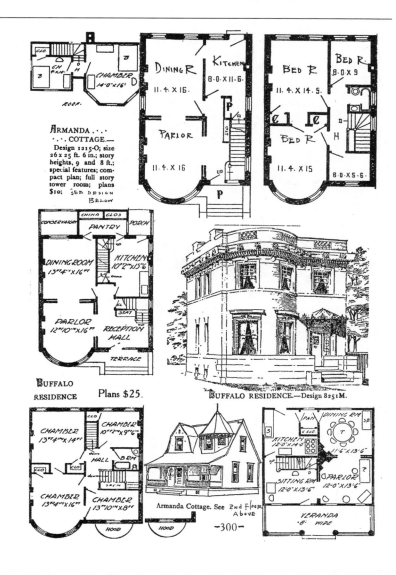

ARMANDA ... COTTAGE.— Design 1215-O; size 26 x 25 ft. 6 in.; story heights, 9 and 8 ft.; special features; compact plan; full story tower room; plans $10; SEE DESIGN BELOW

BUFFALO RESIDENCE. Plans $25.

BUFFALO RESIDENCE.—Design 8251M.

Armanda Cottage. See 2nd Floor Above

—300—

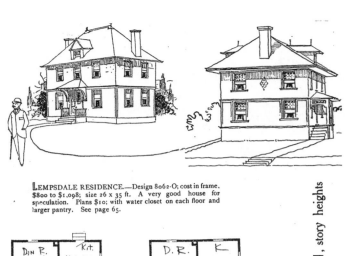

LEMPSDALE RESIDENCE.—Design 8062-O; cost in frame, $800 to $1,098; size 26 x 35 ft. A very good house for speculation. Plans $10; with water closet on each floor and larger pantry. See page 65.

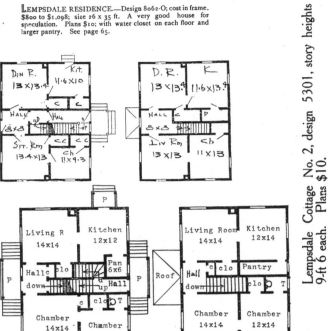

Lempsdale Cottage No. 2, design 5301, story heights 9-ft 6 each. Plans $10.

-301-

NEWPORT COTTAGE.—Design 1042-N; in frame, $976 to $1,089; plans, $5; width, 29 ft. 4 in. by 28 ft. 4 in.; story heights, 8 ft. Special features: Well-ventilated bay-shaped rooms; large central rooms; unique design; attractive, arched porch; very unique.

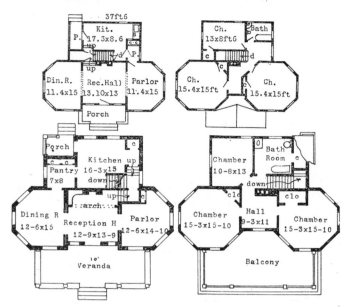

Newport No. 2 design 5302, story 8-ft 6 and 8 ft. Plans $5.

-302-

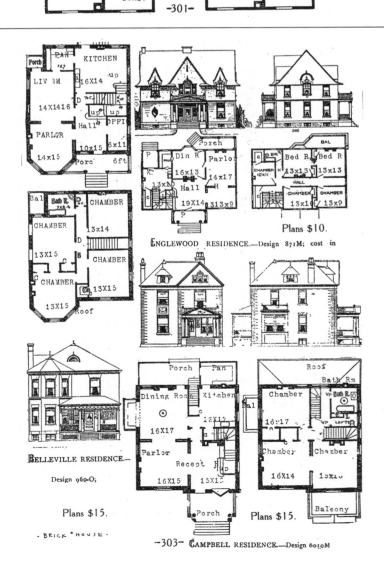

Plans $10.

ENGLEWOOD RESIDENCE.—Design 871M; cost in

BELLEVILLE RESIDENCE.—

Design 960-O;

Plans $15.

· BRICK · HOUSE ·

Plans $15.

-303- CAMPBELL RESIDENCE.—Design 6010M

The plans made by you were all right in design, etc.—W. S. Harman, Joplin, Mo.

COUNTRY HOME. Design 1005-O; in frame, $3,390 to $3,760; plans, $25; story heights, 19 ft. Special features: Large reception hall, semi-circular parlor, 13 ft. 4 in. by 16 ft.; hall, 13 ft. by 20 ft.; library, 13 ft. 4 in. by 16 ft.; dining-room, 15 ft. 4 in. by 14 ft.; kitchen, 13 ft. 4 in. by 16 ft.; chambers all, 13 ft. 4 in. by 16 ft., with the exception of small chamber, 9 ft. by 10 ft. See page 65.

Plans $25.

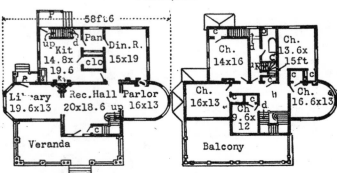

-304-

WINDFALL RESIDENCE.—Design 100,014M; cost $2090 to $2499, plans, $20; size 29x37; Special features large bay on side, combination stairs, attractive exterior, good corner lot design. See page 65.

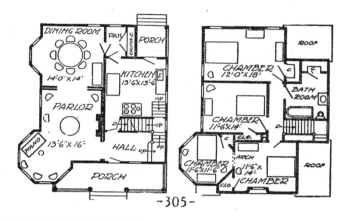

-305-

ELKHORN COTTAGE.—Design 100,023M; plans, $20; cost $2151 to $2366; size 28.6x37, width over all 34 ft; special features: attactrve exterior, large reception hall, side entrance.

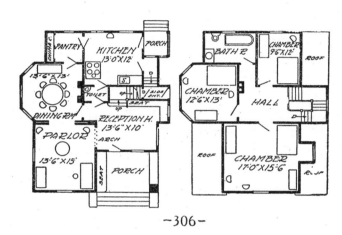

-306-

HE EMPLOYED AN ARCHITECT

HE made a fortune buying lots,
  Converting them to pretty spots,
    And building pleasant homes to sell—
For Roycroft always builded well,
Substantial, healthy, handy homes;
With arches, gables, peaks and domes,
Piazzas, oriels and handsome towers,
Half hidden in the trees and flowers.
Each house was varied from the rest—
Like pretty women, nicely dressed.
He scarce could hold a house till done,
For at least two buyers sought each one.

HOW Roycroft did it, none could learn;
  He was so very taciturn.
    When dying, Roycroft told his spouse
The secret: "When you want a house,
Secure an architect at once."
(He who hires himself, a dunce employes.)
The architect may make one door
Serve where you might put in four or more.
He, knowing laws of heat and light,
Devises rooms so all are bright.
Cuts windows just the size and where,
They yield the utmost light and air.

PROVIDES for all things ample space,
  Keeping everything in proper place;
    Learns what you want before he starts,
Saves adding costly little parts.
Remember, it is not the size—
Arrangement makes the home we prize.
Outside he moulds the charm of "style"
From basement to the topmost tile.
He requires material enough,
Describes the proper sort of stuff,
Everything is clearly specified,
So it is fair to either side.

WHAT is experiment with you,
  He knows precisely how to do.
    What can be done, with what effect;
What not to do, how to select.
Saves steps for housewives' weary feet,
Supplies control of cold and heat,
No house designed with reckless haste
But with distinctiveness and taste.
No tearing-down and building twice,
With "changes" at a fancy price.
Your house will rarely cost you more
Than you have calculated on before.

THE first house I built, I recollect.
  I had an amatuer architect,
    And many often asked me what
Had happened to that vacant lot.
Was it an air-ship that had lit
Or simply an architectural mis-fit?
I patched that house and there it stood
Reflecting on the neighborhood,
Till Providence, in righteous ire,
Redeemed its ugliness with fire.
My buildings, subsequent, were wrought
On paper first, with thorough thought.

THE architect is a prophet who fulfills his own predictions. He foretells the exact formation of a palace or a cottage, a church or a sky-scraper where there is only vacant ground. He conceives to the minutest detail a structure while yet the stone is in the quarry, the bricks are but clay and the lumber is in the tree. Before a dollar has been expended in segregating these materials he has counted the cost and announced the day on which the building will be ready for occupancy.

His client, beholding that the architects former predictions have come to pass, trust him implicitly and provides the means by which the conception of the design shall come into being.

James Russell Lowell says in the Bigelow Papers: "Don't ever prophesy unless you know," and here is where it is important to select an architect who knows. Guess work in building does not pay. Guessing at cost, guessing at time, guessing at appearance and solidity are expensive weaknesses in an architect, that is for the man who pays the bills.

My success is due to my ability to submit a design which embodies the ideas of my client wrought into a plan beyond his conception. My accumulated information, corrected to date, may be relied upon by every client when a positive order is given in advance, thereby justifying my personal attention on matters of exact cost, design, plan arrangement, etc.

It is to this accumulated information and my staff of thoroughly-trained assistants that I owe the position which I occupy in the profession. Each man assistant in my employ being a specialist, thoroughly competent and reliable in the performance of the task assigned to him.

-307-

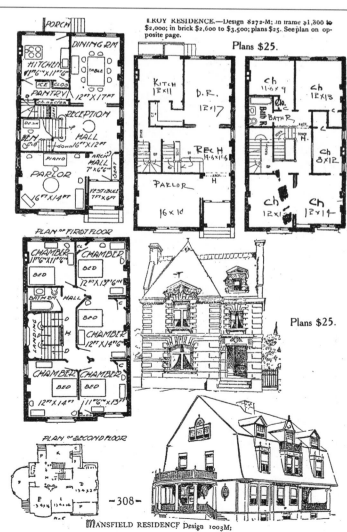

LROY RESIDENCE.—Design 8272-M; in frame $1,300 to $2,000; in brick $2,600 to $3,500; plans $25. See plan on opposite page.

Plans $25.

Plans $25.

MANSFIELD RESIDENCE Design 1003M;

-308-

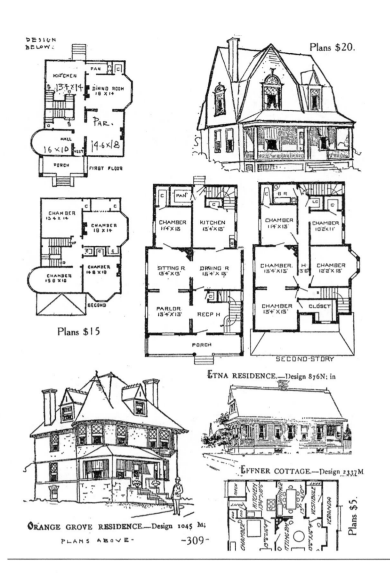

DESIGN BELOW:

KITCHEN 13'4"X14

DINING ROOM 18'X14

PAR.

HALL 16'X10

PORCH

FIRST FLOOR

CHAMBER 13'4"X14

CHAMBER 18'X14

CHAMBER 14'8"X18

CHAMBER 15'8"X18

SECOND

Plans $15

Plans $20.

CHAMBER 11'4"X13

KITCHEN 13'4"X13

SITTING R. 13'4"X13'

DINING R. 13'4"X13'

PARLOR 13'4"X13'

RECP H.

CHAMBER 11'4"X13'

CHAMBER 10'2"X11'

CHAMBER 13'4"X13'

CHAMBER 12'2"X18'

CHAMBER 13'4"X13'

CLOSET

PORCH

SECOND-STORY

ÆTNA RESIDENCE.—Design 876N; in

ORANGE GROVE RESIDENCE.—Design 1045 M;

PLANS ABOVE.

EFFNER COTTAGE.—Design 2332M

Plans $5.

-309-

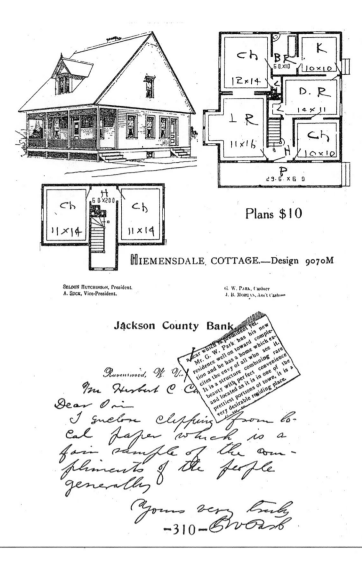

Ch 12X14

BR 6.0X10

K 10X10

D.R 14X11

L R 11X16

Ch 10X10

P 29.6 X 6.0

Plans $10

H 6.0X20.0

Ch 11X14

Ch 11X14

HIEMENSDALE COTTAGE.—Design 9070M

Jackson County Bank

Ravenswood, W. Va.

Mr Herbert C C

Dear Sir

I enclose clipping from local paper which is a fair sample of the compliments of the people generally

Yours very truly

B Park

-310-

Year which we promised Mr. G. W. Park has his new residence well on toward completion and he has a home which excites the envy of all who see it. It is a structure combining rare beauty with perfect convenience and located as it is in one of the prettiest portions of town, it is a very desirable residing place.

The plans you sent were correct in every respect and the work on them something to be admired.
IRA LAUT, Wenona, Ill.

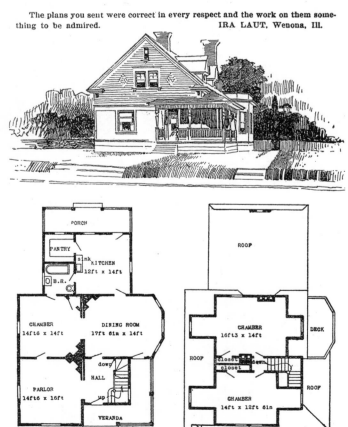

PORCH

PANTRY

sink KITCHEN 12ft x 14ft

B.R.

CHAMBER 14ft6 x 14ft

DINING ROOM 17ft 6in x 14ft

down HALL

PARLOR 14ft6 x 16ft

up

VERANDA

ROOF

CHAMBER 16ft3 x 14ft

DECK

ROOF

Closet down closet

ROOF

CHAMBER 14ft x 12ft 6in

BRUNSWICK RESIDENCE. — Design 1905-N; cost, $1,180 to $1,390; plans, $10. Special features: Convenient bath-room; large dining-room; neat exterior; attractive chimneys and dormer windows; large bath-room.

-311-

OAKLEY COTTAGE.—Design 1213M; size, 23 ft. 6 in. by 31 ft. 6 in.; story heights, 10 ft. and 9 ft.; special features: Nook, side entrance, large reception hall, attractive exterior; cost, $1,269 to $1,398; plans $10. See page 65.

The special plans, specifications and full size details were well worth the investment and I would not build without plans for ten times their cost.
G. R. RUCKER, Checotah, I. T.

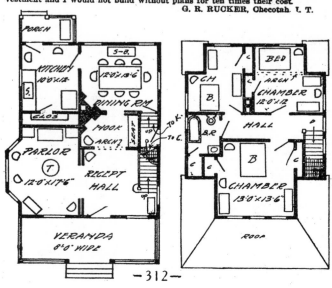

PORCH

KITCHEN 10'0"X13

CLOS.

5-8.

12'0"X15'6

DINING RM.

NOOK ARCH.

PARLOR 12'0"X17'6

RECEPT HALL

VERANDA 8'0" WIDE

BED

CH ARCH.

B.

BR

CHAMBER 12'0"X12

HALL

B

CHAMBER 13'0"X13'6

ROOF

-312-

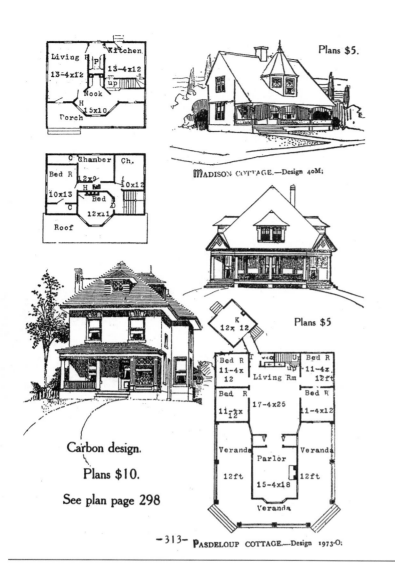

Plans $5.

Living R
13-4x12

Kitchen
13-4x12

P

up

Nook

H
15x10

Porch

MADISON COTTAGE.—Design 40M;

C   Chamber   Ch.

Bed R
10x13
12x9

H   Hall
10x12

Bed
12x11

C

Roof

Plans $5

K
12x12

Bed R
11-4x
12
Living Rm
Bed R
11-4x
12ft

Bed R
11-2x
12
17-4x25
Bed R
11-4x12

up

Veranda
12ft
Parlor
15-4x18
Veranda
12ft

Veranda

Carbon design.

Plans $10.

See plan page 298

—313—   PASDELOUP COTTAGE.—Design 1973-O;

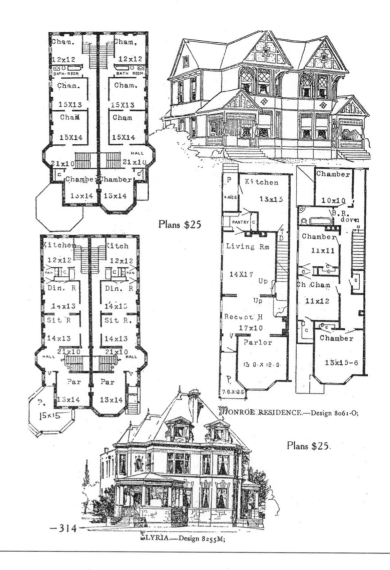

Cham.
12x12
BATH ROOM
Cham.
15x13
Cham
15x14
21x10

Cham.
12x12
BATH ROOM
Cham.
15X13
Cham
15X14
21x10

HALL

Chamber   Chamber
13x14   13x14

Plans $25

Kitchen
12x12
PAR
Din. R
14x13
Sit R
14x13
21x10
HALL
Par
13x14

Kitch
12x12
PAN
Din. R
14x13
Sit R.
14x13
21x10
HALL
Par
13x14

P.
15x15

P
Kitchen
13x15

PANTRY C

Living Rm
14X17
Up

Up

Recpt H
17x10
V
Parlor
13 0 X 12 0

P
7 0 X 12 5

Chamber
10x10
B.R.
down

Chamber
11x11

Ch. Cham
11x12

Chamber

Chamber
13x15-6

MONROE RESIDENCE.—Design 8061-O;

Plans $25.

—314—   ELYRIA.—Design 8255M;

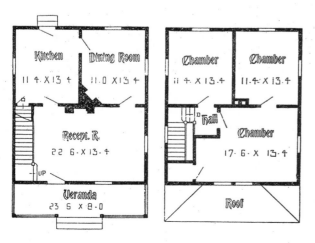

REMONT COTTAGE.—Design 1959-N; in frame, $998 to $1,240; plans, $5; width, 23 ft. 10 in. by 28 ft. 2 in.; story heights, 9 ft. 6 in. and 9 ft. cut down by roof at walls to 5 ft. 6 in. Special features: Large spacious living-room; neat simple exterior.

Kitchen
11 4 X 13 4
Dining Room
11 0 X 13 4

Chamber
11 4 X 13 4
Chamber
11 4 X 13 4

Recpt. R.
22 6 X 13 4

Hall

Chamber
17 6 X 13 4

Veranda
23 5 X 8 0

Roof

—315—

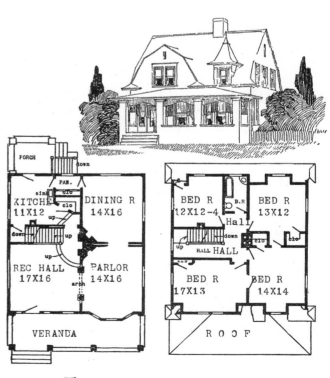

PORCH
down

PAN.
sink   clo
KITCHEN
11X12
clo
up
DINING R
14X16

down
up
REC HALL
17X16
arch
PARLOR
14X16

VERANDA

BED R
12X12-4
B.R
Hall
BED R
13X12

up   down
HALL
HALL   clo

BED R
17X13
BED R
14X14

ROOF

EDON RESIDENCE.—Design 1927-N; cost in frame, $1,492 to $1,590; plans, $10. Special features: Attractive landing at stairs; wide veranda; bay to parlor; good closet space; combination stairs.

—316—

THERE is one way, and one way only, to determine exactly what a house will cost at a particular time in a given locality, and that is to get the actual bids from responsible builders based on complete plans and specifications.

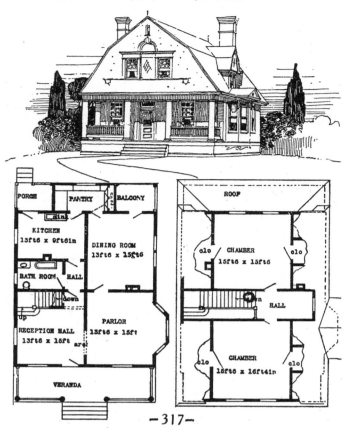

 ELSDON COTTAGE.— Design 1784-N; cost in frame, $ 1,040 to $1,289; plans, $10; story heights, 9 ft. 6 in. and 9 ft.; full story; no cut-off of ceiling by roof. Special features: Bath-room close to kitchen; large full-story rooms on second floor

—317—

 IONA RESIDENCE.—Design 1532-N; cost in frame, $1,459 to $1,789; plans, $15; width, 30 ft. 4 in.; width over all, 36 ft.; story heights, 9 ft. 6 in., cut down at roof to 7 ft. 6 in. Special features: Large reception hall.

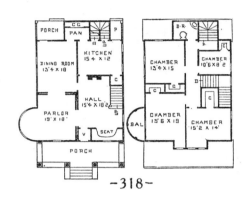

—318—

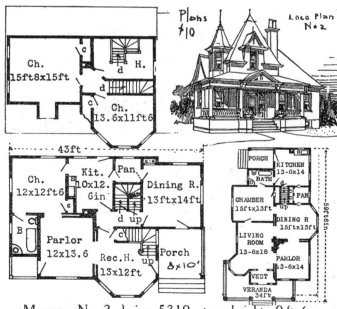

Moscow No. 2 design 5319, story heights 9-ft 6 and 9. See design page 320. Plans $10.

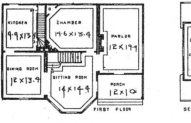 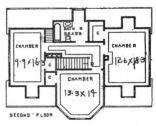

MOSCOW.— Plan No. 3; cost, $1,300 to $1,600; plans, $15. See pages 596 and 65.

—319—

MOSCOW COTTAGE.—Design 1553-O; in frame, plan No. 1, $1,298 to $1,499; plans, $10; width over all, 45 ft. 6 in.; story heights, 9 ft. 6 in.; full story in tower. Special features: Plain, well-proportioned exterior; easy to build; free from "gingerbread" and excessive ornamentation.

Moscow No. 4, Gage design, same as above, with rear stair where marked "C" next to pantry; with closet to rear chamber; with rear stairs landing in store room. See pages opposite

Plans $10.

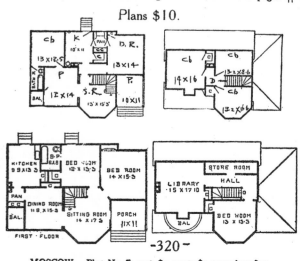

—320—

MOSCOW.—Plan No. 5; cost, $1,200 to $1,500; plans, $10.

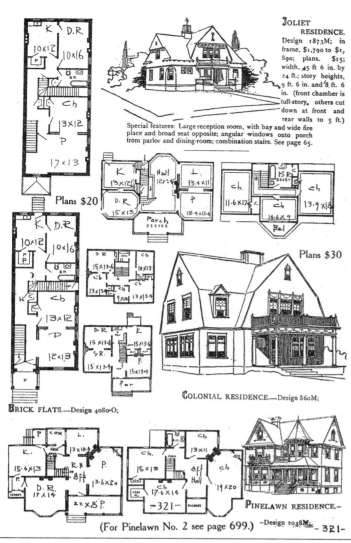

JOLIET RESIDENCE.

Design 1873M; in frame, $1,790 to $1,890; plans. $15; width, 45 ft 6 in. by 24 ft.; story heights, 9 ft. 6 in. and 8 ft. 6 in. (front chamber is full-story, others cut down at front and rear walls to 5 ft.)

Special features: Large reception room, with bay and wide fire place and broad seat opposite; angular windows onto porch from parlor and dining-room; combination stairs. See page 65.

Plans $20

Plans $30

Plans $5.

BRICK FLATS.—Design 4080-O;

COLONIAL RESIDENCE.—Design 860M;

PINELAWN RESIDENCE.—
(For Pinelawn No. 2 see page 699.) —Design 2038M. -321-

-321-

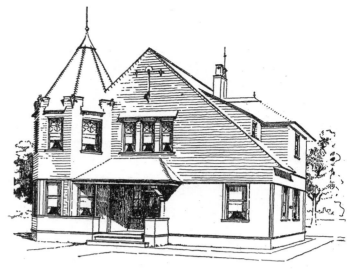

MONTGOMERY RESIDENCE.—Design 4898-N; cost in frame, $1,200 to $1,400; plans, $7.50; story heights, 9 ft. 6 in. and 8 ft. 6 in.; full story. Special features: The building looks well in stained shingles; well-lighted and ventilated parlor.

— BUILDER AND ARCHITECT —

YOU don't go to a blacksmith for watch repairs; to a tailor for dentistry, or to a lawyer when you wish plumbing done. The proper place to get a set of reliable plans and specifications is from a competent architect

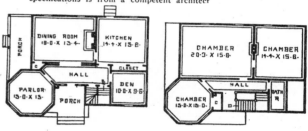

-322-

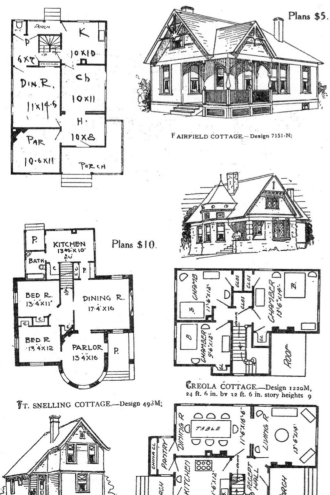

FAIRFIELD COTTAGE.— Design 7151-N;

Plans $10.

FT. SNELLING COTTAGE.—Design 493M;

CREOLA COTTAGE.—Design 1220M, 24 ft. 6 in. by 22 ft. 6 in. story heights 9

-CREOLA-

-323-

KIMBALTEN COTTAGE.—Design 2338M; cost, $1,098 to $1,199; plans, $8; special features: Large dining-room. See page 65.

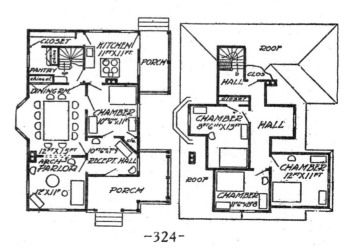

-324-

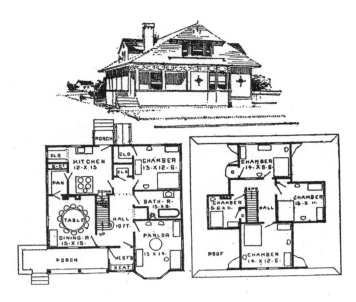

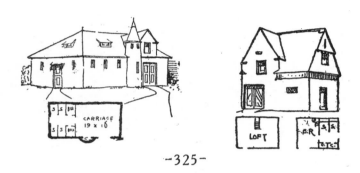

JORDONVILLE COTTAGE.—Design 2422M; cost in frame $1,390 to $1,480 plans $10. See page 65.

ARRIS.—Design 2333-N; cost in frame, $1,490 to $1,590; plans, $10; story heights, 9 ft. 6 in. and 9 ft. Special features: Wide verandas; large parlor; front rooms full story; front of house is not cut up by the customary reception hall.

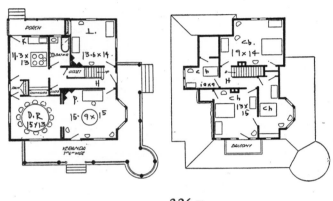

NEW CASTLE COTTAGE. — Design 890-O; in frame, $1,195; plans, $15. New Castle No. 2, Cramer design, same as shown with stairs from kitchen to attic, with 13 ft. 6x10 ft. 6 in. kitchen, with 8 ft. 6x8 servants room, with fire-place in dining-room, opposite bay and not in parlor. See index for Wagoner design. See page 65.

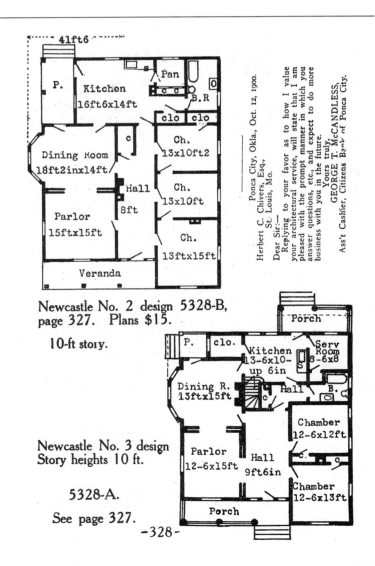

Ponca City, Okla., Oct. 12, 1900.

Herbert C. Chivers, Esq.,
St. Louis, Mo.

Dear Sir:— Replying to your favor as to how I value your architectural service, will state that I am pleased with the prompt manner in which you answer questions, etc., and expect to do more business with you in the future.

Yours truly,
GEORGE T. McCANDLESS,
Ass't Cashier, Citizens Bank of Ponca City.

Newcastle No. 2 design 5328-B, page 327. Plans $15.

10-ft story.

Newcastle No. 3 design
Story heights 10 ft.

5328-A.

See page 327.

CEDAR COTTAGE.—Design 2344M; cost, $1,095 $1,190. Plans, $10. See page 65.

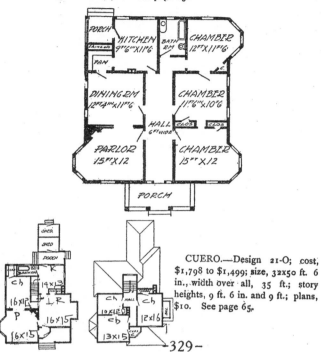

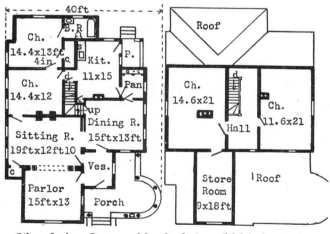

CUERO.—Design 21-O; cost, $1,798 to $1,499; size, 32x50 ft. 6 in., width over all, 35 ft.; story heights, 9 ft. 6 in. and 9 ft.; plans, $10. See page 65.

SPOTTSVILLE COTTAGE.—Design 1788-N; cost in frame, $1,192 to $1,240; plans, $10: 10 ft. and 9 ft. stories. Space for five rooms above.

Style in architecture is that indescribable something which adds to the artistic appearance of a building.

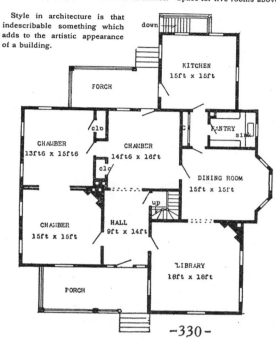

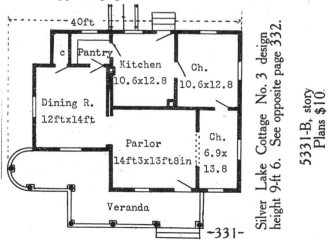

Silver Lake Cottage No. 2 design 5331-A, story 9-ft 6 and 8-ft 6, cut down to 4-ft 6 side wall. See opposite page 332. Plans $10.

Silver Lake Cottage No. 3 design 5331-B, story height 9-ft 6. See opposite page 332. Plans $10.

SILVERLAKE COTTAGE.—Design 7048-N; in frame, $1,292 to $1,496; plans, $10; story heights, 9 ft. 6 in. and 8 ft. 6 in. Special features: Large porch and vestibule. Silverlake No. 2, Livingston design, with no fire-place in parlor; with an additional 14 ft. 4x13 ft. 4 in. chamber at rear, with bath connection. House 36x54 ft. in size. Luzon design No. 3, same as above, but reversed, with porch across front, with 7x14 ft. alcove at side of parlor and no fire-place, bath-room or rear stairs.

Silver Lake design 5332. Plans $10.

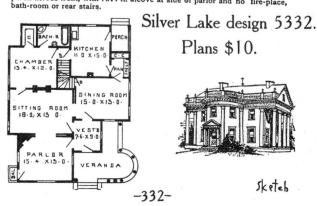

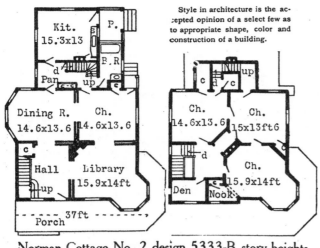

Style in architecture is the accepted opinion of a select few as to appropriate shape, color and construction of a building.

Kit.
15.3x13

P.

B.R

d

Pan

up

Dining R.
14.6x13.6

Ch.
14.6x13.6

c

Hall

Library
15.9x14ft

up

c d c

up

Ch.
14.6x13.6

Ch.
15x13ft6

d

Ch.
15.9x14ft

Den

Nook

37ft

Porch

Norman Cottage No, 2 design 5333-B, story heights
10-ft 8 and 9 ft. Plans $10.

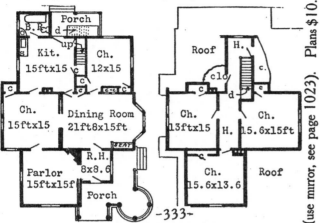

B.R

Porch

d

Kit.
15ftx15

Ch.
12x15

up

c

c c c

Ch.
15ftx15

Dining Room
21ft8x15ft

R.H.
8x8.6

Parlor
15ftx15f

Porch

Roof

H.

clo

c

c

d

c

Ch.
13ftx15

H.

Ch.
15.6x15ft

Ch.
15.6x13.6

Roof

(use mirror, see page 1023). Plans $10.

Enon residence No. 2 design 5333-A, story height:
10 and 9 ft. See reversed design on page 584

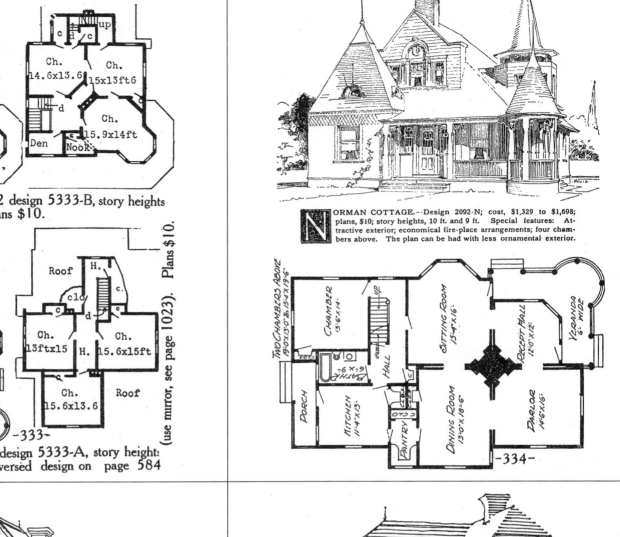

NORMAN COTTAGE.--Design 2092-N; cost, $1,329 to $1,698;
plans, $10; story heights, 10 ft. and 9 ft. Special features: Attractive exterior; economical fire-place arrangements; four chambers above. The plan can be had with less ornamental exterior.

Two Chambers Above
13'-0"x13'-0" & 13'-4"x19'-6"

Chamber
13'6"x14'

up

Hall

Bath Rm
6'x9'

c

Sitting Room
15'4"x16'

Recpt Hall
12'0"x12'

Veranda
6' Wide

Porch

Kitchen
11'-4"x13'

Pantry

Dining Room
13'0"x18'-6"

Parlor
14'6"x16'

-334-

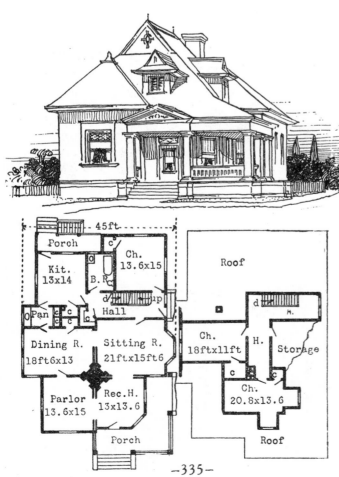

45ft

Porch

c

Kit.
13x14

B.R

Ch.
13.6x15

Roof

Pan

c c c

d

up

Hall

Dining R.
18ft6x13

Sitting R.
21ftx15ft6

Parlor
13.6x15

Rec.H.
13x13.6

Porch

d

H.

Ch.
18ftx11ft

H.

Storage

c

c

Ch.
20.8x13.6

Roof

-335-

Norman Cottage No. 3 design 5335, story heights
10 ft and 8 ft 6, cut to 5 ft side-walls. Plans $10.

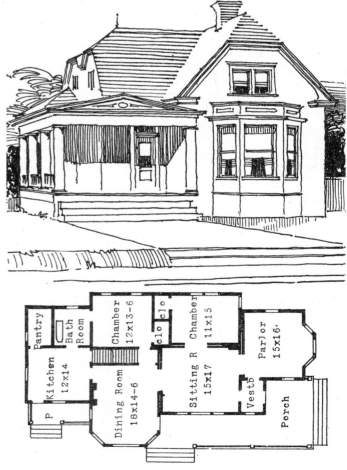

Pantry

P

Kitchen
12x14

Bath Room

Chamber
12x13-6

clo clo

Chamber
11x15

Parlor
15x16

Dining Room
18x14-6

Sitting R
15x17

Vestb

Porch

Besson design 5336, story heights 10-ft 4, width
over all 35 ft. Plans $5. -336-

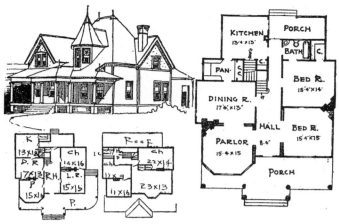

ZEARING. — Fouts design 8-O;

SPRINGDALE COTTAGE.—Design $1,480-O; in frame, $1,699 to $1,889; plans, $10; width, 41 ft. 10 in. by 36 ft. 4 in; width over all, 44 ft. 9 in.; story heights, 10 ft. and 9 ft. 6 in. We have this plan for $10 with bath-room on first floor, located back of chamber and with pantry between kitchen and rear porch. Also a plan with bay in dining-room, a laundry and fuel room back of bath-room, with porch on two sides of kitchen and four chambers above. See index for Springdale cottage (revised). See Woodfield, Roland and Zearing plan on opposite page.

Mr. Herbert C. Chivers,
St. Louis, Mo.

Dear Sir:- Your plans and specifications are very good and met with my approval.
Yours truly,

—337—

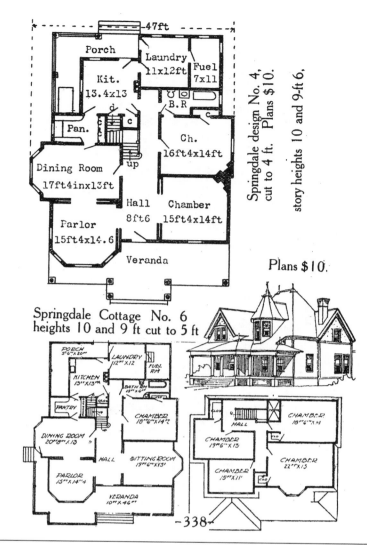

Springdale design No. 4, cut to 4 ft. Plans $10.
story heights 10 and 9-ft 6,

Plans $10.

Springdale Cottage No. 6
heights 10 and 9 ft cut to 5 ft

—338—

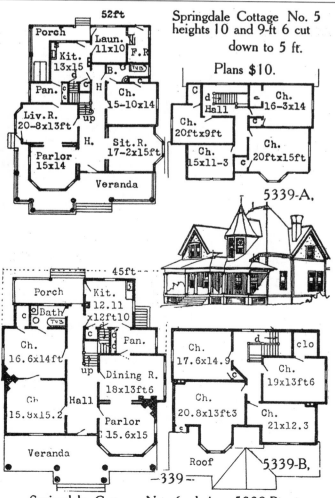

Springdale Cottage No. 5
heights 10 and 9-ft 6 cut down to 5 ft.
Plans $10.

5339-A.

45ft

5339-B,

—339—

Springdale Cottage No. 6 design 5339-B, story
—339— heights 10 and 9 ft cut to 5 ft side walls. Plans $10.

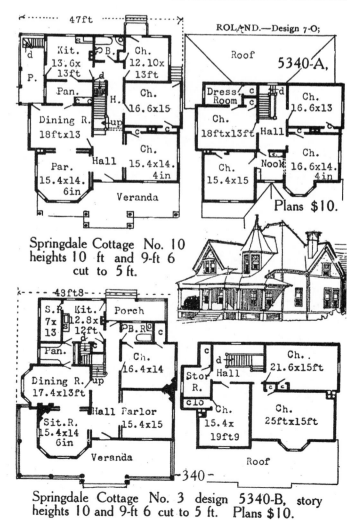

ROLAND.—Design 7-O;

5340-A,

Plans $10.

Springdale Cottage No. 10
heights 10 ft and 9-ft 6 cut to 5 ft.

—340—

Springdale Cottage No. 3 design 5340-B, story
heights 10 and 9-ft 6 cut to 5 ft. Plans $10.

UNIONVILLE COTTAGE.—Design 9066-N; cost in frame, $1,255 to $1,340; plans, $10; width, 22 ft. 4 in. by 39 ft. 2 in.; story heights, 9 ft. 6 in. and 9 ft. in the clear. Special features: Attractive tower-like bay.

RIGHTWOOD COTTAGE.—Design 2366-N; cost, $1,290 to $1,392; plans, $15. Special features: A neat clean-cut design; front chamber full story height; living-room large and well-ventilated; very suitable plan for a narrow lot.

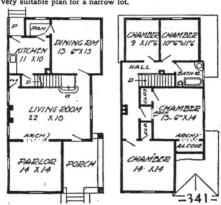

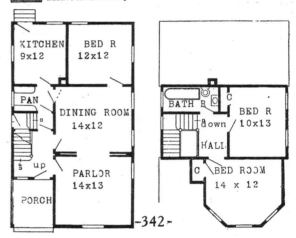

-341-

-342-

RENO COTTAGE.—Design 4230M; in frame, $45 to $598; plans, $7; width, 21 ft. 6 in. by 27 ft. 2 in.; story heights. 9 ft. 6 in. and 9 ft. Modifications—See page 65.

House came out all right as per plans furnished by you. Am pleasantly surprised, with general appearance.—D. M. Spicer, Tiffany, Wis.

FOWLER RESIDENCE.—Design 1538-O; in frame, $1264 to $1500; plans, $10; width. 24 ft. 19 in. x 40 ft.; width over all, 29 ft.; story heights, 10 ft. and 9 ft. 6 in. Modifications; See index for Fowler plan revised. Can furnish $10 plans with brick first story and frame second story. (Erkermeyer Design). See page 65.

We are more than pleased with our home. It is complete in every detail. In fact we would wish for no improvement. We feel that we have the most convenient and modern home in Northern Missouri.
S. L. BROCK, (Dry Goods), Macon. Mo.

ALTOONA RESIDENCE.—Design 1570 M; in frame, $1264 to $1599; plans, $15; width over all. 31 ft.; story heights, 9 ft. 6 in. See page 65.

I am very much pleased with the plans sent and will send you a photo of house at an early date. HARRY SAYLER, Monte Vista, Colo.

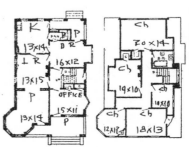

FLEMING. — Design 25-O; cost same as Fowler in brick and frame, $1692 to $2149; size 29 ft. 7 in. x 51 ft. 9 in.; width over all, 36 ft., heights. 9 ft. and 8 ft. 6 in. Plans, $15. See page 65.

-343-

-344-

GYPSUM RESIDENCE.—Design 1834-N; cost in frame, $2,390 to $2,478; plans, $20; story heights, 9 ft. and 9 ft., side walls cut down to 5 ft. Special features: Large bay-shaped rooms; attractive stairs; large rooms to second story.

STYLE IN ARCHITECTURE

Style in architecture is be distinguishing characteristic that makes a well-designed and symmetrical building acceptable to the well-informed artistic taste.

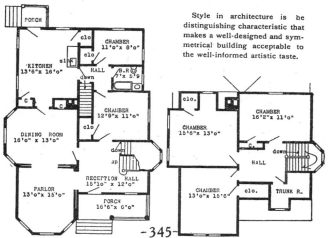

ARLAN COTTAGE.—Design 9393-N; cost in frame, $992 to $1,045; plans, $10; story heights, 9 ft. and 8 ft. Special features: Plain, neat exterior; nique octagonal vestibule and room above; large, well-ventilated rooms.

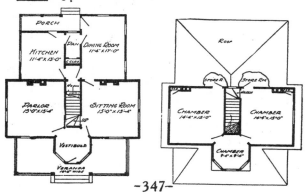

SCIO RESIDENCE.—Design 6009-O; in frame, $1198 to $1390; plans, $10; width over all, 29 ft. 6 in.; See Toledo residence on page 250. See page 65.

ART BUNGALOWS
A Booklet of 100 designs sent postpaid, 50 cents.

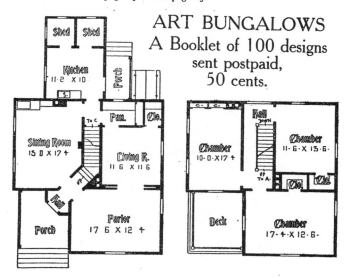

The house which you planned for us is a neat looking affair.
THOMPSON & SIBBEN, (Real Estate), Manistee, Mich.

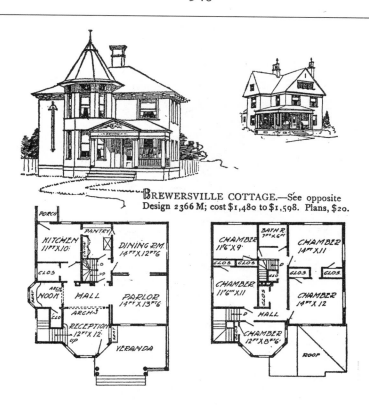

BREWERSVILLE COTTAGE.—See opposite Design 2366 M; cost $1,480 to $1,598. Plans, $20.

Yours at hand and much pleased to hear from you. My house is not completed. The carpenters will finish sometime this week. The contractor was very slow in getting everything ready, but will say your plans were carried out to the letter, and it is pronounced by everyone a showy house. I thought at first you were exhorbitant in your charges, but now would pay you twice that sum than build without your plans, and to say that I am pleased, is putting it mildly, and as soon as it is completed will send you a photo of it, and hope that I may be able to send you more work.

DR. W. S. BRANDON, Daleville, Ind.

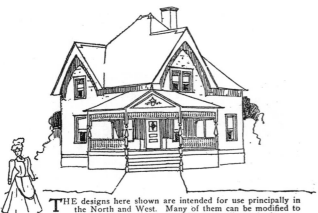

THE designs here shown are intended for use principally in the North and West. Many of them can be modified to meet the requirements of a Southern climate by increasing the heights of ceilings, width of porches, size of halls, changing the kitchen arrangements, omitting vestibules, etc.

LANCASTER RESIDENCE.—Design 1881M; in frame, $1698 to $1790; plans, $20; width 28 ft. 8 iu. x 30; width over all, 36 ft.; story heights, 9 ft. See page 65.

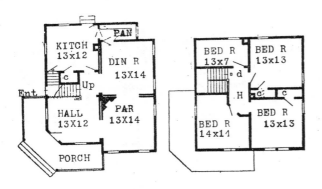

BELMONT RESIDENCE.—Design 6590-O! in frame, $1590 to $1998; plans, $10; width over all, 34 ft.; story heights 9 ft. 6 in.; Special features; Bath on first floor; plain but well balanced design. See page 65.

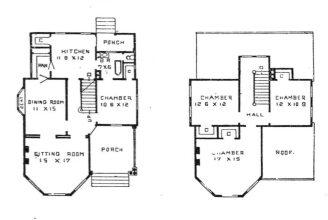

BROOKLYN RESIDENCE.—Design 1872-N; in frame, $1,699 to $1,779; plans, $15; width over all, 45 ft.; story heights, 9 ft. 6 in.; full story. Special features: Wide, imposing frontage; clean-cut, unique design; attractive reception hall, with bay at rear.

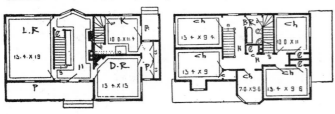

THE WOMAN'S NATIONAL DAILY

HERBERT C. CHIVERS, ARCHITECT

WANATAH COTTAGE.—Design 2375-N; cost in frame, $1,298 to to $1,390; plans, $10. Special features: Built-in range and separate vent-flue in kitchen; attractive reception hall; neat clean-cut exterior; full story heights; attractive bay in front.

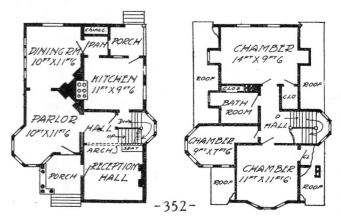

 ARNARD COTTAGE.—Design 9072-N; cost in frame, $1,232 to $1,499; plans, $10; width, 32 ft. 4 in. by 29 ft. 6 in.; story heights, 9 ft. and 9 ft., full story. Special features: Bay in front; large bath-room; unique design. A very compact plan.

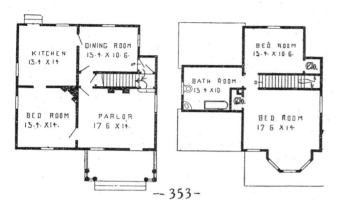

—353—

BIRDSVIEW COTTAGE.—Design 877M; in frame, $1399 to $1598; plans, $10; width over all, 27 ft. 6 in.; story heights, 9 ft. 6 in. and 8 ft. 6 in. (full story). Special features. Gable, as designed, will look well in stained shingles. with white trimmings. Can furnish a very fine color scheme with this cottage. See page 65. See index for Clinton Cottage.

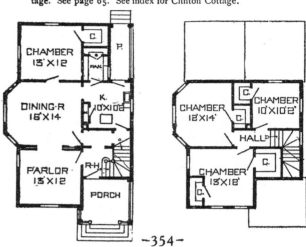

—354—

LUXORIA COTTAGE.—Design 1557-O; in frame, $998 to $1198; plans, $10; width over all 29 ft. 10 in.; story heights, 9 ft. 6 in.; Special features: Compact plan; a good chance to build a fireplace in hall at little expense. See page 65,

LUXORIA plan, Mo. 2. Allen design, plans, $10: with rear stairs; 10 x 14 kitchen; with extra closet and bath room over same and large linen and storage closet over rear porch.

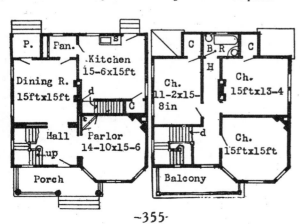

—355—

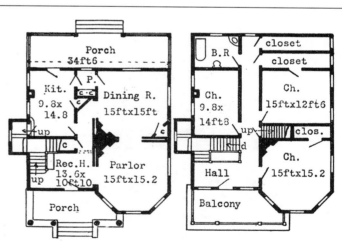

Luxoria Cottage No. 2 design 5356-A, story heights 10 and 10 ft. See design opposite page 355. Plans $10.

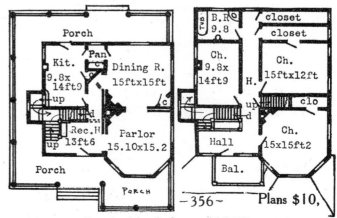

—356—   Plans $10,

Luxoria Cottage No. 2 design 5356-B, story heights 10 and 10 ft. See design on opposite page 355.

 HERRYVILLE COTTAGE.—Design 1958-N; in frame, $1,396 to $1,498; plans, $10; width over all, 34 ft.; story heights, 9 ft. 6 in. and 8 ft. 6 in.; full story in front chamber. Special features: Simple and practical porch; neat detail work; clean-cut exterior.

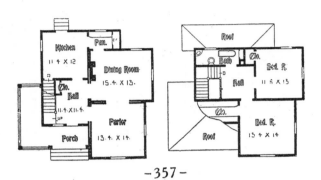

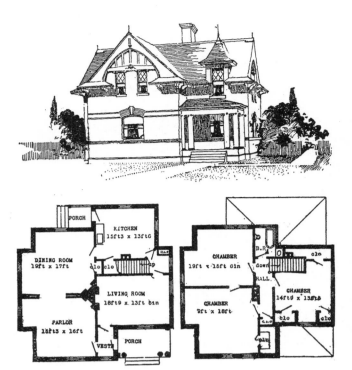

MORO RESIDENCE.—Design 2018-O; cost in frame, $1,492 to $1,580; cost in brick, $2,190 to $2,390; plans $20.

I like the plans very much and they have been admired by all to whom I have shown them.—H. S. Scadding, Kelowana, B. C., Canada.

The plans were satisfactory. No trouble whatever in putting house together.—Mrs. T. S. Osborne, Youngstown, Ohio.

Knowing as I do that my working drawings when they leave the office, go out of reach of my personal supervision I have taken especial pains to make everything very plain and easily understood

Barada design 5359, story heights 9 ft and 9. Full two-story house. See Amity design opposite page 360. Plans $10.

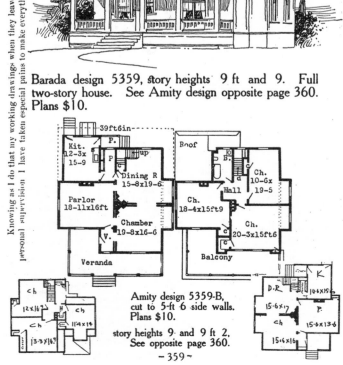

Amity design 5359-B, cut to 5-ft 6 side walls. Plans $10.

story heights 9 and 9 ft 2, See opposite page 360.

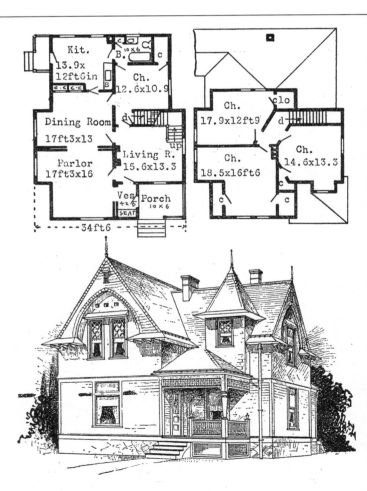

Amity design 5360, story heights 10 and 9 ft cut to 6 ft side-walls. Plans $10. See opposite page.

Piera design 5361, story heights 9-ft 6 and 9 ft. Extreme width 52 ft. Large attractive living room, with fire-place, ingle-nook and conservatory. Plans $10.

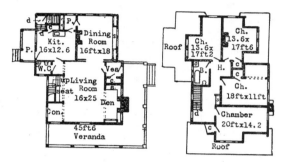

I send you herewith small "Kodak" picture of house. I had no fault to find with your plans, whatever. Your success evidently comes in thoroughly understanding your business.
CHAS. B. YEATON, Boston, Mass.

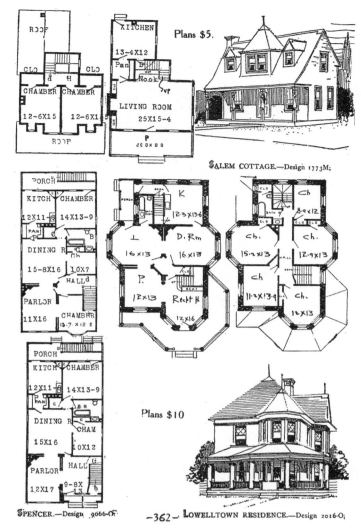

Plans $5.

SALEM COTTAGE.—Design 1773M;

Plans $10

FULTON RESIDENCE.—Design 6005-O; in frame, $1,790 to $1,898; plans, $15; width over all, 27 ft. 4 in.; story heights, 9 ft. 6 in. Modified plan No. 2, Benninger design, with large rear porch; with 4x7 pantry back of kitchen; with first story chamber and room above lengthened 2 feet; with 6x13 ft. bath-room. See pages 364 and 65.

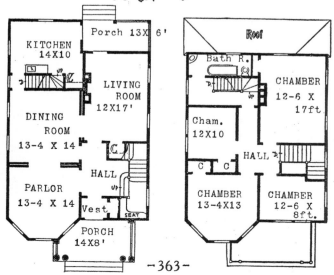

Rushsylvania No. 2 design 5364.
See Fulton Res. 363.
story heights 12 and 9 ft.

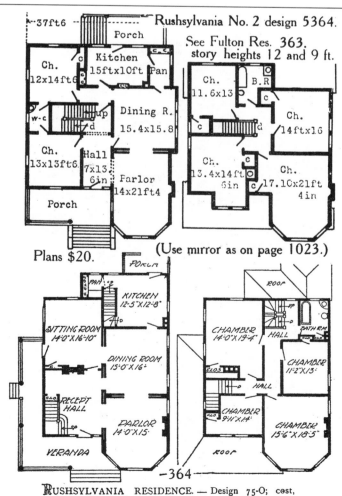

Plans $20. (Use mirror as on page 1023.)

RUSHSYLVANIA RESIDENCE.—Design 75-O; cost, $2,200 to $2,398; size, 30 ft. 6 in. by 48 ft. 6 in.; story heights, 9 ft. 6 in. and 9 ft.; extreme width, 37 ft.; plans, $20. Design similar to Fulton residence on page 363 See page 65.

Rupaki design 5365, story heights 10 and 9 ft, width 48-ft 6. Combination stone and shingle design. Plans

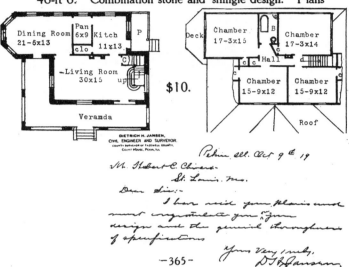

Dining Room 21-6x13 | Pan 6x9 | Kitch 11x13 | P
clo
Living Room 30x15 — up
Veranda

$10.

Chamber 17-3x15 | Chamber 17-3x14
Deck | B
Hall
Chamber 15-9x12 | Chamber 15-9x12
Roof

DIETRICH H. JANSEN,
CIVIL ENGINEER AND SURVEYOR.
COUNTY SURVEYOR OF TAZEWELL COUNTY.
COURT HOUSE, PEKIN, ILL.

Pekin, Ill. Oct 9 ᵗ 19
M. Hubert C. Chivers.
St. Louis, Mo.
Dear Sir:—
I have used your plans and must congratulate you upon your design and the general thoroughness of specifications
Yours very truly,
D. H. Jansen.

—365—

Sambar design 5366, width 40-ft 4, extreme width 44 ft. Story heights 9-ft 6 and 8-ft 6. Plans $10.

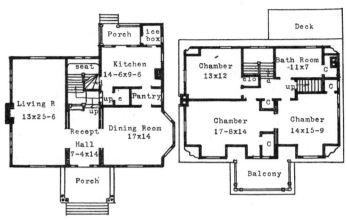

Porch | ice box
seat | Kitchen 14-6x9-6
Living R 13x25-6 | up
Recept | Pantry
Hall 7-4x14 | Dining Room 17x14
Porch

Deck
Chamber 13x12 | Bath Room 11x7
clo | up
Chamber 17-8x14 | Chamber 14x15-9
Balcony

The plans of the house, I had made by you, came very promptly, and I was very much pleased. A. L. NAIL, (Merchant), Chickasha, I. T.

—366—

CLUB HOUSE.—Design No. 2370-M; cost $3,000; plans, $45. See page 65.

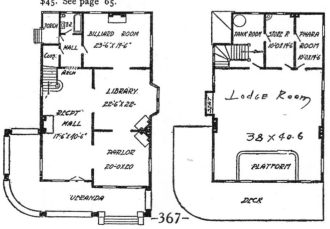

PORCH
HALL | BILLIARD ROOM 23-6" x 19-6"
CLO.
ARCH
RECPT. HALL 17-6"x40-6" | LIBRARY 23-6" x 22-
PARLOR 20-0x20
VERANDA

TANK ROOM | STORE R. 10-0.19-6 | PHARA ROOM 10-0.19-6
Lodge Room 38 x 40.6
PLATFORM
DECK

—367—

NEWPORT RESIDENCE.—Design 9640-N; in frame, $1,499 to $1,580; plans, $15; story height, 9 ft. Special features: Very attractive exterior; nook is suitably arranged for a library with bookcases and bench seats; very large and attractive living-room.

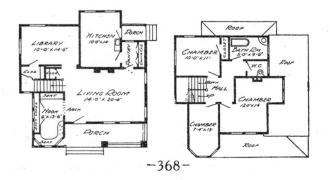

LIBRARY 10-0"x14-6 | KITCHEN 10x14 | PORCH
Pantry
clo
seat | ARCH
NOOK 6x13-6 | LIVING ROOM 14-0"x20-6
seat
PORCH

ROOF
CHAMBER 10-0"x11" | BATH RM 5-0"x9-6
clo
W.C.
up
HALL
CHAMBER 7-4x13 | CHAMBER 12x14
ROOF

—368—

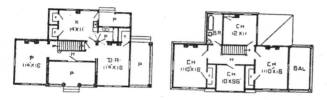

JINGO RESIDENCE.—Design 1020M; in frame, $1,098 to $1,198; plans, $10; width over all, 50 ft.; story heights, 9 ft. in the clear. Special features: Wide imposing frontage; plain simple outlines. See page. 65.

I am just about to move into the house built after your plans. The house suits us in every way and we have no trouble in building after your plans. We wish you success in your efforts to place before the people "natty" and attractive houses
L. D. PEACOCK, Dixon, Ill.

Our St. Louis building which you designed pleases us very much.
THE ST. JOE LEAD COMPANY, New York City.

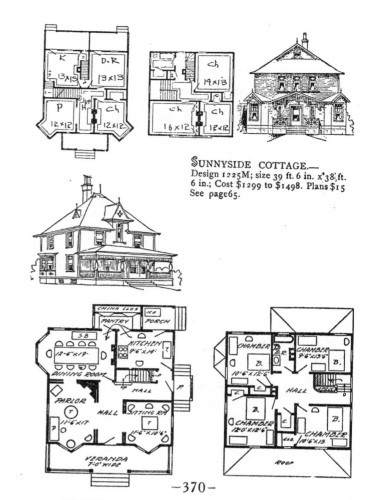

SUNNYSIDE COTTAGE.—Design 1225M; size 39 ft. 6 in. x 38 ft. 6 in.; Cost $1299 to $1498. Plans $15 See page 65.

WALLACE RESIDENCE.—Design 1000M; in frame, $1, 300 to $1499; plans, $20; See page 65.

Linden Cottage —

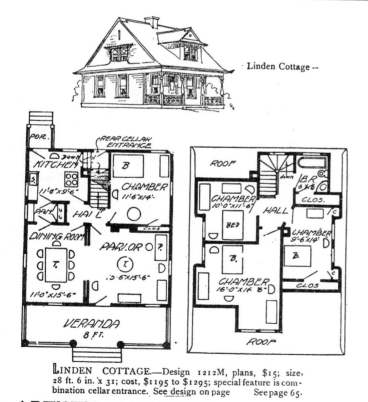

LINDEN COTTAGE.—Design 1212M, plans, $15; size, 28 ft. 6 in. x 31; cost, $1195 to $1295; special feature is combination cellar entrance. See design on page   See page 65.

ARTISTIC CHURCHES
A Booklet of 100 designs
sent postpaid,
50 cents.

Alveda Cottage, See opposite page.

GRANVILLE RESIDENCE.—Design 1525-O; in frame, $1,398 to $1,598; plans, $10; width, 24 ft. 6 in.; special features: Water-closet and basin back of stairs; fireplace in sitting-room; large vestibule; simple roof treatment. See page

CANADIAN AND FOREIGN ORDERS.

Canadian and Foreign plan orders will, upon request, and where feasible, be sent on extra thin tough blue-print paper, by registered mail, in the form of a letter. Specifications can be sent likewise, in separate envelope.

Special attention is given to Foreign orders for the reason that with our unique and distinct style of design and construction every Foreign order seems to bring a great many others.

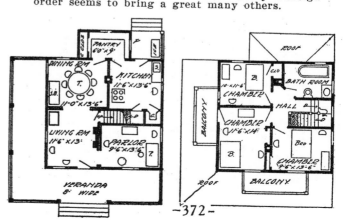

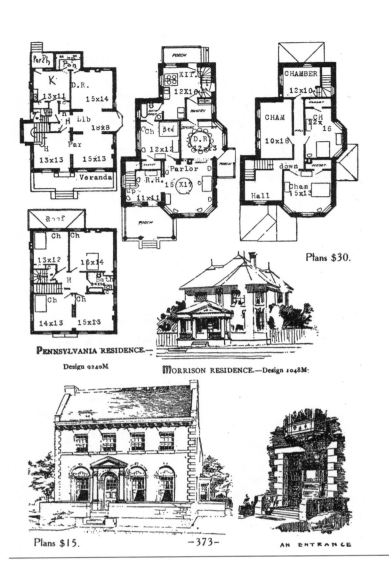

K
13x11

D.R.
15x14

Lib
18x8

Par

13x13 15x13

Veranda

Porch

KIT.
12x10

Parlor
15'X17'

D.R.
12x12

R.H.

up
11x11

Porch

CHAMBER
12x10

CHAM
10x18

CH
12x
16

down

Cham
15x13

Hall

Plans $30.

Roof

Ch Ch
13x12

16x14

Bath

Ch Ch
14x13 15x13

PENNSYLVANIA RESIDENCE.—
Design 9240M

MORRISON RESIDENCE.—Design 1048M.

Plans $15. -373- AN ENTRANCE

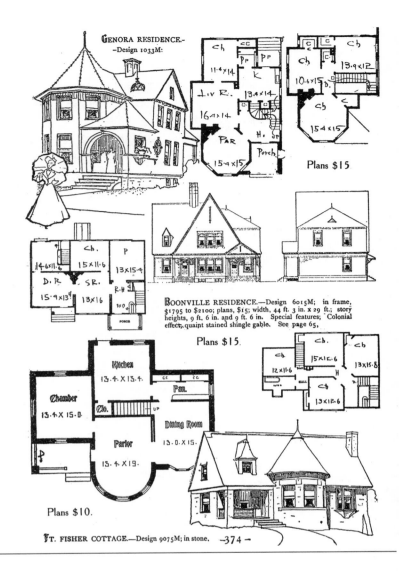

GENORA RESIDENCE.—
—Design 1033M:

ch
11.4×14

Liv R.
16.9×14

Par
15.4×15

K
13.4×14

H. Sr.

Porch

Ch
13.9×12

Ch
10.6×15

Ch
15.4×15

Plans $15

14.6×11.6
D. R.
15.9×13'4

Ch.
15×11.6

SR.
13×16

P
13×15.4

R-H.

BOONVILLE RESIDENCE.—Design 6015M; in frame,
$1795 to $2100; plans, $15; width, 44 ft. 3 in. x 29 ft.; story
heights, 9 ft. 6 in. and 9 ft. 6 in. Special features; Colonial
effect, quaint stained shingle gable. See page 65.

Plans $15.

Kitchen
13.4 X 13.4

Chamber
13.4 X 15.0

Pan.

Clo. up

Dining Room
13.0 X 15.

Parlor
13.4 X 19.

Ch
12×11.6

Ch
15×15.6

Ch
13×12.6

Ch
13×15.8

Plans $10.

FT. FISHER COTTAGE.—Design 9075M; in stone. -374-

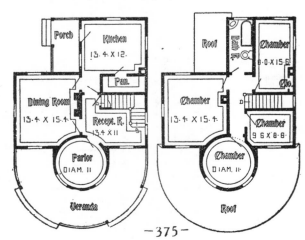

EVANSTON RESIDENCE.—Design 1864 M; in frame,
$1496 to $1580; plans, $12; width over all, 28 ft.: story
heights, 9 ft. 6 in. (front chamber full story). Special features;
Semi-circular porch; See page 65.

Porch

Kitchen
13.4 X 12.

Pan.

Dining Room
13.4 X 15.4

Recept. R.
13.4 X 11

Parlor
DIAM. 11

Veranda

Roof

Chamber
8.0 X 15.6

Clo.

Chamber
13.4 X 15.4

Chamber
9.6 X 8.8

Chamber
DIAM. 11

Roof

-375-

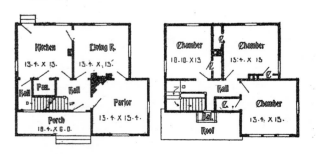

MUNCIE RESIDENCE.—Design 1860 M; in frame,
$1090 to $1180; plans, $10; width over all, 32 ft.; story
heights, 9 ft. 6 in. and 8 ft. 6 in.; (front chamber full story).
Special features; Attractive exterior; plans show a grade en-
trance to cellar in combination with inside cellar stairs. See
page 65.

Kitchen
13.4 X 13.

Living R.
13.4 X 13.

Pan. Hall

Hall up

Porch
18.4 X 6.0

Parlor
13.4 X 15.4

Chamber
10.10 X 13

Chamber
13.4 X 15

Hall

Roof

Chamber
13.4 X 13.

I am very much pleased with special plans. I think you have some fine
ideas. Your designs are certainly very artistic.
MISS AMELIA HAPPELE, Chicago.

-376-

YLVANIA COTTAGE.—Design 1216-N, plans, $10; size, 26 ft. 6 in. by 28 ft. Cost, $899 to $959. Special features: Good corner-lot design; full-story rooms above; economical construction; attractive corner porch.

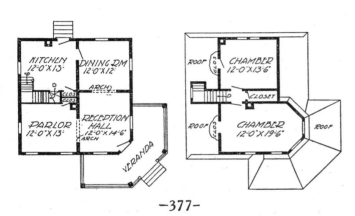

GLOVER COTTAGE.—Design 9082-N; in frame, $1,192 to $1,289; plans; $10; width, 18 ft. by 47 ft. 10 in.; width over all, 18 ft.; story height, 9 ft.

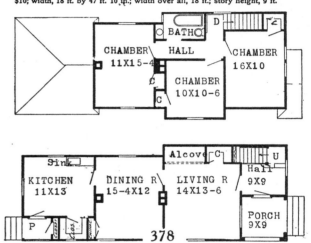

Plans $10.

NEW ROCHEALE RESIDENCE.—
Design 1880M;

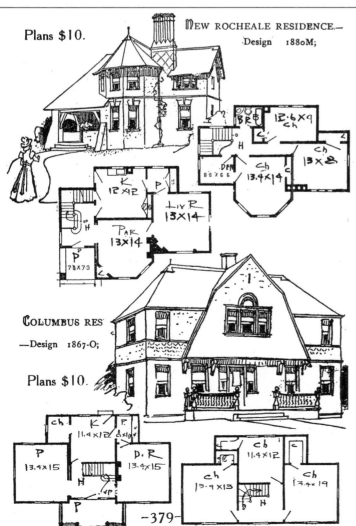

COLUMBUS RES—
—Design 1867-O;

Plans $10.

Plans $15.

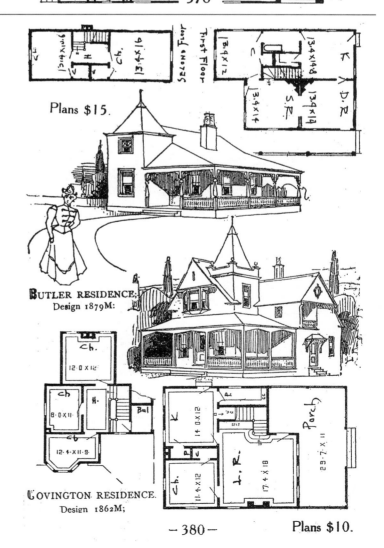

BUTLER RESIDENCE;
Design 1879M:

COVINGTON RESIDENCE.
Design 1862M;

Plans $10.

 TLANTIC CITY RESIDENCE.—Design 9842M; in frame, $2,170 to $2,290; plans, $15; width, 31 ft. by 40 ft. 6 in.; story height, 9 ft. Special features: An all shingle design; very attractive when appropriately colored; and simple to erect.

HERBERT C. CHIVERS · ARCHITECT

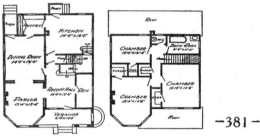

Atlantic City Residence No. 2 design 5385. See plan page 534. Story heights 9-ft 6 and 9.

—381—

BROCTON RESIDENCE.—Design 100;003M; cost $1488 to $1636; plans, $20; size 28 ft. 6 in, x 33 ft.; special features: nook in parlor, large dining room; one chimney stack for entire house, furnace in basemement.

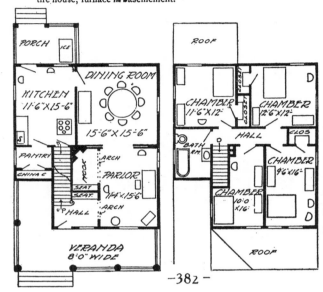

—382—

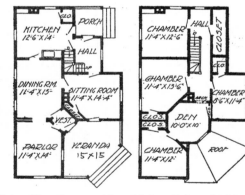

Dykesville Cottage No. 65-0, design 5383. heights 9 ft and 8 ft. Plans $10. Similar Parkdale pages 385 and 384.

The Architect discovers your likes and reduces them to a tangible form; he draws up the specifications so accurately that every variety of material and labor is distinctly set forth as to its quality and kind

If he is able and conscientious, his employment will be a saving of expense. He is not only an artist but a practical man of business. whose duty is to see that his client gets the most of the best for his money.

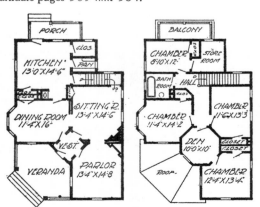

Bowling Green Cottage No. 66-0, design 5383. Story heights 10 and 9 ft. Plans $10. See Parkville, page 385. (Use mirror as shown above on page 1023 to get reversed effect.)

—383—

Tavan design 5384. story heights 10 and 9, similar to Parkdale design 385-6. Plans $15.

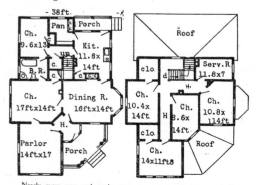

Nearly every man and surely every woman wants a home, and the prettier it is—the more home-like it is, just so much more will the whole family love it.

—384—

PARKDALE COTTAGE.—Design 1634-O; cost in frame, $840 to $1,080; plans, $8; with changes, $15; width, 23 ft. 8 in. by 42 ft. 5 in.; story heights, 9 ft. 6 in. and 8 ft. 6 in.; side walls cut down by roof to 6 ft.; cellar, 7 ft.; special features: Adapted for a corner lot; large veranda. Modifications: Porch treatment could be simplified. Can furnish these plans in stock as shown, or reverse, with the following changes, at $5.

Continued

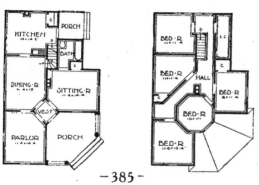

-385-

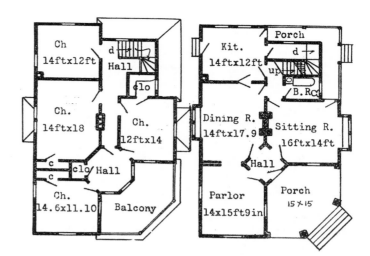

Parkdale Cottage No. 12, design 1634-O; plans, $8; extreme width, 34 ft.; same as "Parkdale" with octagon bay-shape; 13.4x26 ft. parlor, bay-shaped; 23.4x16 ft. sitting-room; 13.4x16 ft. 6 in. dining-room. See page 65.

Parkdale No. 10 design 5386-B story heights 9-ft 6 and 8-ft 6 Plans $8.

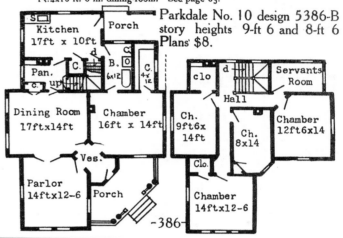

-386-

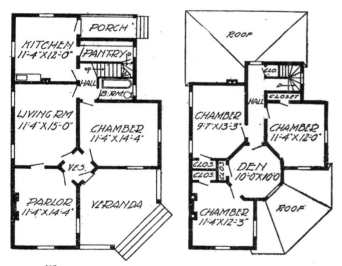

WAPPING COTTAGE.—Design 68-O; cost, $1,499 to $1,599; size, 28 ft. by 42 ft.; story heights, 9 ft. and 8 ft. 6 in. in the clear; plans, $10. Similar in design to Parkdale cottage on page 385.

Wapping plan No. 2, Difani design, with parlor 14x16 ft.; chamber 16x14; 17x14 living room; serving pantry back of this 9x6; kitchen 17x10; 4x10 closet to chamber; and extra closet to kitchen, and six rooms above; and 10 and 9 ft. story heights, cut down to 5 ft. side walls above.

WAPPING RESIDENCE NO. 3.—Sapp design 2329-U; in frame, $2,100; plans, $10; story heights, 9 ft. and 8 ft. 4 in. in the clear.

WAPPING Plan No. 4, Stafford design, same as plan No. 1, with the following changes: Parlor 14x16; living room 14x18, with square window seat bay and fire-place; kitchen 14x12, connected with living room; with kitchen porch extending to chamber; with door into chamber; with chamber enlarged to 16x14; with window-seat bay; with four rooms above 14x12, 14x18, 14x12, 12x14. See page 65.

Wapping Cottage, No. 5; Scott design, same as Wapping No. 1, with 14x15 ft. 9 in. parlor; with 14x17 ft. dining-room with 16x14 ft. sitting-room; with 14x12 ft. kitchen; with 14x12 ft. bed room over kitchen.

-387-

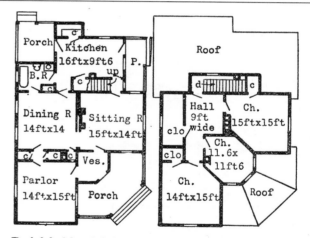

Parkdale No. 11 design 5388-A. See design page 385. Story heights 9-ft 6 and 8-ft 6 cut down to 5 ft, width 31 ft. Plans $8.

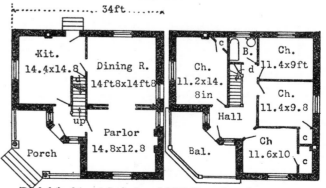

Parkdale No. 12 design 5388-B. See design page 385. Story heights 9-ft 2 and 8-ft 6. Stone house. Plans $8. (Use mirror as on page 1023 for reversed effect.)

-388-

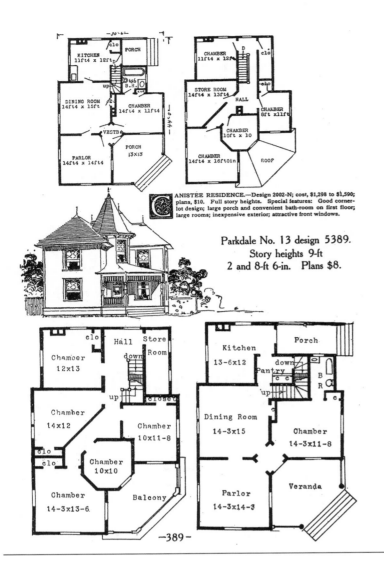

ANISTEE RESIDENCE.—Design 2002-N; cost, $1,298 to $1,590; plans, $10. Full story heights. Special features: Good corner-lot design; large porch and convenient bath-room on first floor; large rooms; inexpensive exterior; attractive front windows.

Parkdale No. 13 design 5389.
Story heights 9-ft
2 and 8-ft 6-in. Plans $8.

—389—

CAPE MAY COTTAGE.—Design 1774-O; in frame, $688 to $898; plans, $5; width, 30.4 x 30; story heights, 9 ft. cut down by roof to 6 ft. 6 in.; Special features: Designed for corner lot; well-lighted stairs; grade entrance to cellar. Modifications—Kitchen could be as dining-room, with a 1-story kitchen addition. See page 65.

A WORD OF CAUTION

Readers of this catalogue of architectural designs are respectfully warned and requested not to build from designs or use portions of plans shown therein. Any duplicity of this kind when found out and reported by our correspondents or travelling representatives will be charged for according to the legal fees of 3½ per cent on the cost of said improvements.

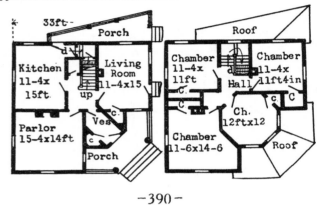

—390—

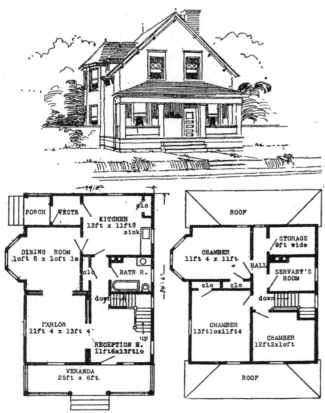

OWASCO RESIDENCE.—Design 2035M; cost in frame $1,392 to $1,480; plans $10. See page 65.

Plans came to hand. We are entirely satisfied, and wish to extend our hearty thanks.—FRANK CANTLON, Everett, Wash.

391

CARROW RESIDENCE.—Design 2390M; cost in brick and frame, $3,500; plans, $30.

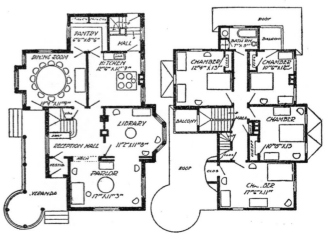

—392—

 LENCOE RESIDENCE.—Design 1039-N; in frame, $1,798 to $1,890; plans, $15; width over all, 33 ft.; story heights, 9 ft. 6 in.; front chamber full story. Special features: Back chamber and ventilated alcove for kitchen range.

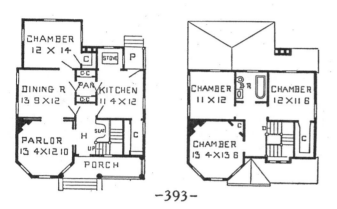

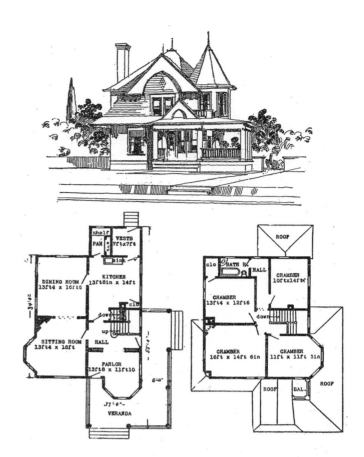

PALASKALA RESIDENCE.—Design 2005M; cost in frame $1,592 to $1,689; plans $15. See page 65.

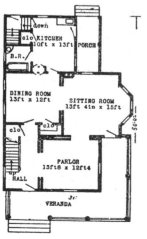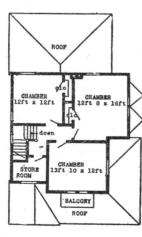

STURGIS RESIDENCE.—Design 1903M; cost in frame $1,922 to $2,098; plans $20. See page 65.

EDINBERG RESIDENCE.—Design 100,015O; cost $1665 to $2798; plans, $10; size 28.6x37.6. Special features: combination side and cellar entrance, conservatory, large pantry. See page 65.

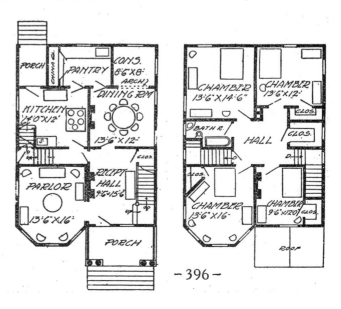

SAINT GEORGE COTTAGE.—Design 1629 O; in frame, $1099 to $1290; plans, $10; width over all 32 ft.; story heights, 9 ft. 6 in. and 9 ft. See page 65.

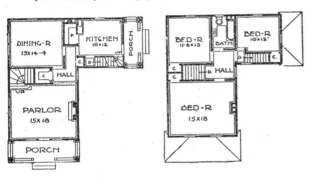

IRONDALE COTTAGE.—Design 588 M; $1298 to $1499; plans, $10. Swiss design; economical roof; good fireplace arrangement. See page 65.

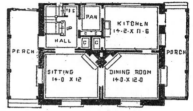

—398—

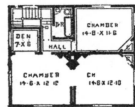

Ah, to build, to build!
That is the noblest art of all the arts.
Painting and sculpture are but images,
Are merely shadows cast by outward things
On stone or canvas, having in themselves
No separate existence. Architecture,
Existing in itself, and not in seeming
A something it is not, surpasses them
As substance, shadow."

—*Longfellow.*

BRAYTON COTTAGE.—Design 100,031-M; size 38x37; cost $1,292 to $1,398; story heights, 1st 10 ft.; 2nd 9 ft.; cellar 6 ft. 6 in.; special features, compact plan. Plans, $10. See page 65.

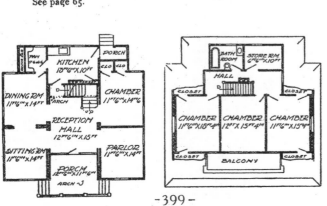

WINAMAC RESIDENCE.—Design 2006M; cost in brick and frame $2,592 to $2,780; plans $25.

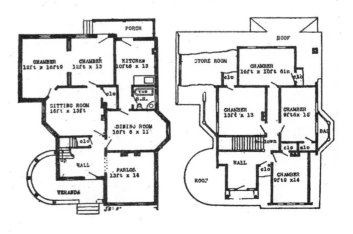

Our house for which you furnished plans is said to be the prettiest in town.
FRED A. MEYER, (P. M.), Boscobel, Wis.

RAVENNA RESIDENCE.—Design 2320-O; cost in frame; $2980 to $3660;   Plans $25;   See page 65.

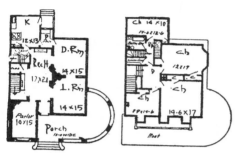

THE EXTENT OF OUR BUSINESS.

We can take only a certain amount of business, turning out plans is not a mechanical operation, as some would presume. It requires good efficient draughtmen and personal attention and my time being entirely devoted to the best interests of my clients I cannot reasonably be expected to give personal attention to sending out "free sketches." I believe it a great injustice to expect an architect, or any other professional man to waste his time in this manner and to send out samples of his work upon approval. A lawyer, physician or any other professional man would not consent to it.

MT. JEWELL RESIDENCE.—Design 2321M; cost $3,200 to $3,570; plans, $30; A very attractive summer home design. See page 65.

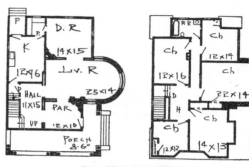

THE CHEAP BUILDER.

The cheap builder is usually antagonistic to the architect. The good builder is generally his friend, for when he figures on a job he knows that his figures will be made on the same basis for material, construction and workmanship as that of his competitors. My professional services cost you nothing when it is considered they come out of and are paid for by the waste which would presumptively result in building without well considered plans.

VILLA RIDGE DESIGN.—Design 100,022M; cost, $2,355 to $2,557; size, 62.6x49 ft.; special features: Large rambling frontage; large reception hall; large bath-room. See page 65.

Bloomfield, Mo., Oct. 12, 19
Mr H. C. Chivers,
   St. Louis, Mo.
Dear Sir:—
   The plans made by you for our Baptist Church here, so far as I can now see, are perfectly satisfactory to me, and the rest of the congregation seem pleased with them.
         Respectfully yours,
(Contractor)   J. A. CLINGINGSMITH.

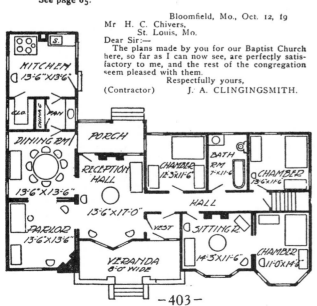

WICKLIFFE RESIDENCE.—Design 1825-N; cost, $3,500 to $4,500; plans, $50. Special features: A very good country home design; would look splendid in stained shingles. A house of this plan shows up large for its cost.

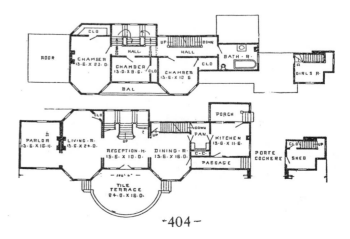

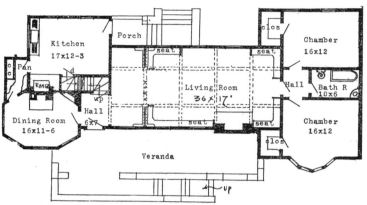

Fusaro design 5405, story height 8-ft 6, width 78 ft. Plans $25. Very suitable for a country home or seaside cottage.

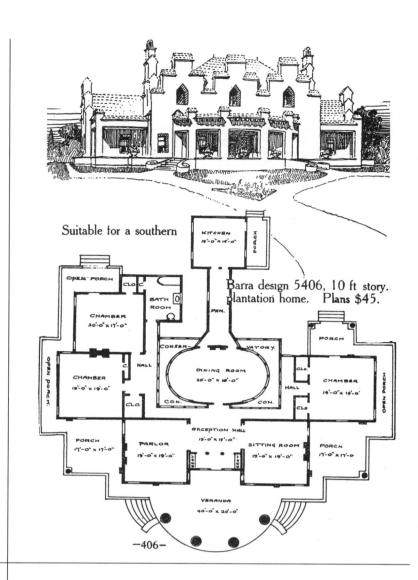

Suitable for a southern

Barra design 5406, 10 ft story. plantation home. Plans $45.

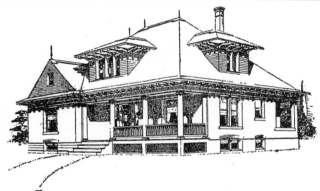

TEXAN COTTAGE.—Design 100,036-O; cost in brick, $1,885 to $2,000; plans, $15. See page 65

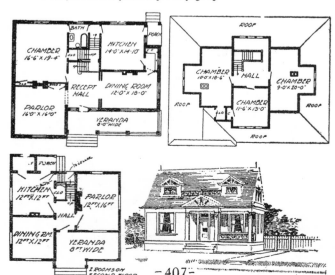

BRAMHALL COTTAGE.—Design 2335M; cost, $698 to $799; plans, $5; special features: Large veranda.

CORUNNA COTTAGE.—Design 1932-N; cost in frame, $1,892 to $1,940; plans, $15; story heights, 9 ft. 6 in. Special features: Full story to tower roof; good exterior; large rooms; neat design; imposing frontage.

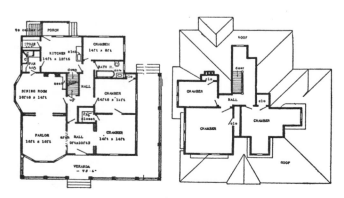

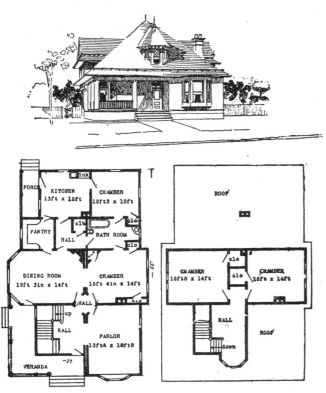

CORONOCA COTTAGE.—Design 2410-O; cost in frame $1,492 to $1,560; plans $10. See page 65.

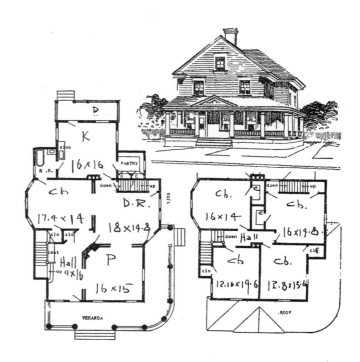

OWASSA COTTAGE.—Design 1931M; cost in frame $1,892 to $1,920; plans $15. See page 65.

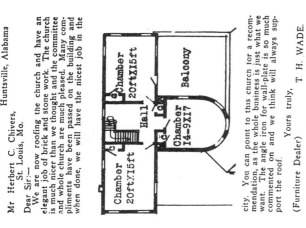

Thornton No. 2 design 5411, high stories suitable for Southern climate. See design page 412. Plans $20. Story heights 10 and 9 ft.

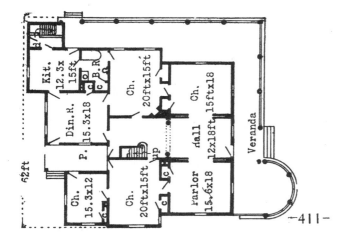

HORNTON COTTAGE.—Design 2358-N; cost, $2,690 to $2,896; plans, $20. Plan No. 2, same as above, with porch around both sides; with bath-room where dining-room now is and 18 ft. by 24 ft.; bay-shape dining-room where bath-room now is, leaving the same number of rooms but making this side of house one room deeper.

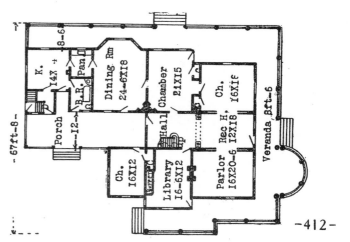

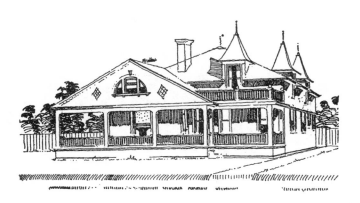

PINDOR COTTAGE.—Design 2242-O; cost in frame $1,392 to $1,590; plans $10. See page 65.

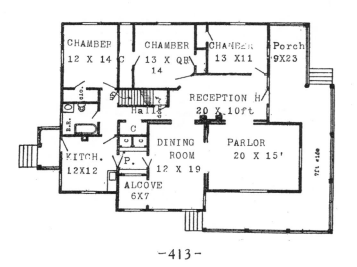

CHAMBER 12 X 14 C
CHAMBER 13 X 14 QR
CHAMBER 13 X11
Porch 9X23
RECEPTION H 20 X 10ft
Hall
KITCH. 12X12
DINING ROOM 12 X 19
PARLOR 20 X 15'
ALCOVE 6X7

-413-

MANETTA COTTAGE.—Anderson design 2341-O; cost, $1,895 to $1,980; plans, $15; 12 ft. story. A good Southern cottage. See page 65.

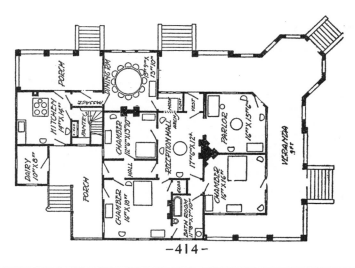

-414-

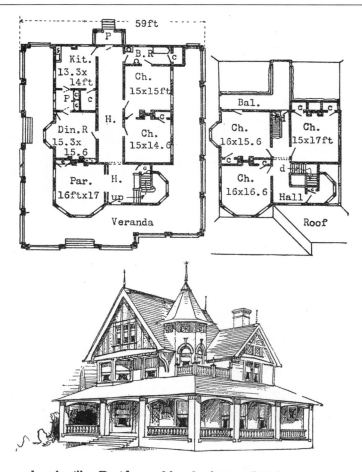

Lambsville Residence No. 3 design 5415, story heights 12 and 11 ft. Suitable for Southern home. See Lambsville design on page 416-417-418. Plans $20.

-415-

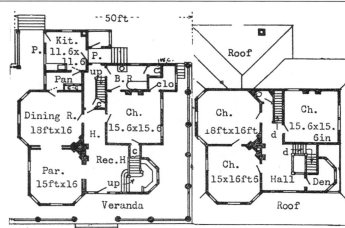

Lambsville Residence No. 2 design 5416-A, story heights 11 ft each. See design opposite page, also pages 417 and 418.

Plans $20.

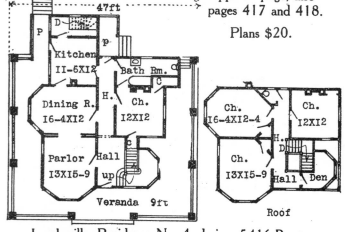

Lambsville Residence No. 4 design 5416-B, story heights 10 and 8 ft. Plans $20. -416-

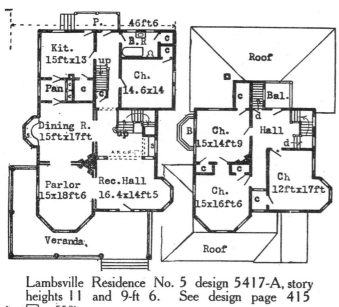

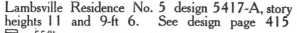

Lambsville Residence No. 5 design 5417-A, story heights 11 and 9-ft 6. See design page 415

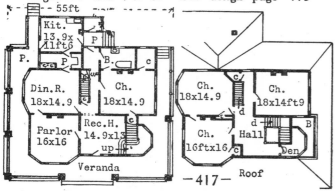

—417—

Lambsville Residence No. 6 design 5417-B, story heights 10-ft 6 and 10 ft. Plans $20. Plans $20.

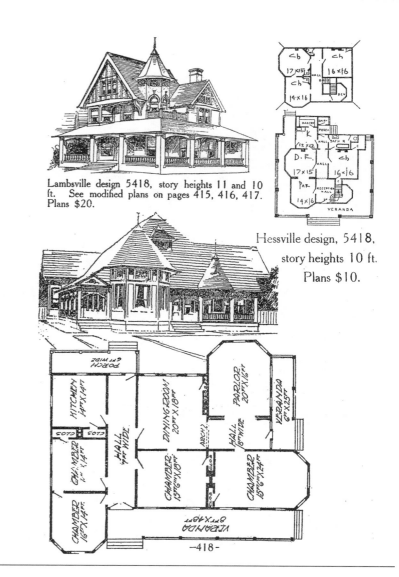

Lambsville design 5418, story heights 11 and 10 ft. See modified plans on pages 415, 416, 417. Plans $20.

Hessville design, 5418, story heights 10 ft. Plans $10.

—418—

 LKTON RESIDENCE.—Design 2246-N; cost in frame, $2,692 to $2,784; plans, $25. Special features: Wide veranda; large pantry; library appears attractively from front hall; attractive wide frontage and balcony.

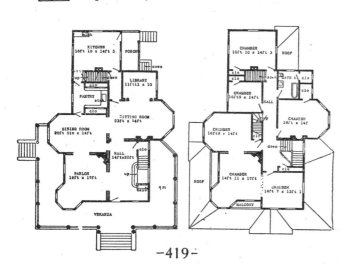

—419—

PITTSBURG RESIDENCE. — Design 1022-N; in frame and stone, $2,800 to $3,000; plans, $35.

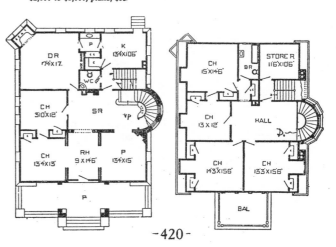

—420—

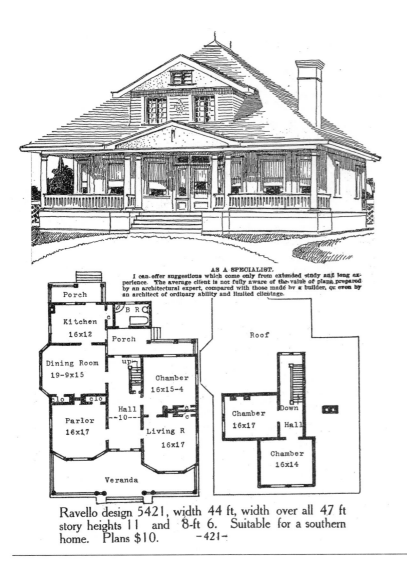

Ravello design 5421, width 44 ft, width over all 47 ft story heights 11 and 8-ft 6. Suitable for a southern home. Plans $10.

-421-

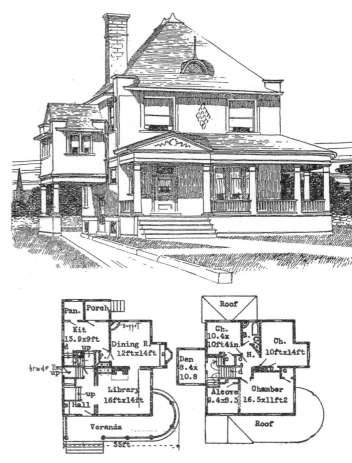

Torino design 5422, general width 27-ft 3, width over all 46 ft. Story heights 9-ft 6 and 9. Attractive den at stairs. Large library. Plans $15.

-422-

SUMMER COTTAGES.

As a number of our cheaper cottages are planned suitable for summer cottages, we have them classified as shown on the succeeding thirty-two pages. These houses are figured for regular construction, except where described as summer construction, and basements are included where cellar stairs are shown. We have a special cheap method of summer-house construction, using beaded partition lumber to inside partitions, running perpendicular around the entire room, and having the room free from the customary exposed posts to outer walls. This method will save 15 to 20 per-cent in cost, and we can prepare special plans of any cheap house for $25. See index for other summer cottages.

LONG ISLAND COTTAGE.—Design 1763M; in frame, $789 to $1,098; plans, $10; width, 35 ft. 6 in. by 25 ft. 2 in.; story heights, 9 ft. 6 in. and 8 ft. 6 in. (cut down at walls by roof to 5 ft. 6 in.).

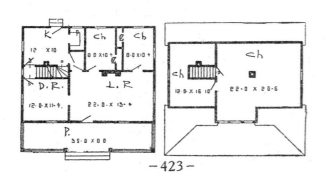

Manresa design 5424, width over all 41-ft 6, story heights 9-ft 6 and 9, second story side-walls slightly cut down. Plans $10.

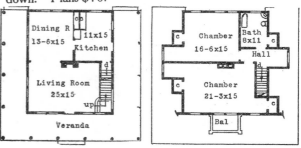

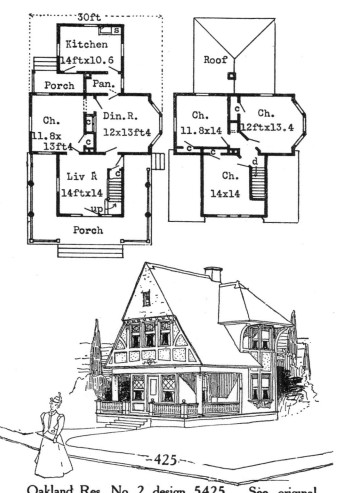

Kitchen 14ftx10.6

Porch Pan.

Ch. 11.8x 13ft4

Din. R. 12x13ft4

Liv R 14ftx14

Porch

30ft S

Roof

Ch. 11.8x14

Ch. 12ftx13.4

Ch. 14x14

-425-

Oakland Res. No. 2 design 5425. See original plans opposite page 426. Story heights 9 and 9 ft. Plans $15.

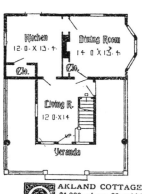

Kitchen 12.0 X 13.4

Dining Room 14.0 X 13.4

Living R. 12.0 X 14

Veranda

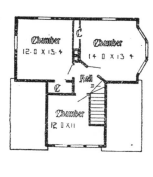

Chamber 12.0 X 13.4

Chamber 14.0 X 13.4

Chamber 12.0 X 11

OAKLAND COTTAGE.—Design 1744-N; in frame, $1,050 to $1,280, plans, $5; width, 27 ft. 6 in. by 28 ft. 6 in.; story heights, 9 ft. and 9 ft. (full story). Special features: Ornamental gable effect; suitable for a summer cottage.

ZION COTTAGE.—Design 1014 M; in frame, $1099 to $1289; plans, $10; width, 42 ft. 8 in.; story heights, 9 ft. (second story walls cut down to 5 ft. 6 in.)

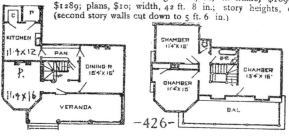

KITCHEN 11.4X12

PAN

DINING-R 15.4X16

CHAMBER 11.4X16

P.

VERANDA

CHAMBER 11.4X12

CHAMBER 11.4X15

B-R

CHAMBER 13.4X16

BAL

-426-

Plans $10

L. R. 22.4X25

K 13.4X17

16X12

REDLANDS RESIDENCE.—Design 1868M

L. R. 13.4X14

K 11.6X15

D R 13X11

P. 13.4X17

Ch 13.4X13

Ch 14X14

Ch 10X13

Bal

Cb 13X15

HANNIBAL RESIDENCE.—Design 1857M

Plans $10.

K 12X11

D. R. 13X13

R.H. 12X17

cb 13X13

l 13X15

P. 5X8X8

QUINCY RESIDENCE.—Design 1875M

Plans $15.

ch 13.9X15

cb

ch

13 X12

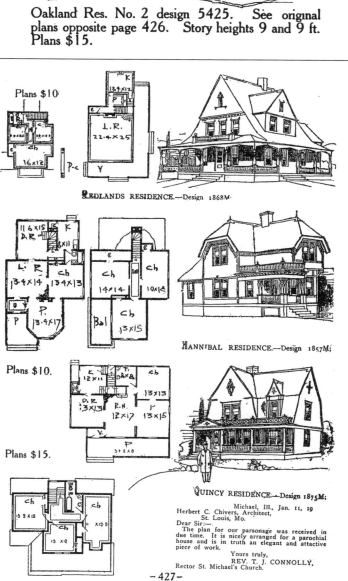

Michael, Ill., Jan. 11, 19

Herbert C. Chivers, Architect, St. Louis, Mo.

Dear Sir:—

The plan for our parsonage was received in due time. It is nicely arranged for a parochial house and is in truth an elegant and attactive piece of work.

Yours truly,

REV. T. J. CONNOLLY.

Rector St. Michael's Church.

-427-

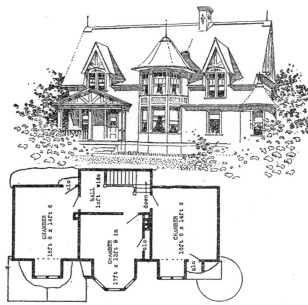

CHAMBER 16ft 6 x 14ft 6

CHAMBER 17ft x 13ft 9 in

CHAMBER 10ft 6 x 16ft 6

HALL 10ft wide

GGERSON COTTAGE.—Design 2353-N; cost in frame, $1,349 to $1,562; plans, $10; story heights, 9 ft. with second story walls cut down to 5 ft. 6 in. except in tower. Special features: A very attractive front. A good farm house plan.

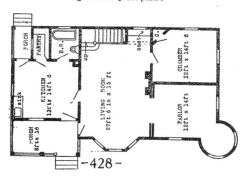

PORCH

PANTRY

B.R

KITCHEN 13ft x 14ft 6

PORCH 6 x 10

LIVING ROOM 27ft 6 in x 15 ft

CHAMBER 12ft x 14ft 6

PARLOR 12ft x 14ft

-428-

The designs given herein will probably serve as a basis on which to express your desires in regard to plans. By referring to a portion of one, and a portion of another, you can give us a clear enough outline from which to work. In this manner we can generally arrive very promptly at about what is wanted.

 SHEVILLE COTTAGE.—Design 9826-N; in frame, $1,662 to $1,283, plans, $10; width over all, 38 ft. 10 in.; story heights, 9 ft. 6 in. Special features: Simple but attractive roof treatment, stained shingle columns, attractive tower.

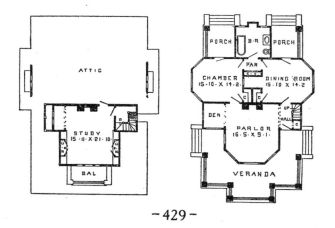

-429-

 ELVA COTTAGE.—Design 1011-N; in frame, $1,480 to $1,598; plans, $15; front chamber full story, others cut down at walls to 5 ft. 6 in.; half of pantry could be used as bath-room, with direct entrance between dining-room and kitchen.

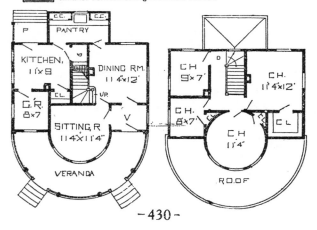

-430-

HARLEM COTTAGE.—Design 1751-O; in frame, $589 to $699; plans, $7; width, 24 ft.; story heights, 10 ft. Special features: Large porch; suitable for a corner lot. See page 65.

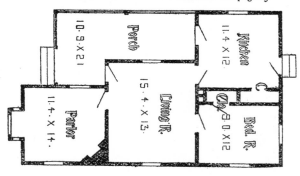

Union City, Tenn. Oct. 23, 1900

Herbert C. Chivers,
　　St. Louis, Mo.

Dear Sir:-

　　Replying to yours 16th. Beg to advise that I built according to your plans and am highly pleased with the results. Regret to say that I have no photo of the house.

　　Yours truly,

-431-

CUYABOGA FALLS COTTAGE.—Design 2342M; cost, $899 to $990, plans $8. A very practical plan See page 65.

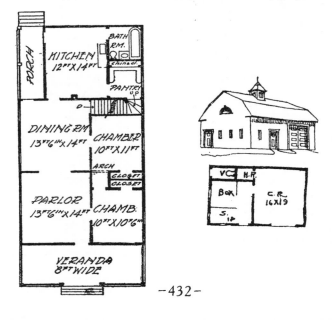

-432-

LOS ANGELES COTTAGE.—Design 1921-N; in frame, $659 to $799; plans, $5; width, 26 ft. by 44 ft. 6 in.; width over all, 28 ft.; story heights, 10 ft. Special features: Very neat exterior. Modifications: Bath-room could be placed between two back chambers. Modification No. 2. Hedden design with bed-room enlarged to 11 ft. 3 in. by 14 ft. 8 in., with 7x7 ft. bath-room adjoining, opening into kitchen, with 4x7 ft. pantry back of both, with kitchen door in rear.

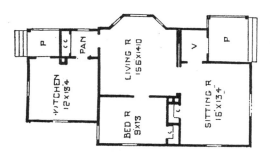

FROM A CONTRACTOR.

Herbert C. Chivers, St. Louis, Mo.:

We very much like our new house, erected from your plans and specifications. It is a thing of beauty for those who look upon it, and a joy for us. One who invests in your judgment, plans and specifications, before building will avoid the many disappointments and discouragements usually met in an effort to build a house. Were we to build to-morrow, you would be selected as our architect. Respectfully,

B. A. DONALDSON,
Contractor and Builder, Edgerton, O.

STOWELL COTTAGE.—Design 2857-N; cost in frame, $1,892 to $1,949; plans, $15; story heights, 9 ft. 6 in. and 9 ft. Special features: Large balcony and large veranda.

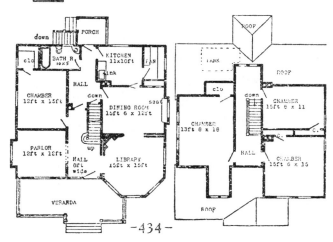

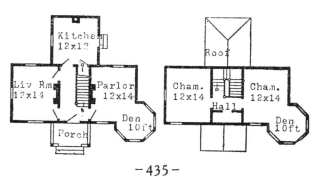

MT. MORRIS COTTAGE.—1952 M; in frame; $798 to $988, in two-story house; plans, $10; story heights, 9 ft. 6 in. and 8 ft. 6 in. Modifications; In two story plan there are dormer windows in front and tower is extended up. See page 65.

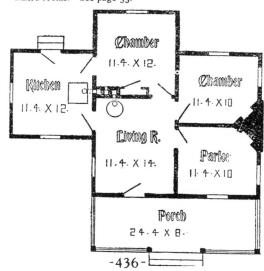

MELVILLE COTTAGE.—Design 1951-O; in frame, $699 to $797; plans, $5; width, 36 ft. by 27 ft, 6 in.; story heights 9 ft. Special features: Attractive stone chimney; well ventilated rooms. See page 33.

 OUNGSTOWN COTTAGE.—Design 1967-N; in frame, $699 to $798; plans, $5; width, 16 ft. 4 in. by 28 ft. 6 in.; story heights, 8 ft. 8 in. and 8 ft. Special features: Combination inside and outside cellar entrance.

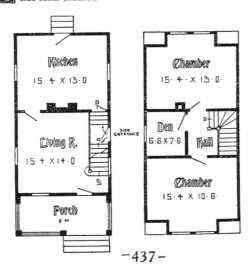

-437-

 ASHINGTON COTTAGE.—Design 1754-N; cost in frame, $689 to $799; plans, $5; width, 36 ft. by 25 ft. 2 in.; story height, 10 ft. Special features: Double porch arrangement would admit of house being used for double-house.

HERBERT C. CHIVERS - ARCHITECT ·

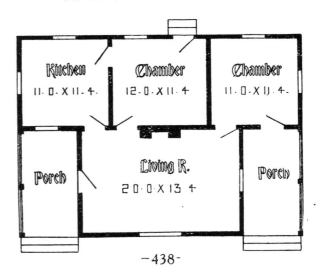

-438-

HORNLAKE COTTAGE.—Design 100193-O; in frame, $650 to $750; plans, $5; width, 22 ft. 1 in. by 42 ft. 10 in.; Story heights, 10 ft. Working plans show a more attractive exterior. See page 65.

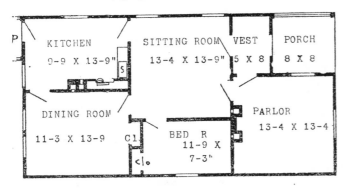

I have enclosed to you by mail under separate cover two photographs of my new house erected from your plans. I must say that my wife and I are highly pleased with it, and find it very convenient and cosy, and thank you for your skill in giving us such a good plan. It is the only house of the kind in the country. The photos I send are not good, but will show the general appearance. C. F. McCOY, West Union, Ohio.

-439-

RICH COTTAGE.—Design 1766-O; in frame, $598 to $679; plans, $5; width, 28 ft. 2 in. by 24 ft.; width over all, 50 ft.; story heights, 10 ft. Special features: Large veranda; quaint roof effect; simple fire-place and chimney arrangement. Modifications: A pleasant room, 20x20, could be placed in attic. See page 33.

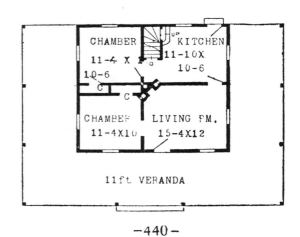

-440-

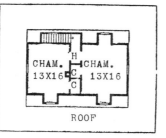

RICHMOND COTTAGE. SEE OPPOSITE PAGE.

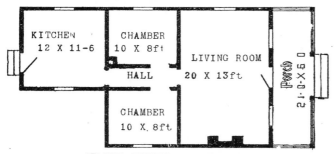

ATLANTA COTTAGE. SEE OPPOSITE PAGE.

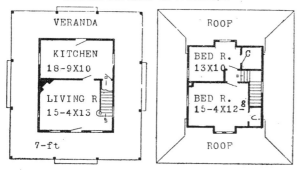

PRINCETON COTTAGE. SEE OPPOSITE PAGE.

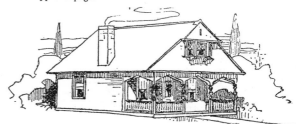

RICHMOND COTTAGE.—Design 1766-O; in frame, $498 to $590; plans, $5; Special features: Economical flue connection and eleven foot veranda. See page 33. See plans on opposite page.

ATLANTA COTTAGE.—Design 1770-O; in frame, $418 to $599; plans, $7. Modifications: Stairs could go up from kitchen in space devoted to hall, with connecting doors through 9x10 ft. bed room. See page 33. See plans on opposite page.

PRINCETON COTTAGE.—Design 1960-O; in frame, $478 to $589; plans, $7.50. See page 33. See plans on opp. page.

We like our house very much as planned by you, and should we ever build again, will certainly favor you with another order.

MRS. FRANK LANE, Boise, Idaho.

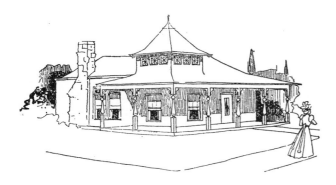

** E**RIE COTTAGE.—Design 1962-N; in frame, $999 to $1,289; plans, $7; width, 26 ft. 2 in. by 40 ft.; width over all, 34 ft.; story heights, 10 ft. Special features: Large veranda; compact connection of rooms to reception room; ornamental stone chimney showing at side. Modifications: An extra room could be added back of back chamber; size, 11 ft. 4 in. by 10 ft., at $75 additional.

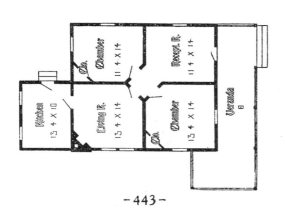

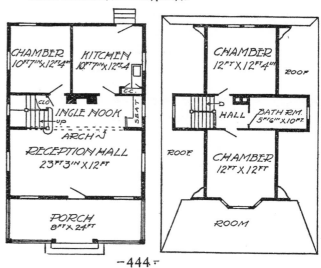

AMHURST COTTAGE.—Design 100,033-N; size, 24.6x32; cost, in summer construction, $650 to 700; plans, $5.

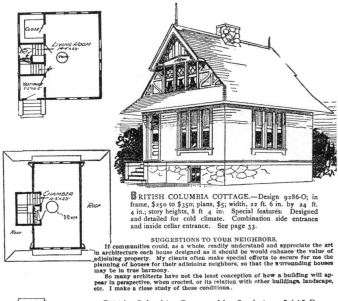

BRITISH COLUMBIA COTTAGE.—Design 9286-O; in frame, $250 to $350; plans, $5; width, 22 ft. 6 in. by 24 ft. 4 in.; story heights, 8 ft 4 in. Special features: Designed and detailed for cold climate. Combination side entrance and inside cellar entrance. See page 33.

SUGGESTIONS TO YOUR NEIGHBORS.

If communities could, as a whole, readily understand and appreciate the art in architecture each house designed as it should be would enhance the value of adjoining property. My clients often make special efforts to secure for me the planning of houses for their adjoining neighbors, so that the surrounding houses may be in true harmony.

So many architects have not the least conception of how a building will appear in perspective, when erected, or its relation with other buildings, landscape, etc. I make a close study of these conditions.

British Columbia Cottage No. 2 design 5445-B, story heights 9 and 8-ft 6. Plans $5.

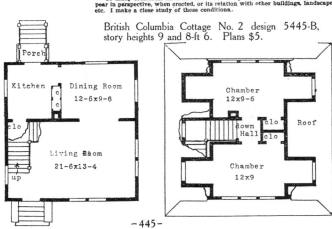

SPOKANE COTTAGE.—Design 1963M; in frame, $385 to $499; plans, $10; width over all, 25 ft. 6 in.; story heights, 9 ft. Suitable for a summer cottage, rustic stone chimney. See page 33.

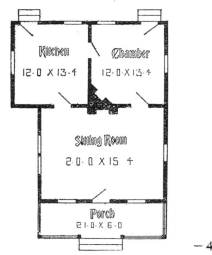

RIVERSIDE COTTAGE.—Design 1758 N; in frame, $559 to $698; plans, $5; width, 39 ft. 6 in. by 16 ft. 4 in.; width over all, 52 ft.; story heights, 9 ft. and 8 ft in the clear. Stairs go up from sitting-room. Special features: Tree-trunk posts, with forked brackets; large brick fire-place in sitting-room; two rooms above can be same size as rooms below. A good summer-house design.

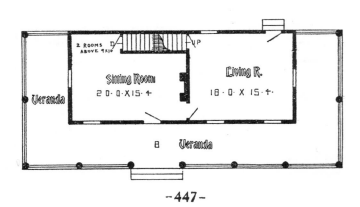

Log hut design 5448, story 9-ft 6. Plans $5.

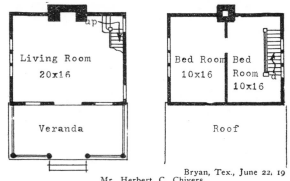

Bryan, Tex., June 22, 19
Mr Herbert C. Chivers
  St. Louis, Mo.
Dear Sir:—
  I am much impressed with the care which you exercise in having a client well pleased.
    Yours truly,
      L. L. McINNIS,
Ass't Cashier, First National Bank

MESA COTTAGE.—Design 1541 M; in frame, $1,000 to $2,000; plans, $15; width. 24 ft. 6 in. by 33 ft.; story heights, 9 ft. and 8 ft. (full story). Special features; Plain, neat exterior; stained shingle gables with white trimmings, very effective. See page 65.

MECCA RESIDENCE.—Design 861 M; in frame, $1498 to $1596; plans, $20; width; 20 ft. 6 in. by 43 ft.; width over all 24 ft. 5 in.; story heights, 9 ft. 6 in. and 9 ft.; sizes of room Parlor, 13 ft. 4 in. by 15 ft.; dining room, 18 ft. by 13 ft. 4 in.; kitchen, 14 ft. 6 in. by 13 ft. 4 in.; front chamber, 13 ft. 6 in. by 15 ft. 6 in.; alcove 6 x 8; with closet; middle chamber, 14 ft. 8 in. x 13 ft. 4 in.; back chamber, 13 ft. 4 in. x 13 ft. 4 in.; bath, 6 x 9. See page 65.

-449-

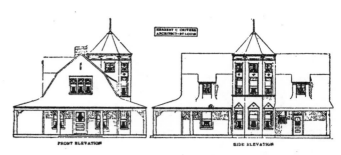

PHILADELPHIA COTTAGE.—Design 6028R; page 267; in frame, $1,198 to $1,399; plans, $5; width, 24 ft. 4 in. by 48 ft.; story heights, 10 ft. and 8 ft. 6 in.; attic, 8 ft. Special features: Wide fire-place in front room; large veranda; suitable for seashore. Plans show post foundation. See page 113.

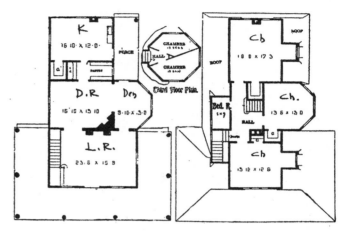

Milwaukee, Wis., June 11, 1904.

Mr Herbert C. Chivers,
St. Louis, Mo.

Dear Sir:—

We to-day received the photograph of the colonial residence and we cannot begin to express our admiration of it. It is truly a thing of beauty, and should be a continuous joy to you, its creator.   Yours truly,

PATTON PAINT CO.

-450-

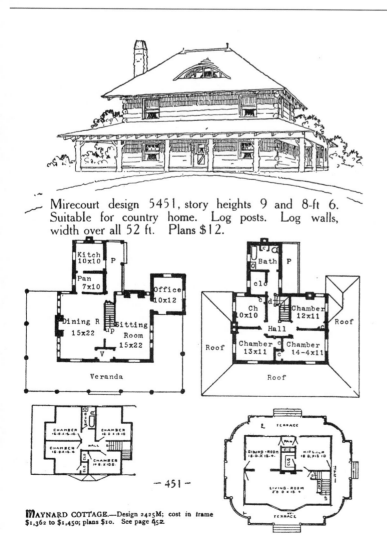

Mirecourt design 5451, story heights 9 and 8-ft. 6. Suitable for country home. Log posts. Log walls, width over all 52 ft. Plans $12.

-451-

MAYNARD COTTAGE.—Design 2425M; cost in frame $1,362 to $1,450; plans $10. See page 452

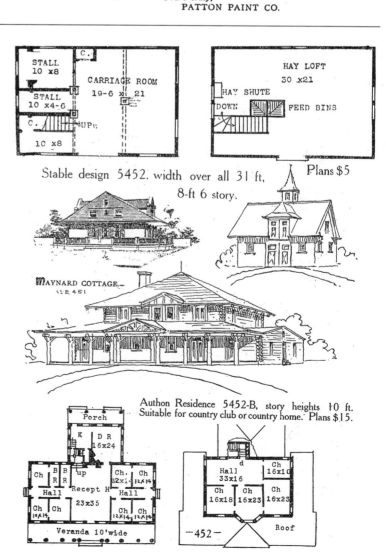

Stable design 5452. width over all 31 ft, 8-ft 6 story.   Plans $5

Author Residence 5452-B, story heights 10 ft. Suitable for country club or country home. Plans $15.

-452-

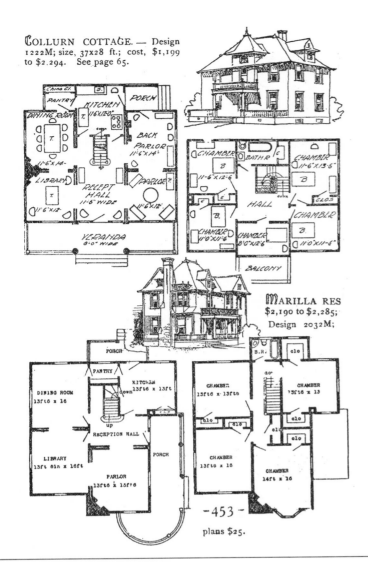

COLLURN COTTAGE. — Design 1222M; size, 37x28 ft.; cost, $1,199 to $2,294. See page 65.

China Cl.
PANTRY
KITCHEN 11'6"x12'0"
DINING ROOM
PORCH
BACK PARLOR 11'6"x14'
LIBRARY 11'6"x12'
RECEPT HALL 11'6" WIDE
PARLOR 11'6"x12'
VERANDA 8'-0" WIDE

CHAMBER 11'6"x12'6"
BATH R.
CHAMBER 11'6"x13'6"
HALL
CHAMBER 11'0"x11'6"
CHAMBER 11'0"x11'6"
CHAMBER 8'0"x12'6"
BALCONY

MARILLA RES $2,190 to $2,285; Design 2032M;

PORCH
PANTRY
KITCHEN down 13ft 6 x 13ft
up
DINING ROOM 13ft 6 x 16
RECEPTION HALL
LIBRARY 13ft 6in x 16ft
PARLOR 13ft 6 x 15ft 6
PORCH

B.R.
clo
CHAMBER 13ft 6 x 13ft 6
CHAMBER 13ft 6 x 13
clo clo
clo clo
clo
CHAMBER 13ft 6 x 18
CHAMBER 14ft x 16

-453- plans $25.

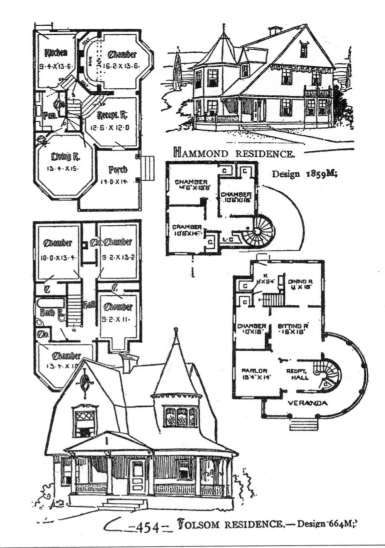

Kitchen 9·4·X·13·6
Chamber 16·2·X·13·6
Pan.
Recpt. R. 12·6·X·12·0
Living R. 13·4·X·15
Porch 14·0·X·14

HAMMOND RESIDENCE.
Design 1859M;

CHAMBER 14·6·X·18·6
CHAMBER 10·6·X·16
CHAMBER 10·6·X·14·

Chamber 10·0·X·13·4
Clo. Chamber 9·2·X·13·2
C.
C.
Bath R.
Clo.
Hall
Chamber 9·2·X·11
Chamber 13·4·X·10

K 8·X·8·4
DINING R. 14·X·15·
C
CHAMBER 10·X·18
SITTING R. 18·X·18·
PARLOR 13·4·X·14·
RECPT. HALL
VERANDA

-454- **FOLSOM RESIDENCE.** — Design 664M;

TEXAS COTTAGE. — Design 1013M; in frame, $1,100 to $1,498; plans, $10; width, 26 ft. 4 in.; story heights, 9 ft. and 8 ft. 6 in. (cut down to 5 ft. at front and rear walls). Special features: Wide front, attractive hall, with wide fire-place for logs. See page 65.

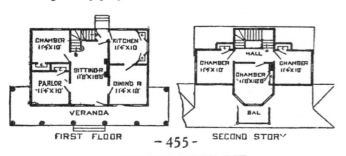

CHAMBER 11'4"x10'
KITCHEN 11'4"x10'
PARLOR 11'4"x10'
SITTING R. 11'8"x16'6
DINING R 11'4"x18'
VERANDA
FIRST FLOOR

HALL
CHAMBER 11'4"x10'
CHAMBER 11'8"x18'8
CHAMBER 11'4"x10'
BAL.
SECOND STORY

-455-

THE TRULY APPRECIATIVE.
The class of clients we desire are the "truly appreciative."

VERMONT COTTAGE. — Design 1211-O; size, 25 ft. 8 in. by 50 ft. 6 in.; story heights, 8 ft. in the clear. Summer construction, $1,200 to $1,400. Special features: Attractive fire-place, two-story effect to living room, stained shingle exterior; very economical construction. Plans $10. See page 33.

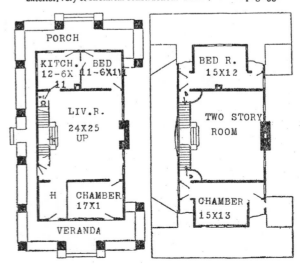

PORCH
KITCH. 12-6X 11-6X 11
BED 11-6X11
LIV.R. 24X25 UP
H
CHAMBER 17X1
VERANDA

BED R. 15X12
TWO STORY ROOM
CHAMBER 15X13

Munich design 5457
Plans $15.

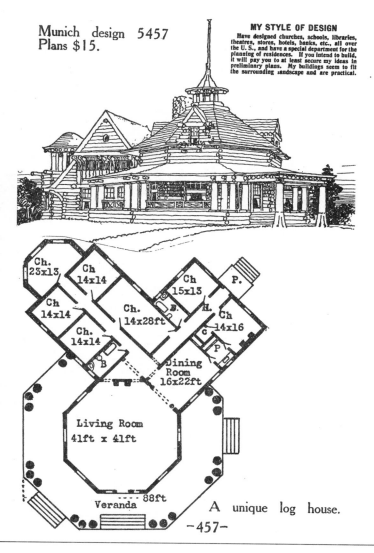

A unique log house.

-457-

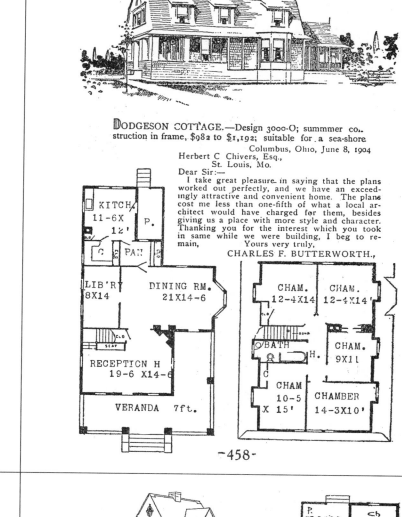

DODGESON COTTAGE.—Design 3000-O; summer construction in frame, $982 to $1,192; suitable for a sea-shore

Columbus, Ohio, June 8, 1904

Herbert C Chivers, Esq.,
St. Louis, Mo.

Dear Sir:—

I take great pleasure in saying that the plans worked out perfectly, and we have an exceedingly attractive and convenient home. The plans cost me less than one-fifth of what a local architect would have charged for them, besides giving us a place with more style and character. Thanking you for the interest which you took in same while we were building, I beg to remain,

Yours very truly,

CHARLES F. BUTTERWORTH.,

-458-

Granite City Cottage No. 2 design 5459-A, story heights 8 and 8 ft. Plans $5

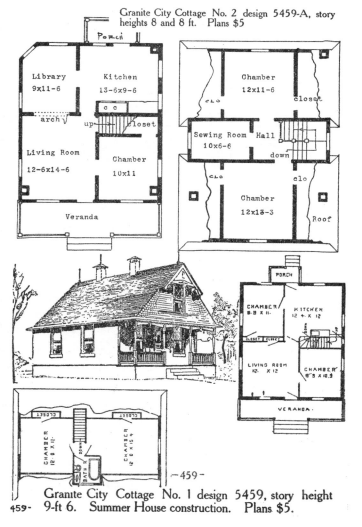

Granite City Cottage No. 1 design 5459, story height 9-ft 6. Summer House construction. Plans $5.

-459-

EUREKA COTTAGE.—Design 1745-O; in frame, $699 to $798; plans, $10; width, 24 ft. 2 in. by 30 ft.; story heights, 9 ft. and 8 ft. (cut down at wall to 5 ft.). Modifications: Closet can be put in between front and back bed-rooms on second floor. See page 65.

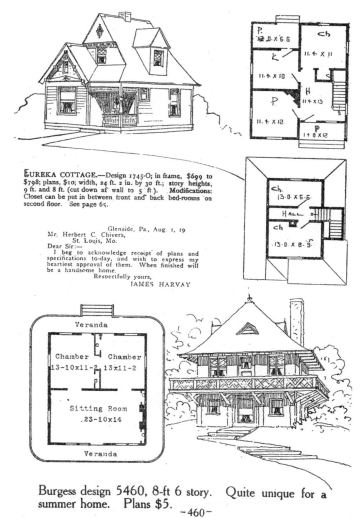

Glenside, Pa., Aug. 1, 19

Mr. Herbert C. Chivers,
St. Louis, Mo.

Dear Sir:—

I beg to acknowledge receipt of plans and specifications to-day, and wish to express my heartiest approval of them. When finished will be a handsome home.

Respectfully yours,

JAMES HARVAY

Burgess design 5460, 8-ft 6 story. Quite unique for a summer home. Plans $5.

-460-

ST. JOSEPH COTTAGE.—Design 1771M; in frame, $499 to $539; plans, $15; width, 18 ft. 4 in. by 44 ft.; width over all, 22 ft. 6 in.; story heights, 9 ft. and 8 ft. (two rooms above). St. Joseph plan No. 2, Andrews design; size, 19. 10x24 ft. with sitting-room 19x12 ft., pantry 6x8 ft., with double flue at kitchen, with single flue to living room, with three rooms above, sizes 11x13 ft., 8, 12x11 ft. and 11x10 ft. with middle room having ventilation on two sides; second-story wall cut down to 5 ft. A very attractive design. See page 65.

Plans $10

A summer home; plans, $10; kitchen under dining-room.

—461—

St. Joseph Cottage No. 2 design 5462-A, story heights 9-ft 6 and 8-ft 6. See design on opposite page 461. Plans $10.

St. Joseph No. 3 design 5462-B, story heights 8-ft 6 and 8. Plans $10.

—462—

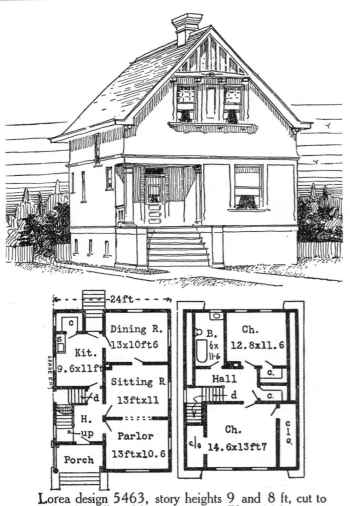

Lorea design 5463, story heights 9 and 8 ft, cut to 6 ft side-walls. Very compact. Plans $10. —463—

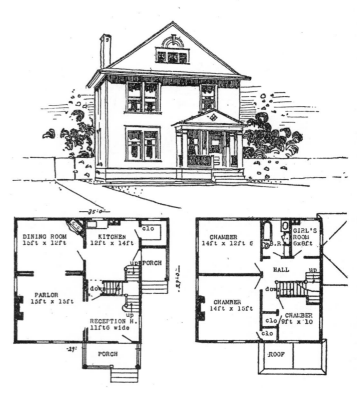

DIMONDALE RESIDENCE.—Design 1977M; cost in frame $1,592 to $1,790; plans $10. See page 65.

POINTS TO LOOK AFTER.

The planning of a house, where expensive materials and labor are considered, should not be left to unskilled hands. Allow the lady of the house to have considerable say-so in the floor arrangement especially. They have to live in the house day and night and a poorly planned house is generally more expensive than a modern practical plan.

464

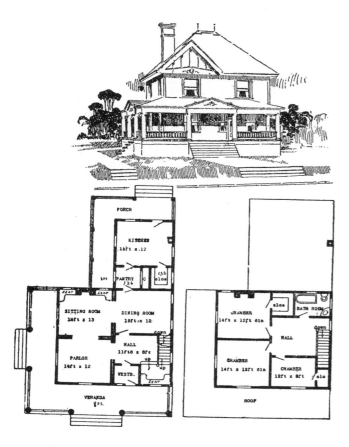

MALTBY RESIDENCE -465- 1925M;

MY TERMS.

I agree to make your plans for a stated sum, and therefore would not be interested in making your building unnecessarily expensive in order to increase my commission, as is often done.

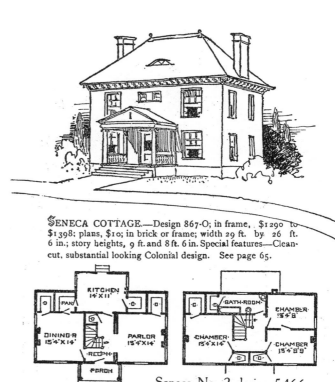

SENECA COTTAGE.—Design 867-O; in frame, $1290 to $1398; plans, $10; in brick or frame; width 29 ft. by 26 ft. 6 in.; story heights, 9 ft. and 8 ft. 6 in. Special features—Clean-cut, substantial looking Colonial design. See page 65.

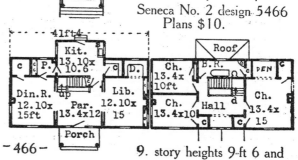

Seneca No. 2 design 5466
Plans $10.

-466-   9. story heights 9 ft 6 and

BLOOFIELD RESIDENCE.—Design 6022-O; in frame, $1200 to $1387; plans, $10; width, 27 ft. 8 in. by 31 ft. 4 in.; story heights, 9 ft. 6 in. and 9 ft. See index for Danville residence: See page 65.

— MY RESPONSIBILITY. —

My professional responsibility and preparedness has been my success and is evidenced by the fact that clients who build year after year invariably come back to me for plans.

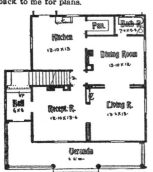 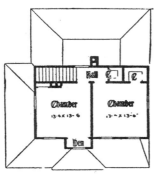

The plans which you prepared for me were in every respect satisfactory as to design, convenience, etc.
B. W. WITT. Mossy Creek. Tenn.

-467-

(second story side walls cut down to 5 ft. 6 in.)

DIXON RESIDENCE.—Design 1540 M;

Plans $15

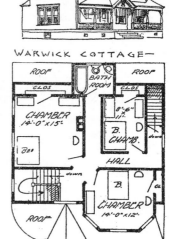

WARWICK COTTAGE—

-468-   Plans $10

SALAMANCA RESIDENCE.—Design 2376M; cost in frame, $2,190 to $2,298; plans, $15. See page 65

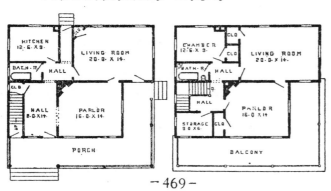

FINCASTLE RESIDENCE.—Design 4001 M; in frame, $792 to $886; plans, $10; story heights, 9 ft. 6 in. and 8 ft. 6 in. cut by roof to 5 ft. 6 in. walls. A neat Colonial design. See page 65.

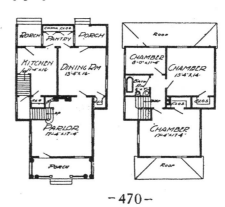

Cadiz design 5471, story heights 9-ft 6 and 8-ft 6, width 26 ft. Plans $10.

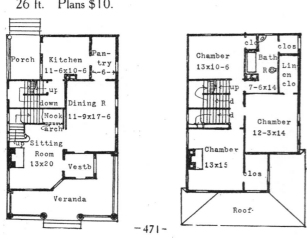

The plans sent me are satisfactory; entirely so. I am much pleased with the house. It is, I think, by far the neatest and most satisfactorily arranged building that I ever saw. ASA BUTLER, Crab Orchard, Tenn.

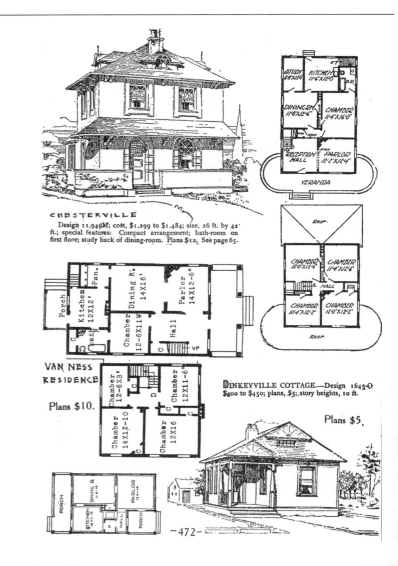

CHESTERVILLE

Design 11,949M; cost, $1,299 to $1,484; size, 26 ft. by 42 ft.; special features: Compact arrangement; bath-room on first floor; study back of dining-room. Plans $12. See page 65.

VAN NESS RESIDENCE

Plans $10.

DINKEYVILLE COTTAGE.—Design 1645-O $400 to $450; plans, $5; story heights, 10 ft.

Plans $5.

SAGINAW COTTAGE.—Design 1202M; Size 36 ft. 6 in.
by 31 ft. Cost $2595 to $1998; plans, $10.

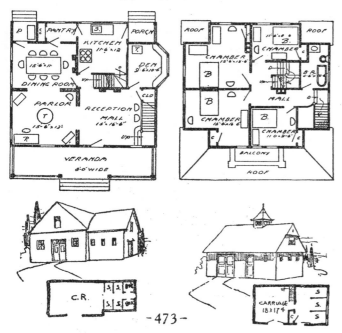

-473-

A greater portion of my work comes from clients who roughly arrive at
the arrangement of plan wanted themselves
and then send their work to me to be put into practical shape.

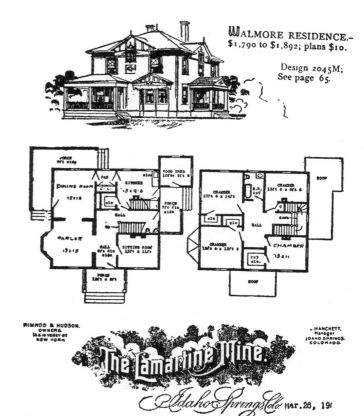

Mr. Herbert C. Chivers,
Wainright Bldg., St. Louis.

Dear Sir:-

Replying to your favor will say plans came satisfactorily.
The color effects specified produced a fine effect.

Yours respectfully,

-474-

"practice makes perfect" this alone should be an incentive for you
to avail yourself of my services.

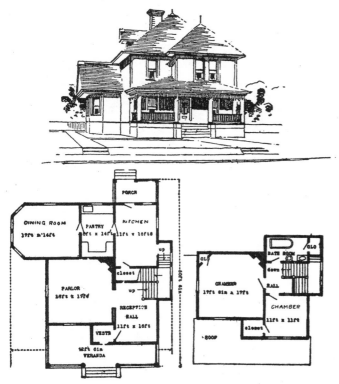

COLOMA RESIDENCE.—Design 1917M; cost in frame
$1,492 to $1,580; plans $10. See page 65.

We are more than pleased with the plans prepared by you.
JOHN P. KEISER, Osceola, Ark.

-475-

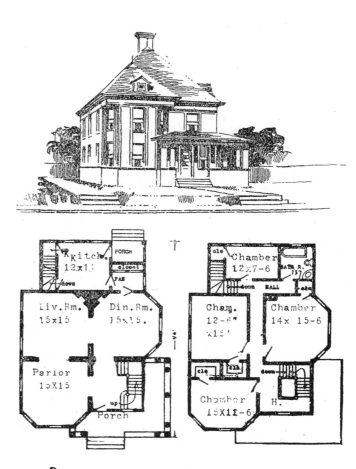

DORSEY RESIDENCE.—Design 1924M; cost in frame,
$1,692 to $1,892; plans $10. See page 65.

-476-

Thames design 5477 heights 9 and 8 ft.

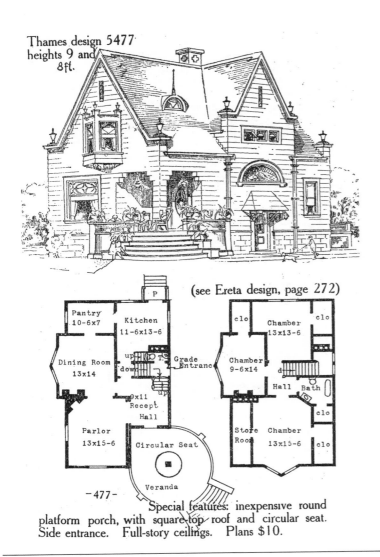

(see Ereta design, page 272)

-477-

Special features: inexpensive round platform porch, with square top roof and circular seat. Side entrance. Full-story ceilings. Plans $10.

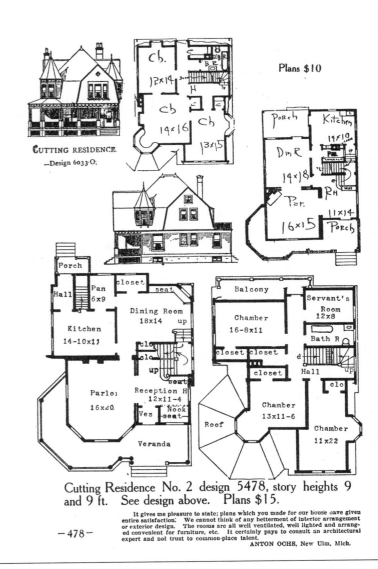

Plans $10

CUTTING RESIDENCE. —Design 6033-O.

Cutting Residence No. 2 design 5478, story heights 9 and 9 ft. See design above. Plans $15.

-478-

It gives me pleasure to state; plans which you made for our house have given entire satisfaction: We cannot think of any betterment of interior arrangement or exterior design. The rooms are all well ventilated, well lighted and arranged convenient for furniture, etc. It certainly pays to consult an architectural expert and not trust to common-place talent.
ANTON OCHS, New Ulm, Mich.

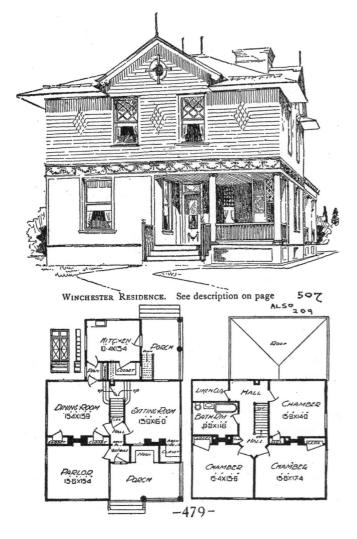

WINCHESTER RESIDENCE. See description on page 507 ALSO 209

-479-

TUSTIN COTTAGE.—Design 2380-O; cost in frame, $1,392 to $1,480. plans, $10. Full story heights. See page 65.

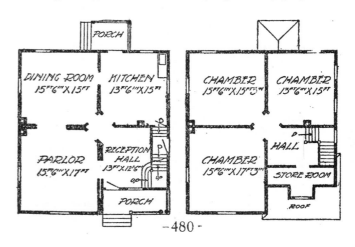

-480-

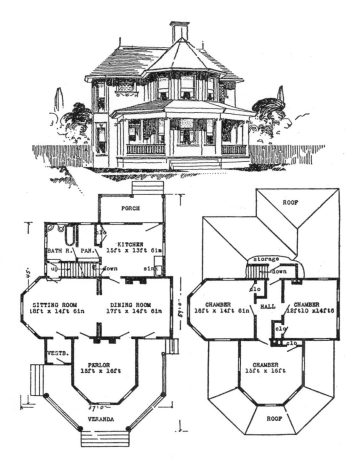

 ORSET RESIDENCE.—Design 1900-N; cost in frame, $2,140 to $2,392; plans, $20. See Chesterton residence. Special features: Attractive parlor and sitting-room; with pleasant outlook and large veranda; front room is well ventilated.

—481—

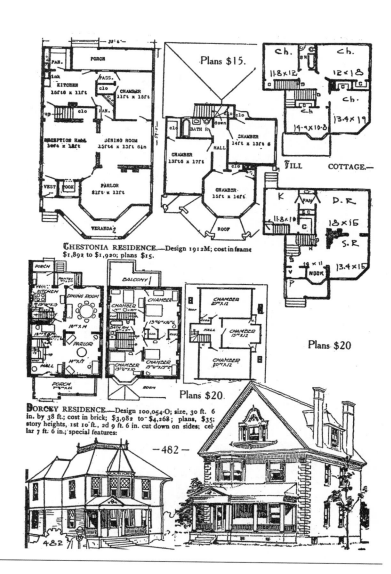

CHESTONIA RESIDENCE.—Design 1912M; cost in frame $1,892 to $1,920; plans $15.

Plans $20

DORCEY RESIDENCE.—Design 100,054-O; size, 30 ft. 6 in. by 38 ft.; cost in brick; $3,982 to $4,268; plans, $35; story heights, 1st 10 ft., 2d 9 ft. 6 in. cut down on sides; cellar 7 ft. 6 in.; special features:

—482—

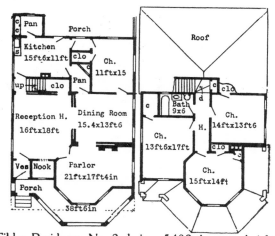

Tilden Residence No. 2 design 5482-A, story heights 9-ft 6 and 8-ft 6. See design opposite page 484. Plans $15.

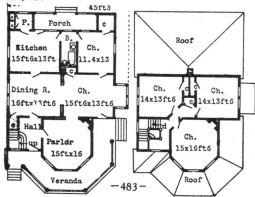

—483—

Tilden Residence No. 3 design 5482-B, story heights 9-ft 6 and 8-ft 6. Round Colonial columns. See similar design with shingle column on opposite page 484. Plans $15.

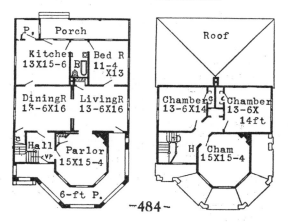

TILDEN RESIDENCE.—Design 361-N; in frame, $1,698 to $1,780; plans, $15; width over all, 31 ft.; story heights, 9 ft. 6 in. and 8 ft. 6 in.; full story. Special features: Octagon parlor and shingle porch; well-ventilated second-story front rooms.

—484—

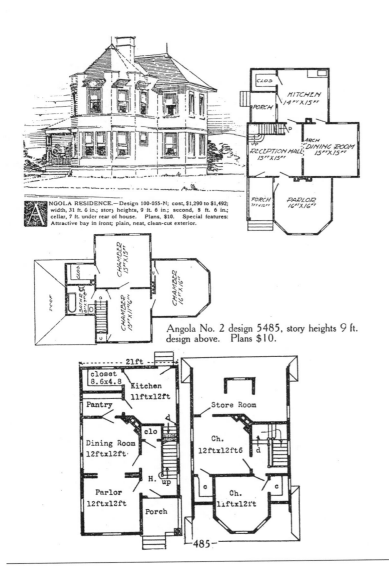

ANGOLA RESIDENCE.—Design 100-055-N; cost, $1,290 to $1,492; width, 31 ft. 6 in.; story heights, 9 ft. 6 in.; second, 8 ft. 6 in.; cellar, 7 ft. under rear of house. Plans $10. Special features: Attractive bay in front; plain, neat, clean-cut exterior.

CLOS
KITCHEN 14"X15"
PORCH
ARCH
RECEPTION HALL 15"X15"
DINING ROOM 15"X15"
PORCH
PARLOR 16"X16"

CHAMBER 15"X15"
CLOS
ROOF
BATH
CHAMBER 13"X11'6"
CHAMBER 16"X16"

Angola No. 2 design 5485, story heights 9 ft. design above. Plans $10.

21ft
closet 8.6x4.8
Kitchen 11ftx12ft
Pantry
clo
d
Store Room
Dining Room 12ftx12ft
Ch. 12ftx12ft6
d
Parlor 12ftx12ft
H. up
c
c
Porch
Ch. 11ftx12ft

—485—

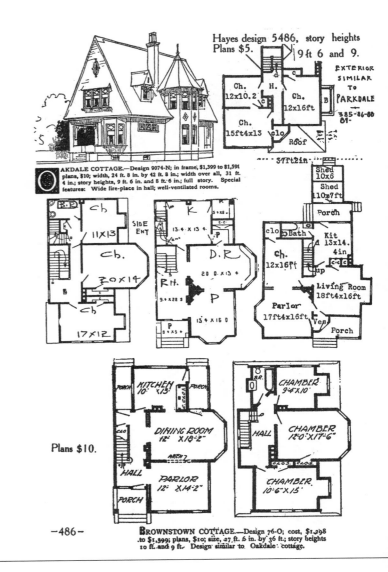

OAKDALE COTTAGE.—Design 9074-N; in frame, $1,399 to $1,599; plans, $10; width, 24 ft. 8 in. by 42 ft. 8 in.; width over all, 31 ft. 4 in.; story heights, 9 ft. 6 in. and 8 ft. 6 in.; full story. Special features: Wide fire-place in hall; well-ventilated rooms.

Hayes design 5486, story heights Plans $5. 9 ft 6 and 9.

EXTERIOR SIMILAR TO PARKDALE 5-85-86-88-89-

Ch. 12x10.2
H.
d
c
Ch. 12x16ft
B
Ch. 15ft4x13
clo
Roof

—37ft2in—

B.R.
Ch. 11X13
Side Ent
K.
Shed 10x6
Shed 10x7ft
Porch
Ch. 20X14
R.H.
D.R.
clo
Bath
Kit 13x14. 4in
17x12
P
Ch. 12x16ft
up
Living Room 18ftx16ft
Parlor 17ftx16ft
Ves
Porch

Plans $10.

PORCH
KITCHEN 10' X15'
PORCH
CLO
B.R.
CHAMBER 9'4X10'
DINING ROOM 12' X18'-2"
CLO
HALL
CHAMBER 12'0"X17'-6"
ARCH
HALL
PARLOR 12' X14'-2"
CHAMBER 10'-6"X15'
PORCH
CLOS

—486—

BROWNSTOWN COTTAGE.—Design 76-O; cost, $1,298 to $1,399; plans, $10; size, 27 ft. 6 in. by 36 ft.; story heights 10 ft. and 9 ft. Design similar to Oakdale cottage.

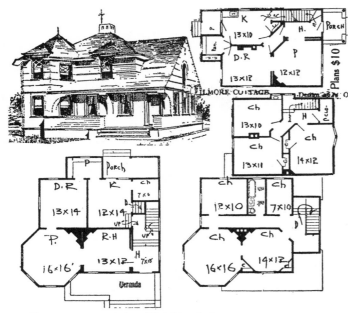

K
13x10
H.
Porch
Pan.
D.R. 13x18
P
12x12
Plans $10

FILMORE COTTAGE. Design 36 N O

Ch. 13x10
H.
Ch. 13x11
Ch. 14x12
Ch.

P. Porch
D.R. 13x14
K. 12x14
7x8
P. 16x16'
R.H. 13x12
7x8
H.
Ch. 12x10
7x10
Ch. 16x16
Ch. 19x12

Veranda

WINDSOR COTTAGE.—Design 9068O; in frame, $1499 to $1498; plans, $20; width, 33 ft. x 26 ft. 4 in.; story heights, 9 ft. 6 in. and 8 ft. 6 in. Special features; Octagon parlor, and wide stair arrangement. Modifications; Kitchen could be used for dining room with small porch back of present dining-room. See page 65.

Plans $20.

Windsor Cottage No. 2 heights 9-ft 6 and 8-ft 6. design 5487.

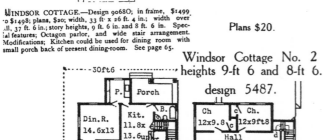

—30ft6—
P. Porch
Din. R. 14.6x13
Kit. 11.8x 13.6
B.
Ch. 12x9.8
Ch. 12x9ft8
Parlor 16ftx16
Rec.H. 14x11ft6
up
Hall
d
Ch. 16ftx16
Ch. 15x11ft6
c
Veranda
Roof

Plans $15.

—487—

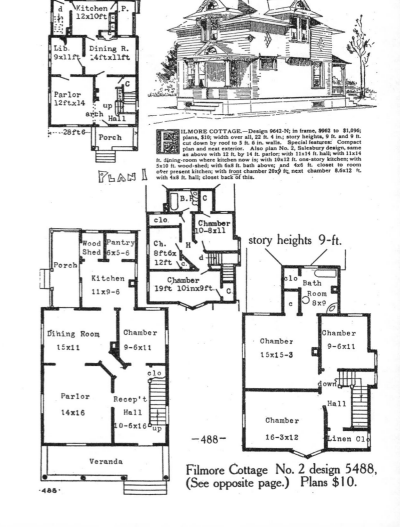

d
Kitchen 12x10ft
P.
Lib. 9x11ft
Dining R. 14ftx11ft
c
Parlor 12x14
up
arch
Hall
—28ft6—
Porch

FILMORE COTTAGE.—Design 9642-N; in frame, $962 to $1,096; plans, $10; width over all, 22 ft. 4 in.; story heights, 9 ft. and 9 ft. cut down by roof to 5 ft. 6 in. walls. Special features: Compact plan and neat exterior. Also plan No. 2, Salesbury design, same as above with 12 ft. by 14 ft. parlor; with 11x14 ft. hall; with 11x14 ft. dining-room where kitchen now is; with 10x12 ft. one-story kitchen; with 5x10 ft. wood-shed; with 6x8 ft. bath above; and 4x6 ft. closet to room over present kitchen; with front chamber 20x9 ft, next chamber 8.6x12 ft. with 4x8 ft. hall; closet back of this.

PLAN I

B.R.
C
clo
Chamber 10-8x11
Wood Shed
Pantry 6x5-6
Ch. 8ftx6 12ft
H.
d
Porch
Kitchen 11x9-6
Chamber 19ft 10inx9ft.
C

story heights 9-ft.

clo
Bath Room 8x9
c

Dining Room 15x11
Chamber 9-6x11
clo
Chamber 15x15-3
Chamber 9-6x11

Parlor 14x16
Recep't Hall 10-6x16
up
down
Hall

Chamber 16-3x12
Linen Clo

—488—

Veranda

—488—

Filmore Cottage No. 2 design 5488, (See opposite page.) Plans $10.

FERNVILLE RESIDENCE. — Design 100,019-O; cost, $1,638 to $1,892; plans, $15; size, 26.6x42 ft.; special features: Compact plan; bay to library, large bath-room, combination cellar entrance at rear.

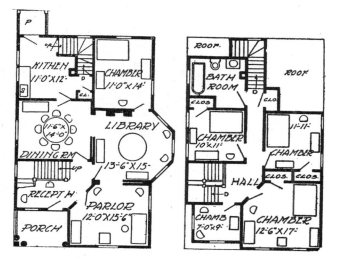

KITHEN 11'0"X12 · CHAMBER 11'0"X14 · ROOF · ROOF · BATH ROOM · CLOS · CLOS · 11-11 · CHAMBER 10'X11' · CHAMBER · LIBRARY · 11'-6"X 14'-0' · 13-6"X15' · DINING RM · up · HALL · CLOS · CLOS · RECEPT H · PARLOR 12'-0"X15'6" · PORCH · CHAMB 7'-0"X9' · CHAMBER 12'-6"X17'

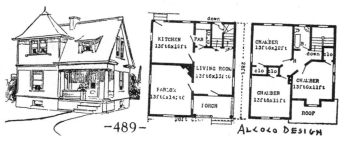

KITCHEN 13ft6x12ft · PAN · down · CHAMBER 13ft6x12ft · down · clo · LIVING ROOM 13ft6x13'6 · clo · clo · CHAMBER 13ft6x11ft · PARLOR 13ft6x14'6 · CHAMBER 12ft6x11ft · PORCH · ROOF

ALCOCO DESIGN

WASHINGTON RESIDENCE.—Design 6014-O; in frame, $1,190 to $1,398; plans, $10; width, 27 ft. 8 in. by 29 ft. 6 in.; width over all, 33 ft.; story heights, 9 ft. 6 in. and 9 ft.; side walls to second story cut down to 8 ft.; special features: Bay to library. Modifications: See St. Louis Cottage on page   Modification 2, Galbreth design, same as Washington Residence, except bay is on side of parlor instead of at library, with combination side entrance and no pantry; full 9 ft story heights. Modification No. 3, Smith design; same as Washington Res., except kitchen flue is at outer corner and stairs to basement go down direct from kitchen. See page 65.

Plans $10.

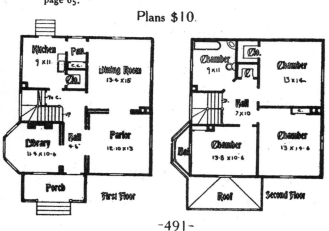

Kitchen 9 x 11 · Pan · Dining Room 13-4 x 15 · Chamber 9 x 11 · Chamber 13 x 14 · Hall 7 x 10 · Library 11-4 x 10-6 · Hall 4' 6 · Parlor 12-10 x 13 · Chamber 13-8 x 10-6 · Chamber 13 x 14-6 · Porch · First Floor · Roof · Second Floor

---

Fernville Cottage No. 2 design 5490-A, story heights 8-ft 6 and 8 ft. See opposite page 489. Plans $15.

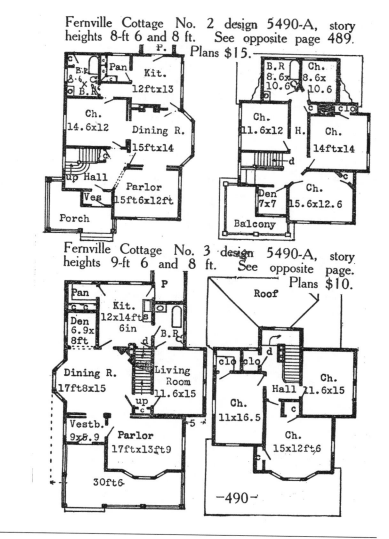

P · B.R. 8.6 x · Pan · Kit. 12ft x13 · B.R. 8.6x 10.6 · Ch. 8.6x 10.6 · Ch. 14.6x12 · Dining R. 15ft x14 · Ch. 11.6x12 · H. · Ch. 14ft x14 · up Hall · Parlor 15ft6x12ft · Veg · Den 7x7 · Ch. 15.6x12.6 · Porch · Balcony

Fernville Cottage No. 3 design 5490-A, story heights 9-ft 6 and 8 ft. See opposite page. Plans $10.

Pan · P · Roof · Kit. 12x14fts 6in · Den 6.9x 8ft · B.R. · d · clo · clo · d · Dining R. 17ft8x15 · Living Room 11.6x15 · Ch. 11x16.5 · Hall · Ch. 11.6x15 · up · c · Vestb. 9x5.9 · Parlor 17ftx13ft9 · Ch. 15x12ft6 · 30ft6

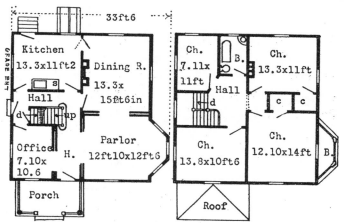

33ft6 · GRADE LINE · Kitchen 13.3x11ft2 · Dining R. 13.3x 15ft6in · Ch. 7.11x 11ft · B. · Ch. 13.3x11ft · Hall · d · Hall · c · c · d · up · Office 7.10x 10.6 · H. · Parlor 12ft10x12ft6 · Ch. 13.8x10ft6 · Ch. 12.10x14ft · B. · Porch · Roof

Washington Residence No. 2 design 5492. Full story heights. See opposite page 491. Plans $10.

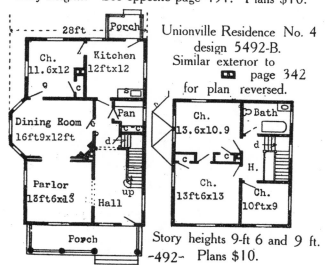

28ft · Porch · Unionville Residence No. 4 design 5492-B. Similar exterior to ☐☐ page 342 for plan reversed. · Ch. 11.6x12 · Kitchen 12ftx12 · Pan · Dining Room 16ft9x12ft · Ch. 13.6x10.9 · Bath · Parlor 18ft6x13 · Ch. 13ft6x13 · up · Hall · H. · Ch. 10ftx9

Story heights 9-ft 6 and 9 ft.

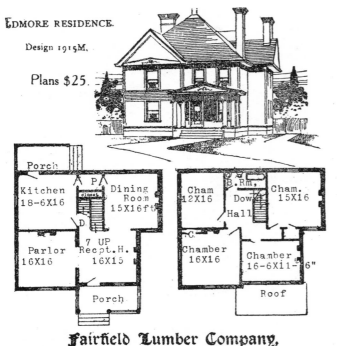

EDMORE RESIDENCE.

Design 1915M.

Plans $25.

Porch

| Kitchen 18-6X16 | P closet | Dining Room 15X16ft |
| Parlor 16X16 | 7 UP Recpt.H. 16X15 | D |

Porch

| Cham 12X16 | B.Rm. Down Hall | Cham. 15X16 |
| Chamber 16X16 | Chamber 16-6X11-6" |

Roof

Fairfield Lumber Company,

Lumber, Lath, Shingles, Sash, Doors, Lime, Cement and
Building Material Generally.

Fairfield, Ill., 10/5/19( ) 1900

Herbert C. Chivers, Esq.,
St. Louis, Mo.
Dear Sir:-

   The plans of my residence prepared by you, also those of
our bank building were very satisfactory in all respects. I thank
you for the interest taken in my work, and the many useful suggestions
offered.

   Yours very truly,

   J.M.Good

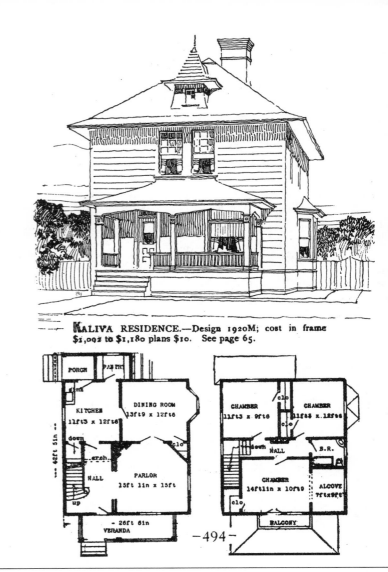

KALIVA RESIDENCE.—Design 1920M; cost in frame
$1,002 to $1,180 plans $10. See page 65.

PORCH	PANTRY		
KITCHEN 11ft3 x 12ft6	DINING ROOM 13ft9 x 12ft6		
HALL	PARLOR 15ft 11in x 15ft		

CHAMBER 11ft3 x 9ft6	CHAMBER 11ft3 x 12ft6	
HALL		B.R.
CHAMBER 14ft11in x 10ft9	ALCOVE 7ft x 9ft

VERANDA — 26ft 6in

BALCONY

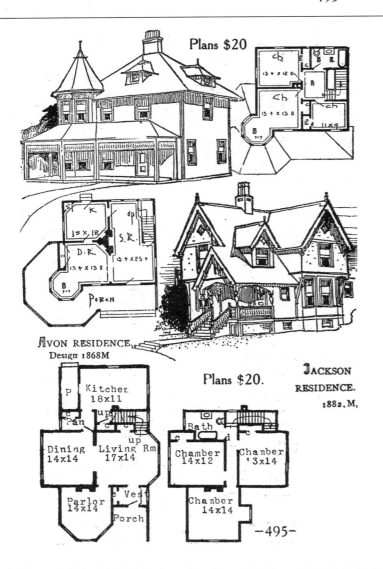

Plans $20

ch 13 + X 12 0		
Ch 13 + X 13 0		ch
		ch 11x9
B 7x7		

| K 15 X 12 | dp |
| S.R. |
| D.R. 13 + X 25 0 |
| B | Porch |

AVON RESIDENCE.
Design 1868M

JACKSON
RESIDENCE.
1882.M.

Plans $20.

P	Kitchen 18x11
c	up
Pan	up
Dining 14x14	Living Rm 17x14
Parlor 14x14	Vest Porch

	Bath
Chamber 14x12	Chamber 13x14
Chamber 14x14	

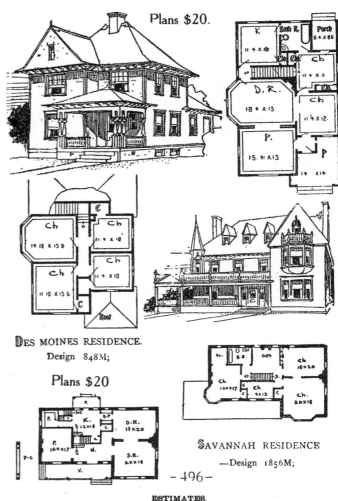

Plans $20.

K 11 + X 20	Bath R.	Porch 8-4 X 25
D.R. 18 + X 13	Ch 11 + X 11
P. 15 + X 13	Ch 11+X 12.
	14 + X 14

| Ch 19-10 X 13 0 | Ch 11 + X 11 |
| Ch 11 10 X 13 6 | Ch 11 + X 10 |

DES MOINES RESIDENCE.
Design 848M;

Plans $20

P.	BR.	Ch
K. 10 X 12ft5	D.R. 15 X 20	Ch 9X13
P. 15+X17	H.	Ch 20X16
P-G	S.R. 20 X 15	
V.		

AL.	B.R.	Ch
Ch 15+X17	C H	15 X 20
	Ch 9X13	
		Ch 20X16

SAVANNAH RESIDENCE
—Design 1856M;

ESTIMATES.
We do not guarantee estimates. This would be absolutely an injustice to our
clients, reputable builders and fellow architects.

Plans $20.

HASTING COTTAGE.—Design 1950-O; in frame, $1250 to $1398; plans, $10; width, 25 ft. 8 in. and 27 ft. 6 in.; story heights, 9 ft. and 8 ft. 6 in. in the clear. Special features— Shingle tower and porch, giving massive effect. See page 65.

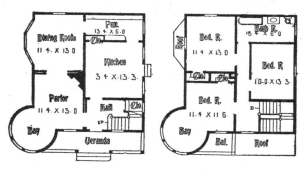

I like your plans better than any others I have seen.
MISS R. KATE GARDINER, Amsterdam, N. Y.

497

HOTELS
My success in Hotels or apartment buildings is in a thorough insight of the many requirements of the public, embodying style, convenience, elegance with view to profitable outlay

SCHOOLS
My success in plans of Schools has given me an advanced and practical training of the exacting requirements of heating, light and ventilation. My style of architecture is educational

ARTISTIC HOMES.
This book is a work of building information, not a highly polished fancy picture book. It contains many plans and all possible information that we can give its readers for the price of same.

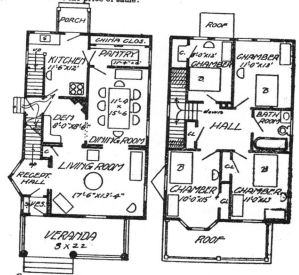

TILTON COTTAGE.—Design 1206M; size 24 x 26 ft. Cost $1298 to $1499; plans, $10. Special features: den with fireplace, side entrance, unique reception hall, large living-room.

—498—

OXBOW RESIDENCE.—Design 2020-O; cost in frame, $3,980 to $4,540; plans, $40. Cost in brick, $6,700 to $7,890; plans, 3 1-2 per cent. on cost.

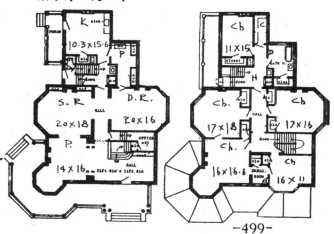

—499—

heights, 10 ft. Special features: Combination side entrance

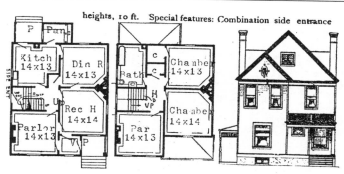

GRAND FOLKS RESIDENCE.—Design 10-O; in frame, $1,399 to $1,486; plans, $10; width over all. 28 ft. 2 in.;

NOTE: SEE No 2 PLAN PAGE 51 4

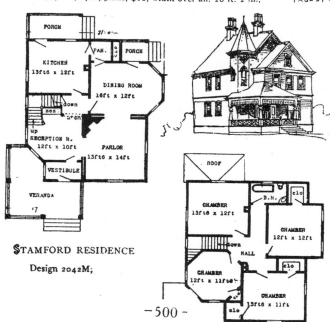

STAMFORD RESIDENCE

Design 2042M;

—500—

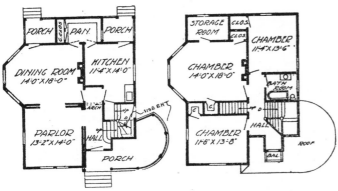

MARLEBORO COTTAGE NO. 2.—Hawke design 55-0; cost, $1,490 to $1,582; size, 26 ft. by 35 ft. See Marleboro design on page   Plans $10.

Marleboro Residence, No. 6, Halzback design, the same as No. 1, on page 502 with barge-board gables;

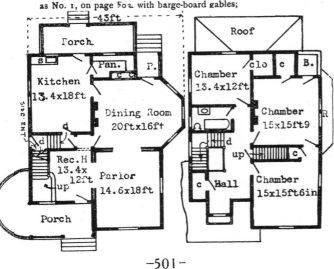

-501-

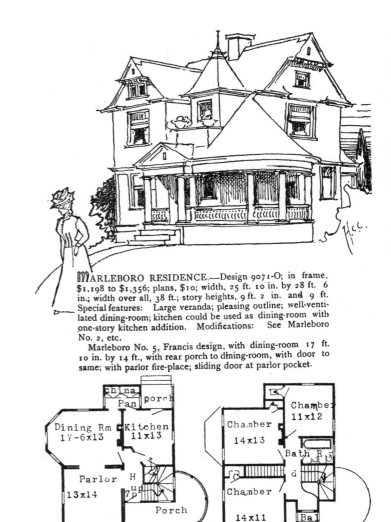

MARLEBORO RESIDENCE.—Design 9071-O; in frame, $1,198 to $1,356; plans, $10; width, 25 ft. 10 in. by 28 ft. 6 in.; width over all, 38 ft.; story heights, 9 ft. 2 in. and 9 ft. Special features: Large veranda; pleasing outline; well-ventilated dining-room; kitchen could be used as dining-room with one-story kitchen addition. Modifications: See Marleboro No. 2, etc.

Marleboro No. 5, Francis design, with dining-room 17 ft. 10 in. by 14 ft., with rear porch to dining-room, with door to same; with parlor fire-place; sliding door at parlor pocket.

-502-

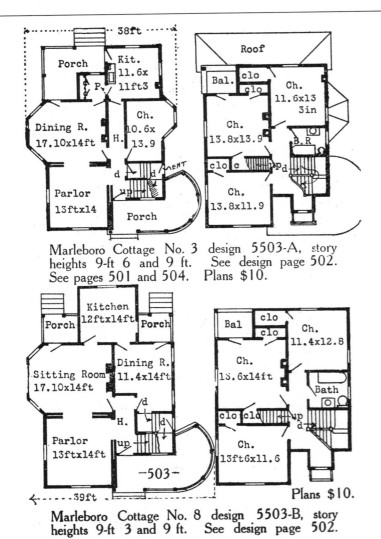

Marleboro Cottage No. 3 design 5503-A, story heights 9-ft 6 and 9 ft. See design page 502. See pages 501 and 504. Plans $10.

-503-

Plans $10.

Marleboro Cottage No. 8 design 5503-B, story heights 9-ft 3 and 9 ft. See design page 502.

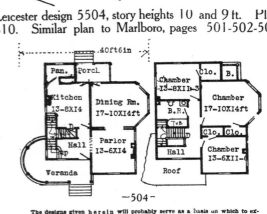

Leicester design 5504, story heights 10 and 9 ft. Plans $10. Similar plan to Marlboro, pages 501-502-503

-504-

The designs given herein will probably serve as a basis on which to express your desires in regard to plans. By referring to a portion of one, and a portion of another, you can give us a clear enough outline from which to work; in this manner we can generally arrive very promptly at about what is wanted.

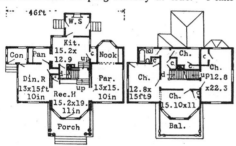

Monaco design 5505, story heights 9-ft 3 and 9. Very attractive, clean-cut front. Unique reception hall, combination stairs and sleeping balcony at side. Plans $15.

-505-

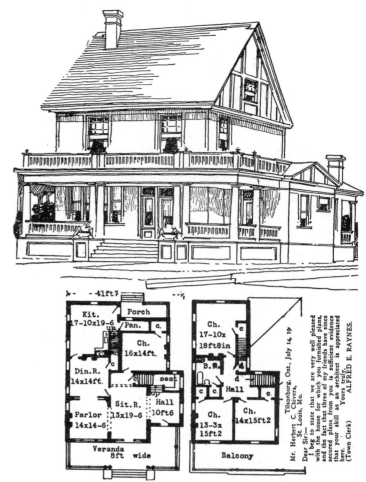

Sardinia design 5506, story heights 10 ft and 9-ft 6. Plain, clean-cut exterior. Can be used as residence or flat. Plans $10. -506-

Reggio design 5507, story heights 9-ft 6 and 9, width over all 36 ft. Large dining room and front chamber. Plans $10.

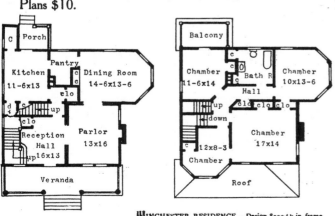

WINCHESTER RESIDENCE.—Design 8099-U; in frame, $1,499 to $1,598; plans, $10; width, 34 ft. by 46 ft.; story heights; 11 ft. in the clear. See page 479
Nemo design on page 209
Winchester plan No. 7, Brand des., parlor, 15.4x14 ft. 6 in.; dining-room, 15.4x14 ft. 6 in. with sliding doors into parlor; with fire-place to sitting-room only. See page 65.
See design on page 479

-507-

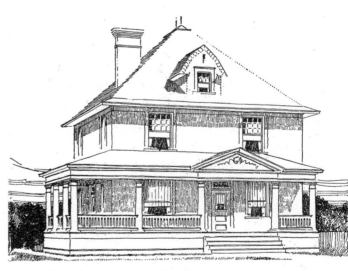

Allepo design 5508, width 36-ft 6, width over all 39 ft. Compact, square, economical plan. Story heights 9-ft 6 and 9. Plans $20.

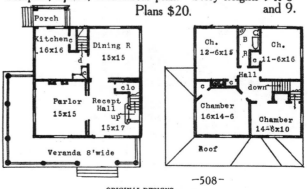

-508-

ORIGINAL DESIGNS.
When you build, it is supposed that you want something original and different to the common-place buildings you see eve.y day. My study is not confined to one locality. I do work in every State in the Union and many foreign countries and a great deal of it, therefore my ideas are not limited.

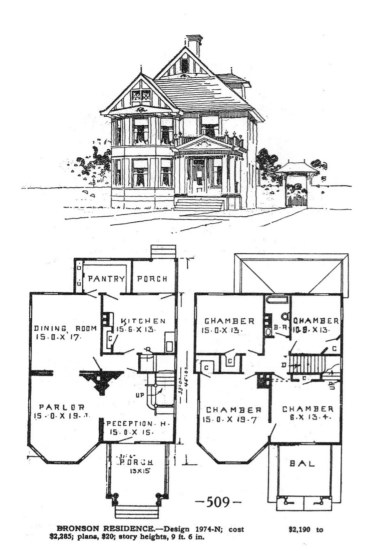

BRONSON RESIDENCE.—Design 1974-N; cost $2,285; plans, $20; story heights, 9 ft. 6 in. $2,190 to

—509—

BEAUFORD RESIDENCE.—Design 100,046-O; plans, $20; size, 36x48; cost in frame, $1,800 to $1,980. Special features: Large vestibule; combination wood-shed; porch and water-closet; comb. cellar stairs; kitchen entrance.

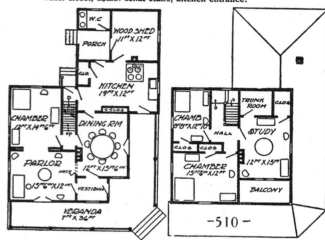

—510—

STATE LEGISLATION AGAINST "BUILDER-ARCHITECTS."
The State of Illinois has recently passed a law compelling architects to undergo a rigid examination before they can practice. They define what an architect is, and self-styled architects, without a license are subject to prosecution and a fine of $500 for each and every offense.

BLACK HILLS RESIDENCE.—Design 960M; in frame, $1,190 to $1,480; in brick, $1,600 to $2,000; plans, $25; special features: Nook and fire-place in connection with stairs. See page 65.

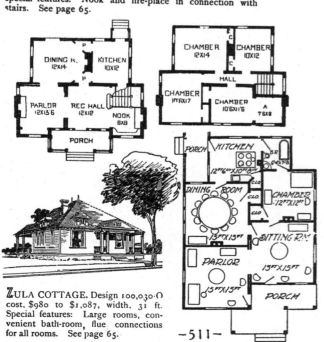

ZULA COTTAGE. Design 100,030-O cost, $980 to $1,087, width, 31 ft. Special features: Large rooms, convenient bath-room, flue connections for all rooms. See page 65.

—511—

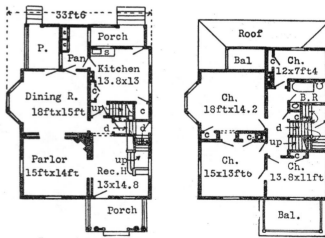

JENISON RESIDENCE.—Design 1908-O; cost in frame $1,892 to $1,920; plans $15. See page 523. See page 65.

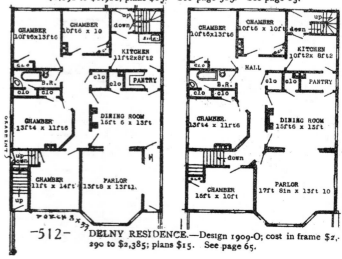

—512— DELNY RESIDENCE.—Design 1909-O; cost in frame $2,290 to $2,385; plans $15. See page 65.

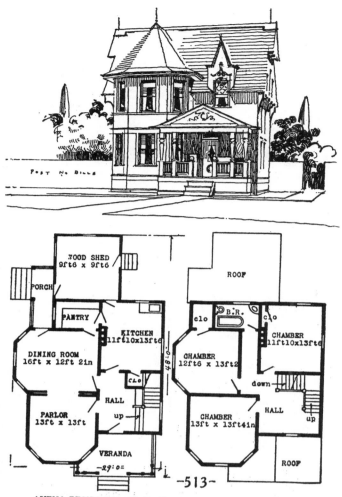

AVENA RESIDENCE.—Design 2011-N; cost, $2,692 to $2,780; plans, $25; story height, 9 ft.

Room labels (design 513):
WOOD SHED 9ft6 x 9ft6
PORCH
PANTRY
KITCHEN 11ft10x13ft6
DINING ROOM 16ft x 12ft 2in
PARLOR 13ft x 13ft
HALL
CLO.
up
VERANDA 29'-0"
ROOF
clo
B.R.
clo
CHAMBER 12ft6 x 13ft2
CHAMBER 11ft10x13ft6
down
CHAMBER 13ft x 13ft4in
HALL
up
ROOF
—513—

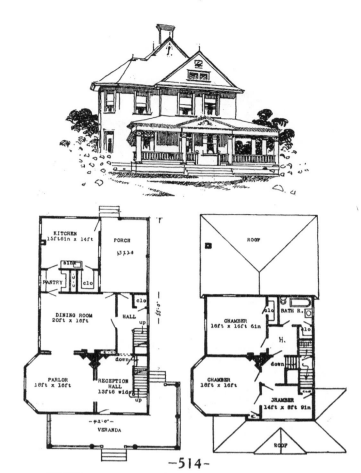

Room labels (design 514):
KITCHEN 15ft6in x 14ft
PORCH 13ft x 8
PANTRY
clo
DINING ROOM 20ft x 16ft
HALL
up
PARLOR 16ft x 16ft
RECEPTION HALL 13ft6 wide
up
VERANDA
ROOF
CHAMBER 16ft x 16ft 6in
clo BATH R.
H.
down
CHAMBER 16ft x 16ft
CHAMBER 14ft x 8ft 9in
ROOF
—514—

ANASTOTA RESIDENCE.—Design 1867-N; cost in frame, $2,190 to $2,239; plans, $20; story heights, 10 ft. and 10 ft. Special features: Attractive, large bay-shape parlor and chamber above; neat, attractive modern exterior design.

OHIO RESIDENCE.—Design 8192-N; in frame, $1,798 to $1,998; plans, $15; width over all, 37 ft. 6 in.; story heights, 9 ft. 6 in. and 8 ft. 6 in., full story at tower. Special features: A good corner lot design; large dining-room.

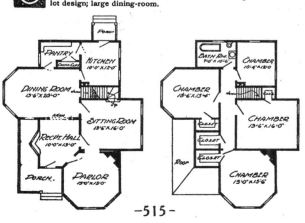

Room labels (design 515):
PORCH
PANTRY
KITCHEN 10'0"X12'0"
DINING ROOM 15'6"X20'0"
SITTING ROOM 13'6"X16'0"
RECPT. HALL 10'0"X13'0"
PORCH
PARLOR 13'0"X16'0"
BATH RM. 7'0"X10'6"
CHAMBER 10'4"X13'0"
CHAMBER 13'6"X15'4"
CHAMBER 13'6"X16'0"
CLOSET
CLOSET
ROOF
CHAMBER 15'0"X15'6"
—515—

JAMESVILLE RESIDENCE. Design 1883M;

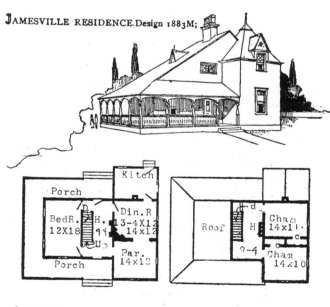

Room labels (design 516):
Kitch
Porch
Din. R 13-4X12
BedR. 12X18
H.
Par. 14x12
Porch
Roof
Cham 14x11
Cham 14x10

—516—

DEXTER PLAN,—Design 1960-Q; in frame, $1290 to $1386; plans, $10; width over all, 27 ft. 10 in.; story heights, 9 ft. 6 in. Special Feature; A very compact plan; easy to construct; bay in front. See page 65.

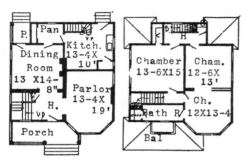

Plan No. 1.—See plan No. 2. opposite page.

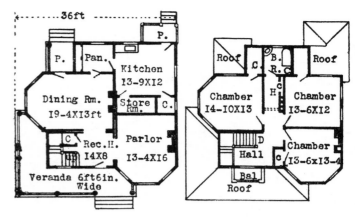

Dexter Plan No. 2 design 5518-A, story heights 10 and 9-ft 6. See design opposite page 517. Large living room. Plans $10.

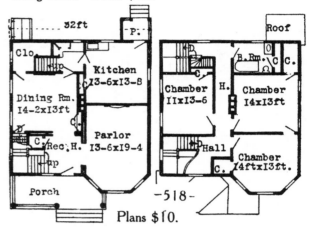

—518—
Plans $10.

Dexter Plan No. 3 design 5518-B, story heights 10 and 9 ft. See design opposite page 517.

SCOTDALE RESIDENCE.—Design 1912M; cost in frame, $1,822 to $1,940; plans, $15.

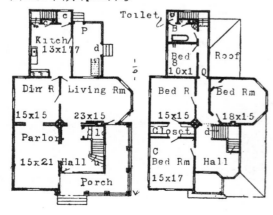

GRAND FOLKS Plans No. 2, Morgan Design reversed, flue holes in place of fire-place and large closets between two main chambers, with 10 ft. 6 in. and 9 ft. 6 in. story heights. See page 500—PLAN No 1.

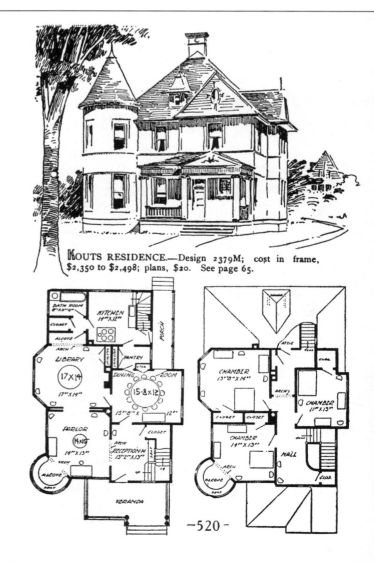

KOUTS RESIDENCE.—Design 2379M; cost in frame, $2,350 to $2,498; plans, $20. See page 65.

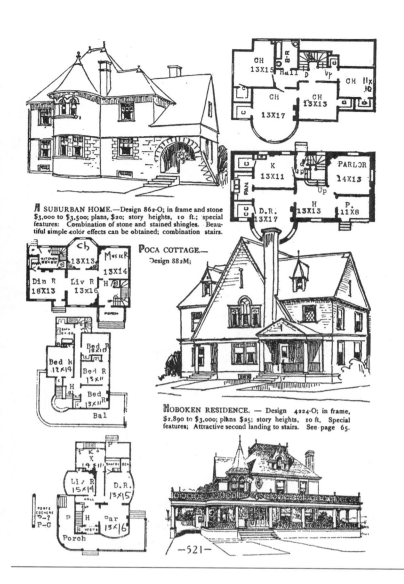

A SUBURBAN HOME.—Design 862-O; in frame and stone $3,000 to $3,500; plans, $20; story heights, 10 ft.; special features: Combination of stone and stained shingles. Beautiful simple color effects can be obtained; combination stairs.

POCA COTTAGE.—Design 882M;

HOBOKEN RESIDENCE. — Design 4224-O; in frame, $2,890 to $3,000; plans $25; story heights, 10 ft, Special features; Attractive second landing to stairs. See page 65.

-521-

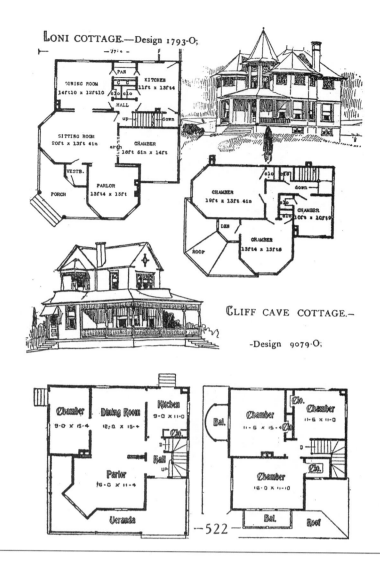

LONI COTTAGE.—Design 1793-O;

CLIFF CAVE COTTAGE.

-Design 9079-O;

-522-

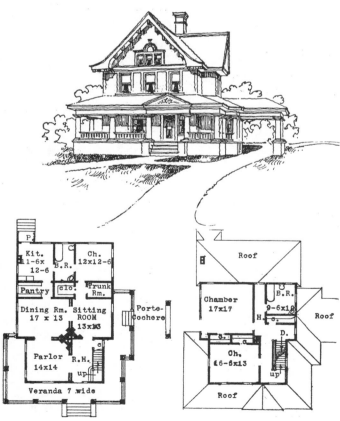

Ealing design 5523, story heights 10 and 9 ft, width 32 ft, width over all 55 ft. Good, plain, practical design. Plans $10.

-523-

Preliminary design. The Edwin Swift Residence, Lake Geneva, Wis.

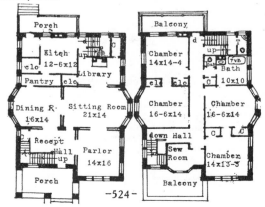

-524-

Beckenham design 5524-B, in brick, width 42 ft, story heights 10 and 9 ft. Plain, neat exterior. Plans $15

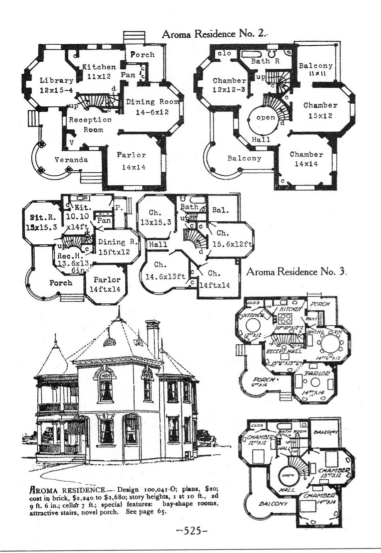

Aroma Residence No. 2.

Library 12x15-4 | Kitchen 11x12 | Pan | Porch
Reception Room
Veranda | Parlor 14x14 | Dining Room 14-6x12

clo | Bath R | Balcony 11x11
Chamber 12x12-3 | up | Chamber 15x12
open Hall
Balcony | Chamber 14x14

Sit. R. 13x15.3 | Kit. 10.10 x14ft | P. | Pan | Ch. 13x15.3 | Bath | Bal.
Dining R. 15ftx12 | Hall | Ch. 15.6x12ft
Rec.H. 13.6x13, 6in | up
Porch | Parlor 14ftx14 | Ch. 14.6x13ft | Ch. 14ftx14

Aroma Residence No. 3.

Barking design 5526, width 29-ft 6, width over all 45 ft, story heights 10 and 9-ft 6. Plans $10.

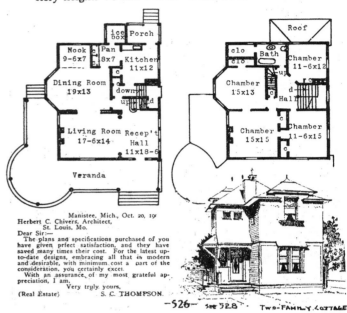

ice box | Porch
Nook 9-6x7 | Pan 8x7 | Kitchen 11x12
Dining Room 19x13 | down up dead
Living Room 17-6x14 | Recep't Hall 11x18-6
Veranda

Roof
clo | clo | Bath | Chamber 11-6x12
Chamber 15x13 | up | Hall
Chamber 15x15 | Chamber 11-6x15

Manistee, Mich., Oct. 20, 19
Herbert C. Chivers, Architect,
St. Louis, Mo.
Dear Sir—
The plans and specifications purchased of you have given prfect satisfaction, and they have saved many times their cost. For the latest up-to-date designs, embracing all that is modern and desirable, with minimum cost a part of the consideration, you certainly excel.
With an assurance of my most grateful appreciation, I am,
Very truly yours,
(Real Estate) S. C. THOMPSON.

AROMA RESIDENCE.— Design 100,041-O; plans, $20; cost in brick, $2,240 to $2,680; story heights, 1 st 10 ft., 2d 9 ft. 6 in.; cellar 7 ft.; special features: bay-shape rooms, attractive stairs, novel porch. See page 65.

AKEMAN RESIDENCE.—Design 1835-N; cost in frame, $2,390 to $2,498; plans, $20. Special features: Pleasant out-look from living-room; lavatory convenient to living-room. A good house for a physician. House appears well on wide lot.

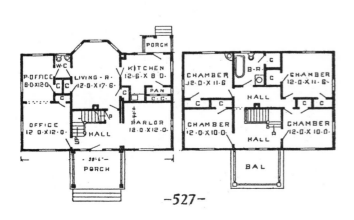

P. OFFICE 8-0x12-0 | w. c | LIVING-R. 12-0x17-6 | KITCHEN 12-6x8-0 | PORCH
Pan
OFFICE 12-0x12-0 | HALL | PARLOR 12-0x12-0
PORCH

CHAMBER 12-0x11-6 | B. R. | CHAMBER 12-0x11-6
HALL
CHAMBER 12-0x10-0 | HALL | CHAMBER 12-0x10-0
BAL

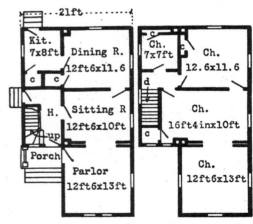

|←---21ft---→|
Kit. 7x8ft | Dining R. 12ft6x11.6 | Ch. 7x7ft | Ch. 12.6x11.6
H. | Sitting R 12ft6x10ft | Ch. 16ft4inx10ft
up
Porch | Parlor 12ft6x13ft | Ch. 12ft6x13ft

Two Family Cottage design 5528-A, story heights 9 and 9 ft. See design 526. Plans $5.

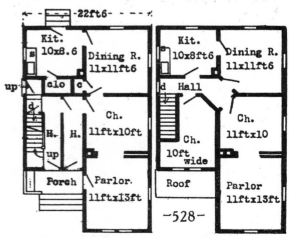

|←---22ft6---→|
Kit. 10x8.6 | Dining R. 11x11ft6 | Kit. 10x8ft6 | Dining R. 11x11ft6
up | clo | Hall
Ch. 11ftx10ft | Ch. 11ftx10
H. | H. | Ch. 10ft wide
up
Porch | Parlor 11ftx13ft | Roof | Parlor 11ftx13ft

Two Family Cottage design 5528-B, story heights 9 and 8-ft 6. See design 523. Plans $5.
528-

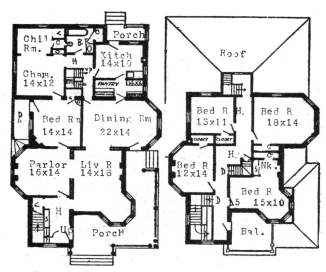

LA FONTAIN RESIDENCE.— Design 2364-M; design on page 529 cost in brick, $6,000 to $6,500. Plans, $65.

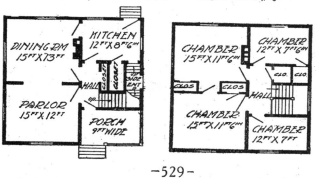

—529—

WARKLENITH COTTAGE.—Design 2363M. See design page 530 See page 65.

LA FONTAIN RESIDENCE.—See plans page 65. See page 65.

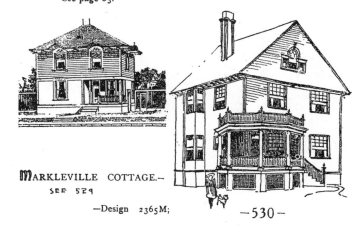

MARKLEVILLE COTTAGE.—
SEE 529

—Design 2365M;

—530—

Plans $15.

Modesto, Cal., June 10, 1902.
Mr. H. C. Chivers,
St. Louis, Mo.
Dear Sir:—
We received plans in good shape, and the church has been built and we are all pleased. Heretofore we have had experience in church plans with Eastern architects, which at first made us skeptical in this case. For a church guaranteed to cost a certain amount, the lowest bid was just double the original estimate.
We feel that you have treated us in a strictly professional and conscientious manner.
Respectfully,
ROBERT S. BOYNS.
Pastor, M. E. Church, South.

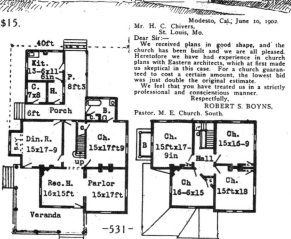

—531—

Chiselhurst design 5531, story heights 10 and 9 ft 6. Well ventilated kitchen. Suitable for southern home.

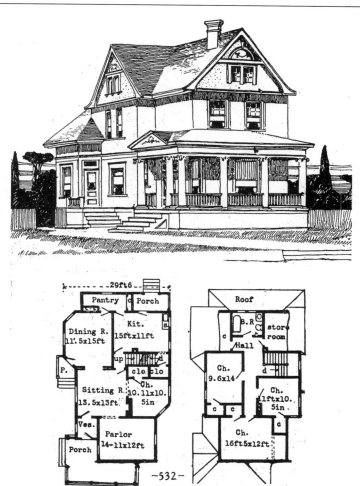

—532—

Amberly design 5532, story heights 11 and 10 ft. Feature, front portion of house not cut-up by stairs. Large closets. Plans $10.

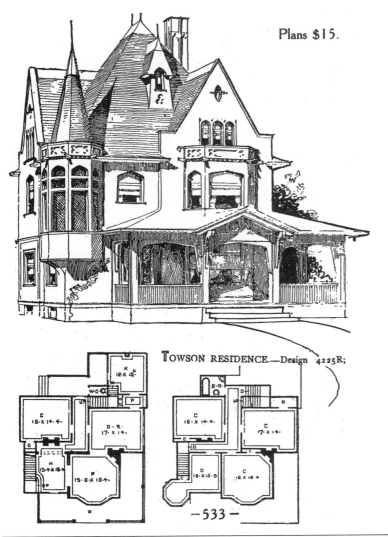

Plans $15.

TOWSON RESIDENCE.—Design 4225R;

—533—

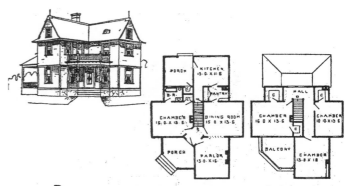

BALLOU RESIDENCE.—Design 9242M; in frame, $1490 to $1598; plans, $10; width, 36 ft. 3 in. x 49 ft.; story heights, 9 ft. 9 in. and 9 ft. 6 in. Special features: A large veranda, Modifications; See index for Parkdale Cottage. See page 65

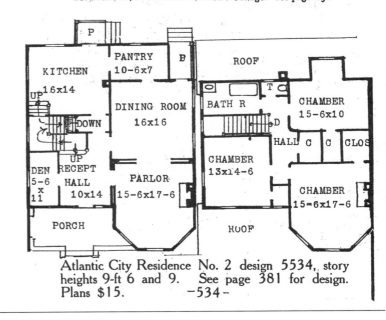

Atlantic City Residence No. 2 design 5534, story heights 9-ft 6 and 9. See page 381 for design. Plans $15.   —534—

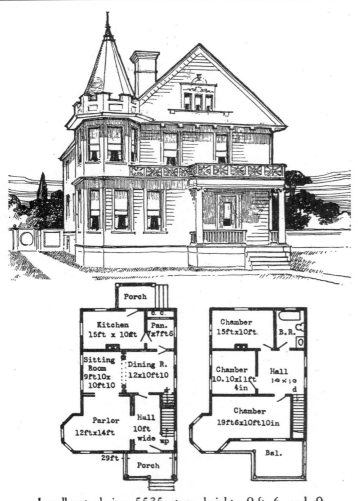

Lyndhurst design 5535, story heights 9-ft 6 and 9. Width 29 ft. Plans $15. —535—

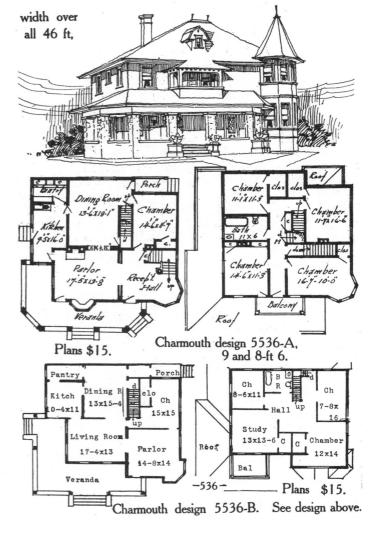

width over all 46 ft,

Plans $15.   Charmouth design 5536-A, 9 and 8-ft 6.

—536—   Plans $15.

Charmouth design 5536-B. See design above.

Plans $10.

Penzance design 5537, width 40 ft 9, over all 46 ft. Story heights 9 and 8 ft. Plain, clean-cut design.

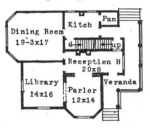

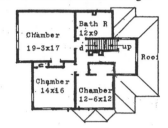

CHARACTER IN ARCHITECTURE.

MAN, emerging slowly through the ages, from his life as a cave-dweller comes in course of time to demand an architect. He is tired of thatched and wattled huts and weary of life in tents. He makes crude efforts at building with wood, with stone and with brick. The structures are unsightly in appearance and uncomfortable to occupy but man does not know it. He is proud of his home. It is the best so far in the history of the world. Presently some original genius erects a house so pleasant to behold and so convenient in arrangement that his neighbors demand that he lay all else aside and build for them. The architect has arrived. He appears at his early best in ancient Egypt and Greece and in Medieval Europe. Emerson once said: "The Egyptian architecture was characterized by breadth of base, the Grecian by adequate support and the Gothic by skyward soaring." Oliver Wendell Holmes, who was present, added: "One is for death, one is for life and one is for immortality." There was character, you see, in each and what you want in modern architecture is character and individuality. These are only possible from a man who has made a thorough study of its past and has ideas of his own which he can adapt to the plans you have formed for your building and the amounts you are prepared to expend.— Herbert C. Chivers.

Shillings design 5538, story heights 12 and 11 ft, width over all 50 ft. Neat, clean-cut exterior. Large rooms. Good southern house. Plans $15.

 WOODBINE RESIDENCE.—Design 1059-N; in frame, $2,298 to $2,500; plans, $20; width, 29 ft. 8 in. by 49 ft. 4 in.; story heights, 9 ft. 6 in. and 9 ft. in the clear. Special features: Compact floor arrangement. This plan can be had with several modifications.

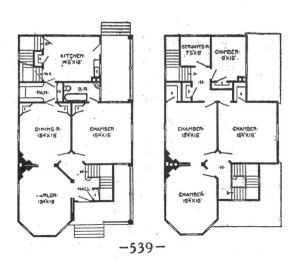

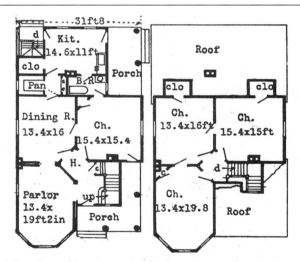

Woodbine No. 5 design 5540-A, story heights 9-ft 6 and 9. See design opposite page 539. Plans $20.

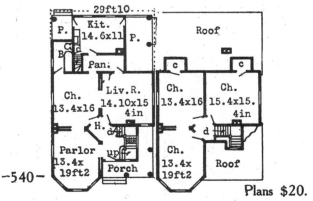

Plans $20.

Woodbine No. 6 design 5540-B, story heights 9-ft 6 and 9-ft 6. See design opposite page 539.

THREE ROOM FLATS—

ROMULUS COTTAGE.—Design 12001M; Size 29 by 45. Cost $1640 to $2199; plans, $20; Special features: economical roof construction, attractive reception hall. See page 65.

For Romulus design No. 2 see page 545.

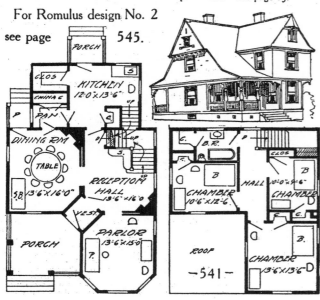

-541-

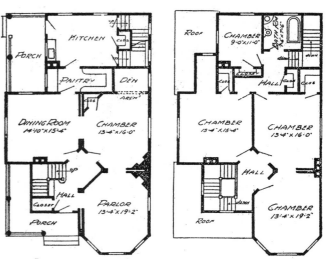

DENTONVILLE RESIDENCE.—Design 27-O; cost, $1,-992 $2,428; plans, $20; size, 30 ft. by 53 ft. 4 in., story heights, 9 ft. 6 in. and 9 ft.

Woodbine Residence No. 2, Miller design, arranged for a physician, with bath-room back of dining-room; with present bath-room space used as 5 ft. rear hall, extending to a dining-room door, with side entrance, and 8x11 office where rear porch now is, with closet, kitchen, pantry and porch in rear and 11x17 ft. chamber in place of 9x12 ft. chamber in rear.

-542-   ART

ART and Architecture go hand-in-hand. The leading architects do not care for moderate-cost residence work, but to meet this demand I have established a special department for the planning of Cozy Homes, and as I do more work in this one department alone, than any three architects, this great practice, extending as it does, to all parts of the United States and Foreign Countries, naturally gives me a knowledge of the best ideas from all parts of the country, and these ideas, for a nominal price, can be incorporated in your plans; and where your neighbor has a cheap carpenter-planned or cheap stock-plan house, that you find duplicated and staring you in the face wherever you go, you, for a few dollars more, can have a house that is stylish, economical, home-like and out of the ordinary.—Herbert C. Chivers.

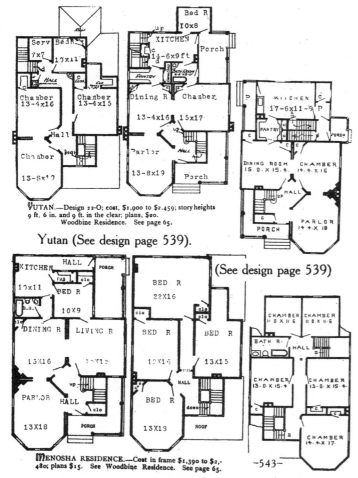

YUTAN.—Design 22-O; cost, $1,900 to $2,459; story heights 9 ft. 6 in. and 9 ft. in the clear; plans, $20. Woodbine Residence. See page 65.

Yutan (See design page 539).

(See design page 539)

MENOSHA RESIDENCE.—Cost in frame $1,390 to $2,-480; plans $15. See Woodbine Residence. See page 65.

Kickapoo (See design 539.)

KICKAPOO RESIDENCE.—Design 60-O; cost, $1,998 to $2,295; plans, $20. See design Woodbine Residence (hold to mirror to reverse). Published in the Nov., 1899, Woman's Home Companion, Springfield, O. See page 65.

-543-

MACKINAW COTTAGE.— Design 29-O; cost, $1,798 to $1,859; size, 30 ft. 2 in. by 43 ft. 8 in.; plans, $15. See page 65.

MACKINAW plan No. 2, Hamilton No. 2, has bath opening direct into sitting-room; with 11x14 ft. kitchen; with 5x12 serving pantry and 6x8 porch in place of bath; without tower, but dormer in its place.

MACKINAW plan No. 3, Hamilton No. 3, same as Mackinaw No. 2, but with pantry omitted.

MACKINAW No. 4, Scherymger design, same as Mackinaw No. 2, cellar stairs on opposite side of kitchen and serving pantry in place of closet, using sitting room as dining-room. Same exterior as Woodbine residence.

Mackinaw Cottage No. 5, Adams design same as Mackinaw, with dining-room where sitting-room is, with 5x11 pantry; 14x11 kitchen, and cellar stairs under porch. The extterior has roof window in place of tower.

Mackinaw Cottage No. 6, McMahon design, Hamilton plan No. 6, same as Mackinaw Cottage, with rear porch on sitting-room side, with door onto same; with 14x17 kitchen; with bath and large pantry in place of present kitchen porch; with one extra 14x17 chamber above kitchen; with exterior same as Woodbine residence, with dormer window in place of tower. See page 65.

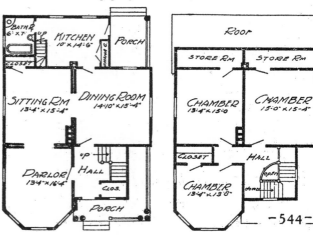

-544-

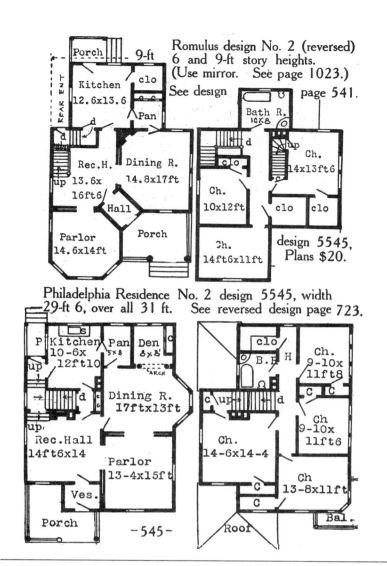

Romulus design No. 2 (reversed)
6 and 9-ft story heights.
(Use mirror. See page 1023.)

See design — page 541.

Porch   9-ft

Kitchen
12.6x13.6

clo

Pan

Bath R.
10x8

Ch.
14x13ft6

Rec.H.
13.6x
16ft6

Dining R.
14.8x17ft

up

Hall

clo

Ch.
10x12ft

clo   clo

Parlor
14.6x14ft

Porch

Ch.
14ft6x11ft

design 5545,
Plans $20.

Philadelphia Residence No. 2 design 5545, width
29-ft 6, over all 31 ft. See reversed design page 723.

P   s

Kitchen
10-6x
12ft10

Pan
5x8

Den
8x8'

clo

B.F   H

Ch.
9-10x
11ft8

up

Dining R.
17ftx13ft

up   d

C   C

Rec.Hall
14ft6x14

Parlor
13-4x15ft

Ch.
14-6x14-4

Ch.
9-10x
11ft6

Ves.

Porch

Ch
13-8x11ft

C

—545—

Roof

Bal.

MONKTON —Des. 100,052-O; cost, $2,498 to $2,892; plans, $20; story
heights, 1st 9 ft. 6 in., 2d 9 ft.; cellar, 7 ft. See Woodbine residence.
Suitable for a physician's office. See page 65.

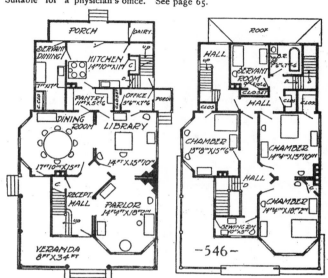

PORCH   PANTRY

SERVANT
DINING

KITCHEN
14'10"X11'

ROOF

HALL

SERVANT
ROOM

PANTRY
11'X5'6"

OFFICE
5'6"X7'6"

PORCH

CLOSET

HALL

DINING
ROOM

LIBRARY

CHAMBER
13'8"X15'6"

CHAMBER
14'4"X15'10"

17'10"X15'

14'X15'10"

RECPT.
HALL

PARLOR
14'4"X18'2"

HALL

CHAMBER
14'4"X18'2"

SEWING RM
10"X15'

VERANDA
8'X34'

—546—

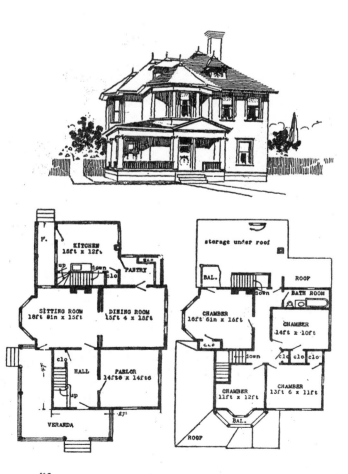

KITCHEN
15ft x 12ft

up   down

PANTRY

storage under roof

BAL.

ROOF

down

BATH ROOM

SITTING ROOM
18ft 8in x 15ft

DINING ROOM
15ft 4 x 15ft

CHAMBER
16ft 6in x 16ft

CHAMBER
14ft x 10ft

HALL

PARLOR
14ft6 x 14ft6

clo   clo   clo

CHAMBER
11ft x 12ft

CHAMBER
13ft 6 x 11ft

VERANDA

BAL.

ROOF

WAWAKA RESIDENCE.—Design 1902M; cost in frame
$2,292 to $2,394; plans $20. See page 65.
—547—

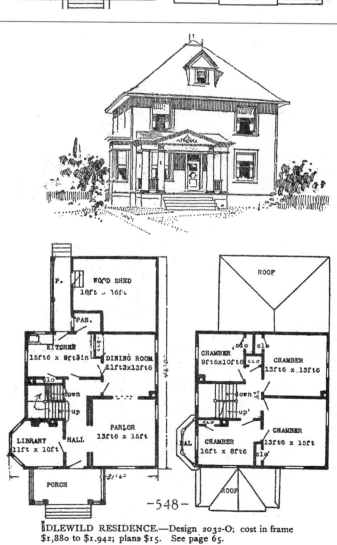

WOOD SHED
18ft x 16ft

ROOF

PAN.

KITCHEN
15ft6 x 9ft3in

DINING ROOM
11ft3x13ft6

CHAMBER
9ft6x10ft6

CHAMBER
13ft6 x 13ft6

down

up

PARLOR
13ft6 x 15ft

CHAMBER
13ft6 x 15ft

LIBRARY
11ft x 10ft

HALL

BAL

CHAMBER
16ft x 8ft6

PORCH

ROOF

—548—

IDLEWILD RESIDENCE.—Design 2032-O; cost in frame
$1,880 to $1,942; plans $15. See page 65.

Grantham design 5549, story heights 10 ft and 9-ft 6.
Suitable for Physician's office, width over porte-cochere and
all 56 ft. Plans $10.

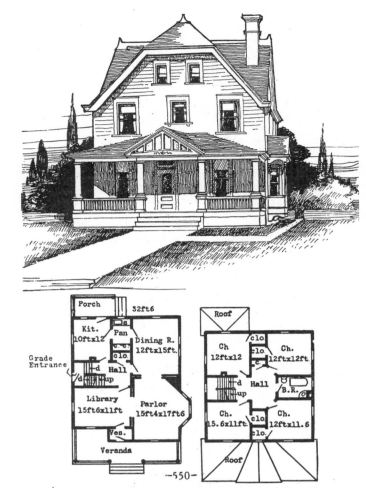

'Hearst design 5550, story heights 9 and 9 ft. Similar
to St. Louis plan, page 787. Plans $10.

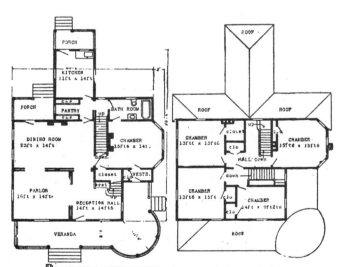

RONDONT RESIDENCE.—Design 2267-O; cost in frame,
$1,922 to $2,198; plans, $15. See Burea Res. for exterior.

BUREA RESIDENCE.—Design 100,058-O; cost, $1,662 to
$1,992; plans, $15; story heights. 9 ft.; cellar, 7 ft.; width, 34
ft.; special features: Down stairs chamber.
  Burea plan No. 2, Doncastle design, same as "Burea",
with 12x18 ft. dining-room extending out to present side
porch space; with 14x14 ft. kitchen; with 4x6 ft. closet where
marked "porch" on side; with extra 14x14 ft. chamber over
kitchen; with 4x6 ft. closet; with 4x9 ft. lavatory where marked
"deck"; with 9 ft. story heights.
  Burea plan No. 3, Park design, same plan with 14x16 ft.
parlor and dining-room; with chamber 14x14 ft.; with fire-place
and bay; with chamber of same size above; rear vestibule at
foot of rear stairs; with door into bath-room.
  Burea plan No. 4, Sprigg design, same as Burea plan No.
2, with four chambers above; with 14x23 ft. dining-room; with
6x11 ft. serving pantry. See page 65.

BUREA RESIDENCE.—Design 100,058-N; cost, $1,662 to $1992; plans,
$15; story height, 9 ft.; cellar, 7 ft.; width, 34 ft. Special features: Down-
stairs chamber. This plan can be had with 12x18 ft. dining-room.

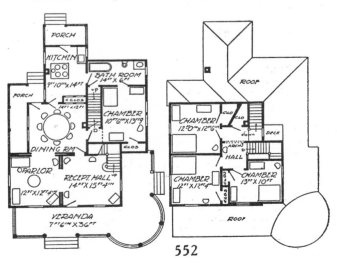

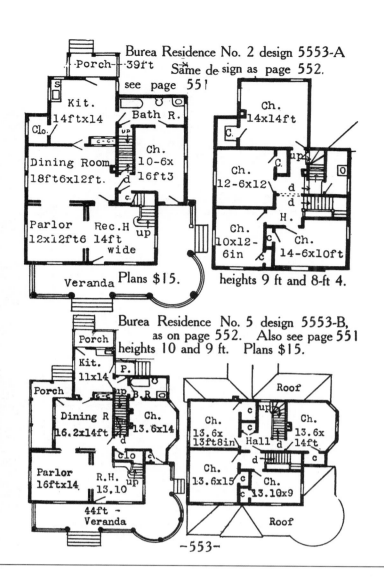

Burea Residence No. 2 design 5553-A
Same design as page 552.
see page 551

Porch—39ft

S

Kit.
14ftx14

Clo.

Bath R.

Dining Room
18ft6x12ft.

Ch.
10-6x
16ft3

Parlor
12x12ft6

Rec.H
14ft
wide

up
d
c

Veranda   Plans $15.

Ch.
14x14ft

C.

Ch.
12-6x12

C.
up
d
d
H.

Ch.
10x12-
6in

Ch.
14-6x10ft

c
c
O

heights 9 ft and 8-ft 4.

Burea Residence No. 5 design 5553-B,
as on page 552.   Also see page 551
heights 10 and 9 ft.   Plans $15.

Porch

Kit.
11x14

P.

Porch

B R

Dining R
16.2x14ft

Ch.
13.6x14

Parlor
16ftx14

R.H.
13.10

clo

up
up

44ft -
Veranda

Roof

Ch.
13.6x
13ft8in

Hall

Ch.
13.6x
14ft

Ch.
13.6x15

Ch.
13.10x9

c
up
d
c
d
c

Roof

-553-

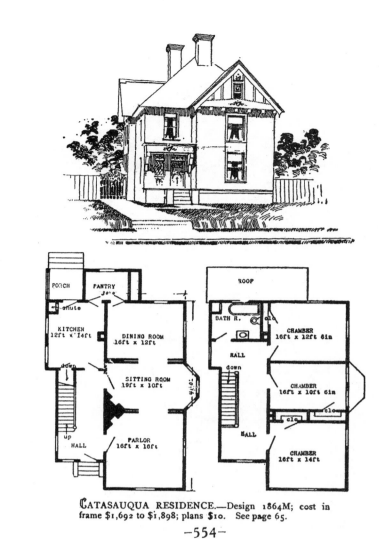

CATASAUQUA RESIDENCE.—Design 1864M; cost in
frame $1,692 to $1,898; plans $10.   See page 65.

PORCH

PANTRY
10x6

chute

KITCHEN
12ft x 14ft

down

up

HALL

DINING ROOM
16ft x 12ft

SITTING ROOM
19ft x 10ft

PARLOR
16ft x 16ft

ROOF

BATH R.   clo

CHAMBER
16ft x 12ft 6in

HALL

down

CHAMBER
16ft x 10ft 6in

clo
clo

HALL

CHAMBER
16ft x 14ft

-554-

OPKINSVILLE RESIDENCE.—Design 1042-N; cost in frame,
$2,298 to $2,669; plans, $20; story heights, 9 ft. 6 in.   Special
features: Fire-place in reception hall; well-ventilated dining-
room; vestibule; attractive V-shape window in front.

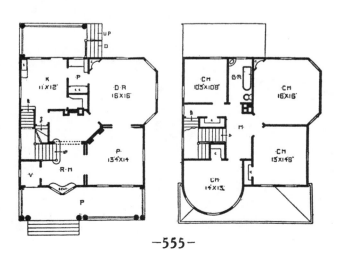

UP
D

K
11'X12'

P

D.R
15'X16'

R.M

P.
13.4'X14'

V

P

CM
10.5'X10.8'

B.R

CM
16'X16'

CM
13'X14.6'

Cm
14'X13'

-555-

ESGARDEN RESIDENCE.—Design 2244N; cost in frame, $2,180
to $2,390; plans, $15.   Special features: A neat exterior; large
library; attractive tower; well-ventilated rooms; attractive angular
window in dining-room.

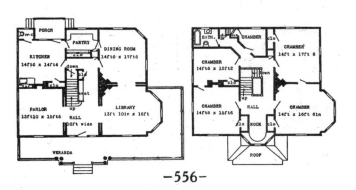

PORCH

PANTRY

KITCHEN
14ft6 x 14ft4

down

PARLOR
13ft10 x 15ft6

DINING ROOM
14ft6 x 17ft6

LIBRARY
13ft 10in x 16ft

HALL
10ft wide

up

seat

VERANDA

BATH.

CHAMBER
14ft6 x 12ft2

CHAMBER
14ft6 x 15ft6

clo
CHAMBER

HALL

CHAMBER
14ft x 17ft 6

clo

down

CHAMBER
14ft x 16ft 6in

NOOK

up

ROOF

-556-

SWINGLEY RESIDENCE.—Design 4090-O; in frame, $1,499 to $1580; plans, $10; size 35 ft. 4 in. square; story heights, 9 ft. 4 in. and 9 ft.; Special features; combination cellar and side entrance at one step above grade. See page 65.

SWINGLEY Plan No. 2, Orr Design: size 35 ft. square; 10 and 9 ft. story heights. side entrance omitted, and bath between corner chambers. See page 65.

SWINGLEY Plan No. 3, Hiles Design, same as above, but in brick, with bath on second floor. See page 65.

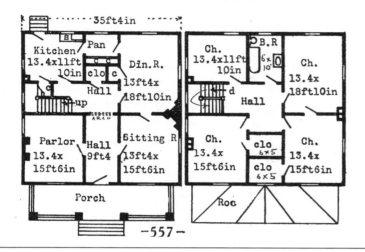

-557-

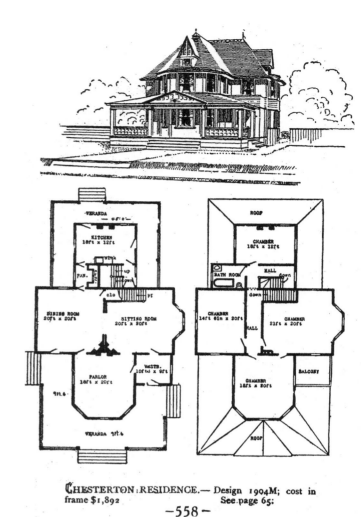

CHESTERTON RESIDENCE.— Design 1904M; cost in frame $1,892   See page 65.

-558-

CLARENDONIA RESIDENCE.—Design 1862M; cost in frame $2,250 to $2,390; plans $20. See page 65.

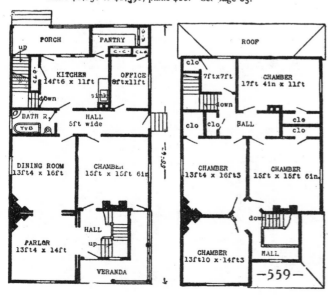

-559-

WHEN you are building a home it will cost you no more, but will be a thousand times more satisfactory, if you will build on the past experience and most modern ideas of an architect of national reputation, and build for the future. It is a fact and a lamentable one, that a hundred times more money has been wasted in mistakes and blunders in building than has ever been paid to architects.

You undoubtedly have some pretty well-defined ideas of the sort of a house you want and there are some things which you have always wanted in your house and now you intended having them. That's right, but don't build a barn, in your haste, and then stick on a lot of warts here and there and expect to get artistic and tasty design.

It will be better for your family, pocket-book, peace-of-mind and temper if you will simply slap all these ideas into a roughly drawn pencil sketch, of the sort of a house you want, and send the same to me with instructions to prepare sketches for you and later to complete the plans. My large experience and information acquired in the satisfaction of thousands of clients is yours for a nominal sum.

It's your house that you are going to build and it's your money that is going to pay for it, but a thing that is worth doing, is worth doing right, and it will not take very much in wasted material to absorb the $45.00 or so you would be trying to save in being your own architect, laying aside the important matter of convenient plan, style and design that an architect of experience can give.

WE ARE FROM MISSOURI AND MUST BE SHOWN

send for book:
HERE IS THE EVIDENCE
OF FAC-SIMILE TESTIMONIALS

I can show you how to make the money you have appropriated for your new house go farther toward meeting your every requirement than you can do for yourself. I have studied these matters in so many phases, and overcome so many obstacles that I am certain I can be of service to you. If you attempt to go it alone you are bound to go it blind. Do not struggle with perplexing preliminary troubles which are the business of your architect. The operation of planning, designing and building a house are too complicated to be successfully undertaken without an architect, even with the co-operation of the best of builders. The professional or expert is needed not only to secure the successful completion of the project but to save money for the client.

Do not hesitate about writing to me for fear of the extra cost. You will find it the truest economy to have my assistance, furthermore, it facilitates my work to start you right in the first place. It is my business and my pleasure to make every dollar of my client's money count for his benefit, to prevent extravagance and waste and enable him to enter at the appointed time a building with which he will be pleased to the end of his days and which will have cost him even less than he expected.

Do not fail to write to me, my office is just as close to you as your nearest mail-box. Besides you have the satisfaction of getting my advice in black and white.

HERBERT C. CHIVERS
ARCHITECT - SAINT LOUIS

-560-

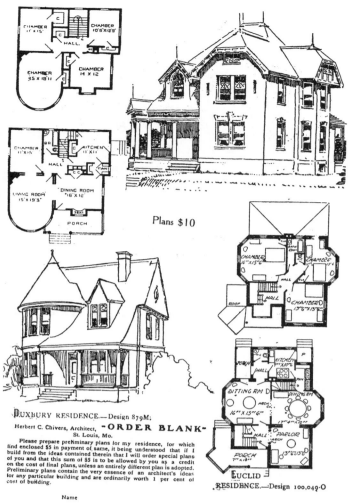

Plans $10

DUXBURY RESIDENCE.—Design 879M;
Herbert C. Chivers, Architect,
St. Louis, Mo.

-ORDER BLANK-

Please prepare preliminary plans for my residence, for which I find enclosed $5 in payment of same, it being understood that if I build from the ideas contained therein that I will order special plans of you and that this sum of $5 is to be allowed by you as a credit on the cost of final plans, unless an entirely different plan is adopted. Preliminary plans contain the very essence of an architect's ideas for any particular building and are ordinarily worth 1 per cent of cost of building.

Name

EUCLID RESIDENCE.—Design 100,049-O

H ONEYHILL COTTAGE.—Design 2420-O; cost in frame, $1,190 to $1,289; plans, $10, story heights, 9 ft. and 8 ft.; full story to main room. Special features: Large veranda; attractive stair landing; large dining-room; well proportioned exterior.

HERBERT C. CHIVERS - ARCHITECT

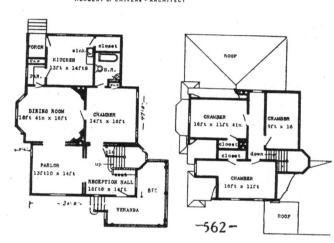

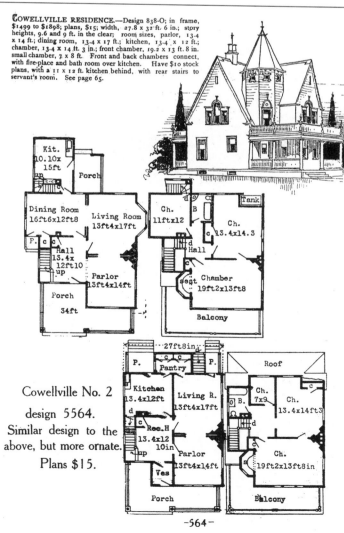

Donington design 5563, heights 9-ft 4 and 8
$10.

Chicago, Ill., Jan. 26, 19
Mr. Herbert C. Chivers,
Wainwright Building,
St. Louis, Mo.
Dear Sir:—
Both Mrs. Hobbs and myself had some brilliant ideas which we wished to embody in a home. The trouble with our brilliant ideas was that no architect would acknowledge that they were even brilliant or usable. Each architect I visited first threw cold water on my ideas and then tried to sell me something I did not want. Having heard a great deal of you and your work during the year I spent in St. Louis, I sent you my sketches, expecting to receive a letter stating that they were worthless. The letter never came, but the plans did, and the plans, well; I think you are a diplomat, but I know you are an architect. If all my ideas are not embodied in these plans, the plans are so complete and well developed, that I do not miss them.
While wishing you success, it occurs to me to mention that there may be many more in Chicago in my predicament, and will certainly refer any prospective builder to St. Louis for his plans.
Sincerely yours,
FRANKLYN HOBBS.

Auburn, Neb., April 17, 1905.
Mr. H. C. Chivers,
St. Louis, Mo.
Dear Sir:—
Please pardon my delay in not writing sooner expressing my appreciation of the plans you made for the remodeling of my residence. The query is, "How did you accomplish such a transformation?" The exterior is far ahead of our expectation, and the interior arrangement fits our needs just about right and makes us a very comfortable home.
The money I paid you for plans was well invested, for they worked out perfectly, saved us money, and a whole lot of worry.
Yours truly,
(Druggist)
E H DORT

C OWELLVILLE RESIDENCE.—Design 838-O; in frame, $1499 to $1898; plans, $15; width, 27.8 x 32 ft. 6 in.; story heights, 9.6 and 9 ft. in the clear; room sizes, parlor, 13.4 x 14 ft.; dining room, 13.4 x 17 ft.; kitchen, 13.4 x 12 ft.; chamber, 13.4 x 14 ft. 3 in.; front chamber, 19.2 x 13 ft. 8 in. small chamber, 7 x 8 ft. Front and back chambers connect, with fire-place and bath room over kitchen. Have $10 stock plans, with a 11 x 12 ft. kitchen behind, with rear stairs to servant's room. See page 65.

Cowellville No. 2
design 5564.
Similar design to the above, but more ornate.
Plans $15.

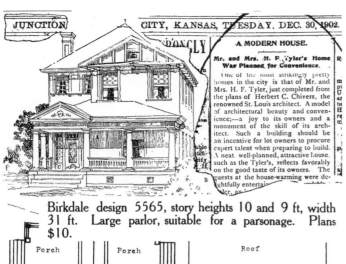

JUNCTION CITY, KANSAS, TUESDAY, DEC. 30, 1902.

A MODERN HOUSE.

Mr. and Mrs. H. F. Tyler's Home Was Planned for Convenience.

One of the most strikingly pretty homes in the city is that of Mr. and Mrs. H. F. Tyler, just completed from the plans of Herbert C. Chivers, the renowned St. Louis architect. A model of architectural beauty and convenience;—a joy to its owners and a monument of the skill of its architect. Such a building should be an incentive for lot owners to procure expert talent when preparing to build. A neat, well-planned, attractive house, such as the Tyler's, reflects favorably on the good taste of its owners. The guests at the house-warming were delightfully entertai

Birkdale design 5565, story heights 10 and 9 ft, width 31 ft. Large parlor, suitable for a parsonage. Plans $10.

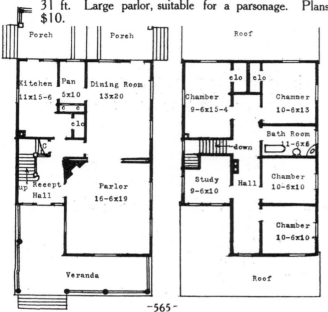

-565-

DOUGLAS RESIDENCE.—Design 1040-N; in frame, $2,500 to $2,850; plans, $35; width, 54 ft. 8 in. by 33 ft. to hall; width over all, 62 ft.; story heights, 10 ft. and 9 ft. in the clear. Special features: Wide, imposing frontage; the rough-stane chimney and arch lends an appearance of solidity; the balcony above works in well. The combination of stone and stained shingles is very attractive.

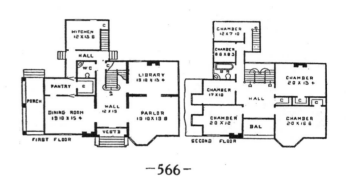

-566-

ONNEAUT RESIDENCE.—Design 1050-N; in frame, $2,280 to $2,460; plans, $20; width over all, 46 ft.; story heights, 10 ft. and 9 ft. 6 in.; attic, 8 ft. Special features: Good-size rooms; attractive outlines to porch and tower:

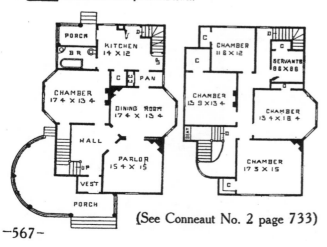

(See Conneaut No. 2 page 733)

-567-

RICHARDSON RESIDENCE.—Design 409M. $2,240 to $2,569; plans, $15.

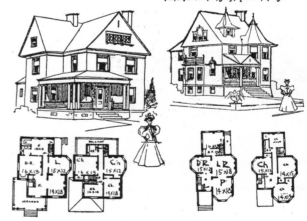

MAGNOLIA RESIDENCE.—Design 904 M; in frame, $2180 to $2290; plans, $15; story heights, 10 ft. Special features, plain neat exterior; parlor, 13 x 18; library, 12 x 15; dining room, 16 ft. x 12 ft. 6 in.; kitchen 13x13. See page 65.

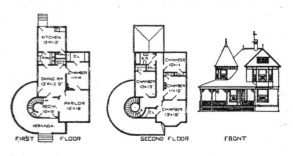

OLIVERVILLE RESIDENCE.—Design 4372M; in frame, $2199 to $2386; plans, $15; width, 25 ft. 10 in., width over all, 32 ft.; story heights, 9 ft. 6 in. and 8 ft 6 in. (full story). Special features, Tower and circular porch. See page 65.

-568-

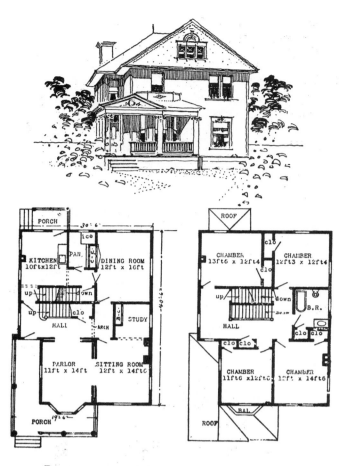

PORT JERVIS RESIDENCE.—Design 2001M; cost in frame $2,092 to $2,190; plans $20. See page 65.

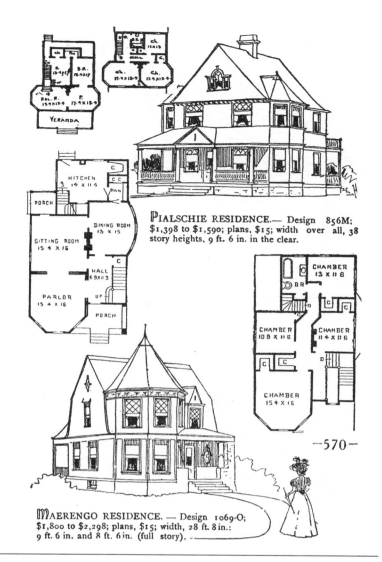

PIALSCHIE RESIDENCE.— Design 856M; $1,398 to $1,590; plans, $15; width over all, 38 story heights, 9 ft. 6 in. in the clear.

MAERENGO RESIDENCE. — Design 1069-O; $1,800 to $2,298; plans, $15; width, 28 ft. 8 in.: 9 ft. 6 in. and 8 ft. 6 in. (full story).

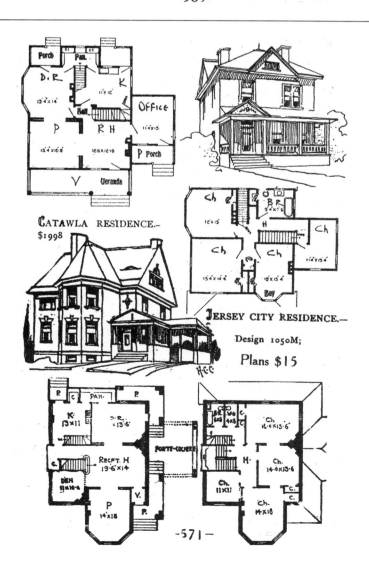

CATAWLA RESIDENCE.— $1998

JERSEY CITY RESIDENCE.—

Design 1050M;

Plans $15

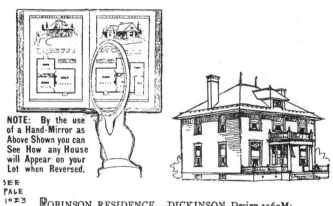

NOTE: By the use of a Hand-Mirror as Above Shown you can See How any House will Appear on your Lot when Reversed.

SEE PAGE 1023

ROBINSON RESIDENCE.—DICKINSON Design 2960M; in frame, $1998 to $2345; plans, $20; width, 47 ft.; story heights, 9 ft. 6 in.; Special features: Wide imposing frontage. Modifications; The modified plan, with porch on side would cost. See page 65.

Robinson Res. No. 3, La Plaute Design same as Robinson residence with 14 x 17 ft. parlor; rear stairs, dumb-waiter, corner china case in dining-room, with space above dining-room used as 12 x 15 ft. screened-in balcony, or summer sleeping compartment, size of building 41 x 32 ft.; story heights, 10 ft.

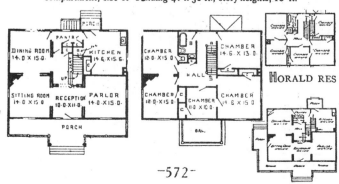

I do not believe that I could be better suited with an architect's plan than I was with yours, W. F. BROWN, (Secretary Tuckahoe Mineral Springs Co.), North Cumberland, Pa.

THE CITY BEAUTIFUL

BY HERBERT C. CHIVERS.
DEVISER OF CIVIC IMPROVEMENTS.

IT is not uncommon to hear the present age condemned as utilitarian and the American people denounced as mere money getters. These sweeping charges are far from being justified by the facts. Professor Emil Reich, in his learned work "Success Among Nations," declares that we are the most liberal spenders on earth and are doing more for the cause of art than is being done in any other country.

It is true that in every city, town, village and hamlet in the land there is a constantly increasing number of business men who are beginning to appreciate the truth of the saying that Civic beauty is a positive asset, that the surest way to increase population and induce the investment of capital is to make the city attractive. Private enterprise is doing much in this direction by the erection of business buildings and residences which it is a pleasure to behold. Municipal authorities, hitherto negligent or indifferent to these high matters, are awakening to an appreciation of the value of the beautiful. In many large cities plans involving the expenditure of many millions have been adopted and are being rapidly executed to produce a purely artistic effect.

There are to be erected during the present year a large number of schools, court houses, churches, city halls, theatres, libraries and other public buildings. There are parks, squares and drive-ways to be laid out. Streets are to be widened and unsightly buildings purchased and torn down. There is a stirring in the direction of aesthetic endeavor such as this country has never before known.

In the latter days of the Second Empire in France when Baron Hausman proposed the remodeling of Paris the ultra-conservatives pronounced his plans extravagant, impracticable and even impossible. "Every Reform" says Emerson "Was once a private opinion and when it shall become private opinion again it will solve the problem of the age." The beautifying of Paris was, first, the private opinion of a German naturalized in France. It came to be the private opinion of Napoleon, III of the members of the Corps Legislativ, of the mayor and his council and of the leading citizens, and the result is, that Paris to-day is the most beautiful city in the world, and its beauty has proved to be a municipal asset of incalculable value. The same is true in a degree of Washington and several other places that are being transformed and regenerated by the substitution of beauty for ugliness. When they wake up to the importance of the movement thousands of towns will follow these good examples.

We are told that "Nothing great was ever achieved without enthusiasm, and to secure adequate civic improvements the newspapers of the place must be sympathetically active in giving publicity to the movement. Boards of Trade and Commercial Exchanges must take an active interest. Business men's clubs organized for this express purpose must aid in the propaganda by the distribution of informative literature and the holding of public mass meetings. Employers of labor should be supplied with reading matter for distribution among the men until the dream of an artist becomes the talk of the streets, the resolution of the conference and finally the decree of the assembly.

The inevitable objection will be raised to any considerable expenditure of money by the city, whether obtained by a direct levy or from the sale of municipal bonds, that taxation will be increased. That is unavoidable. But the grumbling rate-payer must bear in mind the vastly increased value of his property both for rental or sale by the beautifying of the city where it is located.

For years I have been eminently successful as a Deviser of Civic Improvements whether undertaken by the municipality, by corporations or by private individuals. I am prepared to examine and pronounce upon the eligibility of sites and submit plans for administration buildings, schools, hospitals, public baths, parks and play-grounds and for the widening and ornamentation of thoroughfares. Having erected monumental structures in most of the principal cities of the United States and in numerous smaller places I am able to demonstrate my ability to design, construct and decorate in the most satisfactory manner, without a demand for an extravagant outlay, such edifices as railway stations, hotels, churches, theatres, concert halls, exposition buildings, libraries, banks, office buildings and factories, each with due regard to position, use and the accommodation demanded.

I am ready to consult with the projectors of any or all of these enterprises and to prove to them conclusively that my engagement will be to their interest in the adaptability of the designs to their requirements, in the artistic effects which will be produced and in the economy and the promptness with which they will be carried into effect.

We are living in a period of unprecedented prosperity. The harvests throughout the land during the year last past were exceptionally bountiful. The promise of increase in all branches of manufacture and trade is most encouraging. There was never a better time than the present to arouse the public to a realizing sense of the importance of the improvements being made at once. There was never a better time for the carrying out of private plans for the construction of important buildings.

The modern city-dweller, unless he is fortunate enough to reside in one of the places where the beautiful has found acceptance as a necessity, positively suffers from the monotony of his environment. He may not be conscious of this until he visits a more favored community but it is true, nevertheless. The Ancient Athenians and the Romans of the later republic and the early empire understood this. The Florentines in the middle ages provided for the general love of the beautiful and, as we have stated, modern Paris is a noble example of what can be done in this direction. There is an ever growing demand for open spaces, flower gardens, fountains and worthy statues. The public is rapidly becoming more and more appreciative of noble architecture with dignified ornamentation and to demand adequate approaches to monumental edifices. Civic and other authorities are responding to this desire and there is a fair prospect that before the present generation passes from the scene it will be privileged to behold grandeur where there is now naught but the commonplace, and to feast the eyes on beauty where it is at this time only ugliness.

There are difficulties in the way. The obstacles in many instances will not be readily overcome, but to quote again the Sage of Concord. "It is as easy to twist iron anchors and braid cannon as it is to braid straw, to boil granite as it is to boil water if you take all the steps in order. Where there is failure there is some giddiness, some fear, some superstition about luck, some step omitted."

The first step to be taken in this instance is to communicate with me by letter or personal interview. Authorize me to make the necessary investigations and submit preliminary water-color views, plans, designs and estimates. The other steps will be taken in their natural course. Should I be given the contract for the work, it will be completed at the specified time without increase or excess, provided the original outlines remain unchanged.

The results will be, according to the magnitude of the scheme. The transformation of your city, which, becoming "A thing of beauty," will be, in the often quoted words of Keats, "A Joy Forever."

HERBERT C. CHIVERS,

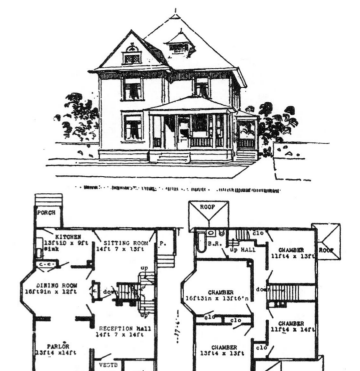

STEUBENVILLE RESIDENCE —Design 1976M; cost in frame $2,192 to $2,240; plans $20. See page 65.

ART

"Such is the strength of art, rough things to shape and of rude commons, rich enclosures make."— James Howell.

SABINA RESIDENCE. — Design 1227-O; size 32 ft. 6 in. by 35 ft. 6 in. Cost, $1,680 to $2,000; plans, $15. Special features: Well-ventilated parlor and chamber above, attractive vestibule entrance. See page 65.

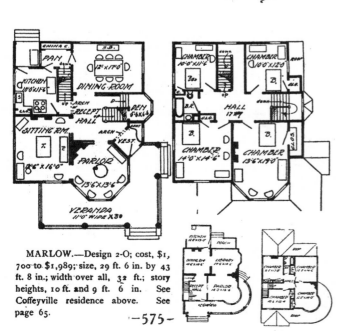

MARLOW.—Design 2-O; cost, $1,700 to $1,989; size, 29 ft. 6 in. by 43 ft. 8 in.; width over all, 32 ft.; story heights, 10 ft. and 9 ft. 6 in. See Coffeyville residence above. See page 65.

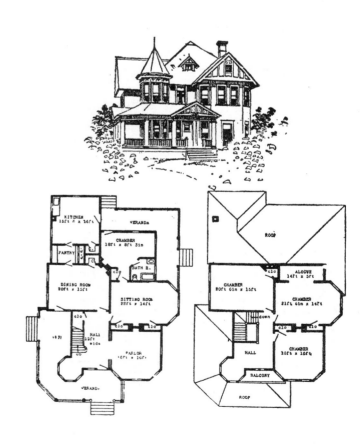

SNODON RESIDENCE.—Design 2041M; cost in frame $2,390 to $2,480; plans $15. See page 65.

MILLBERRY RESIDENCE.—Design 1832-N; cost in frame, $2,490 to $2,982; plans, $25; story heights, 11 ft. and 10 ft. Special features: Large rooms and wide central hall with fire-place; balcony and door to second-story front hall. Good Southern house.

SHAWVILLE RESIDENCE.—Design 1831-N; cost in frame, $2,462 to $2,680; plans, $20; story heights, 9 ft. and 8 ft. 8 in. Special features: Imposing corner-lot design; 9 ft. 6 in. veranda.

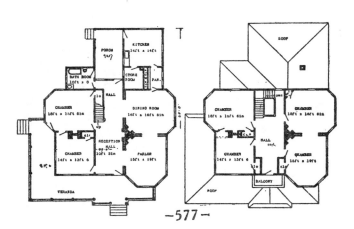

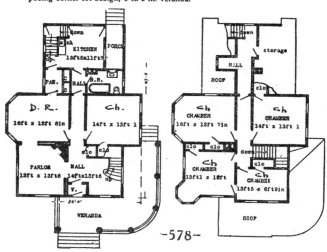

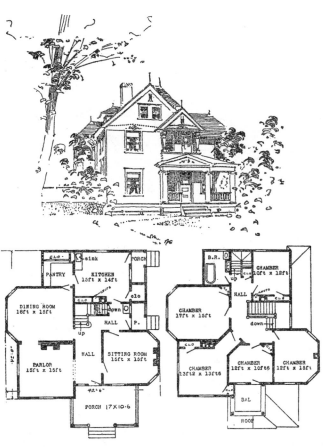

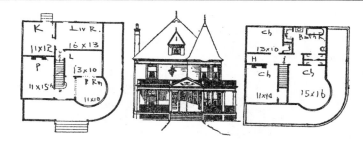

COFFEYVILLE RESIDENCE.—Design 6029-O; in frame, $1,698 to $1,790; plans, $10; width, 37 ft. 6 in. by 40 ft. 6 in.; width over all, 41 ft. 1 in.; story heights, 10 and 8 ft.; special features: A very compact plan. See index for Coffeyville residence revised. We have it with octagon tower. Parlor, 11.4x15 ft. 6 in.; reception room, 11x10 ft.; library, 13x9 ft. 6 in.; living room, 16.6x10 ft.; kitchen, 11x12 ft.

Coffeyville Res. No. 3, White design, with parlor 13x15 ft. 8 in., with stairs to cellar and second floor between parlor and kitchen; with 11x13 kitchen, with 12x12 ft. 6 in library; with 16x11 dining-room, with bay; with 7x10 pantry back of kitchen and rear porch to kitchen. The tower chamber, 12.6x16 ft.; story heights, 10 ft. and 9 ft. 6 in.

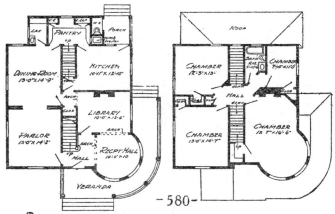

ALEXIS RESIDENCE.—Design 1979-N; cost, $2,190 to $2,298; plans, $20. Special features: Large rooms; central hall; wide frontage; main stairs located in such a way that rear stairs is hardly necessary; wash-basin in rear hall; large front porch.

BEEBE.—Design 1-O; cost, $1,290 to $1,900; size, 31 ft. by 31 ft.; width over all, 39 ft.; story heights, 9 ft. 6 in. and 9 ft.

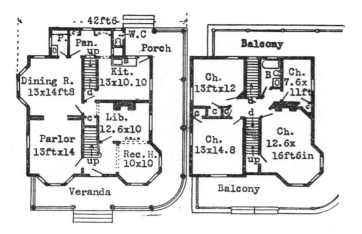

Coffeyville No. 2 design 5581-A, exterior similar to 584, but reversed. (Use mirror on page 1023.) Plans $10.

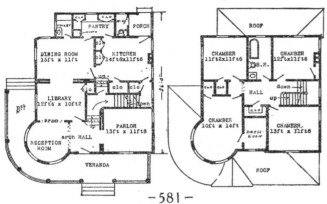

—581—

TAMAROA RESIDENCE.—Design 2254M; cost in frame $1,292 to $1,399; plans $10. See index for Coffeyville Residence. See page 65.

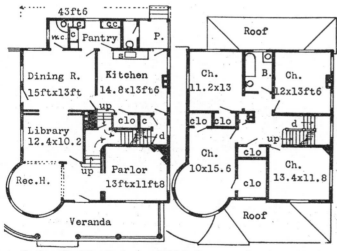

Coffeyville No. 8 design 5583-A, story heights 9-ft 6 and 9. See pages 580-1-2-4.

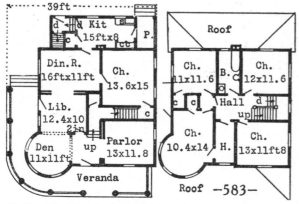

—583—

Coffeyville No. 9 design 5583-B, story heights 9-ft 6 and 9. See pages 580-1-2-4 and 9.

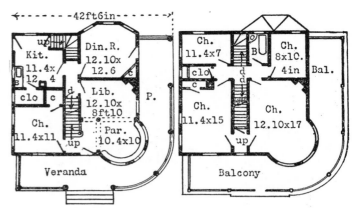

Coffeyville Res. No. 4, Frank design, cost, $1,492 to $1,598; plans, 10; story heights, 9 ft. 6 in. and 9 ft.; same design as No. 1 plan

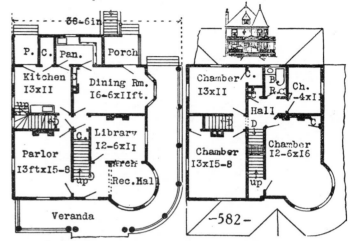

—582—

Coffeyville Residence No. 7 design 5582-B, story heights 10-ft 6 and 9-ft 6. See pages 580-581-582-584. Plans $10.

NON RESIDENCE.—Design 2242-N; cost in frame $2,140 to $2,292; plans $20. Special features: A neat, attractive exterior; inexpensive tower; well-lighted library; two good-size rooms in front. The house has a large, open appearance upon entering. See 333.

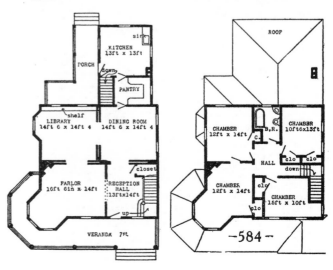

—584—

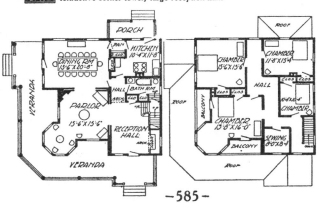

NORWOOD RESIDENCE.—Design 1217-N; size, 28x38; cost, $2,490 to $2,684. Special features: Bath-room on first-floor; large dining-room and veranda; tower and balconies. Plans. $20. Attractive corner tower; large reception hall.

= Dodman residence design 5586, width 44-ft, over all = 52 ft, story heights 9 and 8-ft 6. Combination hall, dining room and kitchen stairs. Neat, clean-cut exterior. Plans $15.

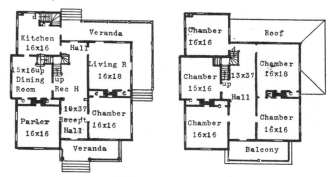

I am very much pleased with plans which you furnished me, and which I selected from one of your series of contributions to the Woman's Home Companion.
HERBERT BUTLER, New Lexington, O.

KOKIMO RESIDENCE.—Design 100,002M; cost $2965 to $3261; Plans, $30; size 35x45. extreme width 50 ft. Special features: Attractive bay; side entrance; vestibule in front; large chamber in front; general outlines of design very good; would make an attractive stained shingle gable. See page 65.

HERBERT C CHIVERS. ARCHITECT.

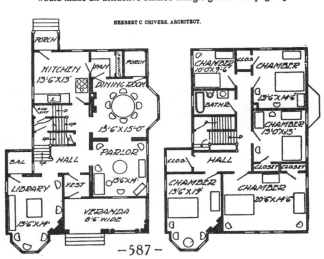

VANCE RESIDENCE.—Design 1007M; in frame, $2190 to $2540; plans, $25; width over all, 41 ft,; story heights 10 ft. Special features: Open porch at sides, fire-place arrangement, semi-circular bays at side. See page 65.

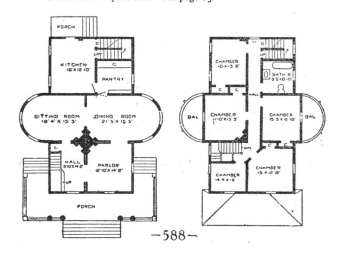

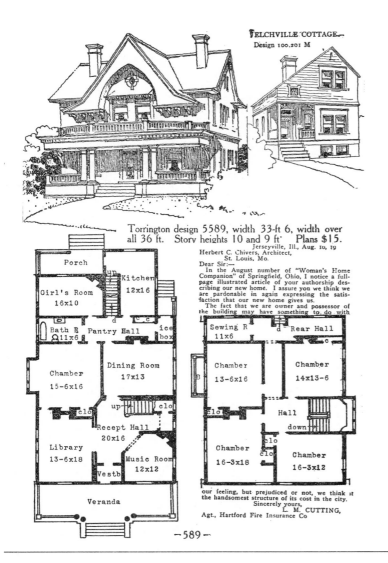

ELCHVILLE COTTAGE
Design 100.201 M

Torrington design 5589, width 33-ft 6, width over all 36 ft. Story heights 10 and 9 ft. Plans $15.

Jerseyville, Ill., Aug. 10, 19

Herbert C. Chivers, Architect,
St. Louis, Mo.

Dear Sir:—
In the August number of "Woman's Home Companion" of Springfield, Ohio, I notice a full-page illustrated article of your authorship describing our new home. I assure you we think we are pardonable in again expressing the satisfaction that our new home gives us.
The fact that we are owner and possessor of the building may have something to do with our feeling, but prejudiced or not, we think it the handsomest structure of its cost in the city.

Sincerely yours,
L. M. CUTTING,
Agt., Hartford Fire Insurance Co

Porch
Kitchen 12x16
Girl's Room 16x10
Bath 11x6
Pantry Hall
ice box
Chamber 15-6x16
Dining Room 17x13
clo
clo
up
Recept Hall 20x16
Library 13-6x18
Music Room 12x12
Vestb
Veranda

Sewing R 11x6
d Rear Hall
Chamber 13-6x16
Chamber 14x13-6
clo
clo
Hall down
Chamber 16-3x18
clo clo
Chamber 16-3x12

—589—

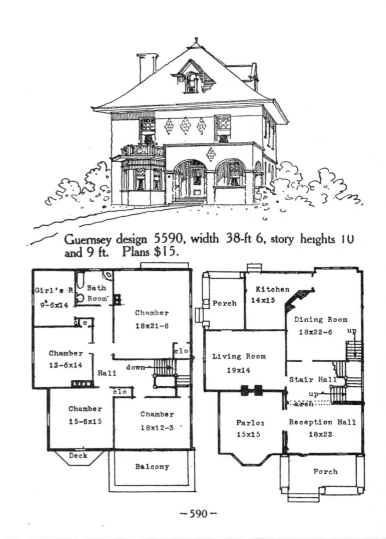

Guernsey design 5590, width 38-ft 6, story heights 10 and 9 ft. Plans $15.

Girl's R 9-6x14
Bath Room
Chamber 18x21-6
c
Chamber 13-6x14
Hall down
clo
Chamber 15-6x15
Chamber 18x12-3
Deck
Balcony

Porch
Kitchen 14x15
Dining Room 18x22-6 up
Living Room 19x14
Stair Hall up arch
Parlor 15x15
Reception Hall 18x22
Porch

—590—

 HENANGO RESIDENCE.—Design 2243-N; cost in frame, $2,390 to $2,462; plans, $20; story heights, 9 ft. 6 in. and 9 ft. Special features: Neat, colonial exterior; large library; large pantry.

Porch
Kitch 13X17'
P
Laun P.
clo up
Dining 20x15
Library 18x20
up
Hall 20x20
P Parlor 18x15
v
Porch 11ft

Ch. 9X 15
Bath
D
Bal
Ch. 12x9
Cham. 16x12
Cham. 15x18
Hall
Chamber 18x14
Chamber 13x13
C
Bal 12x11
Roof

—591—

Plans $20.

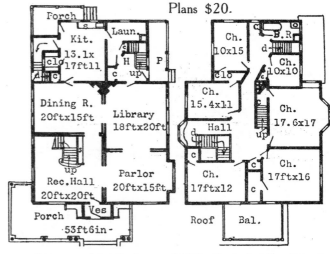

Porch
Kit. 13.1x 17ft11
Laun.
H up P
clo c
Dining R. 20ftx15ft
Library 18ftx20ft
up
Rec. Hall 20ftx20ft
Parlor 20ftx15ft
Porch
Ves
—53ft6in—

Ch. 10x15
B. R.
d
Ch. 10x10
clo
Ch. 15.4x11
Hall up
Ch. 17.6x17
Ch. 17ftx12
Ch. 17ftx16
c
Roof
Bal.

Shenango No. 2 design 5592, story heights 9-ft 6 and 9. See similar design on opposite page, 591

J.T. COOMBS, M.D. Superintendent.
W. L. RAY, M D 1st Asst Physician.
J. MURRAY WILCOX, M.D. 2nd Asst Physician.
EMIL THEILMANN, M.D. 3rd Asst Physician.
W. F. LORD Steward
MRS. M. C. ROBERTS, Matron
W. O. THOMAS, Treasurer
L. M. SUMMERS, Secretary

State Lunatic Asylum No. 1.
Fulton, Mo

July 17

Herbert C. Chivers, Esq.,

Dear Sir:—

Replying to your recent letter will state, I am, and my wife also, exceedingly pleased with plans furnished.

Very respectfully,

W. F. Loyd

—592—

Carno design 5593, story heights 10 and 9 ft, width over steps and all 50 ft. Well-lighted scenic parlor and chamber above. Plans $15.

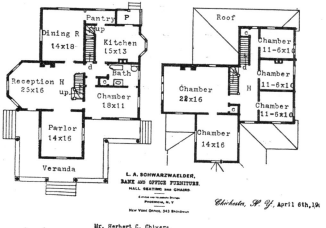

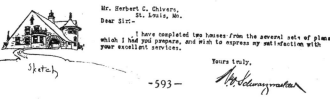

L. A. SCHWARZWAELDER,
BANK AND OFFICE FURNITURE.
HALL SEATING and CHAIRS.

PHOENICIA, N. Y.
NEW YORK OFFICE, 343 BROADWAY

Chichester, N. Y., April 6th, 19t

Mr. Herbert C. Chivers,
St. Louis, Mo.
Dear Sir:-
        I have completed two houses from the several sets of plans
which I had you prepare, and wish to express my satisfaction with
your excellent services.

                Yours truly,
                A. H. Schwarzwaelder

-593-

TESAGE RESIDENCE.—Design 2242M; cost in frame, $2,299 to $2,385; plans, $20. See page 65.

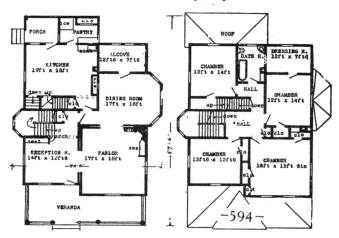

-594-

Dulas design 5595, story heights 9 ft 6 and 9. Large library, with attractive combination fire-place and book cases on one side. Plans $15.

-595-

Cheriton design 5596, story heights 10 ft and 9 ft 6. This exterior can be had with a plain, neat dormer window in roof in place of a gambril roof. Plans $15.

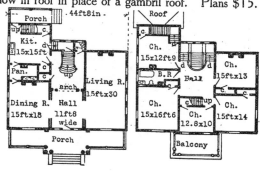

-596-

Compton design 5597, story heights 9 and 9 ft, width 30-ft 6. A particularly clean-cut, well-balanced exterior and a roomy plan.

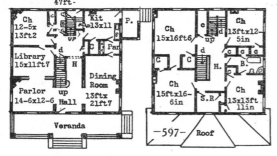

Back chamber on first floor, with separate toilet, very convenient for the aged. Plans $20

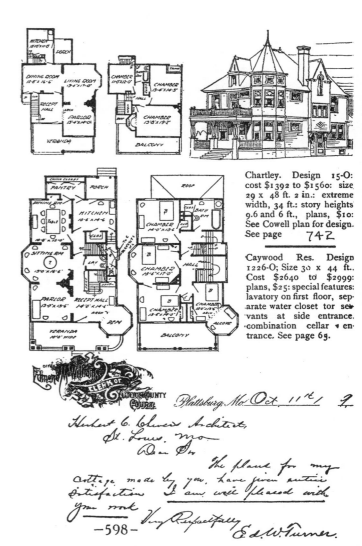

Chartley. Design 15-O: cost $1392 to $1560: size 29 x 48 ft. 2 in.: extreme width, 34 ft.: story heights 9.6 and 6 ft., plans, $10: See Cowell plan for design. See page 742

Caywood Res. Design 1226-O; Size 30 x 44 ft. Cost $2640 to $2999: plans, $25: special features: lavatory on first floor, separate water closet for servants at side entrance. combination cellar entrance. See page 65.

-598-

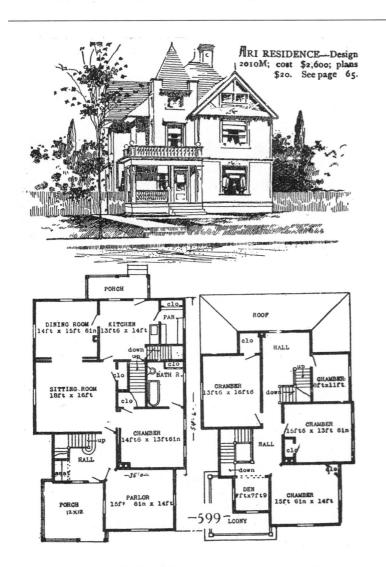

ARI RESIDENCE—Design 2010M; cost $2,600; plans $20. See page 65.

-599-

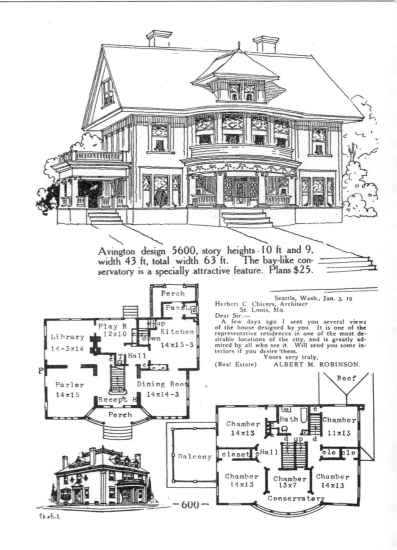

Avington design 5600, story heights 10 ft and 9, width 43 ft, total width 63 ft. The bay-like conservatory is a specially attractive feature. Plans $25.

Seattle, Wash., Jan. 3, 19
Herbert C. Chivers, Architect
St. Louis, Mo.
Dear Sir:—
A few days ago I sent you several views of the house designed by you. It is one of the representative residences in one of the most desirable locations of the city, and is greatly admired by all who see it. Will send you some interiors if you desire them.
Yours very truly,
(Real Estate)   ALBERT M. ROBINSON.

-600-

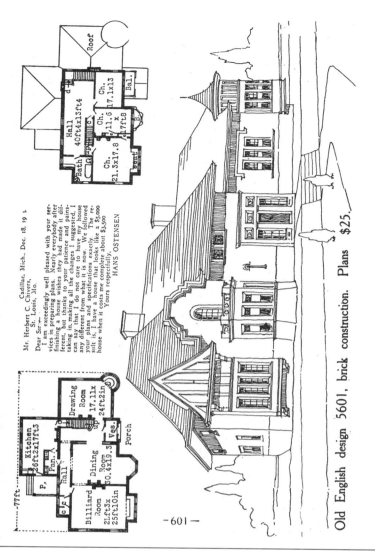

Old English design 5601, brick construction. Plans $25.

Hall 40ft4x13ft4 · Ch. 17.1x13 · Bal. · Ch. 11.6 x 17.8 · B. · Bath · Ch. 21.3x17.8

Mr. Herbert C. Chivers,
St. Louis, Mo.

Dear Sir:—

I am exceedingly well pleased with your services in preparing plans. Nearly everybody after finishing a house wishes they had made it different, but thanks to your patience and painstaking in making all the changes I suggested, I can say that I do not care to have my house any different from what it is now. We followed your plans and specifications exactly to the letter and you know the result is, I have a house that looks like a $5,000 house when it costs me complete about $3,500. Yours respectfully,

HANS OSTENSEN

Cadillac, Mich. Dec. 18, 19 1.

Kitchen 26ft2x17ft3 · Pan. · Drawing Room 17.11x24ft2in · Ves. · Hall · Dining Room 30.4x19.3 · Billiard Room 21ft3x25ft10in · Porch · 77ft.

-601-

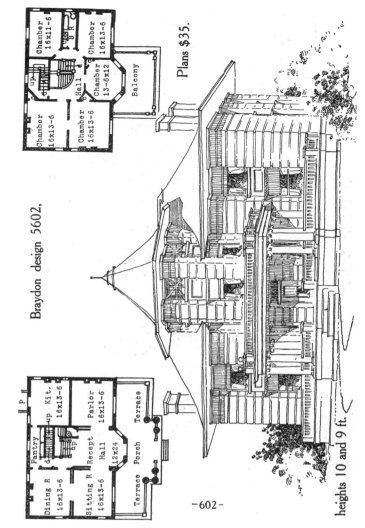

Braydon design 5602, Plans $35. heights 10 and 9 ft.

Chamber 16x11-6 · Chamber 16x13-6 · Chamber 13-6x12 · Hall · Balcony · Chamber 16x13-6 · Chamber 16x13-6

Pantry · Kit. 16x13-6 · Parlor 16x13-6 · Dining R 16x13-6 · Recept Hall 12x24 · Sitting R 16x13-6 · Terrace · Porch · Terrace

-602-

Leafield design 5603, story heights 10 ft and 9 ft 6. Attractive balcony in front. Bath on both floors. Plans $15.

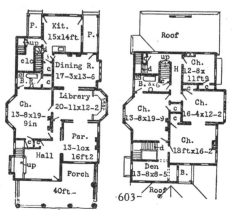

Kit. 15x14ft · P. · Dining R. 17-3x13-6 · Library 20-11x12-2 · Ch. 13-8x19-9in · Par. 13-1ox 16ft2 · Hall · Porch · 40ft.

Roof · Ch. 12-8x 11ft9 · Ch. 13-8x19-9 · Ch. 16-4x12-2 · Ch. 18ftx16-2 · Den 13-8x8-5

603-

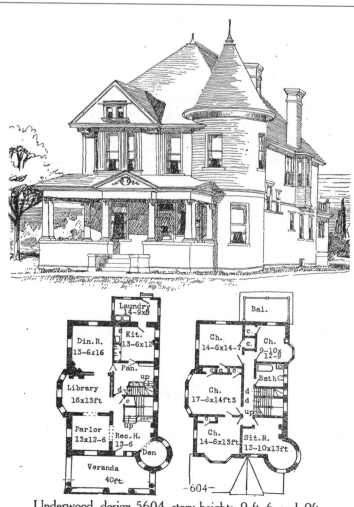

Laundry 14-9x8 · Din.R. 13-6x16 · Kit. 13-6x12 · Pan. · Library 16x13ft · Parlor 13x12-6 · Rec.H. 13-6 · Den · Veranda 40ft.

Bal. · Ch. 14-6x14-7 · Ch. 9-10x12-9 · Bath · Ch. 17-6x14ft3 · Ch. 14-6x13ft · Sit.R. 13-10x13ft

-604-

Underwood design 5604, story heights 9 ft 6 and 9ft.
First story brick and frame above. Plans $15.

Farnboro design 5605, width 48 ft, story heights 10 and 8 ft 6. Wide, pretentious front. Art glass window between hall and dining room, with glass-door closets at side. Plans $25.

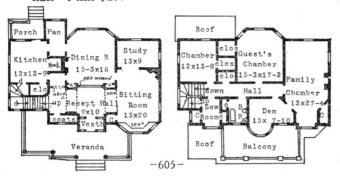

—605—

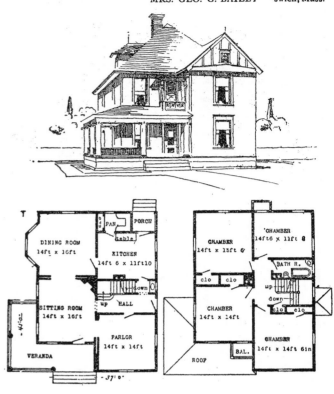

TAPPAN RESIDENCE.—Design 2043M; cost in frame $2,190 to $2,280; plans $10. See page 65.

606

MASSILION RESIDENCE.—Design 1049-O; in frame, $2,200 to $2,500; plans, $20; width, 47 ft. 4 in. by 26 ft. 6 in.; width over all, 47 ft. 4 in.; story heights, 9 ft. in the clear. Special features: Wide imposing frontage. We have plans with projecting Colonial porch, with 4 ft. open porch around to side porch, called (Hill plan). See page 65.

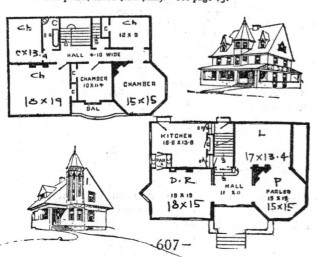

—607—

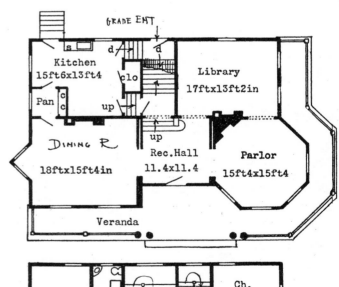

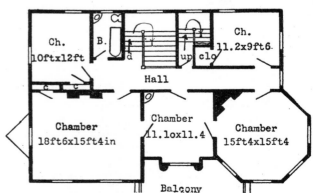

Massillion Residence No. 2 design 5608, story heights 9-ft 6 and 9. See similar design opposite page, 607 but higher cornice, different porch and colonial columns at covered portion of porch. Plans $20.

—608—

 EBENEZER COTTAGE.—Design 2251M; cost in frame
$1,692 to $1,840; plans $10. See page 65.

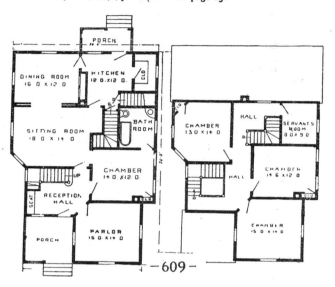

—609—

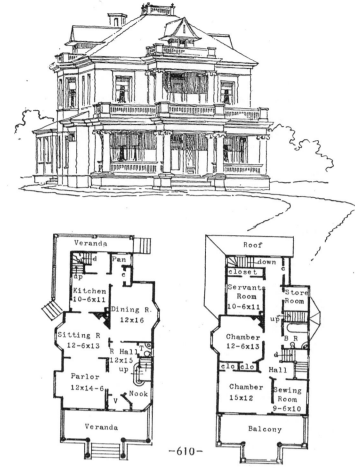

—610—

Loxwood design 5610, width 25-ft 6, width over all 31
ft, story heights 9 and 8-ft 6.   Plans $15.

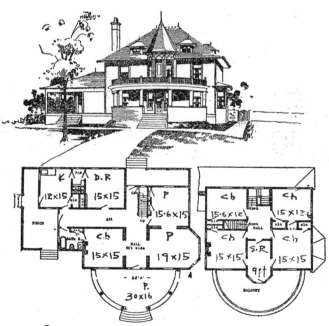

PETERSON RESIDENCE.—Design 1836M; cost in frame
$2,094 to $2,340; plans $15.   See page 65.

THE HARMONIZER.

O know something of everything and everything of something connected with the construction of a building is the business of the architect. The man who pays for the work seldom knows anything about any part of it. What he wants is a harmonized combination. If he is wise he pays a man who is capable of securing this. When a client accepts a design of mine with orders to superintend the work from start to finish he may be assured that from foundation to roof everything will be well done. The stone-mason, the brick-layer, the tiler, the carpenter, the glazier, the plumber and the decorator will have fulfilled to the letter the contracts under which they work. I am the harmonizer. I see the whole where others see but the parts. What to my clients is a posibility is to me a certainty.—Herbert C. Chivers.

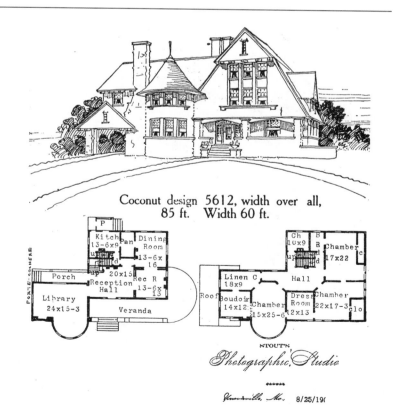

Coconut design 5612, width over all,
85 ft.   Width 60 ft.

STOUT'N
Photographic Studio

Quincyville, Mo.   8/25/19(

H. C. Chivers,
    St. Louis
Dear Sir:—

We like our new brick residence very
much. It is considered the most artistic house
in this part of the country.
    The art glass window which you personally designed for us, is indeed a work of art.

Yours truly,
Thos Stout

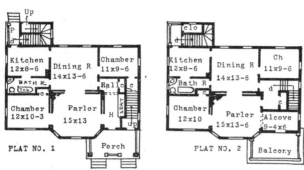

Noyon design 5613, width 39 ft, story heights 9 ft 6 and 9. A good roomy, square, compact residence appearing flat, with first floor chamber and bath. Plans $25.

OZONE RESIDENCE.—Design 1054M; in frame, $2,340 to $2,450, (with stone first story, $950 extra); plans, $20; width, 40 ft. 8 in. by 36 ft.; story heights, 9 ft. 6 in. and 9 ft. in the clear. Special features: Attractive stone (Dutch) gable and chimney effect. Modifications: A front porch could be erected across entrance and front of library, with the main roof extending down over same to good effect. See page 65.

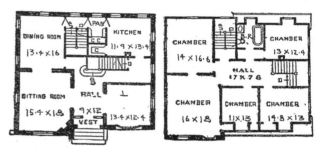

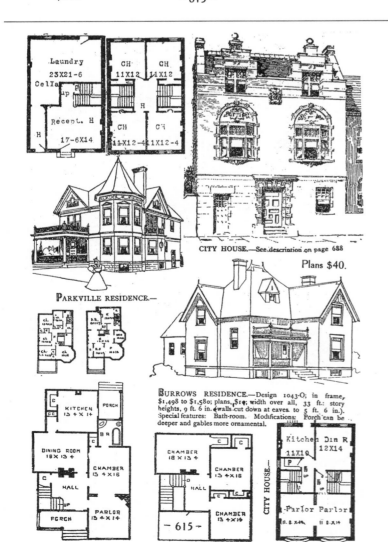

CITY HOUSE.—See description on page 688

Plans $40.

PARKVILLE RESIDENCE.—

BURROWS RESIDENCE.—Design 1043-O; in frame, $1,498 to $1,580; plans, $14; width over all, 33 ft.; story heights, 9 ft. 6 in. (walls cut down at eaves to 5 ft. 6 in.). Special features: Bath-room. Modifications: Porch can be deeper and gables more ornamental.

CITY HOUSE.—

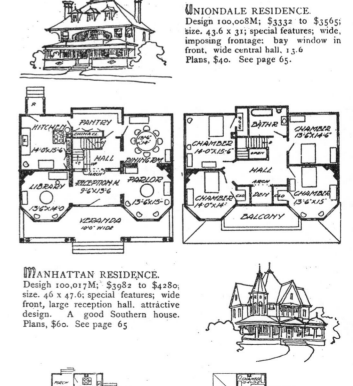

UNIONDALE RESIDENCE.
Design 100,008M; $3332 to $3565; size. 43.6 x 31; special features; wide, imposing frontage; bay window in front, wide central hall, 13.6 Plans, $40. See page 65.

MANHATTAN RESIDENCE.
Desigh 100,017M; $3982 to $4280; size. 46 x 47.6; special features; wide front, large reception hall. attractive design. A good Southern house. Plans, $60. See page 65

DRYDEN RESIDENCE.—Design 1036M; in frame, $2,190 to $2,340; plans, $20; width, 40 ft. by 33 ft. 4 in.; width over all, 43 ft.; story heights, 9 ft. 6 in. and 9 ft. Special features: Side entrance, with direct way to cellar, stairs serve as front and rear stairs, a good feature in cold climates, giving a warm reception hall. See page 65.

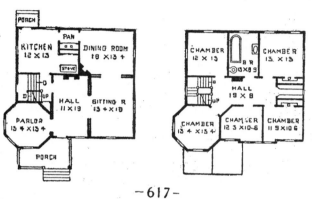

—617—

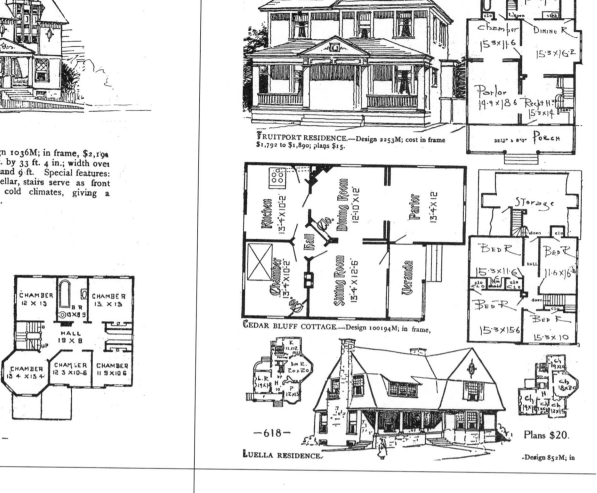

Plans $20

FRUITPORT RESIDENCE.—Design 2253M; cost in frame $1,792 to $1,890; plans $15.

CEDAR BLUFF COTTAGE.—Design 100194M; in frame,

—618—

LUELLA RESIDENCE.

Plans $20

—Design 852M; in

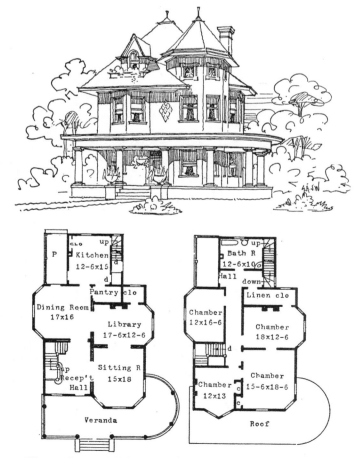

Torota design 5619, story heights 10 and 9 ft 6, width over all 45 ft. Large veranda. Well-balanced exterior. Large rooms. Plans $15. —619—

CHILTON RESIDENCE.—Design 100,059M; size, 37x50; cost in frame, $2,775 to $3,000; story heights, 1st 11 ft., 2d 10 ft.; special features: Bed-room on first floor. See page 65.

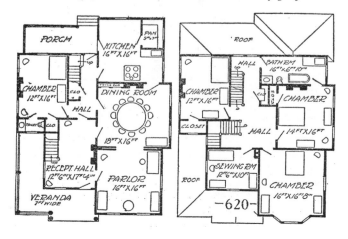

—620—

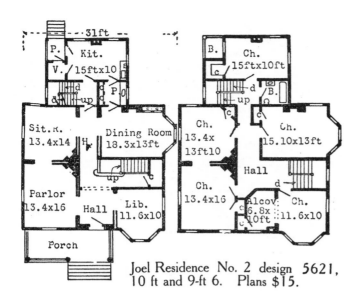

Joel Residence No. 2 design 5621,
10 ft and 9-ft 6. Plans $15.

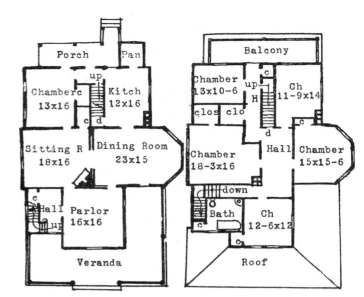

Latimer Residence No. 2 design 5622, see exterior
on page 953, story heights 10 and 9-ft 6, width
43 ft. Plans $20. See Tula Residence No. 2 page
625 and 624.

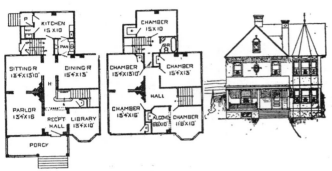

JOEL RESIDENCE.—Design 1005-O; in frame, $2,790 to
$3,000; plans, $25; width over all, 36 ft. 8 in.; story heights,
10 ft. and 9 ft. 6 in. Berietor design, same as above, with
3x6 octogon bay to dining-room.

-621-

PITTSFIELD RESIDENCE.—Design 1528-O; in frame,
$1,198 to $1,389; plans; $10; width, 28 ft. 10 in; by 34 ft.;
story heights, 9 ft. 6 in. and 9 ft.; special features: Inexpensive tower, compact plan; plain, simple design. Modifications:
House would look well with tower eliminated. See page 65.

-622-

FORETHOUGHT IN BUILDING

BUILD on the past experience and new ideas of an
architect of national reputation. You are not
building for the present alone but
for the future. Secure the best designs and plan you can for your
money.

More money has been wasted in
mistakes and blunders in building
than was ever paid to architects.

You probably have well-defined
ideas of the sort of house you want.
There are features you now intend
to insist upon and which you have
heretofore missed in the houses
you have occupied. Have your own
way; but do not, in your haste,
build a home in which you will re-
pent at leisure that it is not different.
This need not occur if you let me
work your ideas into a practical plan
and produce a design which will
meet your approval and your purse.

Many who are about to build,
being inexperienced, do not realize
the importance of securing from a
thoroughly qualified architect regularly drawn plans. They content
themselves with crude outlines prepared by one to whom architecture
is not a fine art, but merely a trade.

The results are coarse, common-
place and unsatisfactory. The
money paid to him would command
the services of an architectural expert possessed of a thorough knowledge of what has been done and
with originality enough to produce
something new.

It is a mistake to suppose that
practical and artistic plans drawn
by a competent architect are necessarily more expensive than are fool-
ish plans, amateurish plans, incor-

rect plans, inartistic plans drawn by
some incompetent architect. The
one would be certain in architectural effect, the other common-place,
experimental and dubious.

The essence of good design is as
much in the details of construction,
as the actual plans, and this is where
the inexperienced are disappointed.
The plain floor plans, exterior views
and specifications do not constitute
complete plans. They are simply
preliminary to the important detailed information which I give as the
work progresses. By all means
employ an architect who works for
art's sake and who is under obliga-
tion to no local interests except
your interests.

The special instructions in the
specifications is a feature the value
of which is too often overlooked.
Only an expert architect is capable
of preparing these and the detailed
drawings.

I cannot give to your plans the
study and considerations they
should have without reasonable assurance of payment when I please
you. To send well-studied designs
and exterior views without this assurance is a speculative chance
which I am unwilling to assume.
My time is given to clients who
place their orders subject to the
above understanding. I then prepare sketches until they are satisfied.

You place your order with me
and I will prepare drawings which
shall enable you to determine what
kind of a house you can build for a
given sum. I am an expert at this
work and my services will cost
you no more than those of a novice
or a blunderer.

623

Gaeta design 5624, width over steps and all 45 ft, story
heights 9 ft and 8 ft. See Tula residence 625. Plans
$15.

-624-

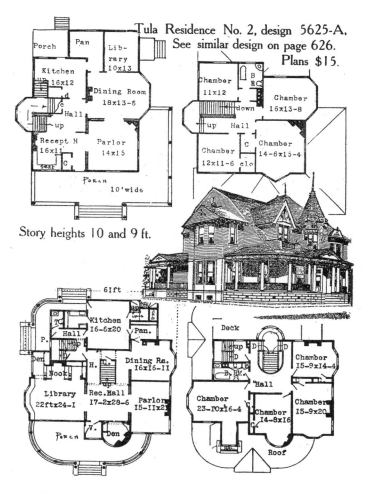

Tula Residence No. 2, design 5625-A,
See similar design on page 626.
Plans $15.

Porch Pan
Library 10x13
Kitchen 16x12
Dining Room 18x13-6
Hall up
Recept H 16x11
Parlor 14x15
Porch 10' wide

Chamber 11x12
Chamber 15x13-8
down up Hall
Chamber 12x11-6 clo
Chamber 14-6x15-4

Story heights 10 and 9 ft.

61ft
Kitchen 16-6x20 Pan.
Hall
Den Nook
Dining Rm. 16x16-11
Chamber 15-9x14-4
Library 22ftx24-1
Rec.Hall 17-2x28-6
Parlor 15-11x21
Deck
Hall
Chamber 23-10x16-4
Chamber 14-8x16
Chamber 15-9x20
Porch Den
Roof

Wauson No. 2 design 5625, story heights 10 ft and 9
ft 6. Plans $30.

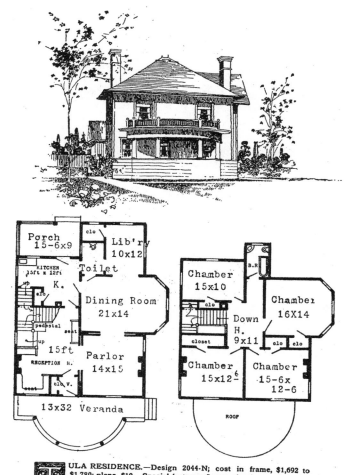

Porch 15-6x9 clo Lib'ry 10x12
Kitchen 15ft x 12ft Toilet
K.
Dining Room 21x14
pedestal
15ft Parlor 14x15
RECEPTION H. clo V.
13x32 Veranda

Chamber 15x10
Chamber 16X14
Down H. 9x11
closet clo clo
Chamber 15x12-6
Chamber 15-6x 12-6
ROOF

TULA RESIDENCE.—Design 2044-N; cost in frame, $1,692 to
$1,780; plans, $10. Special features: Large, circular porch; parlor
in front; combination stairs; large rooms; plain, neat design; large
toilet-room on first floor convenient to library.

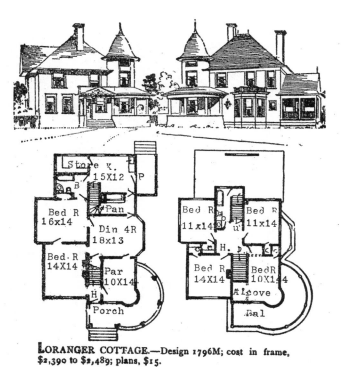

Store K. 15X12 P
B
Bed R 16x14
Pan
Din 4R 18x13
Bed R 11x14
Bed R 11x14
Bed R 14X14
Par 10x14
H
Porch
Bed R 14X14
BedR 10X14
Alcove
Bal

LORANGER COTTAGE.—Design 1796M; cost in frame,
$2,390 to $2,489; plans, $15.

THE PUBLIC VERDICT.

YOU build for yourself a sky-scraper, a theatre, a hotel, a bank, a factory, a
store or a home the passer-by takes possession of it with his eye and claims
it as his to behold. It is to him the city as he sees it. You become known
as the owner of the building and it is to your credit or the reverse. I have
never erected a building for a client which did not redound to his honor as a beau-
tifier of his city. The public verdict on my work is every time: "This building looks
good to us."—Herbert C. Chivers.

CROBRIDGE RESIDENCE.—See opposite page, 318.
Design 1907M; cost in frame $1,892 to $1,920; plans $15.

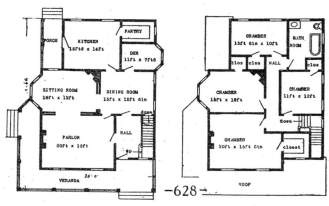

PORCH
KITCHEN 15ft6 x 14ft
PANTRY
DEN 11ft x 7ft6
SITTING ROOM 16ft x 12ft
DINING ROOM 15ft x 12ft 6in
PARLOR 20ft x 15ft
HALL
VERANDA

CHAMBER 15ft 6in x 16ft
BATH ROOM
clos clos HALL clos
CHAMBER 15ft x 12ft
CHAMBER 11ft x 12ft
CHAMBER 20ft x 15ft 6in closet
ROOF

Be as specific when you build as you would in a written contract, for a
"building muddle" is deplorable. The plans, specification and details of construction are necessarily a part of your contract.

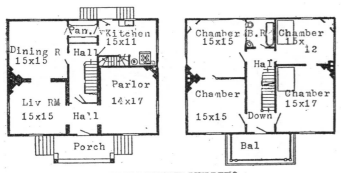

GEORGIA RESIDENCE.—Design 1999-O; in frame, $2,040 to $2,380; plans, $20; width, 37 ft. 6 in. by 29 ft. 8 in.; story heights, 10 ft. and 9 ft.   See page 65.

THE "ARCHITECT-BUILDER."

It is right and proper that all builders should be able to draw more or less, but it is absolutely impossible for a man to be an up-to-date builder and at the same time study architectural plans and design as they should be studied. The fact that "a little knowledge is a dangerous thing" could hardly be more clearly exemplified than with he, who with a smattering of architectural knowledge, self-styles himself "Architect and Builder."

He may be able to make a poor copy of some good design heretofore built, but no copy is as good as an original in the first place, and aside from this, while the copyest is copying, the original man is surging on ahead on something new and better. Did you ever realize this?

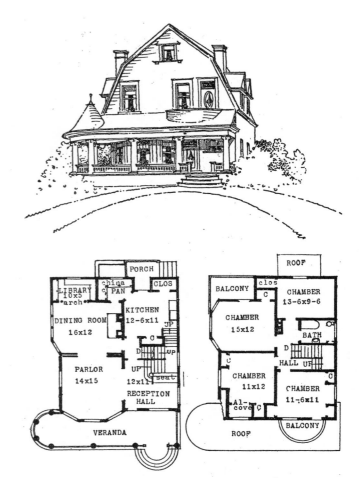

Tulare design 5630, width 27 ft 6. Width over all 5 ft 6. Story heights 10 ft 6 and 9. Neat shingle effect. Plans $10.

Bremen design 5631, width in brick, 33 ft 6, story heights 9 ft 8 and 8 ft 8. Plain, neat exterior. Plans $10.

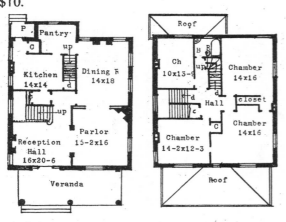

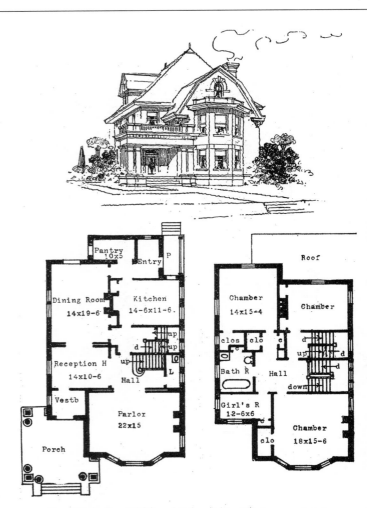

Stettin design 5632 in brick, width 34 ft, story heights 10 and 9 ft. Plans $15.

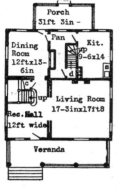

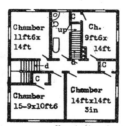

Annotta design 5633, story heights 9 ft 6 and 9. Plans $11

Hyannis, Mass., Jan. 21, 1905.
Herbert C. Chivers, Esq.,
St. Louis, Mo.
Dear Sir:—
In reply to your letter of the 17th inst., would say that plans prepared by you for Catholic Church were complete and very artistically drawn.
Sincerely yours,
REV. D. E. DORAN,
Pastor, St. Francis Xavier Rectory.

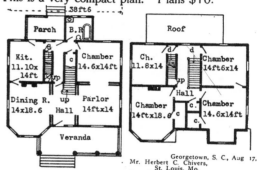

Jacmel design 5634, story heights 10 and 9 ft. We can furnish this with different tower effect if desired. This is a very compact plan. Plans $10.

Georgetown, S. C., Aug 17, 19
Mr. Herbert C. Chivers,
St. Louis, Mo.
Dear Sir:—
The building you planned is all "O. K." I completed same and moved into it the early part of December last and find the plan exceedingly convenient and comfortable. Every one who has been through the house admires it.
Yours very truly,
H. L. SMITH.

Navidad design 5635, story heights 11 and 9 ft, width over all 50 ft. Plans $15. For $28 we will change to suit.

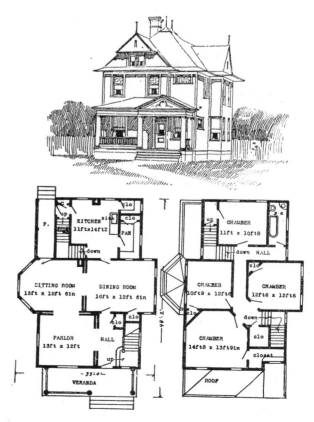

ALPINA RESIDENCE.—Design 1936-N; cost in frame, $1,892 to $1,998; plans, $15; story heights, 10 ft. and 9 ft. Special features: Neat, clean-cut exterior; simple, attractive gable; large dining-room. A practical and inexpensive house.

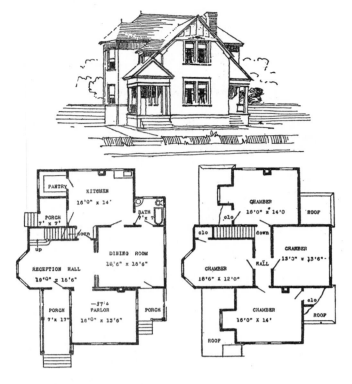

OAKBEACH RESIDENCE.—Design 2034M; cost in frame $1,492 to $1,592; plans $10. See page 65.

We have found the house very convenient for a small family and the outside appearance has been very generally admired by those that have seen it.
—H. W. Damon, Price, Utah.

Plans were very complete and it will make a fine building when complete.
—H. C. McWilliams, Boscobel, Wis.

If there are any churches, schools, stores, libraries, theatres, court houses or other public buildings in your city in contemplation do not fail to put me in communication with the parties. Should I secure any work of this kind I will endeavor to reciprocate,

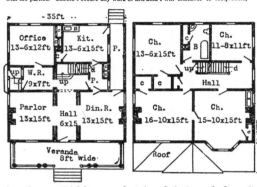

Autlan design 5638, story heights 9-ft 6 and 9. Compact plan, suitable for physician's home, with waiting room at side, Plans $14.

Forsythe design 5639, story heights 10 and 9-ft 6, width 57 ft. Plans $15.

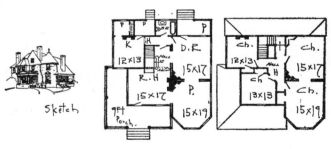

HALLTOWN RESIDENCE. — Design 9112-O; in frame, $1,798 to $2,290; plans, $10; width, 33 ft. 6 in. by 44 ft.; width over all, 37 ft. 6 in.; story heights, 10 ft. 6 in. and 10 ft. in the clear. See page 65.

Sketch

Halltown No. 2 design 5640, See design above, Plans $10.

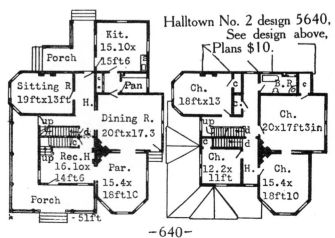

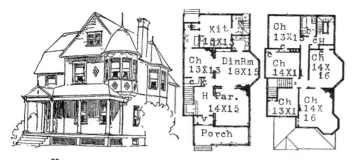

HECLA RESIDENCE.—Design 8298M; in frame, $2,390 to $2,549; plans, $25; story heights, 10 ft; with stone arch and tower $200 extra; plans, $25; width, 57 ft. 4 in. by 29 ft. Width over all, 67 ft.; story heights, 9 ft. 6 in. and 0 ft. in the clear. Special features: Toilet room on first floor; large, convenient rooms, a striking design for a country estate. See page 65.

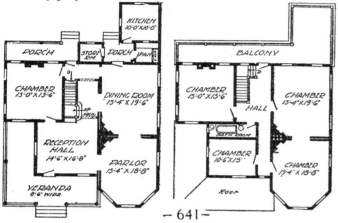

— 641 —

SUNNYSIDE RESIDENCE.—Whelden Design 74-O; (see Halltown design for exterior.); cost, $2,090 to $2,340; size, 42 ft. by 57 ft.; story heights, 10 ft.; plans, $20; special features: Large reception hall, with main stairs so located as to be available for rear stairs, with portiers at arch. See page 65.

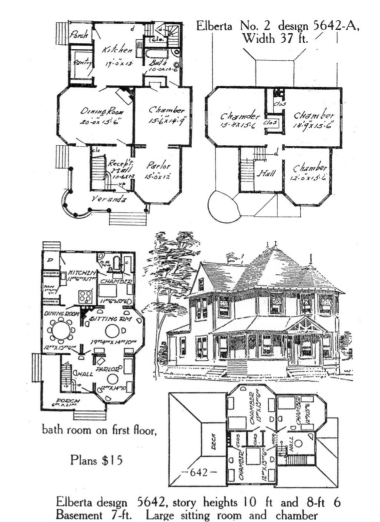

Elberta No. 2 design 5642-A, Width 37 ft.

bath room on first floor,

Plans $15

— 642 —

Elberta design 5642, story heights 10 ft and 8-ft 6
Basement 7-ft. Large sitting room and chamber

Faroe design 5643, in brick, story heights 10 and 9 ft.

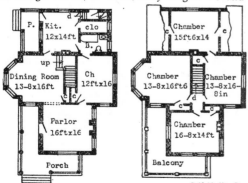

Plans $15.

-643-

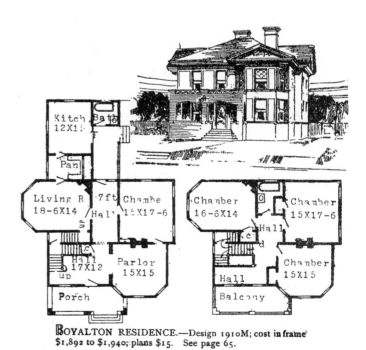

BOYALTON RESIDENCE.—Design 1910M; cost in frame $1,892 to $1,940; plans $15. See page 65.

-644-

 EWBERRY RESIDENCE.—Design 2332-N; cost in frame, $1,692 to $1,898; plans, $10; full story heights. Special features: A very compact house. This plan can be had in many modifications. Stairs can go up direct from reception hall without rear hall, and plans can be had with less expensive roof.

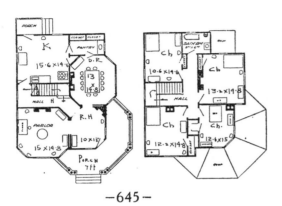

Hampton design No. 14, design 5646-B, story heights 10 and 9 ft, width 32-ft 6, over all 35 ft. Plans $10. (Other Hampton Residences pages 645 and nine following pages.)

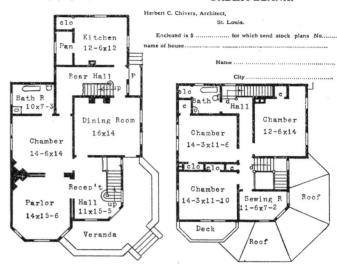

— ORDER BLANK.—

Herbert C. Chivers, Architect, St. Louis.

Enclosed is $ .... for which send stock plans No........
name of house...
Name ....
City ....

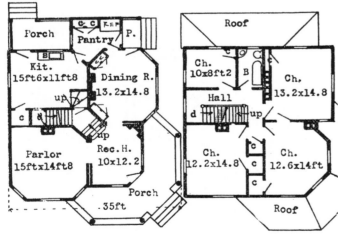

Hampton-Earlsboro No. 13 design 5647-A, story heights 10 and 9-ft 6, in the clear. See Hampton design page 646. Plans $10.

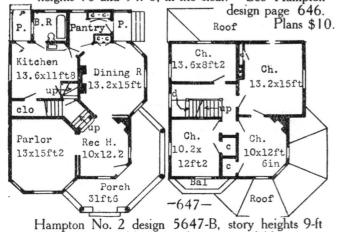

Hampton No. 2 design 5647-B, story heights 9-ft 6 and 9. See Hampton design page 646.

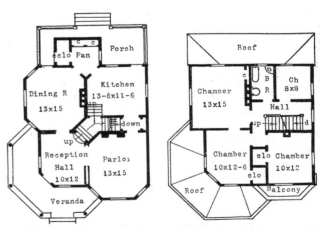

Hampton (reversed) design 5648-A, width over all 31 ft, story heights 9-ft 6 and 9. See design page 646 and following pages. Plans $10. (Use mirror to get reversed effect, See page 1023.)

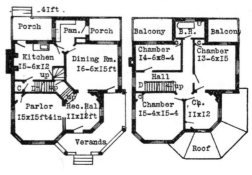

Hampton (Brick) design 5648-B, story heights 10 and 9-ft 6. See design page 646 and following pages. Plans $10.

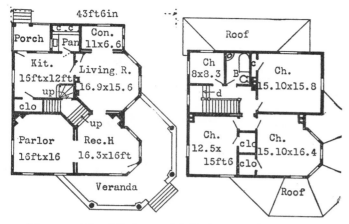

Hampton No. 12 design. 5649-A, story heights 11 and 10 ft. Plans $10.

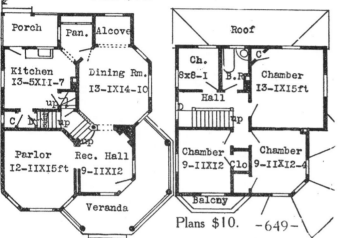

Hampton No. 4 design 5649-B, story heights 9-ft 6 and 9. See design page 646 and following pages.

Plans $10. -649-

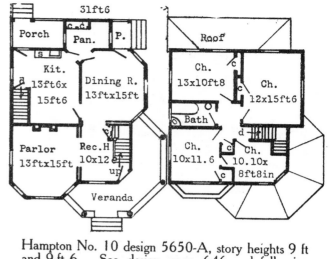

Hampton No. 10 design 5650-A, story heights 9 ft and 9-ft 6. See design page 646 and following pages. Plans $10.

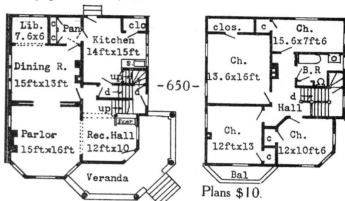

-650-

Plans $10.

Hampton No.19 design 5650-B, story heights 9 ft and 8 ft. See design page 664 and following

650

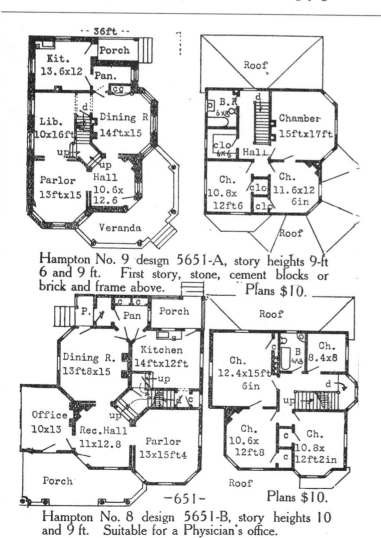

Hampton No. 9 design 5651-A, story heights 9-ft 6 and 9 ft. First story, stone, cement blocks or brick and frame above. Plans $10.

-651-

Plans $10.

Hampton No. 8 design 5651-B, story heights 10 and 9 ft. Suitable for a Physician's office.

Hampton No. 7 design 5652-A, story heights 9 ft each. See page 646 and following pages. Plans $10.

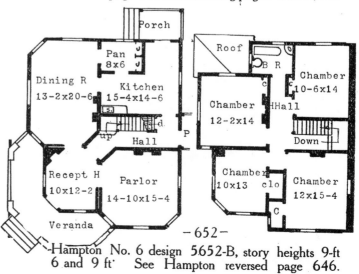

-652-

Hampton No. 6 design 5652-B, story heights 9-ft 6 and 9 ft. See Hampton reversed page 646.

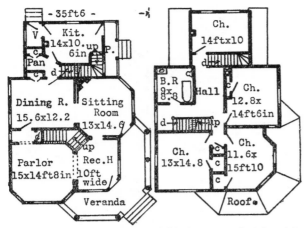

Hampton No. 5 design 5653-A, story heights 10 and 9-ft 6. Large parlor. See design page 646
Plans $10.

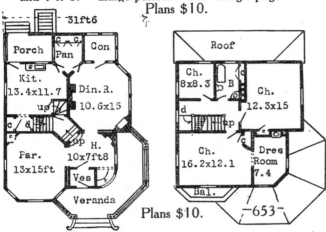

Hampton No. 15 design 5653-B, story heights 9-ft 6 and 9. See design page 646 and following

Plans $10. —653—

653—

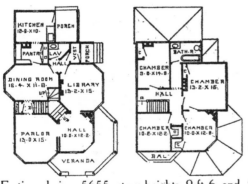

Festina design 5655, story heights 9-ft 6 and 9. See design page 646 and following pages. Plans $10.

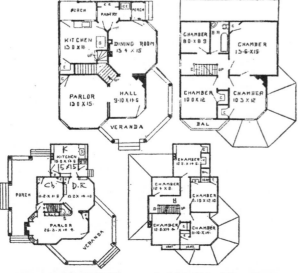

Maga design 5655-B, story heights 9 and 9. See page 646. Plans $15.
—655—

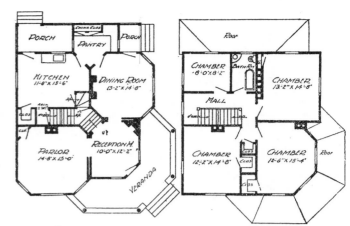

EARLSBORO COTTAGE.—Design 51-O; cost, $1,600 to $1,700; story heights, 10 ft. and 9 ft. 6 in. in the clear; plans $10. See Hampton design on page 218.

Earlsboro No. 2, Dexheimer design, with arch at reception hall in place of door to parlor; with dining-room used as library, connecting by sliding door with 15.6x12 ft. dining-room in place of kitchen; with 14x10 kitchen in rear; with pantry and rear stairs; plans $10. Continued

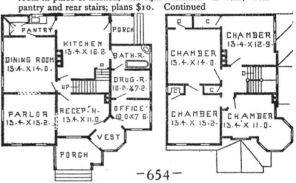

—654—

PHYSICIAN'S HOME.—Design 48-O; cost $1,800 to $2,200; plans $20; size 38x33 ft. 10 in.; story heights, 9 and 8 ft. 6 in. Same design as Pekin residence. See index for other physician's houses.

Linda Vista design 5656, width over all 44 ft, story heights 10 and 9-ft 6. Large southern-like rooms. Conservatory at rear. First story brick, stone or concrete blocks. Frame above. Plans $15.

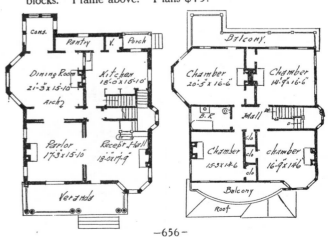

—656—

I consider your designs prettier than most others.—Albert O. Parker.

Lindley design 5657, width over all 40 ft. Clean-cut, plain exterior. Story heights 10 and 9 ft. Two splendid chambers in front. Plans $10.

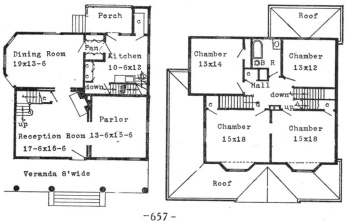

I had no fault to find with your plans. Everything fitted together well. I send photo today.—A. R. Welsh, Enfield, Wis.

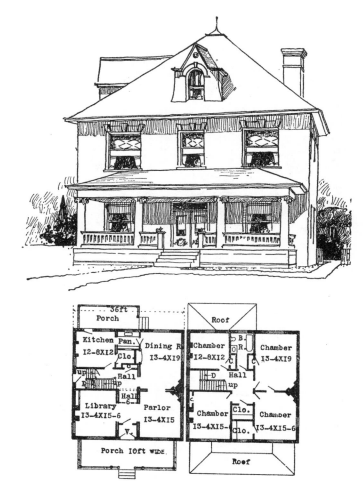

Lintha design 5658, story 9 ft each. Suitable for brick or concrete blocks. Plans $10.

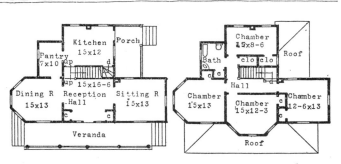

Brewster design 5659, extreme width 47 ft, 10-ft veranda, story heights 9 and 8 ft 6. Wide, imposing frontage, Plans $15.

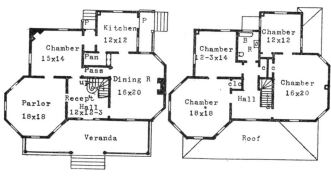

Lenoxdale design 5660, width over all 48-ft, story heights 10 and 9-ft 6. Fine clean cut exterior. Plans $10.

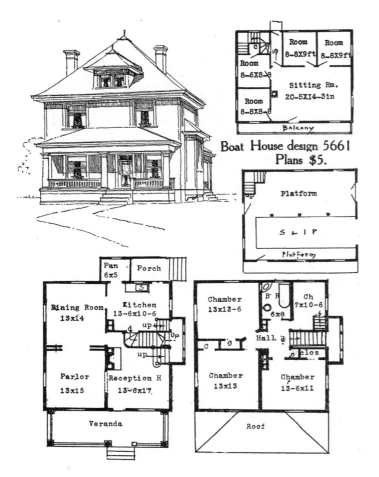

Boat House design 5661
Plans $5.

Lemoyne design 5661, width 28-ft 6, story heights 10 and 8-ft 6. Combination front and rear stairs. Plain practical plan and design. Plans $12.

EULA RESIDENCE.—Design 100,042-O; cost $1392 to $1498; story heights, 9 ft. 6 in.; size, 30x31; special features, large bay to dining-room. See page 225. Plans, $10, a very compact house, suitable for a parsonage.

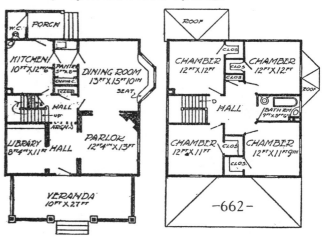

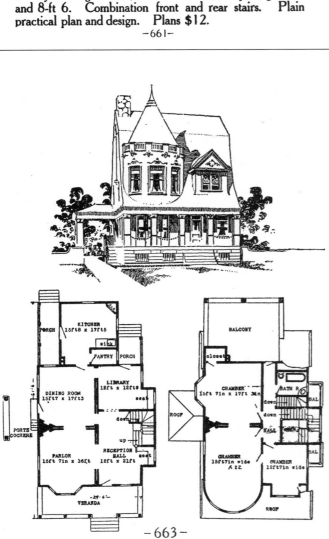

NAPOLEON RESIDENCE.—Design 2000-O; cost $2,690 to $2,770; plans $25. See page 65.

PIQUA RESIDENCE.—Design 8080M; in frame,$1898 to $1996, plans, $15; story heights, 9 ft. 6 in. Special features: Neat combination stairs with seat and bay; well-ventilated dining-room. See page 65.

Piqua No. 2 design 5664, story heights 9-ft 6. See design above. Plans $10.

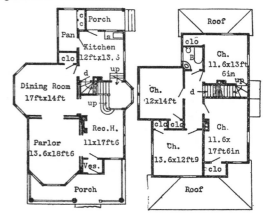

Harrisburg, Ark., May 11, 19(
Mr. Herbert C. Chivers,
    St. Louis, Mo.
Dear Sir:—
    The school house has been completed and is satisfactory in every respect.
    The cost of the building was just $59.00 below your estimate
    The members of the school board send you their hearty thanks for furnishing us with such a good building for the money
            Yours respectfully,
                    L. D. FREEMAN

DORSEY RESIDENCE.—Design 1846-N; cost in frame, $2,490 to $2,562; plans, $26; story heights, 9 ft. 6 in. and 8 ft. Special features: Large parlor; combination stairs; two good chambers in front; nook or space for conservatory back of dining-room.

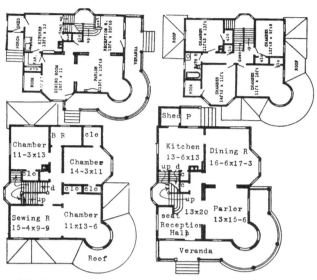

Sulphur Springs, Colo., May 19, 190
Mr Herbert C. Chivers,
St. Louis, Mo.
Dear Sir:—
The plans have arrived and I am very much pleased with them. So is everyone else that has seen them. I am now figuring with contractors and expect to have the house built by August.
Yours very truly,
J. N. PETTINGELL,
(County Clerk and Recorder)

Dorsey No. 2 design 5665-B, Plans $25.

story heights 9-ft 6 and 8.

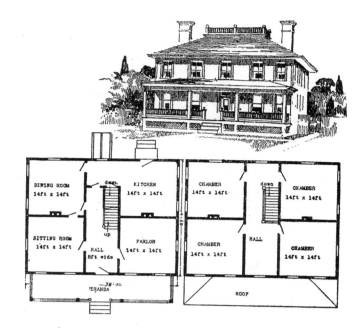

LENNON RESIDENCE.—Design 1935M; cost in frame $1,092 to $1,280; plans $10. See page 65.

ROWELL RESIDENCE. — Brock design 12-O; cost, $2,100 to $2,450; story heights, 9 ft. 6 in. and 9 ft.; plans, $20. See design on page 502.

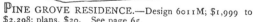

PINE GROVE RESIDENCE.—Design 6011M; $1,999 to $2,298; plans, $20. See page 65.

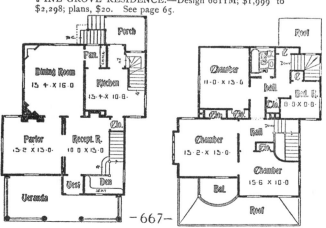

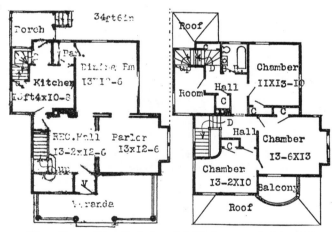

Pine Grove No. 2 design 5668-A, story heights 10 and 9 ft. See reversed design opposite page 667. Plans $20.

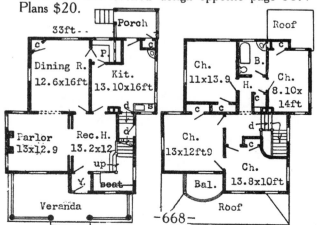

Pine Grove No. 3 design 5668-B, story heights 9 ft and 9. See design page 667. Plans $20.

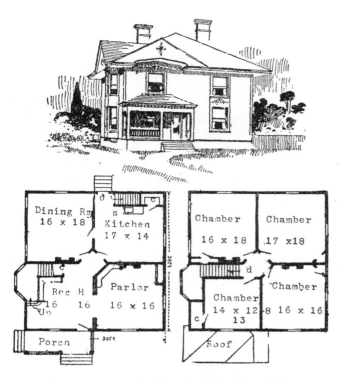

JENNVILLE RESIDENCE.—Design 1919.O; cost in frame $1,192 to $1,285, plans $10. We have this without front gable; with neat dormer window in front. See page 65.

We are now contemplating building again at no distant date and when we do will build a two-story house, and at that time I shall write you, as I think "Chivers" is there with the goods when it comes to artistic and practical homes. Mrs. McC. thinks likewise.

GEORGE T. McCANDLESS, Ponca City, Okla.

669

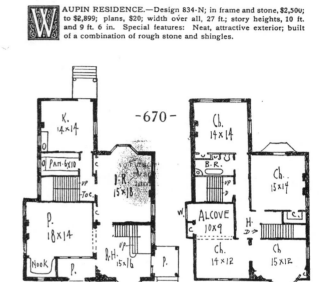

WAUPIN RESIDENCE.—Design 834-N; in frame and stone, $2,500; to $2,899; plans, $20; width over all, 27 ft.; story heights, 10 ft. and 9 ft. 6 in. Special features: Neat, attractive exterior; built of a combination of rough stone and shingles.

-670-

AKDALE RESIDENCE.—Design 1044-N; in frame, $2,198 to $2,498; plans, $15; width, 33 ft. 6 in. by 39 ft.; width over all, 38 ft. 4 in.; story height, 10 ft. Special features: Corner bay; central reception hall; large pantry, 6x13 ft. Modifications: Nook space could be used as an additional chamber; linen closet would be large enough for girl's room.

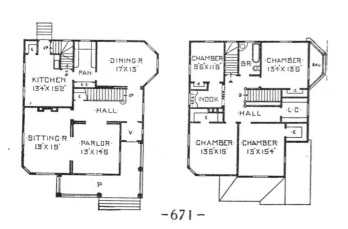

-671-

Rathburn design 5672, story heights 10 and 9-ft. 6. Colonial design. Pretentious reception hall and stairs, side entrance and conservatory. Plans $25.

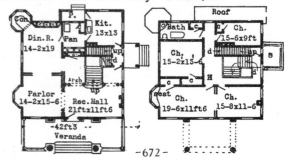

-672-

Plans, specifications and details of residence are here. I think they are fine. Am well satisfied.—G. W. Buchanan, Chippewa Lake, Ohio.

Ratna design 5673, width 33-ft., width over steps and all 55-ft., story heights 10 and 9-ft.   Plans $15.

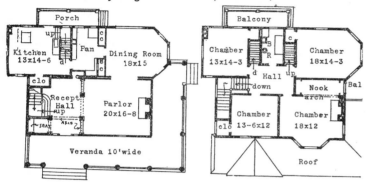

Porch

up

Kitchen
13x14-6

Pan

Dining Room
18x15

clo

Recept
Hall
up

Parlor
20x16-8

SEAT

Veranda 10' wide

Balcony

B
R

Chamber
13x14-3

Chamber
18x14-3

Hall
down

up

Nook
arch

Bal

clo

Chamber
13-6x12

Chamber
18x12

Roof

Paragould, Ark., April 15, 19(
Mr. Herbert C. Chivers,
    St. Louis, Mo.
Dear Sir:—
    You will see from the enclosed picture that
I built the house according to plans as furnished by you. It is just as complete as a small
house could be. I am much pleased with the
floor plan as well as the exterior, and as the
building has a south frontage it will be an ideal
summer home.
                        Yours truly,
                        A. G. DICKSON, M. D.

—673—

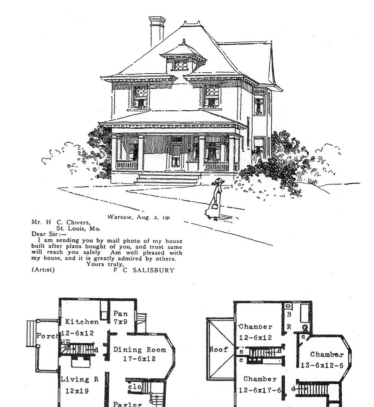

Kitchen
12-6x12

Pan
7x9

Porch

Dining Room
17-6x12

Living R
12x19

clo

Parlor
14x14-7

up

Veranda

Roof

Chamber
12-6x12

B
R

c

Chamber
13-6x12-6

Chamber
12-6x17-6

d

Chamber
11-4x8-6

clo

Roof

—674—

Rangeley design 5674, widtd 28-ft, width over steps and all 40-ft., story heights 9 and 8-ft. 6.   Plans $10.

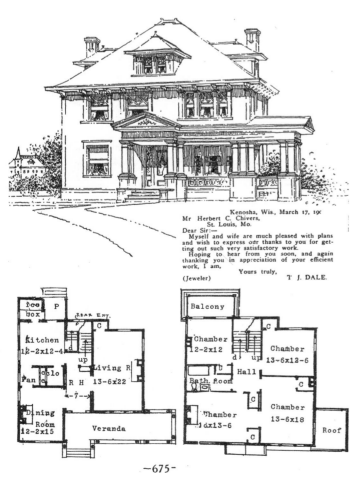

Ice
Box

P

REAR ENT.

c

Kitchen
12-2x12-4

up

Living R
13-6x22

Pan

clo

R H

7

Dining
Room
12-2x15

Veranda

Balcony

Chamber
12-2x12

up

Chamber
13-6x12-6

Hall

Bath Room

c

c

Chamber
16x13-6

c

Chamber
13-6x18

c

Roof

Kenosha, Wis., March 17, 19(
Mr Herbert C. Chivers,
    St. Louis, Mo.
Dear Sir:—
    Myself and wife are much pleased with plans
and wish to express our thanks to you for getting out such very satisfactory work.
    Hoping to hear from you soon, and again
thanking you in appreciation of your efficient
work, I am,
                        Yours truly,
(Jeweler)   T J. DALE.

—675—

Ramirena design 5675, width 35-ft., width over all 42-ft, story heights 10 ft. and 9-ft. 6.   Plans $15.

Quintana design 5676, width 28-ft. 6, width over porch and all 36-ft, story heights 9-ft. and 8-ft. 6.   Plans $10.

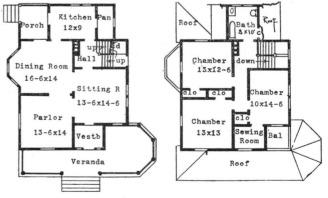

Porch

Kitchen
12x9

Pan

up

d

Hall

up

Dining Room
16-6x14

Sitting R
13-6x14-6

Parlor
13-6x14

Vestb

Veranda

Roof

Bath
8x10

c

Chamber
13x12-6

down

clo

clo

Chamber
10x14-6

Chamber
13x13

clo

Sewing
Room

Bal

Roof

ORDER BLANK.

Dear Sir:
    Please make preliminary drawings (for approval) complete working
drawings, details and legally worded specifications for which I agree to pay
you $............. upon delivery of the completed work.   Respectfully,

Name.....................

—676—

 OMASTON RESIDENCE.—Design 1830-N; cost in frame, $2,290 to $2,498; plans, $20. Special features: Large parlor; combination front and rear stairs; attractive corner window; large pantry; balcony in rear.

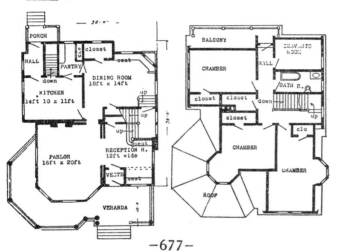

Mr. Herbert C. Chivers,
St. Louis, Mo.
Dear Sir:—
The house for which you prepared plans suits me exactly. I could not be better pleased. I consider distance no barrier when dealing with an architect of your ability, as you seem to know intuitively what pleases one.
Very truly yours,
W. S. McGUNNEGLE,
Cashier, Merchants Nat. Bank of Meadville.

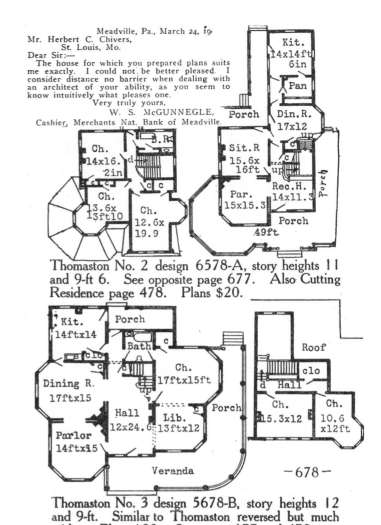

Thomaston No. 2 design 6578-A, story heights 11 and 9-ft 6. See opposite page 677. Also Cutting Residence page 478. Plans $20.

Thomaston No. 3 design 5678-B, story heights 12 and 9-ft. Similar to Thomaston reversed but much wider. Plans $20. See pages 677 and 478.

Quita design 5679, width 36-ft. 6, story heights 9-ft. 6 and 9. Plans $10.

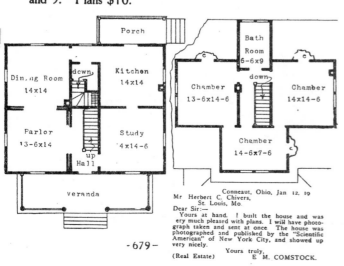

Conneaut, Ohio, Jan 12, 19
Mr Herbert C. Chivers,
St. Louis, Mo.
Dear Sir:—
Yours at hand. I built the house and was very much pleased with plans. I will have photograph taken and sent at once The house was photographed and published by the "Scientific American" of New York City, and showed up very nicely.
Yours truly,
(Real Estate) E. M. COMSTOCK.

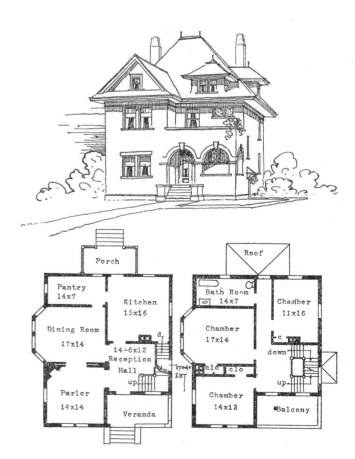

Quitaque design 5680, width 30-ft. 6, width over all 33-ft. 6, story heights 9-ft. 6 and 9. Suitable for brick or concrete blocks. Plans $10.

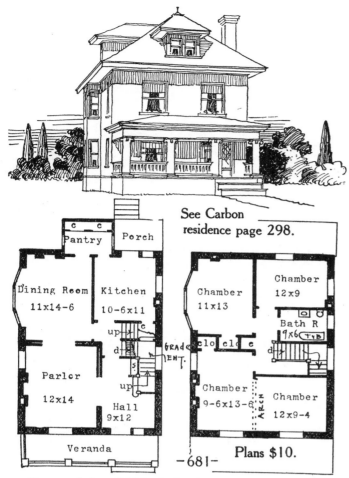

See Carbon
residence page 298.

Poynor design 5681, in brick, width 24-ft, story
heights 9-ft 6 and 9. Combination stairs, well-
lighted dining room and chamber above.

-681-

Plans $10.

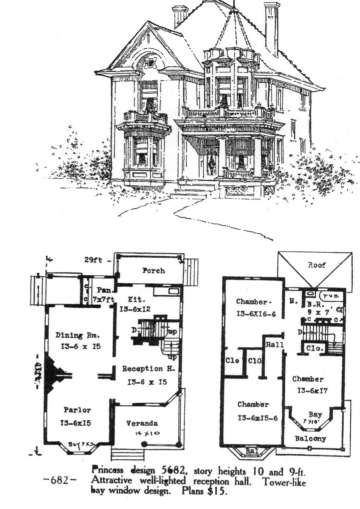

Princess design 5682, story heights 10 and 9-ft.
Attractive well-lighted reception hall. Tower-like
bay window design. Plans $15.

-682-

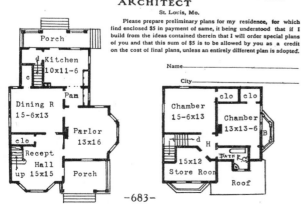

PRELIMINARY PLAN
HERBERT C. CHIVERS PROPOSICION
ARCHITECT
St. Louis, Mo.

Please prepare preliminary plans for my residence, for which
find enclosed $5 in payment of same, it being understood that if I
build from the ideas contained therein I will order special plans
of you and that this sum of $5 is to be allowed by you as a credit
on the cost of final plans, unless an entirely different plan is adopted.

Name_____
City_____

-683-

Plano design 5683, width 30-ft., width over all 33-ft.,
story heights 9 and 8-ft. 6. Neat bay-like effect at Reception Hall, Plans $15.

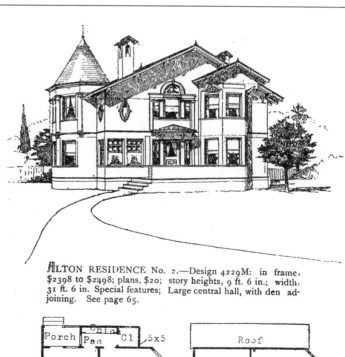

ALTON RESIDENCE No. 2.—Design 4229M: in frame,
$2398 to $2498; plans, $20; story heights, 9 ft. 6 in.; width,
31 ft. 6 in. Special features; Large central hall, with den adjoining. See page 65.

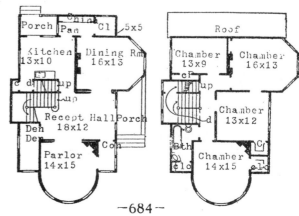

-684-

HARTWOOD RESIDENCE.—Design 2030-O; cost in frame, $2,090 to $2,280; plans $20. See page 65.

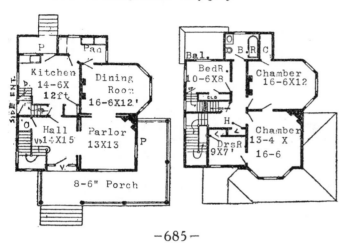

SOLON RESIDENCE.—Design 2242-N; cost in frame, $1,392 to $1,456; plans, $10; full story heights. Special features: Inexpensive yet attractive tower-like corner; neat, clean-cut exterior. The best portion of this house is not cut up with stairs.

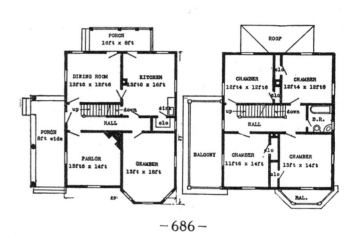

JOY RESIDENCE.—Design 1560-N; in frame, $1,500 to $1,800; plans, $10; width, 27 ft. 10 in. by 45 ft.; width over all, 27 ft. 10 in.; story heights, 9 ft. 6 in. and 9 ft.; no attic. Special features: A neat, clean-cut colonial exterior; easy to erect; attractive tower.

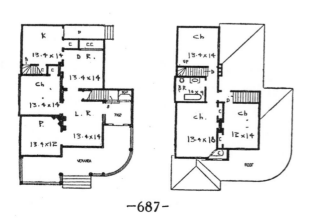

heights 9-ft 6 and 8-ft 6.

A good corner-lot house.

Plans $25.

Thornburg design 5688-A.

See plans on page 689.

Plans $25.

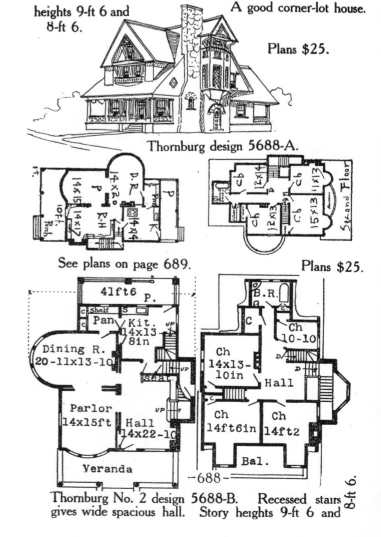

Thornburg No. 2 design 5688-B. Recessed stairs gives wide spacious hall. Story heights 9-ft 6 and 8-ft 6.

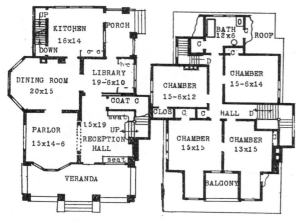

Thornburg No. 3 design 4689-A, story heights 10 and 9-ft. 6. See design page 688. Width 31-ft. 6, width over all 44. Plans $25.

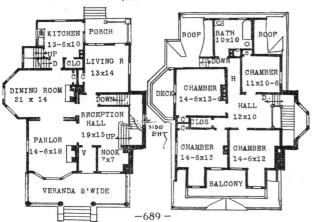

Thornburg No. 4 design 4689-B, story heights 10 and 9-ft.-6. See design page 688. Plans $25.

—689—

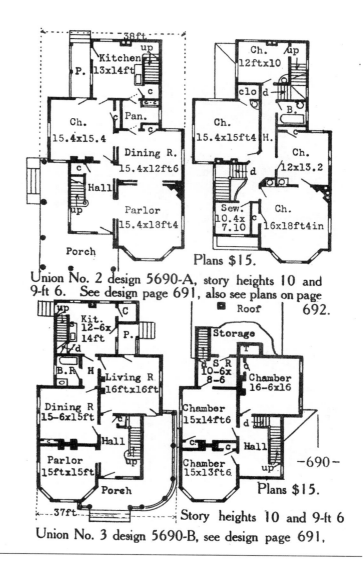

Plans $15.

Union No. 2 design 5690-A, story heights 10 and 9-ft 6. See design page 691, also see plans on page 692.

Plans $15.

Story heights 10 and 9-ft 6

Union No. 3 design 5690-B, see design page 691,

—690—

UNION RESIDENCE.—Design 6013-O; in frame, $2309 to $2480; plans, $25; width over all, 32 ft. 2 in. x 52 ft. 2 in.; story heights, 10 ft. and 9 ft.; Attic 8 ft. See Mineola Residence—See Frogmore Residence page 692.

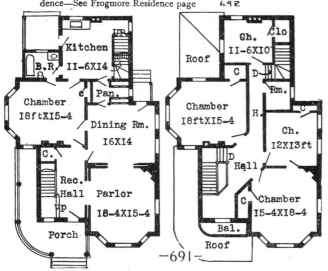

—691—

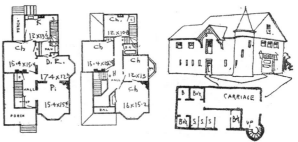

FRAGMORE RESIDENCE. — Boyd Design 38M; cost $2480 to $2970; story heights, 10 ft. and 9 ft; plans, $25 see Union Residence page

—691—

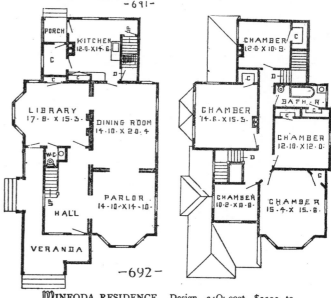

—692—

MINEODA RESIDENCE.—Design 240; cost $2399 to $2499; 36 ft. 6 in. x 52 ft. 2 in.; story heights, 10 and 9 ft. 6 in. Design similar to Union Residence on page but more attractive. Plans, $25.

GALVA COTTAGE.—Design 2393M; cost in frame, $3,-500 to $4,500; plans, $45. Special features: Well lighted, cheerful chamber next to dining-room and library; this could be used as an office. See page 65.

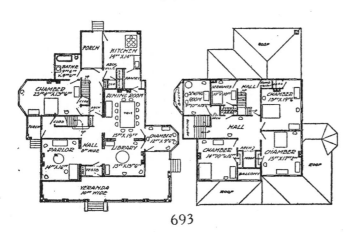

693

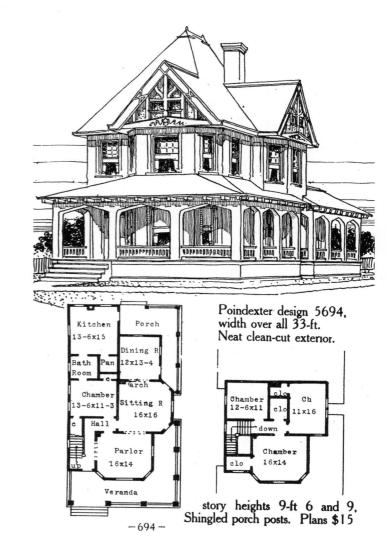

Poindexter design 5694, width over all 33-ft. Neat clean-cut exterior.

story heights 9-ft 6 and 9. Shingled porch posts. Plans $15

—694—

Perdue design 5695, width 38 ft, story heights 9-ft 6 and 8-ft 6. Plain clean-cut exterior. Plans $10.

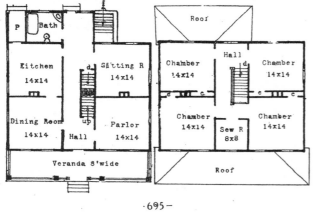

·695·

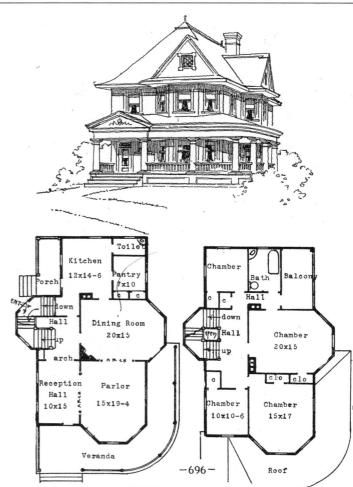

Tancitaro design 5696, width 26-ft 6, extreme width 39 ft. Story heights 10 and 9 ft. Large rooms, suitable for southern climate. Plans $10.

—696—

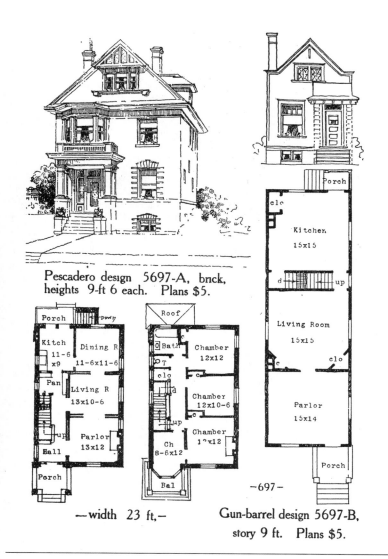

Pescadero design 5697-A, brick, heights 9-ft 6 each. Plans $5.

Kitchen 15x15

Porch

clo

d   up

Living Room 15x15

clo

c

Parlor 15x14

Porch

—697—

Porch   powdy

Kitch 11-6 x9

Dining R 11-6x11-6

Pan

Living R 13x10-6

Parlor 13x12

Hall   up

Porch

—width 23 ft,—

Roof

Bath

Chamber 12x12

clo

c

Chamber 12x10-6

up

Chamber 12x12

Ch 8-6x12

Bal

Gun-barrel design 5697-B, story 9 ft.   Plans $5.

ELMTON RESIDENCE.—Design 1787M; in frame, $1,892 to $1,925; plans, $10. In brick, $2,980 to $3,590; plans, $45.

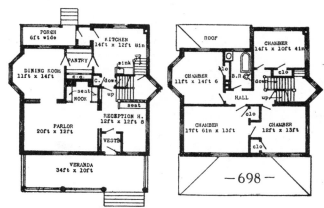

PORCH 6ft wide

KITCHEN 14ft x 12ft 8in

PANTRY

DINING ROOM 11ft x 14ft

c.c.   C. down

seat
NOOK   up

RECEPTION H. 12ft x 12ft 8

PARLOR 20ft x 12ft

VEST

VERANDA 34ft x 10ft

ROOF

CHAMBER 14ft x 10ft 4in

CHAMBER 11ft x 14ft 6   B.R   clo

HALL   up

CHAMBER 17ft 6in x 13ft

CHAMBER 12ft x 13ft

clo

—698—

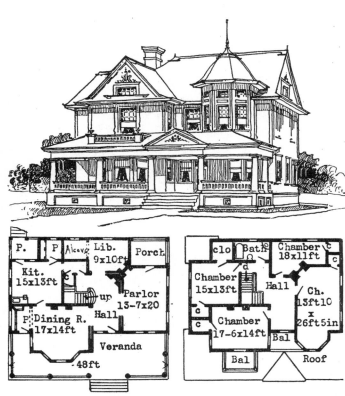

P.   P   Alcov   Lib. 9x10ft   Porch

Kit. 15x13ft   up   Parlor 13-7x20

P Dining R. 17x14ft   Hall

Veranda

—48ft—

clo   Bath

Chamber 15x13ft   Hall

Chamber 17-6x14ft

Bal

Chamber 18x11ft

Ch. 13ft10 x 26ft5in

Bal   Roof

Pinelawn No. 2 design 5699, wide dignified front. See page 321. Plans $25

The house I built last year from your plans is much admired.
B. F. SHEETS, Oregon, Ill.

—699—

We believe our house is exactly right in plan and design.. We have no fault to find whatever.   It looks pretty and cozy.
MRS. WILLIAM PETERS, Wenewoc, Wis.

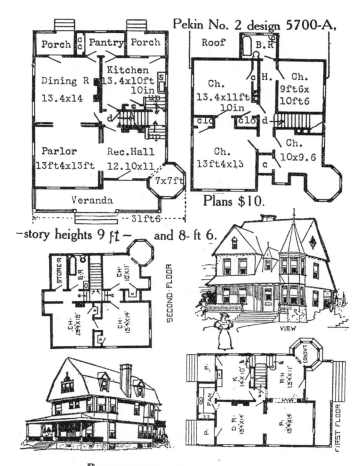

Pekin No. 2 design 5700-A,

Porch   Pantry   Porch

Dining R 13.4x14

Kitchen 13.4x10ft 10in

Parlor 13ft4x13ft

Rec.Hall 12.10x11

7x7ft

Veranda

—31ft6—

—story heights 9 ft—   and 8-ft 6.

Roof   B.R

Ch. 13.4x11ft 10in

clo

Ch. 13ft4x13

Ch. 9ft6x 10ft6

clo

Ch. 10x9.6

c

Plans $10.

STORE R   B.R   CH. 10'X12'

CH. 13'4"X12'   CH. 13'4"X14'

SECOND FLOOR

VIEW

D.R. 13'4"X14'   K. 14'X10'   R.H. 13'4"X11'

P.   PAN   P.   CONS'V'T

FIRST FLOOR

PEKIN RESIDENCE.—Design 1005-O; in frame, $1450 to $1598; plans; $10; width, 27.10 x 28 ft. 2 in.; width over all, 32 ft; story heights, 9 and 8 ft. 6 in.; Special features: compact plan; attractive exterior; can furnish floor plans for either design. See page 65.

700—

MOBERLY RESIDENCE.—Design 4369M; in frame, $1,500 to $1,800; plans, $15; story heights, 10 ft.; special features: Large, well-ventilated dining-room.

Moberly Res. No. 2, Russell design, same plan as above, with porch extending around across front of sitting-room; with 13-in. brick walls on first story and frame above; a very attractive design; with front rooms enlarged to 13x15 ft.; with w. c. separate from bath-room; with extra closet to front chamber; with two chambers in attic. See pgae 65.

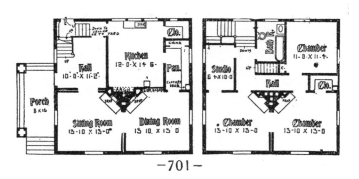

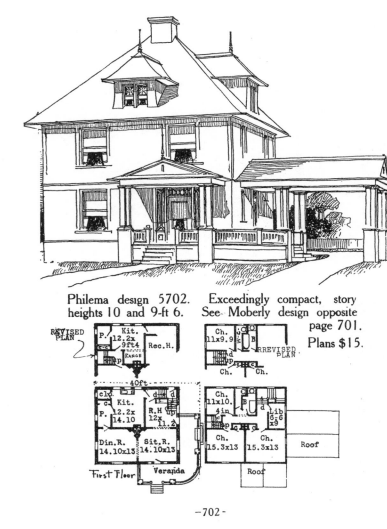

Philema design 5702. Exceedingly compact, story heights 10 and 9-ft 6. See Moberly design opposite page 701. Plans $15.

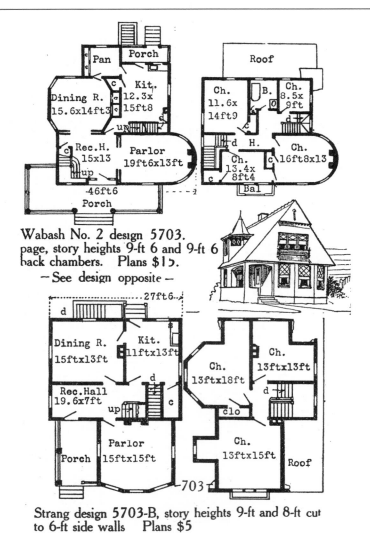

Wabash No. 2 design 5703. page, story heights 9-ft 6 and 9-ft 6 back chambers. Plans $15.

— See design opposite —

Strang design 5703-B, story heights 9-ft and 8-ft cut to 6-ft side walls   Plans $5

WABASH RESIDENCE.—Design 1876-O; in frame, $1,660 to $1,976; plans, $15; with octagon bay, which is more practical to construct; width, 29 ft. 9 in. by 27 ft.; width over all, 38 ft.; story heights, 8 ft. 6 in. and 8 ft.; special features: Pleasing outlines; designed for a stained shingle effect; fire proof closet in kitchen; quaint window effect in reception room. Wabash No. 2, Tyler des., with central fire-places left out; with rear stairs up from kitchen; with built-in china closet in dining-room; with front porch extending around to stair side of house; with fire-place in bay to parlor and room above. See page 65.

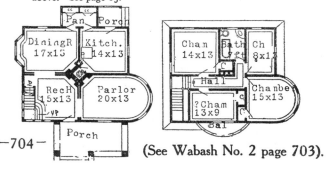

(See Wabash No. 2 page 703).

Dafner Residence design 5705. Plans $10.

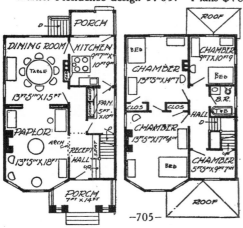

-705-

DAFTER RESIDENCE.—Design 100.048-O; size 34:6x32.
cost $1030 to $1190; story heights, 1st 9 ft. 6 in. and 9 ft.
special features pleasant outlook in front, large pantry, neat
design; plans,$10. See page 365.

ERGUSON RESIDENCE.—Design 4229-N; in frame, $1,298 to
$1,399; plans, $10; width over all, 40 ft. Special features: Good
outlines to roof. Modifications: Small chamber below, can be
a part of reception hall, with arch in line with front door. Ferguson Residence No. 2; in frame, $2,390 to $2,480; plans, $20;
story heights, 10 ft. and 9 ft. in the clear. Special features: Striking design; well-ventilated parlor. Have $10 stock plans with the following
changes: Kitchen back of parlor as dining-room; also with kitchen wing
eliminated. Ferguson No. 3, Gladson design, similar to this with den
back of a circular-shaped parlor, and bath back of this.

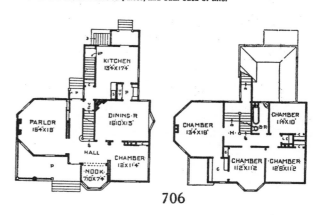

706

Ferguson No. 4 design 5707-A, 9-ft 6 and
9-ft 6, width over all 40 ft.
See pages 707-708. Plans $10.
See reversed design below.

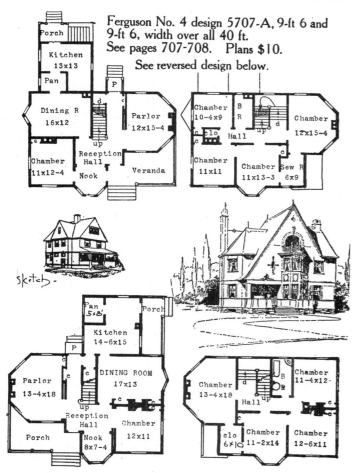

Ferguson No. 5 design 5707-B, story heights 9-ft 6 and
9-ft 6. Extreme width 40 ft. See design above. See
pages 706-708. Plans $10.
-707-

Portland No. 2 design 5708, see exterior page 709.
story heights 9-ft 6 and 9. Plans $15.

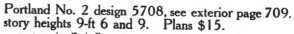

Ferguson No. 2 design 5708, story heights 10-ft and
9-ft in the clear. See pages 706-707. Plans $20.

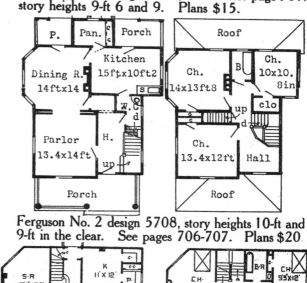

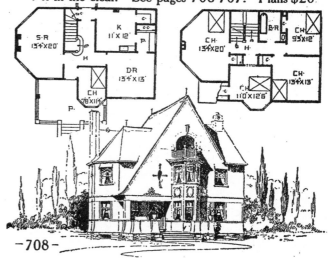

-708-

PORTLAND RESIDENCE.—Design 6012-N; in frame, $1,598 to $1,879; plans, $15; width, 23.6x35 ft. 7 in.; story heights. 9.6 and 9 ft.; attic, 8 ft. Portland Residence No. 2, Stephenson design, side porch left off, covered porch across front; porch in place of den; kitchen, 15x11 ft. 2 in. projecting on side; stairs to attic in place of hall closet.

ELMWOOD RESIDENCE.—Design 9060-N; in frame, $1,500 to $1,989; plans, $15; story heights, 9 ft. 6 in. and 9 ft.; full story except 18 inches cut off to outer corner of front chamber. Elmwood reversed; width, 28 ft. 8 in. by 33 ft. 9 in.; width over all, 36 ft. Special features: Front rooms are not cut off by stairs as customary.

—709—

(See Portland No. 2 page 708).

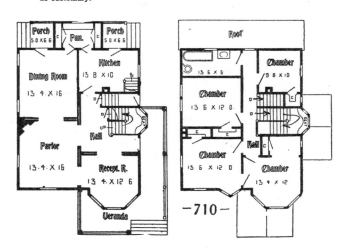

—710—

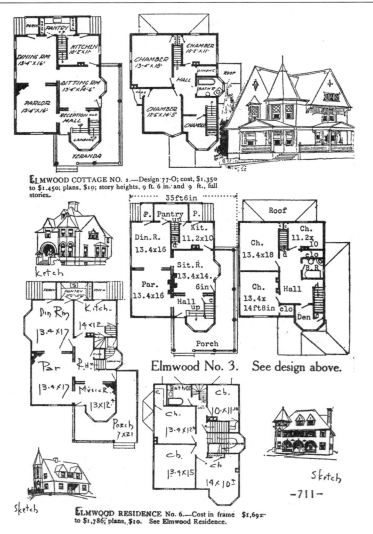

ELMWOOD COTTAGE NO. 2.—Design 77-O; cost, $1,350 to $1,450; plans, $10; story heights, 9 ft. 6 in. and 9 ft., full stories.

Elmwood No. 3. See design above.

—711—

ELMWOOD RESIDENCE No. 6.—Cost in frame $1,692 to $1,786; plans, $10. See Elmwood Residence.

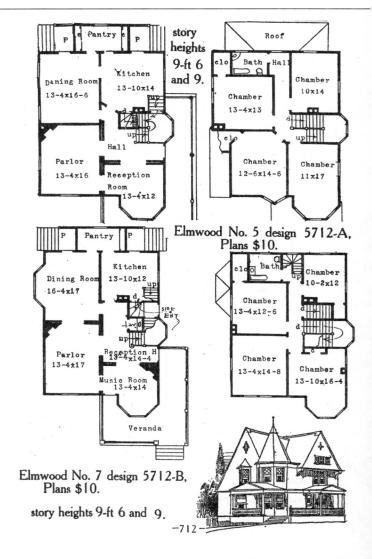

Elmwood No. 5 design 5712-A, Plans $10.

Elmwood No. 7 design 5712-B, Plans $10.

story heights 9-ft 6 and 9.

—712—

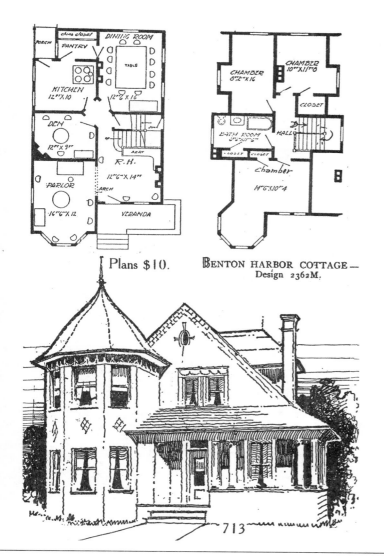

Plans $10.

BENTON HARBOR COTTAGE.—
Design 2362M.

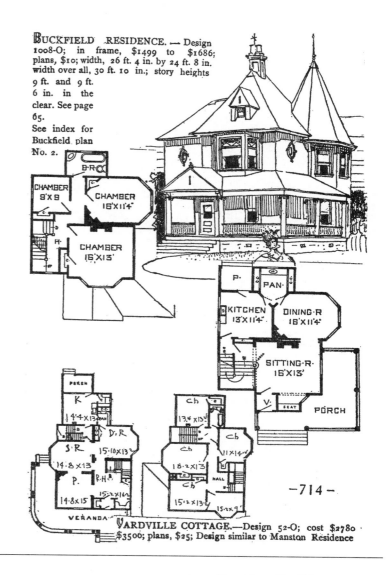

BUCKFIELD RESIDENCE.—Design 1008-O; in frame, $1499 to $1686; plans, $10; width, 26 ft. 4 in. by 24 ft. 8 in. width over all, 30 ft. 10 in.; story heights 9 ft. and 9 ft. 6 in. in the clear. See page 65.
See index for Buckfield plan No. 2.

YARDVILLE COTTAGE.—Design 52-O; cost $2780 $3500; plans, $25; Design similar to Manston Residence

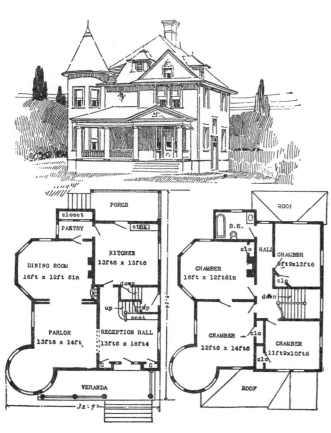

BELVIDEN RESIDENCE.—Design 1793M; cost in frame, $1,892 to $1,990; plans, $10. See page 65.

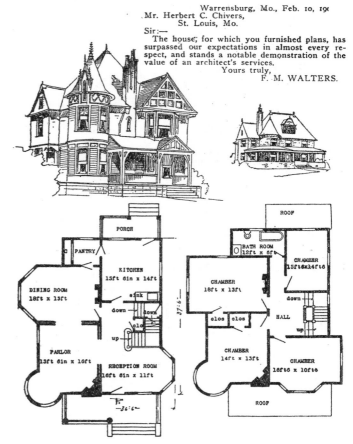

Warrensburg, Mo., Feb. 10, 19(
Mr. Herbert C. Chivers,
St. Louis, Mo.
Sir:—
The house, for which you furnished plans, has surpassed our expectations in almost every respect, and stands a notable demonstration of the value of an architect's services.
Yours truly,
F. M. WALTERS.

STEMO RESIDENCE.—Design 1847-N; cost in frame, $2,290 to $2,480; plans, $25 Special features: Attractive chimney and tower; neat, clean-cut exterior; well-lighted reception room.

I take pleasure in saying the plans you made for me were entirely satisfactory in every respect.
CHARLES SHINKLE (Southern Ice & Coal Co.) NASHVILLE.

(2nd testimonial)

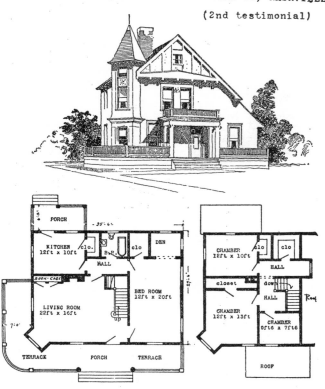

CONSTANTINE RESIDENCE.—Design 1981-N; cost in frame, $1,492 to $1,598; plans, $10. Special features: Large living-room; good sensible and home-like arrangement on first floor; large bed-room; wide spacious veranda.

--Plans $20--

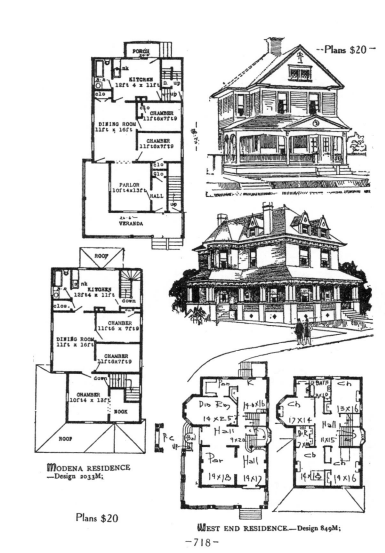

MODENA RESIDENCE
—Design 2033M;

Plans $20

WEST END RESIDENCE.—Design 849M;

PALO RESIDENCE.—Design 903M; in frame, $3,550 to $3,990; plans, $30; story heights, 10 ft. Special features: Semi-circular colonial porch; the sizes of rooms are: Parlor, 17x23 ft.; library, 17x14 ft.; dining-room, 17x23 ft.; kitchen, 15x13 ft.; hall, 15x30 ft. See page 65.

PROMPTNESS IN REPLIES.

IN doing business by mail I feel that I can serve you more promptly than local talent, as I make it a point to be very prompt in replies, especially after positive final instructions are obtained. The economy in construction which I practice is of considerable importance, besides you won't see that everlasting "sameness" in my designs.

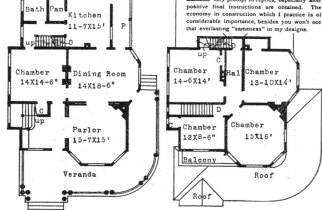

Cragmont design 5719, story heights 10 and 9-ft. Large rooms. Plans $10. Neat clean-cut exterior.

ILLINOIS STATE-LICENSED ARCHITECT

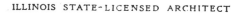

CITY RESIDENCE.—Design 1025-O; plans, $75 with any changes; cost $7,500 to $8,500.

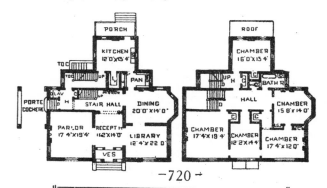

SPECIAL ATTENTION GIVEN TO BUILDINGS OF SPECIAL REQUIREMENTS ✠ ✠ BUILDINGS OF A MONUMENTAL AND ORNAMENTAL CHARACTER FINELY EXECUTED IN DESIGN AND DETAIL ✠ ✠ ✠ ✠

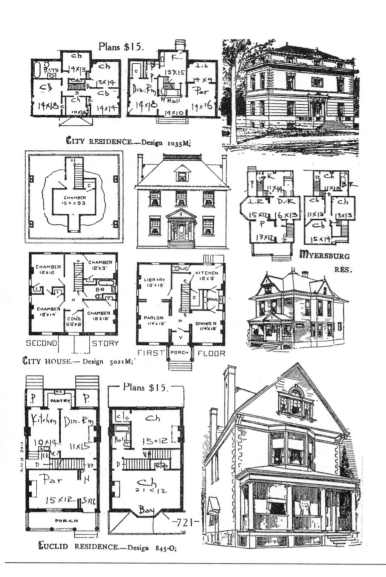

Plans $15.

CITY RESIDENCE.—Design 1035M;

CITY HOUSE.—Design 5021M;

SECOND STORY

FIRST PORCH FLOOR

MYERSBURG RES.

Plans $15.

EUCLID RESIDENCE.—Design 845-O;

—721—

HILLSBORO RESIDENCE.—Design 4221M; in frame, $2,690 to $3,500; plans, $30, with changes; width over all, 49 ft.; story heights, 10 ft.; special features; Attractive and striking outlines, yet modest in detail. See page 65.

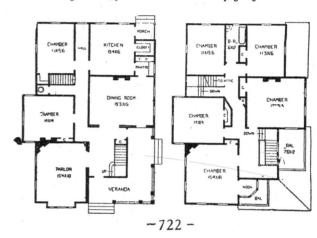

—722—

 HILADELPHIA RESIDENCE.—Design 866-O; in frame, $1,998 to $2,498; in brick veneer, $2,200 to $3,500; plans, $20. Philadelphia Residence No. 2, Westling design, with 14 ft. 8 in. by 13 ft. dining-room; with 8x9 ft. den where pantry is; with 5x8 ft. serving pantry where kitchen closet is; with additional 10x12 ft. chamber over dining-room; with 4 ft. stairs; with entire plan reversed.

For Philadelphia Residence No. 2 see page 723.

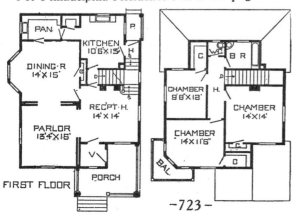

FIRST FLOOR

—723—

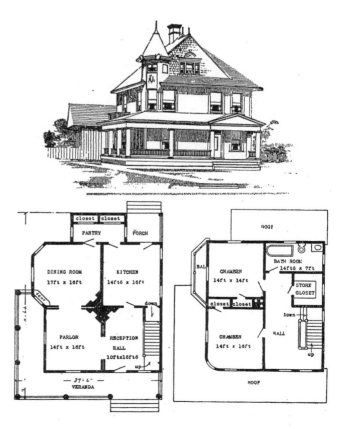

 GNEW RESIDENCE.—Design 1792-N; cost in frame, $1,692 to $1,780; plans, $10. Special features: Large rooms; simple, neat tower effect; large veranda. A good corner-lot house.

724

You can very readily realize that an architect at a distance would be likely to design something novel and different to the common-place, he would be disinterested as to who was contractor, and would probably save you the cost of plans many times over.

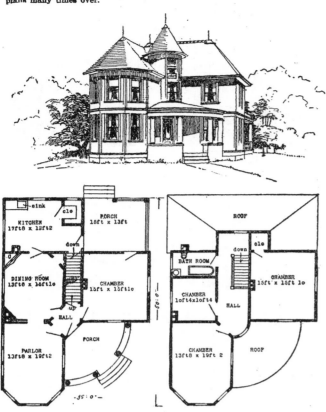

ENCORCES RESIDENCE.—Design 1978M; cost in frame $1,890 to $1,998; plans $15. See page 65.

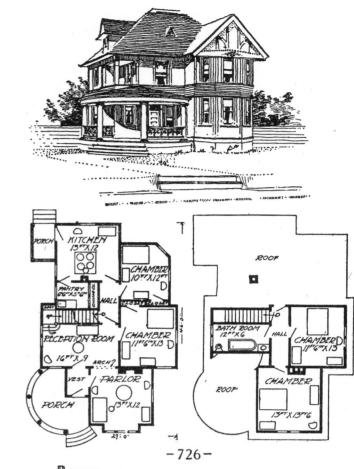

—726—

BRYSON RESIDENCE.—Design 2007M; cost in frame $2,290 to $2,382; plans $25. See page 65.

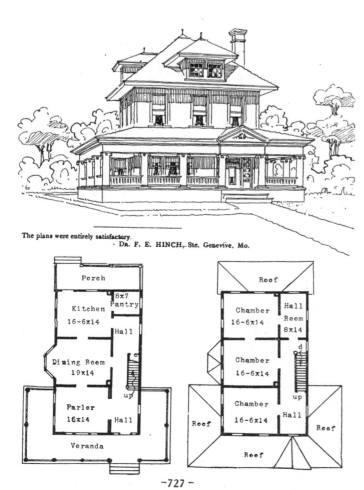

The plans were entirely satisfactory.
— Dr. F. E. HINCH, Ste. Genevieve, Mo.

Paskenta design 5727, story heights 10 ft, width 26 ft. Extreme width 42 ft. Plans $10.

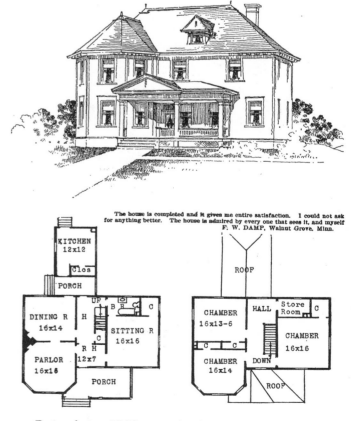

The house is completed and it gives me entire satisfaction. I could not ask for anything better. The house is admired by every one that sees it, and myself
F. W. DAMP, Walnut Grove, Minn.

Parina design 5728, story heights 10 and 9 ft. Extreme width 46 ft. Plans $10.

DESIGN 841.

Pamlico design 5729, story heights 9-ft 6 and 9. Stately dignified stone house. Adaptable to many plans. This design could be built to good effect in concrete blocks, brick or even shingles. Plans $35.

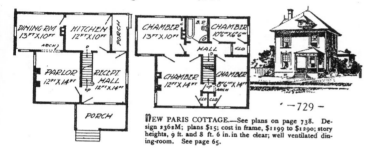

—729—

NEW PARIS COTTAGE.—See plans on page 738. Design 236M; plans $15; cost in frame, $1199 to $1290; story heights, 9 ft. and 8 ft. 6 in. in the clear; well ventilated dining-room. See page 65.

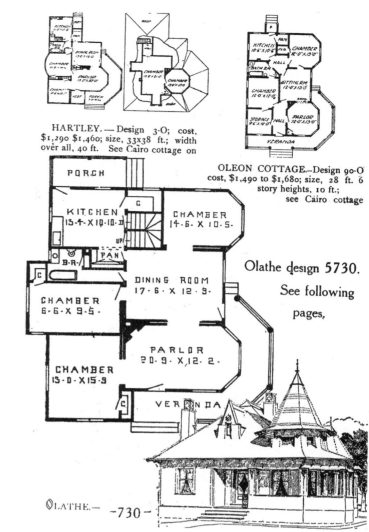

HARTLEY.— Design 3-O; cost, $1,290 $1,460; size, 33x38 ft.; width over all, 40 ft. See Cairo cottage on

OLEON COTTAGE.—Design 90-O cost, $1,490 to $1,680; size, 28 ft. 6 story heights, 10 ft.; see Cairo cottage

PORCH

KITCHEN 13·4·X 10·10·

CHAMBER 14·6· X 10·5·

DINING ROOM 17·6· X 12·9·

CHAMBER 6·6· X 9·5·

PARLOR 20·9· X 12·2·

CHAMBER 13·0· X 15·9

VERANDA

Olathe design 5730. See following pages.

OLATHE.— —730—

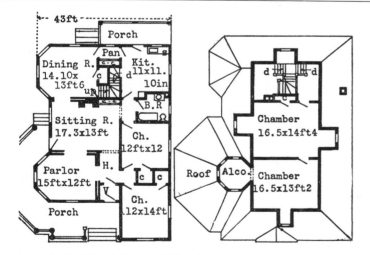

43ft

Porch

Pan.

Dining R. 14.10x 13ft6

Kit. 11x11. 10in

B.R

Sitting R. 17.3x13ft

Ch. 12ftx12

Parlor 15ftx12ft

H.

Ch. 12x14ft

Porch

Roof Alco.

Chamber 16.5x14ft4

Chamber 16.5x13ft2

Cairo No. 2 design 5731-A, story heights 9-ft and 8-ft 6. See design page 730. Plans $10.

46ft

Porch

Kit. 13.5x 10.8

Ch. 13.9x10

Dining R. 17.3x12.7

Ch. 17ftx13ft

Parlor 21ftx12ft

Ch. 13x15.5

Porch

B.R

Ch. 14.5x13ft

Stor 9.4x 9ft4

Ch. 12.10x 12ft6

Ch. 16.4x12ft

Roof

—731—

Cairo No. 3 design 5731-B, story heights 9-ft. See design page 730. Plans $10.

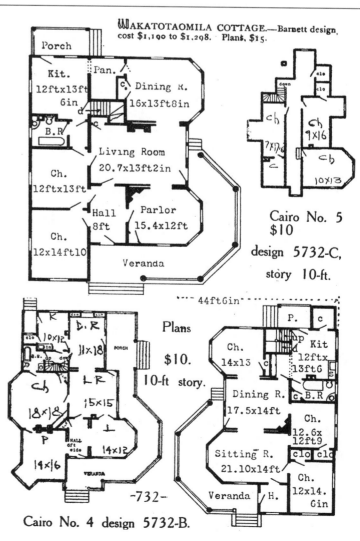

WAKATOTAOMILA COTTAGE.—Barnett design, cost $1,190 to $1,298. Plans $15.

Porch

Kit. 12ftx13ft 6in

Pan.

Dining R. 16x13ft8in

B.R

Ch. 12ftx13ft

Living Room 20.7x13ft2in

Ch. 12ftx13ft

Hall 8ft

Parlor 15.4x12ft

Ch. 12x14ft10

Veranda

ch 7x17

ch 9x16

ch 10x13

Cairo No. 5 $10

design 5732-C, story 10-ft.

44ft6in

K 10x12

D.R 11x18

P.

c

Ch. 14x13

Kit 12ftx 13ft6

Dining R. 17.5x14ft

c B.R

LR 15x15

Ch. 12.6x 12ft9

18x18

Plans $10. 10-ft story.

14x12

Sitting R. 21.10x14ft

clo clo

Ch. 12x14. 6in

14x16

P

VERANDA

H.

Veranda

—732—

Cairo No. 4 design 5732-B.

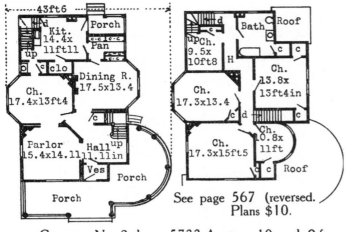

Conneaut No. 2 design 5733-A, story 10 and 9-ft 6.

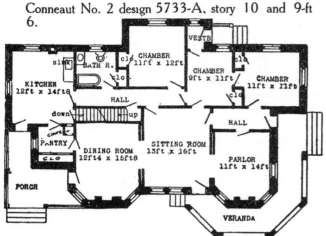

Cairo No. 6 design 5733-B in stone. Fairbanks design. $10 plans.

CAIRO COTTAGE.—Design 1557-N; in frame, $1,300 to $1,590; plans, $10. story heights, 9 ft. 6 in. and 8 ft. 6 in. attic. Special features: Semi-octagon porch; novel design; easy to construct. We have plan No. 1, called O'Brien design, with 20-inch stone walls; with stairs in front hall and fire-place in dining-room and sitting-room; with rear porch 6x36 ft.

Cairo Cottage No. 7 design 5734.

Plans $10.

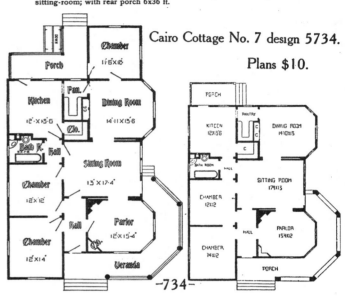

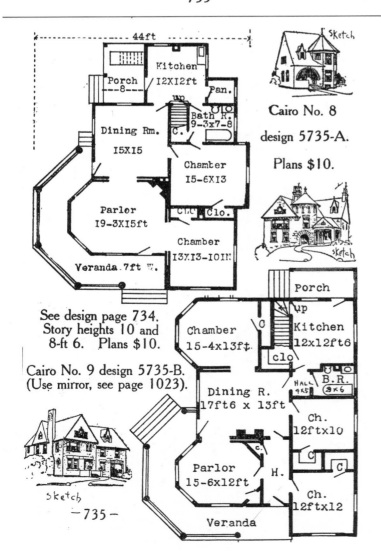

Cairo No. 8 design 5735-A.

Plans $10.

See design page 734. Story heights 10 and 8-ft 6. Plans $10.

Cairo No. 9 design 5735-B. (Use mirror, see page 1023).

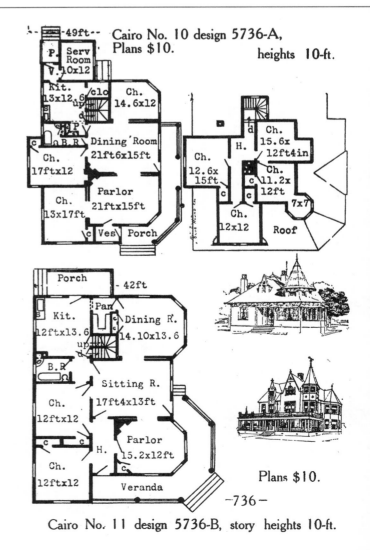

Cairo No. 10 design 5736-A, Plans $10.

heights 10-ft.

Plans $10.

Cairo No. 11 design 5736-B, story heights 10-ft.

Cairo Cottage No. 12 design 5737, full story heights 10 ft 6 and 10. See pages 730 to 738. Plans $15.

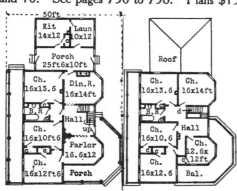

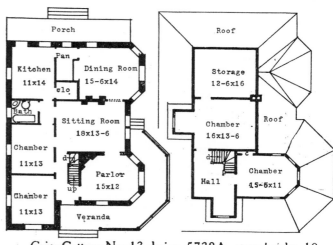

Cairo Cottage No. 13 design 5738A, story heights 10 and 8 ft. In stone. See pages 730 to 738. Plans $10.

Cairo No. 15 design

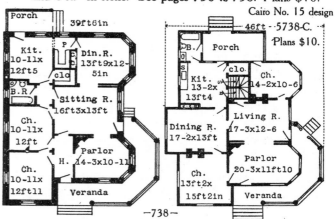

Plans $10.

—738—

Cairo Cottage No. 14 design 5738-B. Plans $10. In stone.

—737—

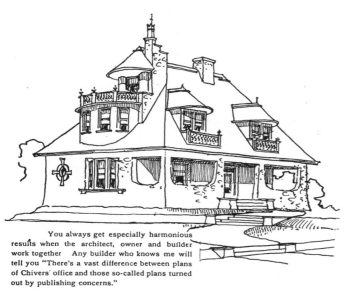

You always get especially harmonious results when the architect, owner and builder work together. Any builder who knows me will tell you "There's a vast difference between plans of Chivers' office and those so-called plans turned out by publishing concerns."

WILLOW PAMT RESIDENCE, —Design 2324M; Cost in stone and shingles, $2947 to $2499; plans, $45. See page 65

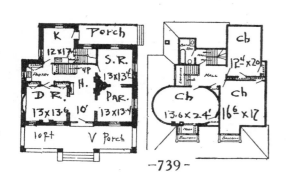

—739—

SERVIA RESIDENCE.—Design 2245-N; cost in frame, $2,390 to $2,495; plans, $35. Special features: Large rooms; attractive veranda; good flue connections to all rooms.

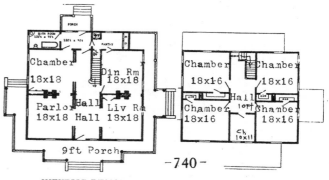

—740—

INFERIOR DESIGNS ARE MONUMENTAL EYE-SORES.

A modern and progressive up-to-date individual would not think of wearing a garment unless taken from some authoritive plate of fashion, and at that, a new garment is usually in use less than a year's duration. Yet many will allow a novice to draft plans of their building, which will be an eye-sore for generations, when for less money, at the outset they can secure ideas and drawings of an architectural expert whose aim, for reputation's sake alone, will be to produce the best possible effects for the least sum of money.

PITTSFIELD RESIDENCE.—Design 528-O; in frame, $1,268 to $1,489; plans, $10; width, 28 ft. 10 in. by 34 ft.; story heights, 9 ft. 6 in. and 9 ft. Special features: Inexpensive tower, compact plan, plain, simple design. Modifications: House would look well with tower eliminated. See page 65.

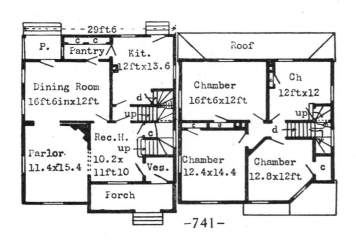

-741-

OREGON RESIDENCE.—Design 839M; in frame, $1,490 to $1,598; plans, $15; width; 35 ft. 10 in. by 30 ft. 10 in.; width over all, 39 ft. Story heights, 9 ft. Special features: Plain, simple roof treatment and a well-balanced, easy to construct design.

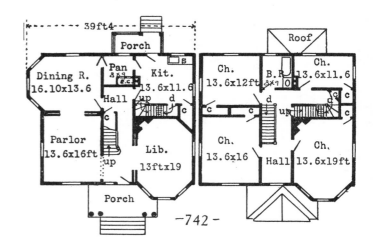

-742-

WELLS RESIDENCE.—Design 4371M; in frame, $1,498 to $1,600; plans, $15; width over all, 31 ft. 8 in.; story heights, 9 ft. Special features: Large reception hall; a door can be put in direct to dining-room. Modifications: The plans show a more attractive exterior. See page 65.

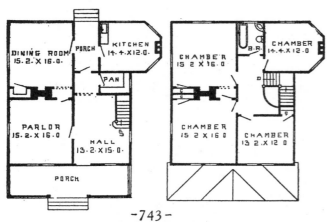

-743-

THESTONIA RESIDENCE.—Design 1914-O; cost in frame, $1,492 to $1,580; plans, $10. See page 65.

MARSELLES RESIDENCE.—Design 100,027M; cost $2203 to $2406; plans, $25; size 34x36. Special features: wide reception hall, with fire place, attractive combination front and rear stairs.

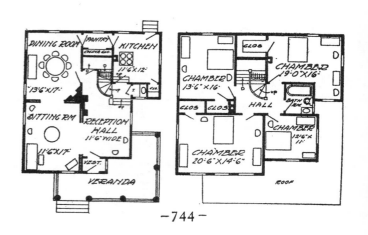

-744-

ESTON RESIDENCE.—Design 4898-N; in frame, $1,900 to $2,200; plans, $20; width over all, 47 ft.; story height, 10 ft. in the clear. Special features: Large veranda; attractive colonial design; good outlines; bay in front; combination stairs. A good Southern house.

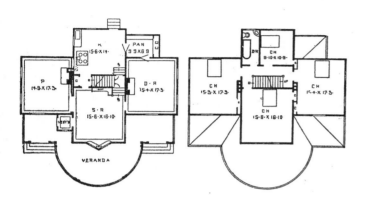

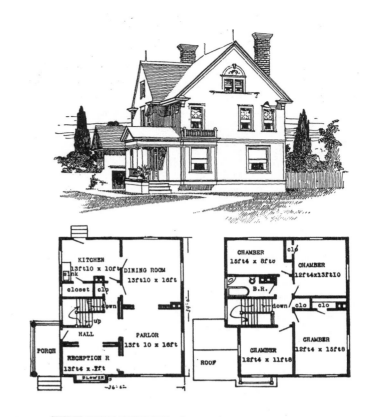

AMSEY RESIDENCE.—Design 1929-N; cost in frame, 1,492 to $1,580; plans, $10. Special features: Large chambers; attractive reception room; a good corner-lot design; a square, compact house; economical to build.

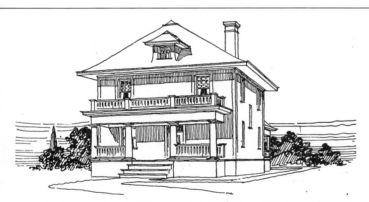

Pacheco design 5747, story heights 10 and 9-ft., width 30-ft., 6. Square compact economical house. Plans $12

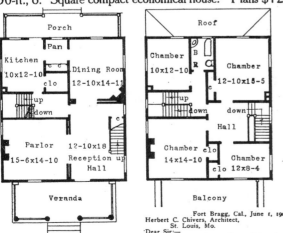

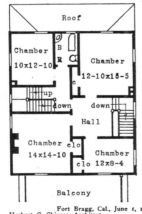

Fort Bragg, Cal., June 1, 1906.
Herbert C. Chivers, Architect,
St. Louis, Mo.
Dear Sir:—
I take extreme pleasure in certifying that the photograph sent you herewith is that of my cottage built from your plans. This picture was taken subsequent to the great California earthquake. Most all structures in this town which were hit terrifically were either demolished or damaged. I am as proud as a peacock of your work and have received many congratulations on possessing an earthquake-proof house.
Sincerely yours,
ROBERT GARDNER, D. D. S.

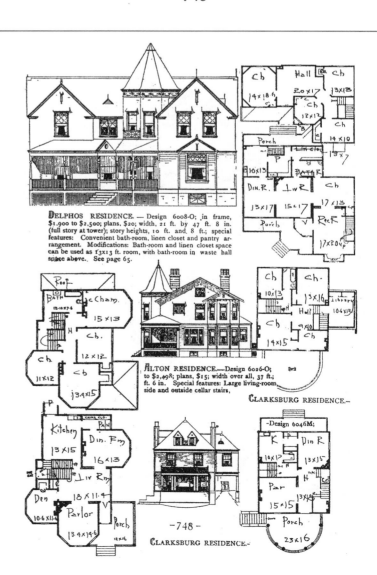

DELPHOS RESIDENCE. — Design 6008-O; in frame, $1,900 to $2,500; plans, $20; width, 21 ft. by 47 ft. 8 in. (full story at tower); story heights, 10 ft. and 8 ft.; special features: Convenient bath-room, linen closet and pantry arrangement. Modifications: Bath-room and linen closet space can be used as 13x13 ft. room, with bath-room in waste hall space above. See page 65.

ALTON RESIDENCE.—Design 6026-O; to $2,498; plans, $15; width over all, 37 ft.; ft. 6 in. Special features: Large living-room, side and outside cellar stairs.

CLARKSBURG RESIDENCE.—

-Design 6046M;

CLARKSBURG RESIDENCE.—

I send you herewith photo of the house which you planned for me. I found the special advice given of great benefit, and you shall certainly hear from me when I build again.   MRS. MARCUS B. ALLEN, Tom's River, N. J.

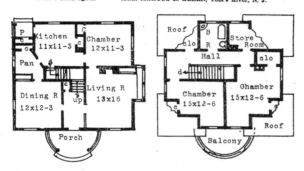

Pahranagha design 5749, width 34-ft., width over all 36-ft., story 9-ft. 6 and 9-ft.   Plans $15.

Not until too late, does the average owner realize how easy a building can be utterly ruined, and possibly then he will not notice it until it is pointed out. Yet, if Tom, Dick and Harry's suggestions are followed, in preference to those of the original designer, who understands and sees the building in its completeness, there will always be something to it that will appear common-place.

Otero design 5750, story heigdts 9-ft. 6 and 9.   Clean-cut exterior, large rooms, den off dining room.   Plans $10

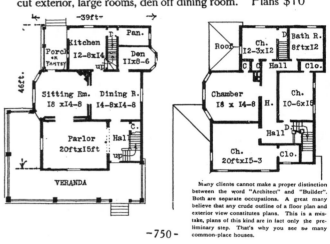

Many clients cannot make a proper distinction between the word "Architect" and "Builder." Both are separate occupations. A great many believe that any crude outline of a floor plan and exterior view constitutes plans. This is a mistake, plans of this kind are in fact only the preliminary step. That's why you see so many common-place houses.

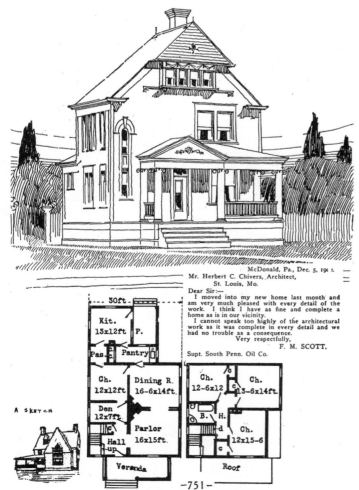

McDonald, Pa., Dec. 5, 190 .
Mr. Herbert C. Chivers, Architect,
St. Louis, Mo.
Dear Sir:—
I moved into my new home last month and am very much pleased with every detail of the work. I think I have as fine and complete a home as is in our vicinity.
I cannot speak too highly of the architectural work as it was complete in every detail and we had no trouble as a consequence.
Very respectfully,
F. M. SCOTT.
Supt. South Penn. Oil Co.

Osso design 5751, story heights 9 and 8-ft. 6, suitable for pastor's home.   Chamber on first floor.   Plans $15.

Physicians Office design 5752, story heights 10-ft. 6.
Plans $25.

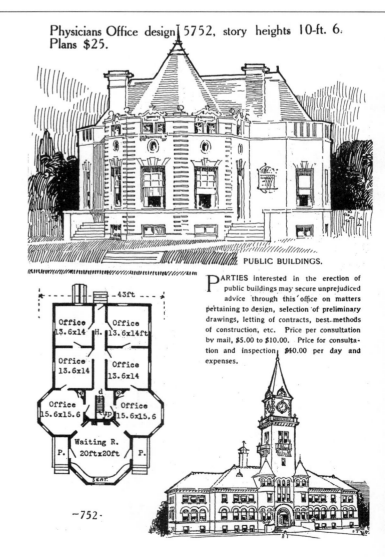

PUBLIC BUILDINGS.

PARTIES interested in the erection of public buildings may secure unprejudiced advice through this office on matters pertaining to design, selection of preliminary drawings, letting of contracts, best methods of construction, etc.   Price per consultation by mail, $5.00 to $10.00.   Price for consultation and inspection, $40.00 per day and expenses.

DUVALL RESIDENCE.—Design 4999-O; in frame, $1225 to $1398; plans, $15; width, 20 x 31; story heights, 9 ft. 6 in. and 8 ft. 6 in. Special features; Compact plan, attractive and well ventilated dining-room, convenient servant's room.

Duvall Residence No. 2. Moore Shower design, same design as above, but gable is not out off, with 12 x 13 parlor; 13 x 15 sitting-room with bay; 13 x 15 dining-room with bay, 10 x 10 pantry, 12 x 12 kitchen, rear stairs to basement, large rooms to second story, with bay over dining-room, and water-closet seperate from bath-room.   See page 65.

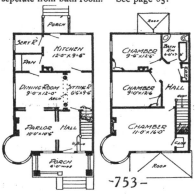

—753—

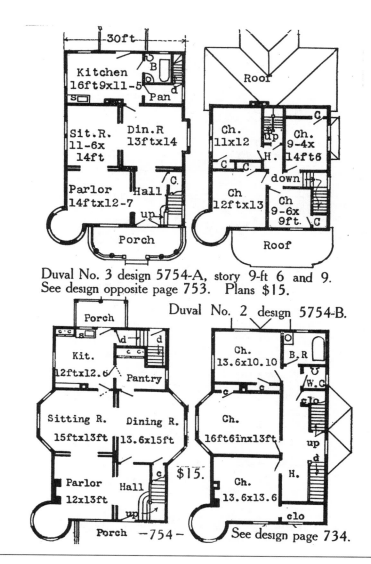

Duval No. 3 design 5754-A, story 9-ft 6 and 9. See design opposite page 753.   Plans $15.

Duval No. 2 design 5754-B.

$15.

Porch   —754—   See design page 734.

Oseuma design 5755, story heights 10 and 9-ft. 6. — Large pretentious looking home.   Plans $15.

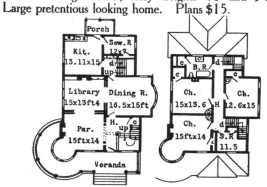

—755—

Orosi design 5756, story heights 9-ft. 6 and 8 ft.-6. Plain neat exterior.   Plans $10.

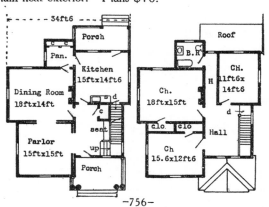

—756—

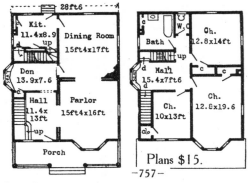

Plans $15.

-757-

Oronfino design 5757, story heights 9 and 9-ft. Suitable for Pastor's home. The den and bay-shaped hall above are particularly unique features for such a compact plan.

Oneta design 5758, story heights 9-ft. 6 and 9 Square compact plan. Plans $10.

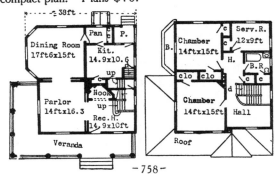

-758-

Goodlady design 5759, width over all 46-ft, story heights 9-ft. 6. A particularly unique English half-timber gable design.

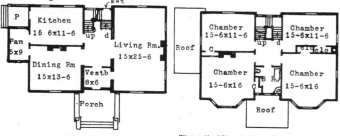

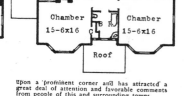

-759-   Agt. S. E. and S. F. R. R.

Anchiota design 5760, story heights 9-ft. 6, width 28-ft. 6. Well-lighted Reception Hall. Plans $15.

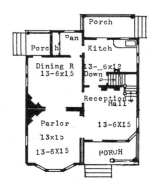

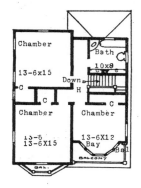

—Sketch

-760-

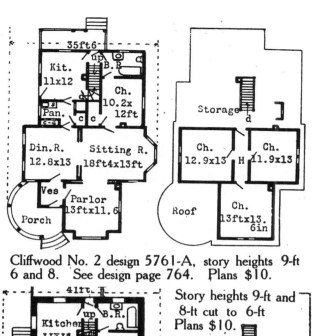

Kit.
11x12

up   B.R.

Ch.
10.2ft
12ft

Pan.

Din.R.
12.8x13

Sitting R.
18ft4x13ft

Ves

Parlor
13ftx11.6

Porch

35ft6

Storage

Ch.
12.9x13

H

Ch.
11.9x13

Roof

Ch.
13ftx13.
6in

Cliffwood No. 2 design 5761-A, story heights 9-ft 6 and 8. See design page 764. Plans $10.

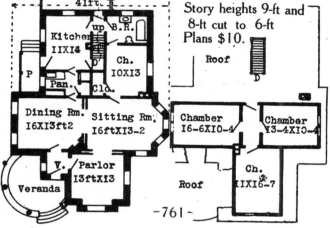

Kitchen
11X14

up   B.R.

Ch.
10X13

P

Pan.

Clo.

Dining Rm.
16X13ft2

Sitting Rm.
16ftX13-2

V.

Parlor
13ftX13

Veranda

41ft

Story heights 9-ft and
8-ft cut to 6-ft
Plans $10.

Roof

Chamber
16-6X10-4

Chamber
13-4X10-4

Ch.
11X16-7

Roof

-761-

Cliffwood No. 4 design 5761-B.

K
10-6x
16ft

up   B.R.
11-6x

P

PAN

CH.
11-6x14

C

C

D.R.
18x15-4

S.R.
18-6x15-4

V

P
15x15

V

**Cliffwood Cottage No. 5
heights 9-ft 6 and 8.
Plans $10.**

**design 5762-A,
See pages 761-763-764**

-38ft0in-

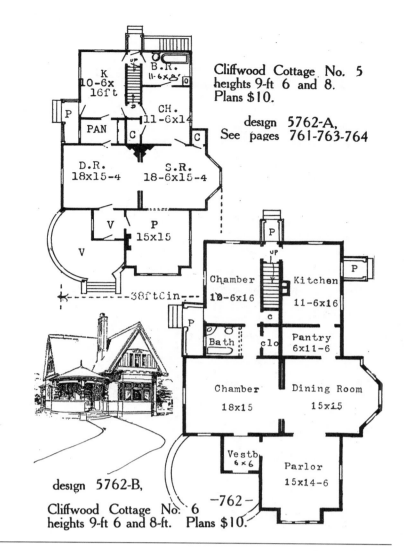

Chamber
19-6x16

P

UP

Kitchen
11-6x16

P

c

Bath

clo

Pantry
6x11-6

Chamber
18x15

Dining Room
15x15

Vestb
6x6

Parlor
15x14-6

-762-

**design 5762-B,
Cliffwood Cottage No. 6
heights 9-ft 6 and 8-ft. Plans $10.**

Cliffwood No. 7 design 5763-A, story heights 10 and 10-ft. See pages 761-762-764. Plans $10.

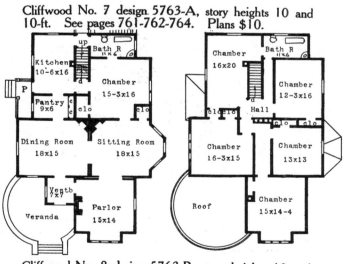

up   Bath R
11x6

Kitchen
10-6x16

P

Chamber
15-3x16

Pantry
9x6

clo

Dining Room
18x15

Sitting Room
18x15

Vestb
7x7

Parlor
15x14

Veranda

Chamber
16x20

Bath R
11x6

Hall

Chamber
12-3x16

Chamber
16-3x15

Chamber
13x13

Roof

Chamber
15x14-4

Cliffwood No. 8 design 5763-B, story heights 10 and 9-ft. 6. See pages 761-763-764. Plans $10.

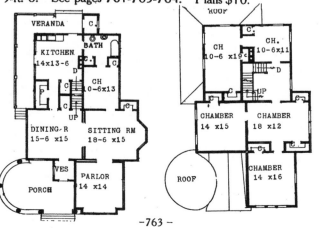

VERANDA

C

KITCHEN
14x13-6

BATH

CH
10-6x13

DINING-R
15-6 x15

SITTING RM
18-6 x15

VES

PARLOR
14 x14

PORCH

Roof

C

CH
10-6 x19

CH
10-6x11

D

UP

CHAMBER
14 x15

CHAMBER
18 x12

ROOF

CHAMBER
14 x16

-763-

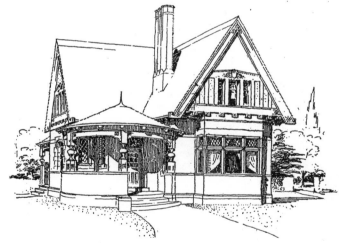

CLIFFWOOD COTTAGE.—Design 7058-O; in frame, 10 ft. story, $1,099 to $1,198; plans, $10; story heights, 9 ft. 6 in. and 8 ft. Modification No. 2: Garfield design; parlor 12x13 ft.; sitting-room 13x15 ft.; dining-room 12x13 ft.; chamber 10x12 ft.; kitchen 12x11 ft., and three rooms above; plans $10. Modification No. 3: Johnson design; parlor 13x12, with fireplace; sitting-room 12x13 ft.; dining-room 19x16; kitchen 13x12, with open stairs; bath-room and two 12x10 chambers above with no rear stairs; plans $10. See page 65.

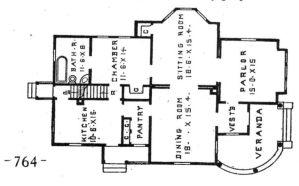

BATH-R.
11-6 x8

CHAMBER
11-6 x14

SITTING ROOM
18-6 x15-4

KITCHEN
10-6 x16

PANTRY

DINING ROOM
18- x15-4

PARLOR
15-0 x15

VESTB

VERANDA

-764-

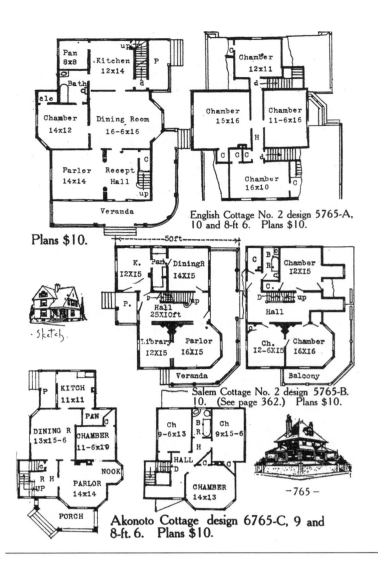

Pan 8x8 .Kitchen 12x14 P

Bath clo

Chamber 14x12 Dining Room 16-6x16

Parlor 14x14 Recept Hall

Veranda

Chamber 12x11 d

Chamber 15x16 Chamber 11-6x16

H

C C C d

Chamber 16x10 C

Plans $10.

English Cottage No. 2 design 5765-A, 10 and 8-ft 6. Plans $10.

K. 12X15 Pan DiningR 14X15

P.

Hall 25X10ft up

Library 12X15 Parlor 16X15

Veranda

B C R C Chamber 12X15

C.

D up

Hall

Ch. 12-6X15 Chamber 16X16

Balcony

Salem Cottage No. 2 design 5765-B. 10. (See page 362.) Plans $10.

P KITCH 11x11

PAN C

DINING R 13x15-6 CHAMBER 11-6x19

R H NOOK

up PARLOR 14x14

PORCH

Ch 9-6x13 B R Ch 9x15-6

H

HALL C C D

CHAMBER 14x13

-765-

Akonoto Cottage design 6765-C, 9 and 8-ft. 6. Plans $10.

DINING R KITCHEN

c

PARLOR

PORCH

FIRST STORY

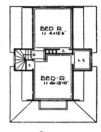

BED R.

c

BED R.

SECOND STORY.

Georgetown, S. C., Aug. 17, 19
Mr Herbert C. Chivers,
St. Louis, Mo.
Dear Sir:—
The building you planned is all "O. K." I completed same and moved into it the early part of December last and find the plan exceedingly convenient and comfortable. Every one who has been through the house admires it.

-766- Yours very truly,
H. L. SMITH.

Enclosed please find photo of church, the first one I took of the building. As far as your work is concerned I am well pleased.
REV. FR. TH. A. WOLTERS, Annawan, Ill.

San Diego No. 4, Hackman design, same as above, with 12x12 ft. kitchen addition, with large pantry, and large 8x8 ft. rear porch back of present kitchen; with first arrangement of plan as in San Diego No. 2 except parlor is 15x15; dining-room 14x13; bed-room 13x13. See page 65.

San Diego No. 5, Swavely design, same as San Diego, with the following changes: Porch across front only; parlor, 15x12; side hall at stairs, extending to front porch; kitchen 11x14 back of hall; dining-room in place of present kitchen 12x12; with 5x12 pantry back of this; three chambers above sizes, 13x12, 12x14, 10.6x14 ft.

SAN DIEGO COTTAGE NO. 2.—Design 100,190-O; in frame, $750 to $850; plans, $5; width, 27 ft. 10 in. by 39 ft. 4 in.; story heights, 9 ft. 6 in. and 8 ft. (cut down at sides to 5 ft.). See view on opposite page, See page 65.

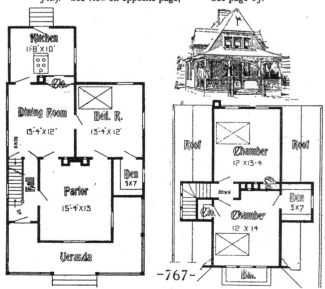

Kitchen 11-8'x10'

Clo

Dining Room 13'-4"x12' Bed. R. 13'-4"x12'

Parlor 15'-4"x13' Den 5'x7'

Veranda

Roof Roof

Chamber 12 x13-4

DOWN Den 5'x7'

Clo

Chamber 12 X 14

B.

-767-

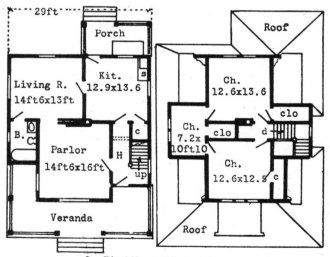

29ft

Porch

Roof

Living R. 14ft6x13ft Kit. 12.9x13.6 s

B. C

Parlor 14ft6x16ft

H

up

Veranda

Ch. 12.6x13.6

clo

Ch. 7.2x 10ft10 clo d

Ch. 12.6x12.5 c

Roof

San Diego No. 6, Geiseke design, same as San Diego, with 8 ft. veranda; parlor, 14.6x16 ft.; with large front window;

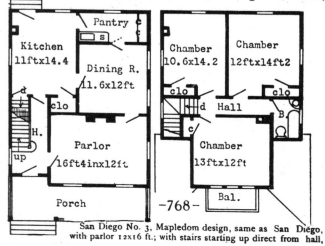

Pantry c

Kitchen 11ftx14.4 s c

Dining R. 11.6x12ft

d clo

H.

up

Parlor 16ft4inx12ft

Porch

Chamber 10.6x14.2 Chamber 12ftx14ft2

clo

clo d Hall

c

B.

Chamber 13ftx12ft

Bal.

-768-

San Diego No. 3, Mapledom design, same as San Diego, with parlor 12x16 ft.; with stairs starting up direct from hall,

ENGLISH HOUSE.—Design 878 M; in frame, $1298 to $1498; plans, $25; width, 32 ft. 10 in. by 32 ft 8 in.; width over all, 40 ft.; story heights, 9 ft. 6 in. and 8 ft. 6 in. (full story). Special features; Plain neat exterior. See page 65.

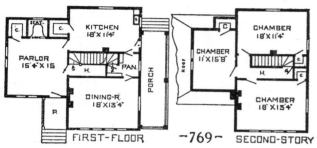

About three years ago I erected a dwelling all complete from plans prepared by you. It has proved very satisfactory and has received more complimentary notices than any structure of the kind in the city as to style and inside arrangement and finish. We are highly pleased with your work. MR. AND MRS. R. M. ROBERTS, RED OAK, IOWA.

OAKLAND RESIDENCE.—Design 1877 M; in frame, $1608 to $1799; plans, $15; story heights, 9 ft. cut down to 5 ft. 6 in. walls to second story. Special features—Stone front, ornamental English gables; other walls covered with shingles. See page 65.

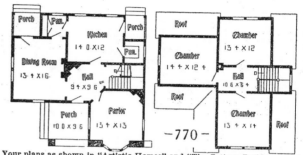

Your plans as shown in "Artistic Homes" and "The Cottage Builder" are the best we have seen.

MRS. T. W. GIBSON MOSS, (Monterey Co.). Cal.

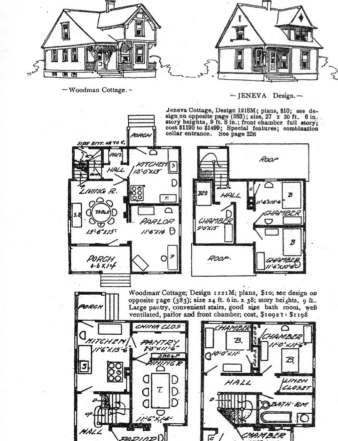

—Woodman Cottage.—

— JENEVA Design.—

Jeneva Cottage, Design 1218M; plans, $10; see design on opposite page (383); size, 27 x 30 ft. 6 in. story heights, 9 ft. 8 in.; front chamber full story; cost $1190 to $1499; Special features; combination cellar entrance. See page 226

Woodman Cottage; Design 1221M; plans, $10; see design on opposite page (383); size 24 ft. 6 in. x 38 ft.; story heights, 9 ft.. Large pantry, convenient stairs, good size bath room, well ventilated, parlor and front chamber; cost, $1092 to $1198

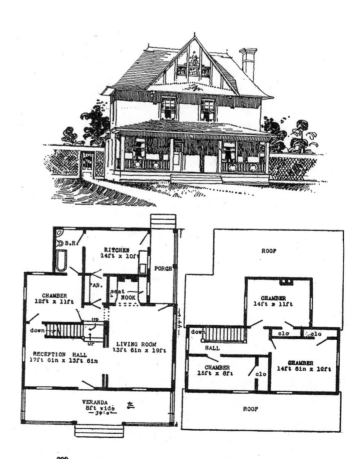

MARENCE RESIDENCE.—Design 1980M; cost in frame $1,492 to $1,590; plans $10. See page 65.

RICH RESIDENCE.—Design 1871M; in frame, $1,298 to $1496; plans, $15; width, 28.2 x 36.19; story heights, 9.6 and 8.6 in nearly full story. Special features; Plain,—neat exterior, suitable for stained shingles; combination inside and outside cellar entrance. See page 65.

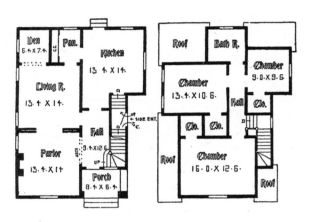

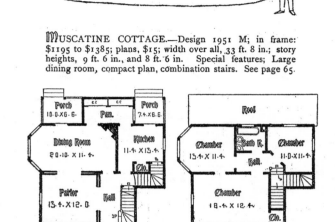

MUSCATINE COTTAGE.—Design 1951 M; in frame: $1195 to $1385; plans, $15; width over all, 33 ft. 8 in.; story heights, 9 ft. 6 in., and 8 ft. 6 in. Special features; Large dining room, compact plan, combination stairs. See page 65.

I am thoroughly pleased and regard your plans a work of art. Your specifications are also full and completely protect the owner from a legal standpoint.
H. W. POGUE, Attorney at Law, Jerseyville, Ill.

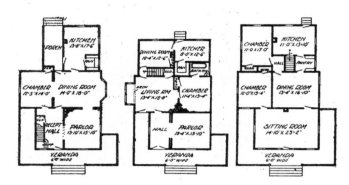

DEADWOOD COTTAGE.—Hill Design 1810-O; in frame, $950 to $1,150; plans, $8; (see index for Deadwood plan No. 2); width, 31 ft.; width over all, 39 ft.; story heights, 10 ft.; (space for two rooms above). Special features: Simple roof treatment; a very practical plan. See page 65.

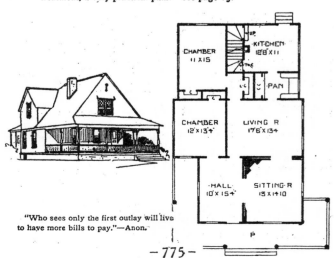

"Who sees only the first outlay will live to have more bills to pay."—Anon.

Deadwood No. 4 design 5776-A.
Plans $8.

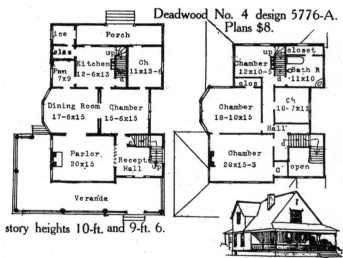

story heights 10-ft. and 9-ft. 6.

Gypsum No. 2 design 5776-C, Plans $20. See reversed exterior 345.

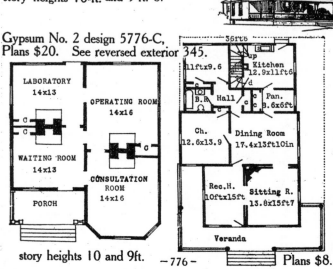

story heights 10 and 9ft. Plans $8.

Deadwood No. 5 design 5776-B, story heights 10-ft.

DYERSBURG COTTAGE NO. 2.—Design 6030 O; in frame $1200 to $1398; plans, $5; width over all, 30 ft. 7 in.; story heights, 10 ft. and 9 ft. Special features; well ventilated rooms. See Dyersburg No. 1 on page 779 See page 65.

Cardington, Ohio, June 14, 19
Mr. Herbert C. Chivers,
St. Louis, Mo.
Dear Sir:—
I am sending you this day under separate cover a photo of house taken soon after it was completed.
We think a great deal of our home, and should I ever build again it would certainly be from plans prepared by Herbert C. Chivers.
Yours respectfully,
FRANK S. JONES.
(Dry Goods)

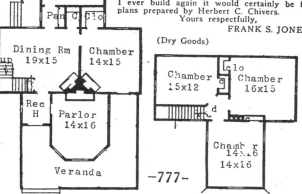

-777-

DYERSBURG COTTAGE.—Design 1621 O; in frame, $699 to $799; plans $5; width 27 ft. by 39 ft. 4 in.; story heights, 9 ft. and 8 ft. cut down by roof at walls to 5 ft. Modifications See index for Dyersburg plan No. 2. See page 65.

DYERSBURG Modification plan, No. 1. Pool Design, with 13 ft. 5 in. x 15 ft. parlor; 12 ft. x 14 ft. 6 in. bed room; 13 ft. by 14 ft. 6 in. dining room; 6 ft. by 8 ft. bath room in place of closet at rear hall, with fire place in parlor and in extra bed room direct above parlor.

DYERSBURG MODIFIED No. 2. HOUGH plan, Parlor 16 ft. x 13 ft. Vestabule entrance on opposite side of house to 18 ft. x 15ft. dining room with stairs, with 14 ft. x 15 ft. bed room in place of present dining room, with door to front porch, with triple triangulor fire place at intersection of parlor, dining room and bed room, with 5 ft. x 10 ft. bath room at rear hall, 13 ft. x 14 ft. and three rooms above, with balcony roof to porch.

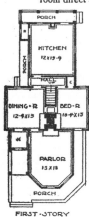

FIRST STORY

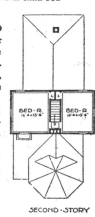

SECOND STORY

-779-

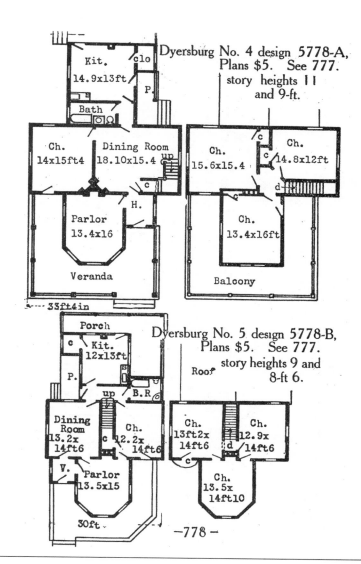

Dyersburg No. 4 design 5778-A,
Plans $5. See 777.
story heights 11 and 9-ft.

Dyersburg No. 5 design 5778-B,
Plans $5. See 777.
story heights 9 and 8-ft 6.

-778-

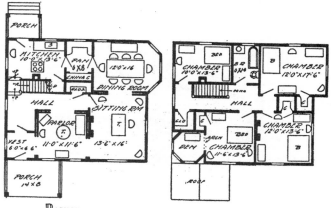

PAYNE COTTAGE.—Design 1209M; size. 24 ft. 6 in. x 30.; story heights, 10 ft. 9 in.; special features; small conspicuoust parlor, large sitting room, well-ventilated chambers, combination stairs, den on second floor. Cos $2098 to $2290; plans, $20. See design opposite page for design.

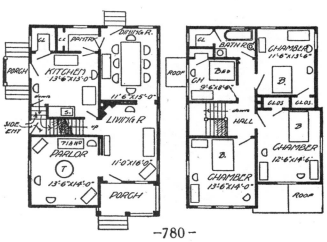

-780-

SLANDISH COTTAGE.—

CLIFTON RESIDENCE.—Design 6019-O; in frame, $1298 to $1499: plans, $5; width, 25 ft. 6 in. by 35 ft.; Modifications.   See index Birdsville Cottage.   See page 65.

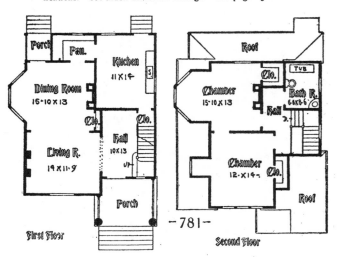

CARONDELET COTTAGE.—Design 6016-O; in brick and frame, $1298 to $1464; plans, $10; width, 30 ft. 8 in: by 27 ft. 8 in.; full story heights, 9 ft. in the clear,   Special features—Large living room; full story the upper rooms: 9 in. walls.   See page 65.

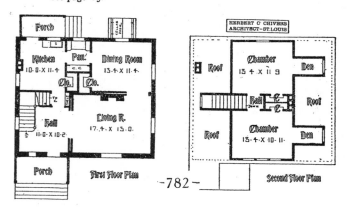

FAIRFIELD COTTAGE—Design 1857 O in frame, $676 to $799; plans, $10; width, 28 ft. 2 in. x 29 ft.; story heights, 9 ft. and 9 ft. (full story.)   Special features—Cottage like gable effect in front; economical porch roofing.   See page 65.

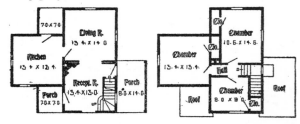

House is just completed. It is the talk of the town. As it is different to anything yet built here, we have received many favorable comments on same. The house is up-to-date in every respect.
J. A. ADAMS, North Yakima, Wash.

The plans which you prepared for our new bank and office building have worked out all right. We are well pleased with the building.
ASHER R. COX, (Vice-President Orchard City Bank) Xenia, Ill.

Your plans of County Jail Building are complete in every respect and we are well pleased with them.   J. W. SHIELDS, (Real Estate), Pineville, Mo.

REDLANDS COTTAGE.—Design 9061M; in frame, $989 to $1,096; plans, $10; width, 30 ft. by 30 ft. 6 in.; story heights, 9 ft. and 9 ft. (front chamber full story.)   Special features: A plain, practical house.   See page 65.

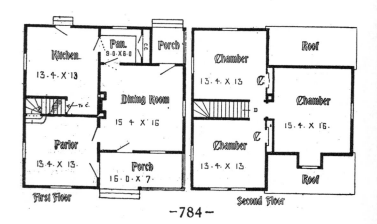

STONEBURY RESIDENCE.—Design 153-O; in frame, $989 to $1,185; plans, $10; width, 21 ft.; story heights, 9 ft. and 8 ft. 6 in. Special features: Large pantry and closets; combination inside and outside cellar entrance. Modifications: Hall can connect with kitchen by leaving out closet. See page 65.

GRAYSBORO COTTAGE.—Design 4228-O; in frame, $375 to $475; plans, $5; width, 22 ft. by 28 ft.; story heights, 9 ft. and 9 ft. 6 in., (front and rear walls 6 ft. high.) Special features: First story weatherboards, second story shingles. See page 65.

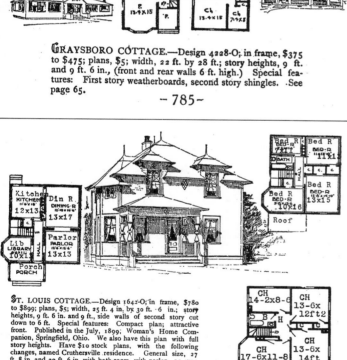

ST. LOUIS COTTAGE.—Design 1641-O; in frame, $780 to $899; plans, $5; width, 25 ft. 4 in. by 30 ft. 6 in.; story heights, 9 ft. 6 in. and 9 ft., side walls of second story cut down to 6 ft. Special features: Compact plan; attractive front. Published in the July, 1899; Woman's Home Companion, Springfield, Ohio. We also have this plan with full story heights. Have $10 stock plans, with the following changes, named Cruthersville residence. General size, 27 ft. 8 in. and 29 ft. 6 in. with bath-room, with parlor, 13.4x13 ft.; library, 12x10 ft. 6 in.; dining-room, 13.4x15 ft.; story heights, 10 ft. and 9 ft. in the clear. See pages 197 and 198. See page 65.

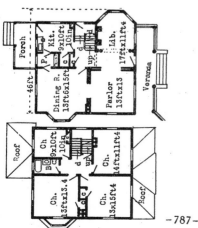

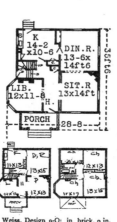

PUNBINEE RESIDENCE.—Design 2268M; cost in frame, $1,702 to $1,820, plans, $10. See St. Louis Cottage. Above

Weiss, Design 9-O; in brick, 9 in. wall; cost, $1790 to $1998; plans, $10. See St. Louis Cottage. Above

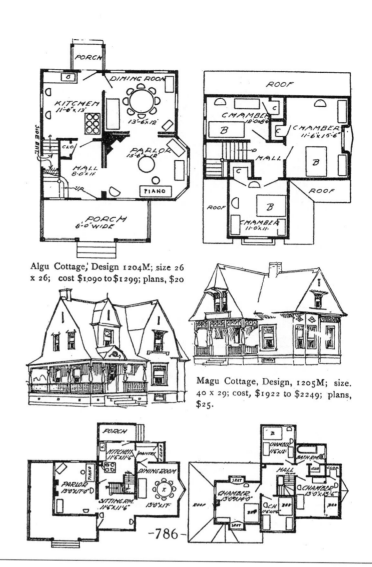

Algu Cottage, Design 1204M; size 26 x 26; cost $1,090 to $1299; plans, $20

Magu Cottage, Design, 1205M; size. 40 x 29; cost, $1922 to $2249; plans, $25.

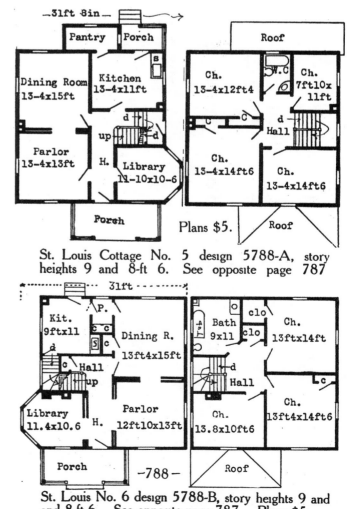

St. Louis Cottage No. 5 design 5788-A, story heights 9 and 8-ft 6. See opposite page 787

St. Louis No. 6 design 5788-B, story heights 9 and and 8-ft 6. See opposite page 787. Plans $5.

St. Louis No. 10.   Plans $5.

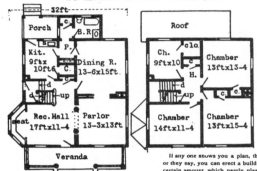

If any one shows you a plan, that you. know, or they say, you can erect a building from for a certain amount, which nearly pleases you, send me the particulars, etc., and I will clearly indicate to you where you can save at least the cost of my fee, and I will furthermore look after the design and important constructive details, which, if followed out, insures the best results, giving your building a distinctive clean-cut appearance.

—789—

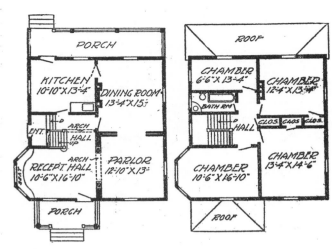

DARBY COTTAGE.—Design 59-O; cost, $998 to $1,198; size, 28 ft. 2 in. by 30 ft.; story heights, 6 ft. and 8 ft., full story; plans, $8.   See design of St. Louis cottage on page 787 A special feature of this plan is attractive stairs and combination side entrance and cellar entrance.

DARBY NO 2, Likins design, same as above, with 4 ft. pantry between dining-room and kitchen; with 6x7 bath-room on first floor; with general dimensions 32x30 ft.; with no bay to second story chamber; with full stories and dormer on roof; similar to Washington Residence. 491 – Also See 787

Darby plan No. 3, reversed Finley design, same as above, with sliding doors to parlor; with arch and large brick fire-place to library; with 5 ft. central hall; with 11.4 x 17 ft. library where reception hall now shows; with bay omitted to front chamber above; with pantry and pot-closet between kitchen and dining-room; with 3x8 bay to dining-room; with bath-room between two rear chambers; with porch across front; with open porch extending to dining-room bay.

Norcatur, Design 10-O; cost, $1,098 to $1192; size, 27.8 x 29.6 width over all, 31 ft.; plans, $8; See design on page

—790—

See design and description below
Plans $12.

The detail drawings of economical and ornamental construction alone which I send out are worth ten times the value that ordinary plans are. In fact you cannot successfully put up a building of any kind without these details.   Any competent and well-meaning builder will tell you this, and how much it facilitates matters.

Brison design 5791.
Story heights 9-ft 3 and 9.

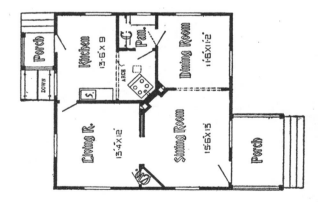

EAST SIDE COTTAGE.—Design 1295M; see Carrytown design on page 72 for exterior; in frame, $450 to $590; plans, $15; width over all, 28 ft. 4 in.; story heights, 9 ft. Special features: Square economical plan; ventilating hood for kitchen stove (see arch); good flue arrangement.   See page 65.

HARVARD COTTAGE.—Design 870-O; in frame, $1,198 to $1,289; plans, $5; width, 24 ft. 6 in. by 28 ft. 2 in.; story heights, 9 ft. 3 in. and 9 ft. in the clear.   Special features: Compactness of plan; simplicity of exterior; a very practical plan; pleasing roof lines.   Have modified $5 plan No. 2, Brison design, with back door entering out into 7 ft. by 13 ft. 6 in. rear porch, with 10x9 ft. kitchen addition and bath-room and closet space above (Brison design), cost $250 additional.   See page 65.

—791—

Cheap cottages.   Plans, $10.

—792—

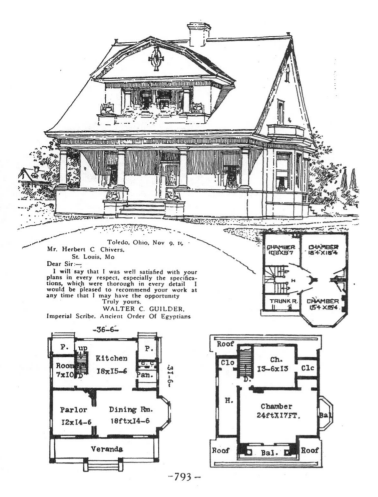

Mulato design 5793, story heights 9-ft. 6.   Neat bunga-
low-like cottage.   Plans $10.

— 793 —

Nowesta design 5794, story heights 10 and 8-ft. 6.
Similar design to Romulus design 541.   Plans $10.

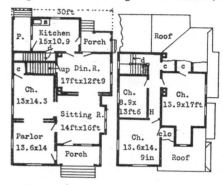

MY experience in designing large estates throughout the country has necessitated my doing the landscape work in connection with same.   I therefore now keep regularly in my
employ a competent engineer and surveyor and can furnish real
estate agents, municipalities and owners of country estates complete landscape lay-outs.   By reason of my architectural experience I can lay-out such work to the very best advantage for the
proper setting of buildings.—HERBERT C. CHIVERS,
                                    Landscape Architect.

— 794 —

HRISMAN RESIDENCE.—Design 1849-N; cost in frame, $2,890
to $3,282; plans, $25.   A very compact house.   Note large size
of rooms, central location of stairs; door to dining-room can be
placed in later.

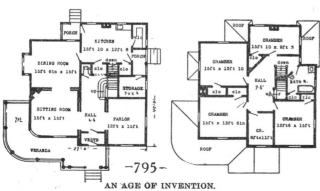

— 795 —

AN AGE OF INVENTION.

    Look around you, see what is being done in mechanical inventions, then look
at some of the buildings which go up now-a-days, many of them being copies of
plans built thirty and forty years ago.   The reason of this is that many a person is content with ordinary results, and usually having no one to advise them
otherwise, go ahead on the same old outlines.   Nothing expresses your progressive individuality more than a modern place of abode.   It talks volumes for you
to every passer-by

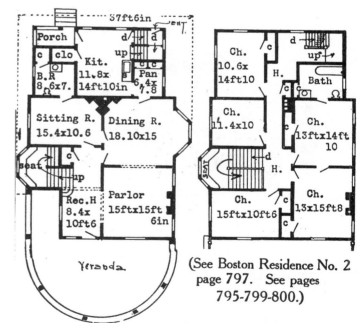

(See Boston Residence No. 2
page 797.   See pages
795-799-800.)

Boston Residence No. 2 design 5796.   Full semi-
circular porch.   See exterior page 797.   Also see
pages 798-799-800.   Story heights 10 and 9-ft. 6.
Plans $30.

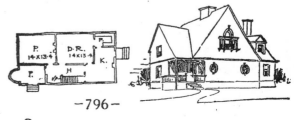

— 796 —

BYESVILLE.—Design No. 2339; cost, $560; plans, $8.

BOSTON RESIDENCE.—Design 1052-O; in frame, $2800 to $3250; plans, $30; width, 28 x 47 ft. 4 in.; story heights, 9 ft. 6 in. and 9 ft.; attic, 8. Special features; Large porch.

Boston Residence No. 2. Have $10 stock plan of this with rear porch to kitchen, with 9 x 8 laundry, where porch now is, with out-side door, with bay to front chamber, and separate water-closet in back hall. See Manston Resiuence page 933.

Boston Residence No. 2. Modified;—Lott design, with dining room space used as sitting room, 15 x 16; with 16 x 20 octogan shape dining-room back of this, with first story bath room in place of den, with kitchen back of this, with bath-room between front two chambers and bath-room over first story bath.

Continued

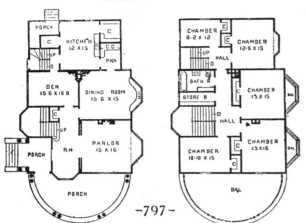
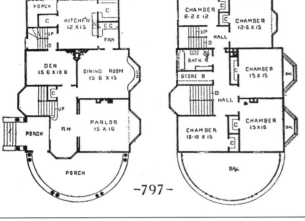

-797-

RARDEN RESIDENCE.—Design 1835-O; cost in frame $2,780 to $2,940; plans $25. A good southern house. See page 65.

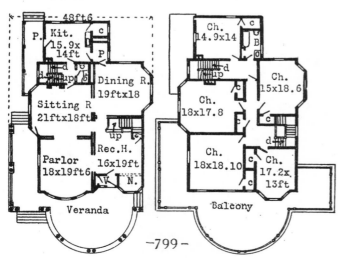

-799-

WALTHA.—Design 35-O; cost $1498 to $1880; size 32 ft. and 37 ft 6 in.; width over all, 38 ft. See Boston designs on page 480.

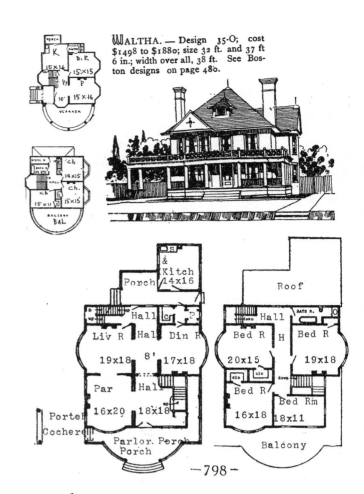

-798-

GOWEN RESIDENCE.—Design 1845M; cost in frame $2,690 to $2,982; plans $25. See page 65.

The plan was quite satisfactory and we like our cottage very much.—Wyllys Pettit, Ridge Road, N. Y.

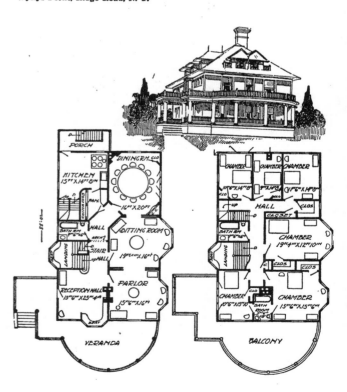

 ERSHON RESIDENCE.—Design 1916-N; cost in frame, $3,489 to $4,680; plans, $25. See Manston residence on page 152, from which this is a modification.

-800-

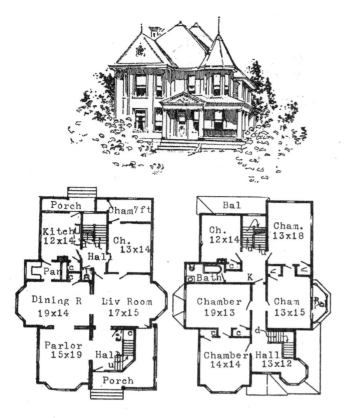

APPLEGATE RESIDENCE.—Design 1841M; cost in frame $2,690 to $2,882; plans $25. See page 65.

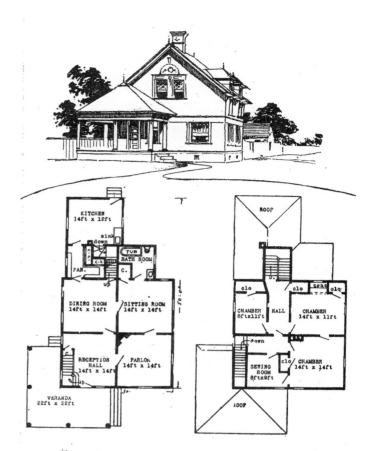

BORDEAUX COTTAGE.—Design 2410M; cost in frame $1,392 to $1,480; plans $10. See page 65.

Noresta design 5803, story heights 9-ft. each. Bay-like sitting room and first-floor chamber. Plans $10.

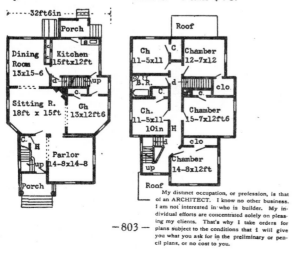

My distinct occupation, or profession, is that of an ARCHITECT. I know no other business. I am not interested in who is builder. My individual efforts are concentrated solely on pleasing my clients. That's why I take orders for plans subject to the conditions that I will give you what you ask for in the preliminary or pencil plans, or no cost to you.

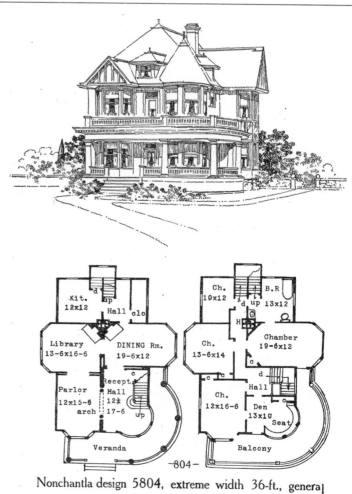

Nonchantla design 5804, extreme width 36-ft., general width 26-ft., story heights 9-ft. 6 and 8-ft. 6. A plain clean-cut corner-lot residence. Plans $15.

Very roomy plan.

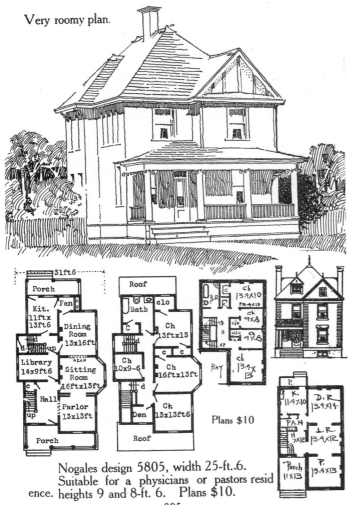

Nogales design 5805, width 25-ft..6.
Suitable for a physicians or pastors resid
ence. heights 9 and 8-ft. 6. Plans $10.

Plans $10

—805— CAMPBELL RESIDENCE.—Design 6027M;

Naknek design 5806, width 31-ft., story heights 9 and
8-ft. Convenient parlor-like first floor chamber. Plans $10.

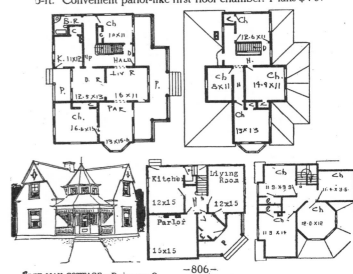

CAPE MAY COTTAGE.—Design 1774-O; —806—

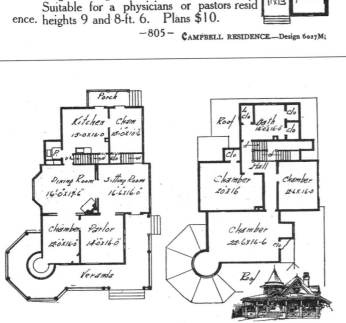

Nacora design 5807, width over all 44-ft., story heights
10-ft. and 8-ft. 6. Large rooms. Suitable for a corner-
lot house. Plans $10.

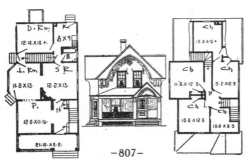

—807—

STOCKTON COTTAGE.—Design 1872-O; in frame, $1,-
290 to $1,498; plans, $10. We also have this in two full
stories, called Morris design. See page 65.

Narkeeta design 5808,
heights 12 and 11-ft.

Plans $15.

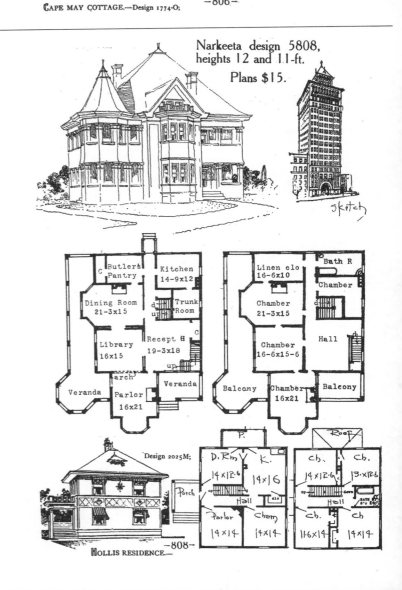

Design 2025M;

—808—

HOLLIS RESIDENCE.—

Nashawena design 5809, width over steps and all 50-ft. story heights 10 and 9-ft. Plans $15.

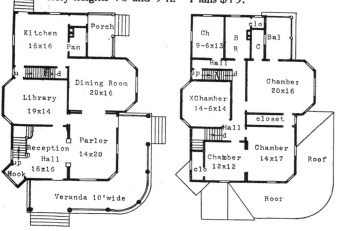

Natrona design 5810, story heights 9 and 8-ft 6. Plain, neat exterior. Plans $10.

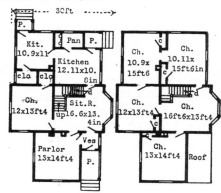

ANGOLA RESIDENCE.—Design 2250-N; cost in frame, $2,392 to $2,480; plans, $15. Special features: Front bay brakes into front gable attractively; octagon roof to porch is attractive; large fireplace in front hall shows up conspicuously; a clean-cut design.

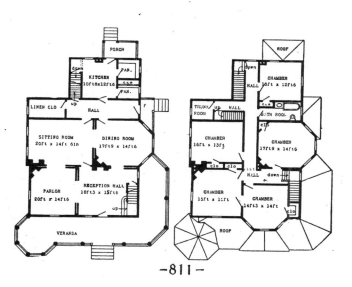

Bluepoint design 5812. See Angola Residence for exterior, pages 485-811-812-813, width 34ft, width over all 40 ft. (See Bluepoint plan, pages 812, also 813-814. Plans $15. Story heights 9 ft 9 and 9 ft 6.

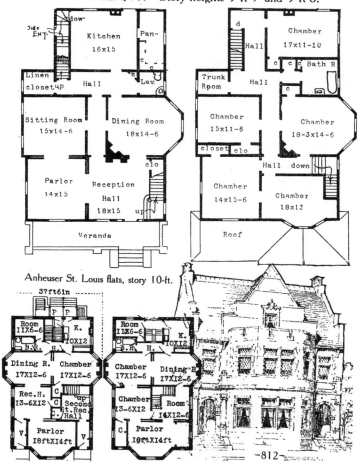

Anheuser St. Louis flats, story 10-ft.

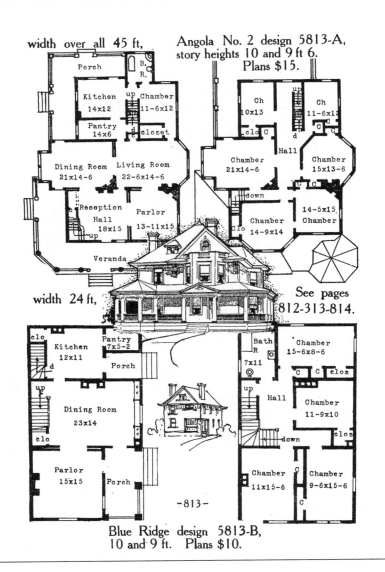

width over all 45 ft,

Angola No. 2 design 5813-A, story heights 10 and 9 ft 6. Plans $15.

Porch

Kitchen
14x12

B.
R.

up Chamber
11-6x12

closet

Ch
10x13

up

Ch
11-6x12

Pantry
14x6

C

C

d

Dining Room
21x14-6

Living Room
22-6x14-6

Chamber
21x14-6

Hall

Chamber
15x13-6

Reception
Hall
18x15

Parlor
13-11x15

down

up

Chamber
14-9x14

Clo

14-5x15
Chamber

Veranda

See pages
812-313-814.

width 24 ft,

clo

Kitchen
12x11

Pantry
7x5-2

Porch

d

Bath
R
7x11

Chamber
15-6x8-6

C

C

clos

up

Dining Room
23x14

up

Hall

Chamber
11-9x10

clo

down

clos

Parlor
15x15

Porch

Chamber
11x15-6

C

Chamber
9-6x15-6

C

-813-

Blue Ridge design 5813-B,
10 and 9 ft. Plans $10.

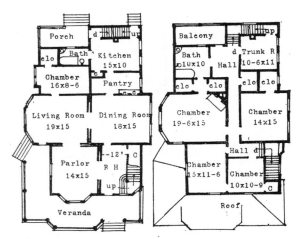

Porch

d

up

clo

Bath

Kitchen
15x10

Balcony

Bath
10x10

d

Trunk R
10-6x11

Hall

Chamber
16x8-6

Pantry

clo

clo

clo

clo

Living Room
19x15

Dining Room
18x15

Chamber
19-6x15

Chamber
14x15

Parlor
14x15

-12'
R H

C

Hall

d

Chamber
15x11-6

Chamber
10x10-9

C

up

Veranda

Roof

Angola No. 3 design 5814-A, width over all 60 ft,
story heights 10 and 9-ft 6. Plans $15.

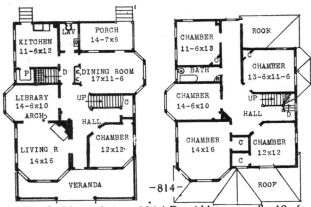

KITCHEN
11-6x12

LAV

PORCH
14-7x6

CHAMBER
11-6x13

ROOF

P

D

DINING ROOM
17x11-6

BATH

CHAMBER
13-6x11-6

LIBRARY
14-6x10

ARCH

UP

C

CHAMBER
14-6x10

UP

HALL

D

LIVING R
14x16

HALL

CHAMBER
12x12

CHAMBER
14x16

C

CHAMBER
12x12

C

VERANDA

-814-

ROOF

Angola No. 4 design 5814-B, width over all 40 ft,
story heights 10 and 9 ft 6. See pages 812-813-814.
Plans $15.

GAYBROOK RESIDENCE. —
100,004M; cost $2424 th $2666;
plans. $25; size 31x45; special features;
semi-circular in front; novel
dormer windows, shingle porch, bay
front. See page 65.

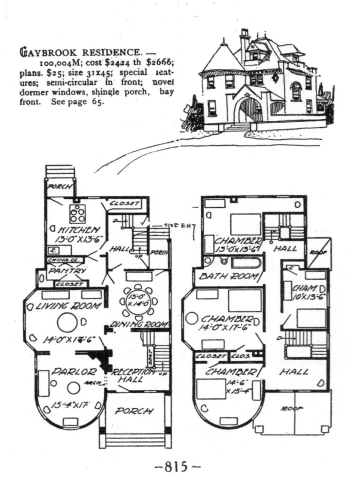

PORCH

CLOSET

Q

FRONT ENT

D

KITCHEN
13'-0"X13'-6"

HALL

up

PORCH

ROOF

CHAMBER
13'-0"X13'-6"

HALL

S.

CHINA CL.

PANTRY

15'-0"
X14'-6"

BATH ROOM

CHAM D
10'X13'-6"

CLOSET

LIVING ROOM
14'-0"X17'-6"

DINING ROOM

CHAMBER
14'-0"X17'-6"

PARLOR

RECEPTION
HALL

up

CLOSET CLOS.

CHAMBER
14'-6"
X15'-4"

HALL

15'-4"X17'

ARCH

PORCH

ROOF

-815-

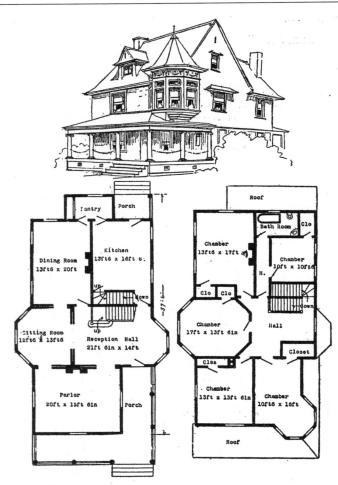

Roof

Pantry

Porch

Bath Room

Clo

Dining Room
13ft6 x 20ft

Kitchen
13ft6 x 16ft 6

up

Chamber
13ft6 x 17ft

Chamber
10ft x 10ft

down

H.

Clo

Clo

Sitting Room
12ft6 x 13ft6

Reception Hall
21ft 6in x 14ft

Chamber
17ft x 13ft 6in

Hall

down

Clo

Clos

Parlor
20ft x 15ft 6in

Porch

Chamber
13ft x 13ft 6in

Closet

Chamber
10ft x 15ft

Roof

PIFFARD RESIDENCE.—Design 2037M; cost in frame
$1,492 to $1,585; plans $10. See page 65.

-816-

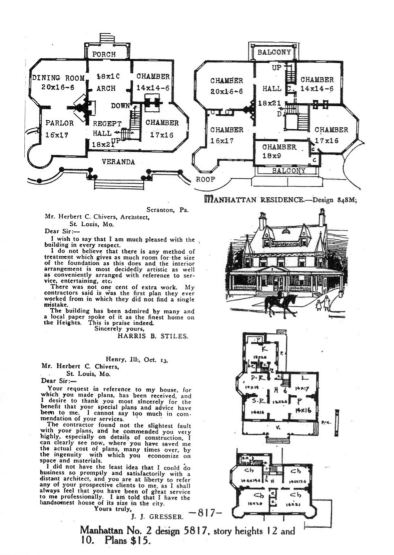

PORCH

| DINING ROOM 20x16-6 | 18x1C | CHAMBER 14x14-6 |
| PARLOR 16x17 | ARCH / DOWN / RECEPT HALL 18x21 / UP | CHAMBER 17x16 |

VERANDA

| CHAMBER 20x16-6 | BALCONY / UP / HALL C. 18x21 / D | CHAMBER 14x14-6 |
| CHAMBER 16x17 | CHAMBER 18x9 | CHAMBER 17x16 |

BALCONY

ROOF

MANHATTAN RESIDENCE.—Design 848M;

Scranton, Pa.

Mr. Herbert C. Chivers, Architect,
St. Louis, Mo.

Dear Sir:—

I wish to say that I am much pleased with the building in every respect.

I do not believe that there is any method of treatment which gives as much room for the size of the foundation as this does and the interior arrangement is most decidedly artistic as well as conveniently arranged with reference to service, entertaining, etc.

There was not one cent of extra work. My contractors said is was the first plan they ever worked from in which they did not find a single mistake.

The building has been admired by many and a local paper spoke of it as the finest home on the Heights. This is praise indeed.

Sincerely yours,
HARRIS B. STILES.

Henry, Ill., Oct. 13.

Mr. Herbert C. Chivers,
St. Louis, Mo.

Dear Sir:—

Your request in reference to my house, for which you made plans, has been received, and I desire to thank you most sincerely for the benefit that your special plans and advice have been to me. I cannot say too much in commendation of your services.

The contractor found not the slightest fault with your plans, and he commended you very highly, especially on details of construction, I can clearly see now, where you have saved me the actual cost of plans, many times over, by the ingenuity with which you economize on space and materials.

I did not have the least idea that I could do business so promptly and satisfactorily with a distant architect, and you are at liberty to refer any of your prospective clients to me, as I shall always feel that you have been of great service to me professionally. I am told that I have the handsomest house of its size in the city.

Yours truly,
J. J. GRESSER. —817—

Manhattan No. 2 design 5817, story heights 12 and 10. Plans $15.

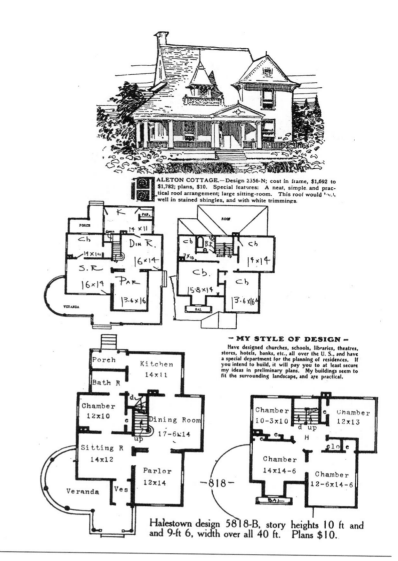

ALETON COTTAGE.—Design 2356-N; cost in frame, $1,692 to $1,782; plans, $10. Special features: A neat, simple and practical roof arrangement; large sitting-room. This roof would look well in stained shingles, and with white trimmings.

K	PAN
Ch	14 x 11
11x14	Din R. 16 x 14
S. R. 16 x 19	PAR / 13.6 x 16

VERANDA / BAL

Cb	B R
7 x 10	Cb 14 x 14
Cb 15.8 x 14	Cb 13.6 x 16.4

— MY STYLE OF DESIGN —

Have designed churches, schools, libraries, theatres, stores, hotels, banks, etc., all over the U. S., and have a special department for the planning of residences. If you intend to build, it will pay you to at least secure my ideas in preliminary plans. My buildings seem to fit the surrounding landscape, and are practical.

Porch	Kitchen 14x11
Bath R	
Chamber 12x10	d / Dining Room 17-6x14
Sitting R 14x12	up
Veranda / Ves	Parlor 12x14

Chamber 10-3x10	Chamber 12x13
	H
Chamber 14x14-6	Chamber 12-6x14-6

—818—

BAL

Halestown design 5818-B, story heights 10 ft and and 9-ft 6, width over all 40 ft. Plans $10.

width over all 40

Yalmer design No. 2 design 5819-A story heights 9 ft 6 and 9 ft.

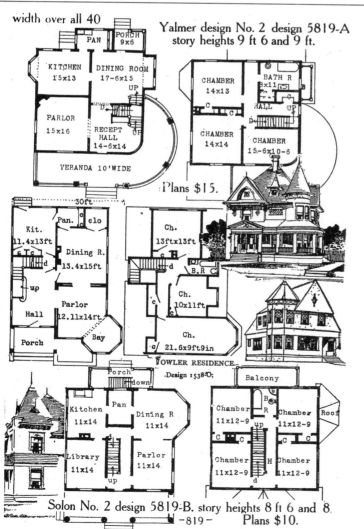

PAN	PORCH 9x6
KITCHEN 15x13	DINING ROOM 17-6x15 / UP
PARLOR 15x16	RECEPT HALL 14-6x14

VERANDA 10' WIDE

CHAMBER 14x13	BATH R 8x11
	HALL / UP
CHAMBER 14x14	CHAMBER 15-6x10-6

Plans $15.

30ft

Kit. 11.4x13ft	Pan. / clo
	Dining R. 13.4x15ft
Hall / up	Parlor 12.11x14ft
Porch	Bay

| Ch. 13ftx13ft |
| B.R |
| Ch. 10x11ft |
| Ch. 21.6x9ft9in |

FOWLER RESIDENCE.
Design 15380;

Porch / down	Balcony
Kitchen 11x14	Pan / Dining R 11x14
Library 11x14	Parlor 11x14 / up

Chamber 11x12-9	B / R / Chamber 11x12-9	Roof
	up	
Chamber 11x12-9	H / Chamber 11x12-9

Solon No. 2 design 5819-B. story heights 8 ft 6 and 8. —819— Plans $10.

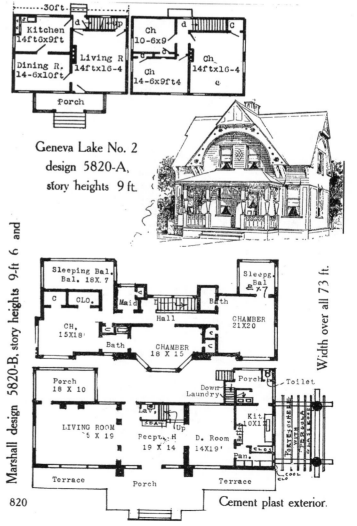

30ft

| Kitchen 14ft6x9ft | d |
| Dining R. 14-6x10ft | Living R 14ftx16-4 |

Porch

| Ch. 10-6x9 | C |
| Ch. 14-6x9ft4 | Ch. 14ftx16-4 |

Geneva Lake No. 2 design 5820-A, story heights 9 ft.

Marshall design 5820-B, story heights 9-ft 6 and

Sleeping Bal. Bal. 18X 7		Sleepg. Bal. X 7
C / CLO.	Maid / Hall / Bath	
CH. 15X18	Bath	CHAMBER 21X20
	CHAMBER 18 X 15	

Porch 18 X 10	Down Laundry	Porch	Toilet
	La.		Kit. 10X1
LIVING ROOM 5 X 19	Recep. H 19 X 14	D. Room 14X19'	PORTE WITH PERGOLA
Terrace	Porch	Terrace	

Width over all 73 ft.

820

Cement plast exterior.

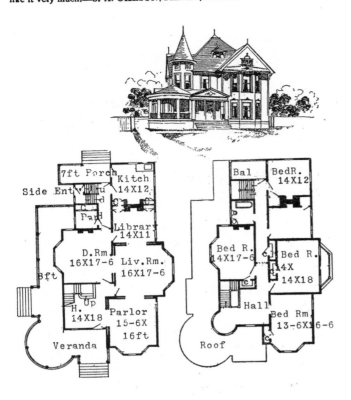

NEOGA RESIDENCE.—Design 1840M; cost in frame $2,-980 to $3,240; plans $25. Good size rooms; large side porch. See page 65.

DUNFEE RESIDENCE.—Design 1850-O; cost in stone and frame $3,440 to $4,260; plans $40.

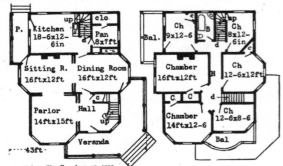

Bonner Springs design 5823, story heights 10 and 9 ft. Good corner-lot house.   Plans $15.

Blakeman design 5824, story heights, 10 and 9 ft 6. Attractive octagonal balcony.   Plans $10.

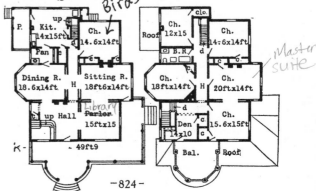

Gainesville, Ga., Aug. 15, 1902.
Mr. Herbert C. Chivers,
St. Louis, Mo.
Dear Sir:—
The plans which you furnished are admirable for small cottages and everybody in town wants to rent one. They have been occupied ever since they were built and I could rent several others like them if I had them
Very truly yours,
A. W. VAN HORN.

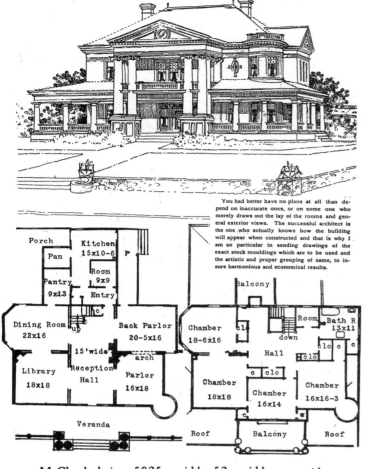

You had better have no plans at all than depend on inaccurate ones, or on some one who merely draws out the lay of the rooms and general exterior views. The successful architect is the one who actually knows how the building will appear when constructed and that is why I am so particular in sending drawings of the exact stock mouldings which are to be used and the artistic and proper grouping of same, to insure harmonious and economical results.

McCloud design 5825, width 52, width over side porches and all 73 ft, story heights 11-ft 6 and 10-ft 6. Plans $35.

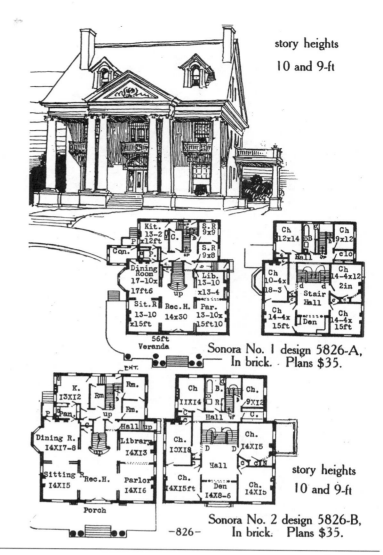

story heights 10 and 9-ft

Sonora No. 1 design 5826-A, In brick. Plans $35.

story heights 10 and 9-ft

Sonora No. 2 design 5826-B, In brick. Plans $35.

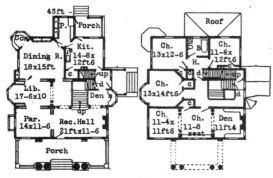

Zoni design 5827, story heights 10 and 9-ft 6. Attractive hall and den at side. Attractive chamber suite in front. Plans $35.

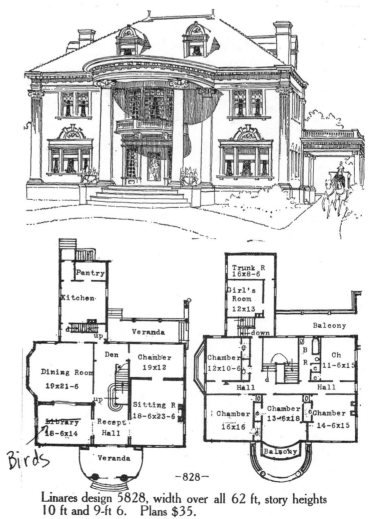

Birds

Linares design 5828, width over all 62 ft, story heights 10 ft and 9-ft 6. Plans $35.

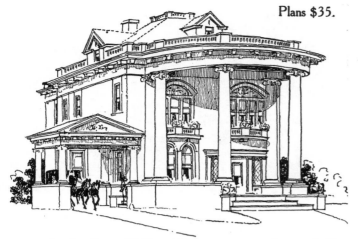

Juanito design 5829, width over porte-cochere and all 52 ft, story heights 10 and 9 ft. Good colonial effect.

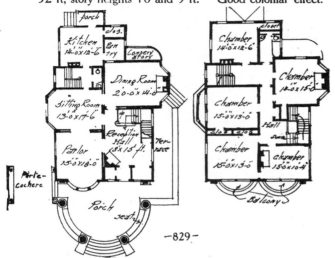

−829−

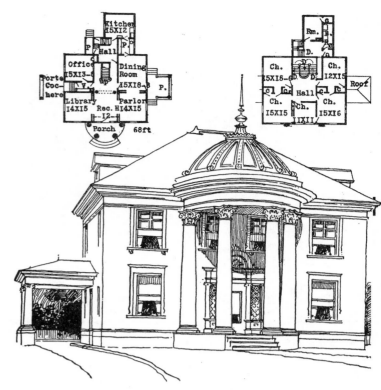

Rossland design 5830, story heights 10 and 9-ft 6. Good roof effect with greenish slate or shingles painted to match and galvanized iron dome painted to represent light greenish antique copper. Plans $35.

I am very much pleased with plans which you furnished me, and which I selected from one of your series of contributions to the Woman's Home Companion.
HERBERT BUTLER, New Lexington, O.

−830−

SSEN RESIDENCE.—Design 2247-N; cost in frame, $2,890 to $2,990; plans, $25. Special features: Attractive hall and inglenook at the heavy column effect to hall is very attractive; rear stairs is separate from second story so that main portion of house can be locked up and yet leave access for servants from kitchen to attic.

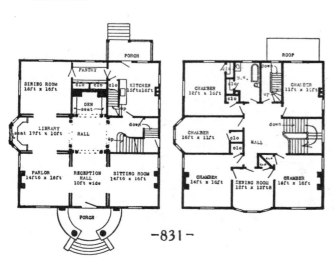

−831−

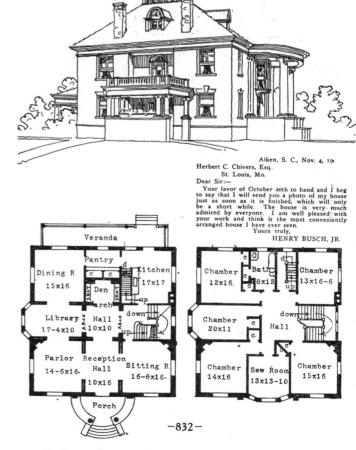

Aiken, S. C., Nov. 4, 19
Herbert C. Chivers, Esq.
St. Louis, Mo.
Dear Sir:—
Your favor of October 20th to hand and I beg to say that I will send you a photo of my house just as soon as it is finished, which will only be a short while. The house is very much admired by everyone. I am well pleased with your work and think it the most conveniently arranged house I have ever seen.
Yours truly,
HENRY BUSCH, JR.

−832−

Shelburne design 5832 in brick, width 44, story heights 11 and 10 ft. Plans $20.

PAYALTON RESIDENCE.—Design 1779-N; cost in frame, $2,690 to $2,980; plans, $25

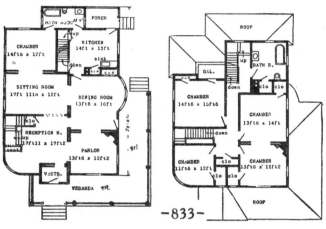

-833-

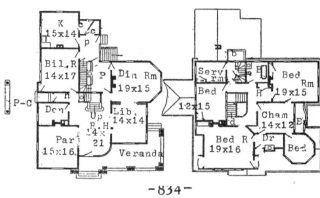

TUSCALOOSA RESIDENCE.—Design 2389-O; cost in frame, $2,980 to $3,500; plans, $30. Story heights, 12 and 11 ft. See page 65.

-834-

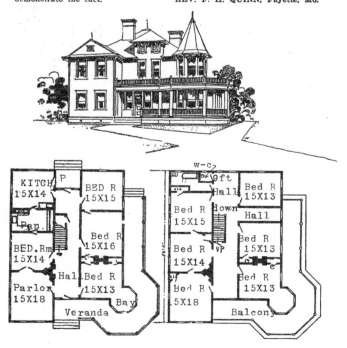

CRAIGVILLE RESIDENCE.—Design 1832M; cost in frame $2,780 to $2,940; plans $25. A good southern house. See page 65.

-835-

SARATOGA RESIDENCE.—Design 6030R; page 406; in frame, $2,490 to $2,670; plans, $10; width over all, 38 ft.; story heights, 10 ft. and 9 ft. 6 in. Special features: Plain, neat design; large rooms, wide open porch at side. See page 113.

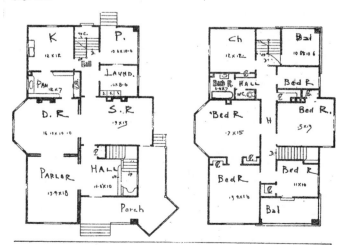

-836-

ALDRICH RESIDENCE.—Design 100,001-O; Cost, $4,-043 to $4.447; plans, $40; Special features: large dining room and varanda. Suitable for a Southern home. High stones. See page 65.

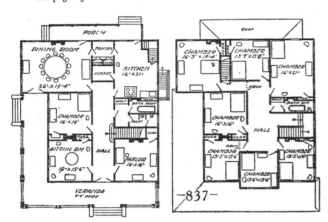

—837—

ROYALTON RESIDENCE.—Design 1911M; cost in frame $2,390 to $2,492; plans $20. See page 65.

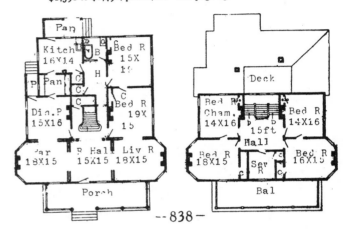

—838—

My residence at Maywood has been erected and I am pleased with it. The plans worked out well. GUSTAVUS M. FITZER, New York City.

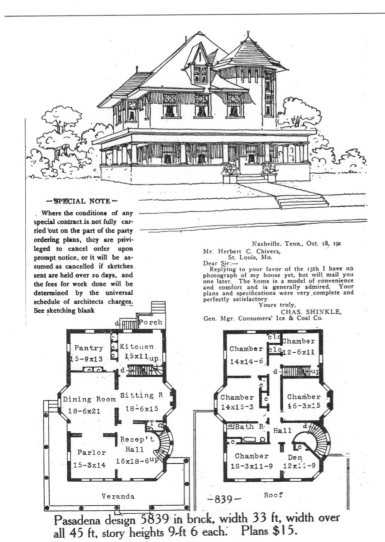

Nashville, Tenn., Oct. 18, 19(
Mr. Herbert C. Chivers,
    St. Louis, Mo.
Dear Sir:—
    Replying to your favor of the 15th I have no photograph of my house yet, but will mail you one later. The home is a model of convenience and comfort and is generally admired. Your plans and specifications were very complete and perfectly satisfactory.
        Yours truly,
            CHAS. SHINKLE,
Gen. Mgr. Consumers' Ice & Coal Co.

—839—

Pasadena design 5839 in brick, width 33 ft, width over all 45 ft, story heights 9-ft 6 each. Plans $15.

San Benito design 5840, width 43 ft, story heights 9-ft 6 each. Dignified colonial effect. Plans $35.

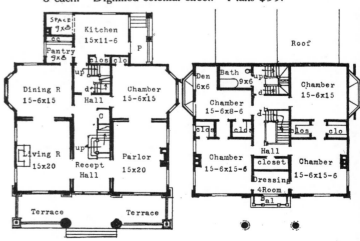

—840—

REDBEACH RESIDENCE.—Design 2021M; cost in frame $2,090 to $2,180; plans $25. Cost in brick. $3,204 to $3,800; plans, $45.

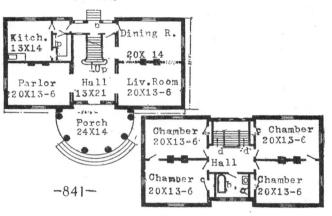

—841—

Our home is neat and tasty and is admired by everybody. I send you photo by to-day's mail. W. BUTLER, (Sec. Fruit Packing Co.), Shelby, Mich.

Redondo design 5842, width 34 ft (over all 43 ft) well-lighted front rooms, story heights 9 and 8-ft 6. Plans $20.

—842—

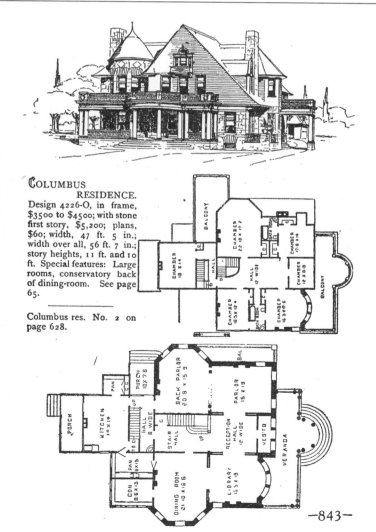

COLUMBUS RESIDENCE.

Design 4226-O, in frame, $3500 to $4500; with stone first story, $5,200; plans, $60; width, 47 ft. 5 in.; width over all, 56 ft. 7 in.; story heights, 11 ft. and 10 ft. Special features: Large rooms, conservatory back of dining-room. See page 65.

Columbus res. No. 2 on page 628.

—843—

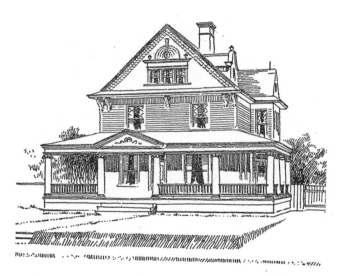

KENTON RESIDENCE.—Design 2382-N; cost in frame, $2,492 to $2,589; plans; $25.

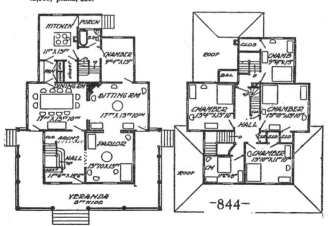

—844—

NEW YORK RESIDENCE.—Design 1031M; in frame, $4,599 to $5598; plans, $68; width, 63.6 x 39.8.; width over all, 30 ft.; story heights; 10 and 8.6. Special features; Wide imposing front, well ventilated, good size room, a good plan for a large country estate. See page 65.

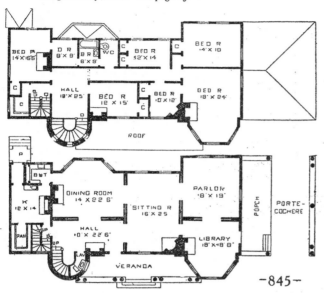

-845-

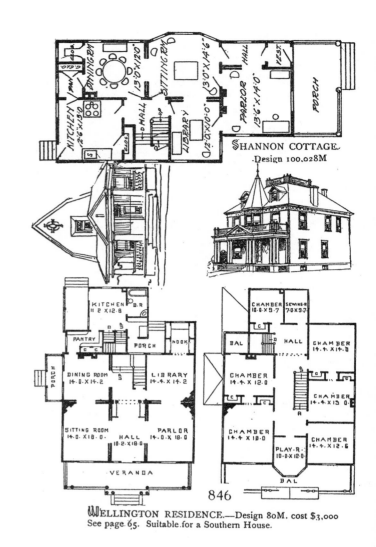

SHANNON COTTAGE.
Design 100.028M

846

WELLINGTON RESIDENCE.—Design 80M. cost $3,000
See page 65. Suitable for a Southern House.

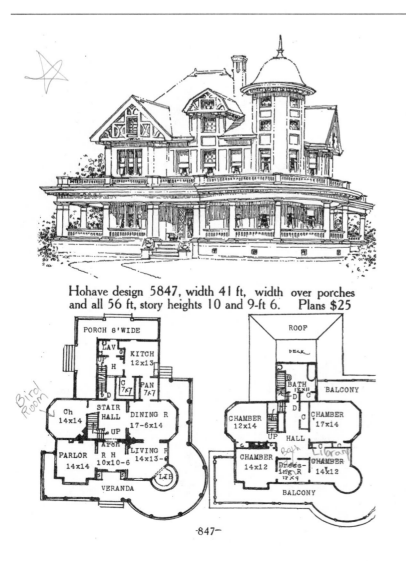

Hohave design 5847, width 41 ft, width over porches and all 56 ft, story heights 10 and 9-ft 6. Plans $25

-847-

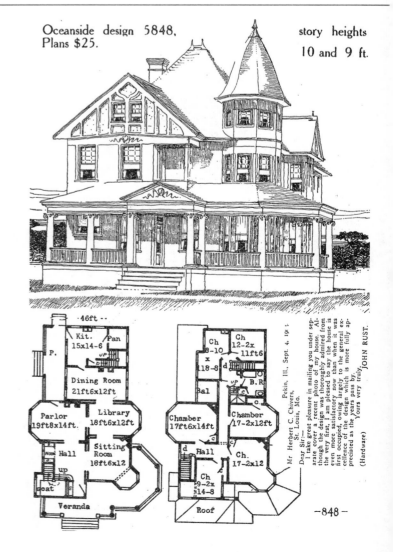

Oceanside design 5848, Plans $25.

story heights 10 and 9 ft.

-848-

DEVON RESIDENCE.—Design 1064M; in frame, $2,690 to $2,898; plans, $25; width, 38 ft, 11 in. by 32 ft. 6 in.; story heights, 9 ft. 6in. Special features: All rooms open into a large central hall; large fire-place in sitting-room. See page 65.

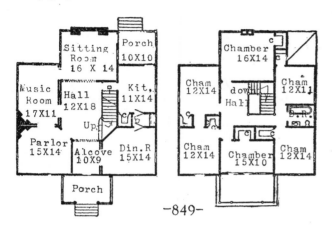

—849—

WREN RESIDENCE.—Design 1047M; in frame, $1800 to $2200; plans, $20; width, 30 ft. 8 in.; story heights, 9 ft. Special features: Attractive reception hall; vestibule coat and cloak closet; bay in front and side; See page 65.

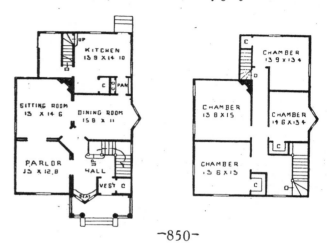

—850—

THORNHILL COTTAGE.—Design 100 906M; cost $2379 to $2758; plans, $25; size 28.6x48. Special features: attractive side tower, large pantry, combination rear stairs.

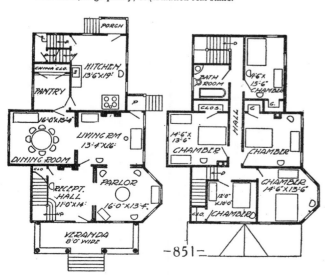

—851—

VIRGINIA RESIDENCE.—Design 856M; in frame, $3,490 to $3,960; plans, $25; width, 56 ft. 4 in. by 35 ft.; width over all, 70 ft.; story heights, 11 ft. Special features: Porte-cochere in rear, stairs do not crowd back of hall, parlor, 20 ft. by 17 ft.; library, 20x17 ft.; dining-room, 20x14 ft.; kiitchen 14x13 ft. See page 65.

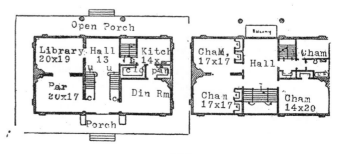

—852—

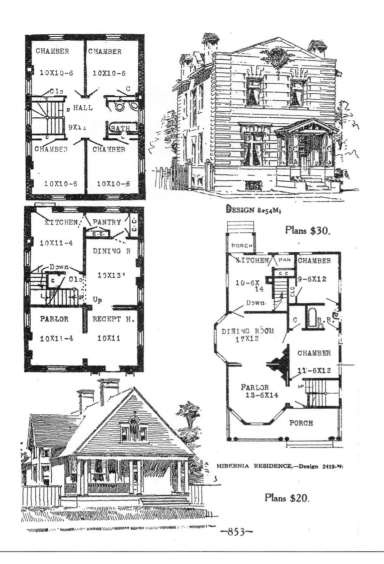

CHAMBER 10X10-6 | CHAMBER 10X10-6
HALL 9X12
BATH
CHAMBER 10X10-6 | CHAMBER 10X10-6

KITCHEN 10X11-4 | PANTRY
DINING R 10X13'
PARLOR 10X1!-4 | RECEPT H. 10X11

DESIGN 8254M;

Plans $30.

KITCHEN 10-6X14 | PAN | CHAMBER 9-6X12
DINING ROOM 17X12
CHAMBER 11-6X12
PARLOR 13-6X14
PORCH

HIBERNIA RESIDENCE.—Design 2419-N;

Plans $20.

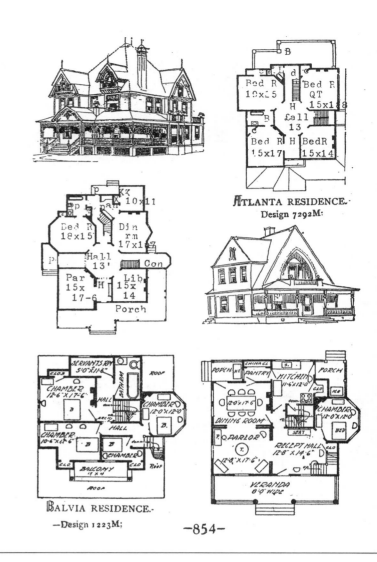

B
Bed R 10x15 | Bed R QT 15x18
Hall 13
Bed R 15x17 | BedR 15x14

ATLANTA RESIDENCE.
Design 7292M;

K 10x11
Bed R 18x15 | Din rm 17x14
Hall 13' | Con
Par 15x17-6 | Lib 15x14
Porch

SERVANTS RM 5'0"X11'6" | ROOF
CHAMBER 12-6 X 17-6 | CHAMBER 12-0 X 12-0
CHAMBER 10-6 X 17-6 | CHAMBER
BALCONY 19 X 4 | ROOF

PORCH | PANTRY | KITCHEN 11-6X12-0 | PORCH
DINING ROOM 10X17-6 | CHAMBER 12-0 X 12-0
PARLOR 12-0 X 17-6 | RECEPT HALL 12-6 X 14-6
VERANDA 8'-0" WIDE

BALVIA RESIDENCE.
—Design 1223M;

—853—

—854—

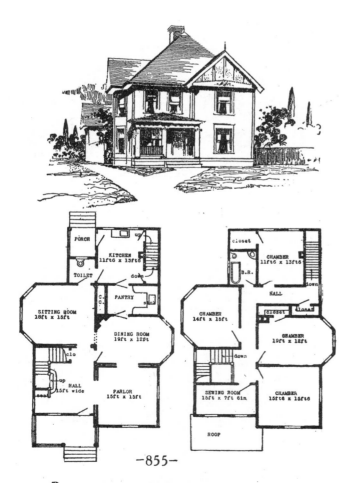

PORCH | | up
KITCHEN 11ft6 x 13ft6
TOILET
SITTING ROOM 18ft x 15ft
DINING ROOM 19ft x 12ft
PANTRY
HALL 15ft wide
PARLOR 15ft x 15ft

closet
CHAMBER 11ft6 x 13ft6
B.R.
HALL
CHAMBER 14ft x 15ft
CHAMBER 19ft x 12ft
SEWING ROOM 15ft x 7ft 6in. | CHAMBER 15ft6 x 15ft6
ROOF

—855—

RIMERTON RESIDENCE.—Design 2004M cost $2,295 to $2,385; plans $20. See page 65.

Calera, Ala., June 30, 1896.

Mr. Herbert C. Chivers, Architect, St. Louis Mo.:
Dear Sir:—In regard to plans and specifications drawn by you for my dwelling now nearing completion, will say, that same have fully come up to my expectations, and I consider it a very good investment for any one desiring to build, to have plans. The house is considered convenient and substantial, and I am very well satisfied.   Yours truly,
C. H. O'NEAL.

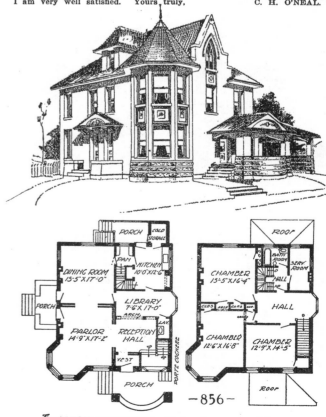

PORCH | COLD STORAGE | ROOF
DINING ROOM 15-5"X17-0" | PAN | KITCHEN 10'0"X12-6"
LIBRARY 7-6 X 17-0 | CHAMBER 15-5 X 16-4
PORCH
PARLOR 14-9"X17-2" | RECEPTION HALL
HALL
CHAMBER 12-6 X 16-8 | CHAMBER 12-9 X 14-5
PORCH | ROOF

—856—

HAUSTON RESIDENCE.—Design 64 on page 696; cost $3,250 to $3,999 in brick: size 33 ft. 5 in. by 38 ft.; story heights 10 ft. Special features: Very complete plans $15

CERESCO RESIDENCE.—Design 1923M; cost in frame $2,022 to $2,180; plans $15. See page 65.

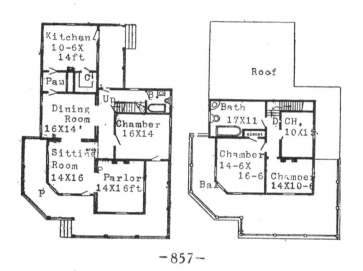

Kitchen 10-6X14ft
Pan
Dining Room 16X14'
Sitting Room 14X16
Chamber 16X14
Parlor 14X16ft

Roof
Bath 17X11
CH. 10X15
Chamber 14-6X 16-6
Chamber 14X10-6

—857—

RUDYARD RESIDENCE.—Design 2384M; cost in frame, $2,782 to $2,930; plans, $25. See page 65.

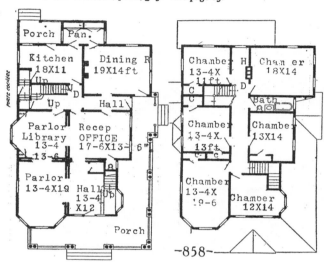

Porch   Pan.
Kitchen 18X11   Dining R 19X14ft
Up   Hall
Parlor Library 13-4 13-6   Recep OFFICE 17-6X13-6"
Parlor 13-4X19   Hall 13-4 X12
Porch

Chamber 13-4X 11ft   Chamer 18X14
Bath
Chamber 13-4X 13ft   Chamber 13X14
Chamber 13-4X 19-6   Chamber 12X14

—858—

 DAUGHTON RESIDENCE.—Design 2374-N; cost in brick veneer and frame, $3,500; plans, $30. Special features: Conservatory adjoining kitchen; attractive bay to reception hall; separate water-closet in connection with bath-room.

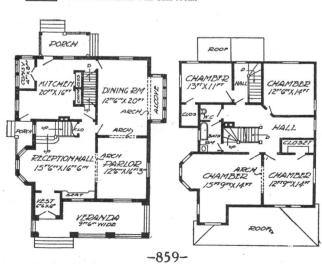

PORCH
Kitchen 20"X16"
Dining Rm 12"6"X20"
Reception Hall 15"6"X16"6"
Parlor 12"6"X16"3"
VERANDA 9"6" WIDE

ROOF
CHAMBER 13"X11"
CHAMBER 12"6"X14"
HALL
CHAMBER 15"9"X14"
CHAMBER 12"9"X14"
ROOF

—859—

KALKASKA COTTAGE.—Design 1783M; $1,292 to $1,348; plans, $15.

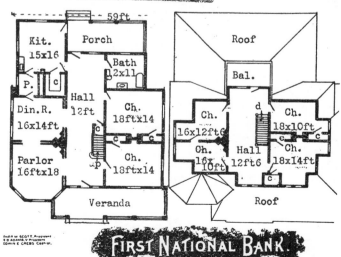

59ft
Kit. 15x16   Porch
P.
Hall 12ft   Bath 12x11
Din. R. 16x14ft   Ch. 18ftx14
Parlor 16ftx18   Ch. 18ftx14
Veranda

Roof
Bal.
Ch. 16x12ft6   Ch. 18x10ft
Ch. 16x10ft   Hall 12ft6   Ch. 18x14ft
Roof

Mr. Herbert C. Chivers,
St. Louis, Mo.   Fairfield. Ills.   10--24" 190
Dear Sir:-   Plans of our new bank are very finely executed. We are pleased with the general design and arrangement.

Yours sincerely,

Edw.E.Crebs Cashier.

—860—

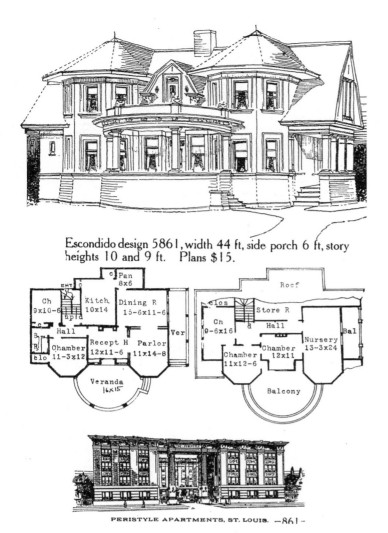

Escondido design 5861, width 44 ft, side porch 6 ft, story heights 10 and 9 ft.   Plans $15.

Ch 9x10-6 | Pan. 8x6 | Kitch. 10x14 | Dining R 15-6x11-6 | Ver

Hall | Chamber 11-3x12 | Recept H 12x11-6 | Parlor 11x14-8

Veranda 16x15

Clos | Store R | Cn 9-6x16 | Hall | Nursery 13-3x24 | Bal

Chamber 11x12-6 | Chamber 12x11

Balcony

PERISTYLE APARTMENTS, ST. LOUIS. —861—

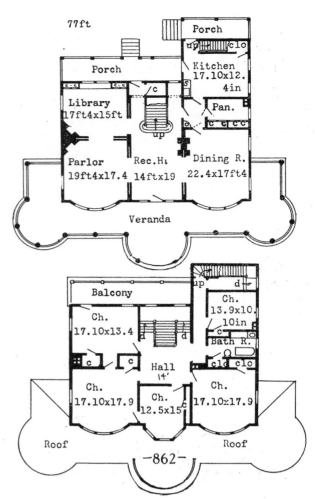

77ft

Porch

Porch | Kitchen 17.10x12.4in

Library 17ft4x15ft | Pan.

Parlor 19ft4x17.4 | Rec.H 14ftx19 | Dining R. 22.4x17ft4

Veranda

Balcony | Ch. 13.9x10.10in

Ch. 17.10x13.4 | Bath R.

Hall 14' | Ch. 17.10x17.9 | Ch. 12.5x15 | Ch. 17.10x17.9

Roof | Roof

—862—

Pinckneyville No. 4 design 5862, story heights 10-ft each.   Width 58-ft.   See design page 863.

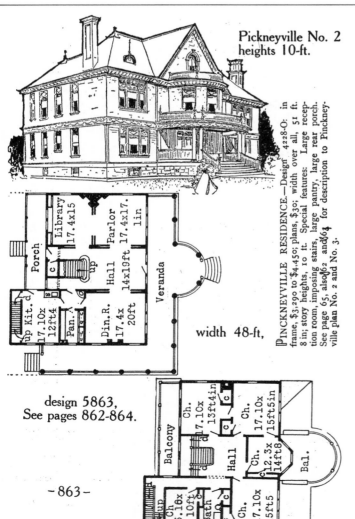

Pickneyville No. 2
heights 10-ft.

PINCKNEYVILLE RESIDENCE.—Design 4228-O: in frame, $3,290 to $4,450; plans, $30; width over all, 51 ft. 8 in; story heights, 10 ft. Special features: Large reception room, imposing stairs, large pantry, large rear porch. See page 65, also 862 and 864 for description to Pinckneyville plan No. 2 and No. 3.

Porch | Library 17.4x15 | Hall | Parlor 14x19ft 17.4x17. 1in

Kit. 17.10x 12ft4 | Pan. | Din.R. 17.4x 20ft | Veranda

width 48-ft,

design 5863,
See pages 862-864.

Balcony | Ch. 17.10x 13ft4in | Ch. 17.10x 15ft5in

Hall | Ch. 12.3x 14ft8 | Bal.

Ch. 13.16x 10ft | Bath | Ch. 17.10x 15ft5

—863—

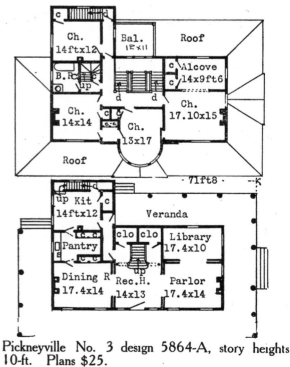

Ch. 14ftx12 | Bal. 12x11 | Roof

B.R. | Alcove 14x9ft6

Ch. 14x14 | Ch. 13x17 | Ch. 17.10x15

Roof

—71ft8—

Kit 14ftx12 | Veranda

Pantry | clo clo | Library 17.4x10

Dining R 17.4x14 | Rec.H. 14x13 | Parlor 17.4x14

Pickneyville No. 3 design 5864-A, story heights 10-ft.   Plans $25.

THE USE OF PLANS.
Plans are to be used but once, and parties purchasing plans of this office are priviledged to build only one building from them. This is a universal custom among architects, and for plans used a second time we are entitled to 3½ per cent on the total cost of each building erected from them.

Some are of the opinion that these plans may be used, provided changes are made, but where it can be shown that a prospective client purchased books containing certain ideas embodied in such plans as may be built from, without payment to the originator it is sufficient evidence on which to prosecute. This notice is simply to protect those who might endeavor to use "ignorance of the law" as an excuse for duplicating plans.

It is admitted, even by many architects, that the facilities of this office to produce practical plans and artistic designs is superior to that of any other in the United States.

If any of our stock plans should exceed estimate I will exchange them within 10 days after shipping for any other plans of less cost which I may have in stock, if returned in good shape, for $2 additional.

—864—

KALEVA RESIDENCE.—Design 100021M; cost $3026 to $3331; plans, $35; size 33x51 width over all, 36 ft. special features: bay in front and side. compact plans, large kitchen closet. See page 65.

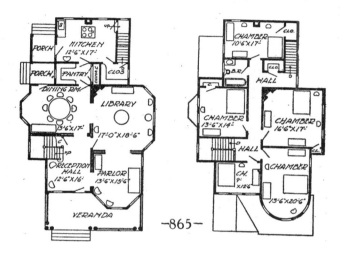

LOMERA RESIDENCE.—Design 2382M; cost in frame, $2,690 to $2,782; plans, $25. See page 65·

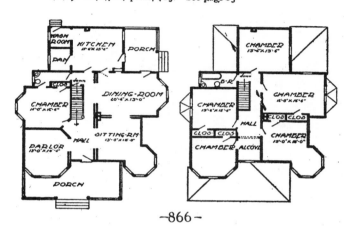

Shenango No. 4 design 5867-A, story heights 9-ft 6 and 9. Plans $20. See page 591.

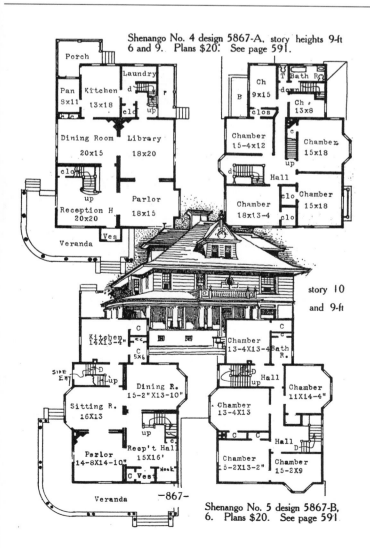

story 10 and 9-ft

Shenango No. 5 design 5867-B, 6. Plans $20. See page 591.

Gustonia No. 6 design 5868, width 30 ft 6, width over all 38 ft, story heights 10 and 8 ft 6. See pages 869-870-871. Plans $15.

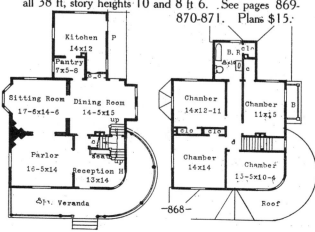

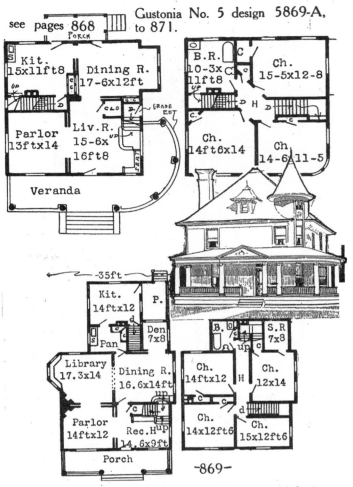

Gustonia No. 5 design 5869-A, to 871.

see pages 868

PORCH

Kit. 15x11ft8 — Dining R. 17-6x12ft

B.R. 10-3x 11ft8 — C — Ch. 15-5x12-8

Parlor 13ftx14 — Liv. R. 15-6x 16ft8

Ch. 14ft6x14 — Ch. 14-6 11-5

Veranda

-35ft

Kit. 14ftx12 — P.

Den 7x8 — Pan — S.R. 7x8

Library 17.3x14 — Dining R. 16.6x14ft

Ch. 14ftx12 — Ch. 12x14

Parlor 14ftx12 — Rec. H 14.6x9ft — Ch. 14x12ft6 — Ch. 15x12ft6

Porch

-869-

Gustonia No. 4 design 5869-B, story heights 9-ft 6 each. See pages 868 to 871.

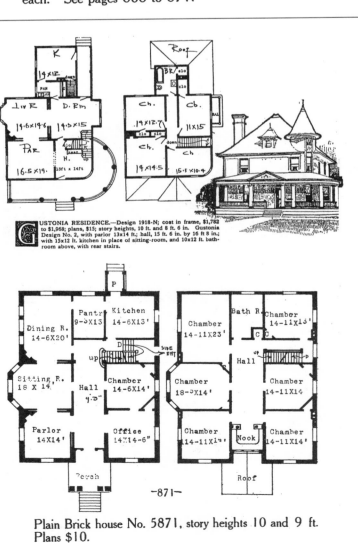

K 19x12

Liv R 19-6x19-6 — D. Rm 19-5x15

PAR 16.5x19 — H.

Roof

BR clo

Ch. 19x12-7 — Cb. 11x15

Ch. 19x14-5 — Ch 15-5x10-4

GUSTONIA RESIDENCE.—Design 1918-N; cost in frame, $1,782 to $1,968; plans, $15; story heights, 10 ft. and 8 ft. 6 in. Gustonia Design No. 2, with parlor 13x14 ft.; hall, 15 ft. 6 in. by 16 ft 8 in.; with 15x12 ft. kitchen in place of sitting-room, and 10x12 ft. bath-room above, with rear stairs.

P

Dining R. 14-6X20' — Pantry 9-5X13 — Kitchen 14-6X13'

Sitting R. 18 X 14' — Hall — Chamber 14-6X14'

Parlor 14X14' — Office 14'X14-6"

Porch

Chamber 14-11X23' — Bath R. — Chamber 14-11X13'

Hall

Chamber 18-5X14' — Chamber 14-11X14'

Chamber 14-11X14' — Nook — Chamber 14-11X14'

Roof

-871-

Plain Brick house No. 5871, story heights 10 and 9 ft. Plans $10.

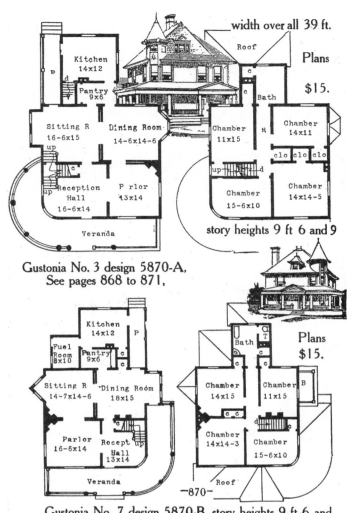

width over all 39 ft.

Plans $15.

Kitchen 14x12 — Roof

Pantry 9x6 — Bath

Sitting R 16-6x15 — Dining Room 14-6x14-6 — Chamber 11x15 — Chamber 14x11

Reception Hall 16-6x14 — P rlor 13x14 — Chamber 15-6x10 — Chamber 14x14-5

Veranda

story heights 9 ft 6 and 9

Gustonia No. 3 design 5870-A, See pages 868 to 871,

Kitchen 14x12 — P

Fuel Room 8x10 — Pantry 9x6

Sitting R 14-7x14-6 — Dining Room 18x15

Parlor 16-6x14 — Recept Hall 13x14

Veranda

Plans $15.

Bath

Chamber 14x15 — Chamber 11x15

Chamber 14x14-3 — Chamber 15-6x10

Roof

-870-

Gustonia No. 7 design 5870-B, story heights 9 ft 6 and 9, width over all 39 ft. See pages 868 to 871.

Alviso design 5872, width 33 ft, width over all 40 ft, story heights 9 ft 6 and 9. Large, spacious hall, neat stairs, large front room. Plans $10.

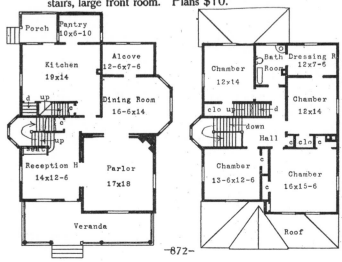

Porch — Pantry 10x6-10

Kitchen 19x14 — Alcove 12-6x7-6

Dining Room 16-6x14

Reception H 14x12-6 — Parlor 17x18

Veranda

Chamber 12x14 — Bath — Dressing R 12x7-6

Chamber 12x14

Hall

Chamber 13-6x12-6 — Chamber 16x15-6

Roof

-872-

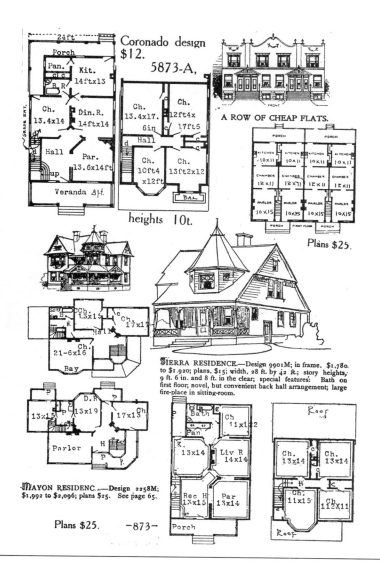

Coronado design $12.

5873-A,

24ft
Porch
Pan. | Kit. 14ftx13
B. R.
Ch. 13.4x14 | Din. R. 14ftx14
Hall
up
Par. 13.6x14ft
Veranda 8ft.

heights 10t.

Ch. 13.4x17. 6in | Ch. 12ftx4x 17ft5
Hall
Ch. 10ft4 x12ft | Ch. 13ft2x12

BAL.

A ROW OF CHEAP FLATS.

PORCH | PORCH
KITCHEN 10 X 11 | KITCHEN 10 X 11 | KITCHEN 10 X 11 | KITCHEN 10 X 11
CHAMBER 12 X 11 | CHAMBER 12 X 11 | CHAMBER 12 X 11 | CHAMBER 12 X 11
PARLOR 10 X 15 | PARLOR 10 X 15 | PARLOR 10 X 15 | PARLOR 10 X 15
PORCH | FIRST FLOOR | PORCH

Plans $25.

Ch. 13x15 | Ch. 17x17
Ch. 21-6x16
Bay

SIERRA RESIDENCE.—Design 9901M; in frame, $1,780. to $1,920; plans, $15; width, 28 ft. by 42 ft.; story heights, 9 ft. 6 in. and 8 in. in the clear; special features: Bath on first floor; novel, but convenient back hall arrangement; large fire-place in sitting-room.

D. R.
13x15 | P 13x19 | 17x13 Ch.
Parlor

Bath | Ch 11x12
Pan
K. 13x14 | Liv R 14x14
Rec H 13x15 | Par 13x14

Roof
Ch. 13x14 | Ch. 13x14
Ch. 11x15 | Ch. 112x11
Roof
Porch

MAYON RESIDENC.—Design 2258M; $1,992 to $2,096; plans $25. See page 65.

Plans $25.   —873—

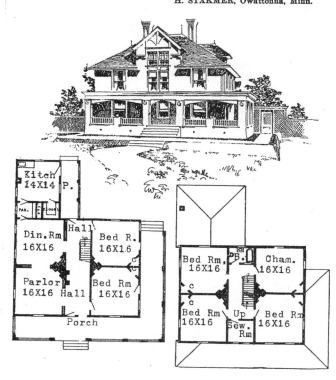

Kitch 14X14 | P.
PAN. | closet
Din. Rm 16X16 | Hall | Bed R. 16X16
Parlor 16X16 | Hall | Bed Rm 16X16
Porch

Bed Rm 16X16 | P. | Cham. 16X16
Bed Rm 16X16 | Up Sew. Rm | Bed Rm 16X16

WIXOM RESIDENCE.—Design 1843-N; cost in frame, $2,990 to $3,198; plans, $25. Large, well-ventilated rooms. Spacious veranda; ample fire-places.

—874—

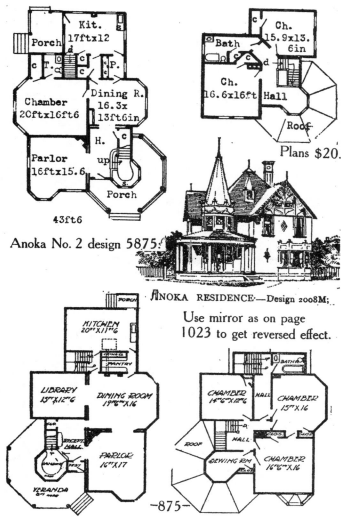

Porch | Kit. 17ftx12
Chamber 20ftx16ft6 | Dining R. 16.3x 13ft6in
Parlor 16ftx15.6 | up
Porch

Bath | Ch. 15.9x13. 6in
Ch. 16.6x16ft | Hall
Roof

Plans $20.

43ft6

Anoka No. 2 design 5875.

ANOKA RESIDENCE.—Design 2008M;

Use mirror as on page 1023 to get reversed effect.

KITCHEN 20"X17"6
DINING R.
PANTRY
LIBRARY 15"X12"6 | DINING ROOM 19'6"X16
RECEPTION HALL
PARLOR 16"X17
VERANDA

CHAMBER 14'6"X12"6 | HALL | CHAMBER 15"X16
ROOF | HALL
SEWING RM | CHAMBER 16'6"X16

—875—

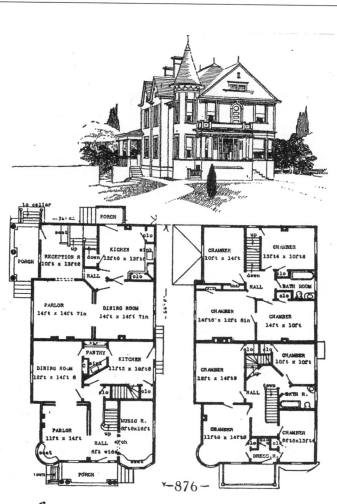

to cellar
PORCH
RECEPTION R 10ft x 13ft6 | KICHEN 13ft6 x 13ft6
HALL
PARLOR 14ft x 14ft 7in | DINING ROOM 14ft x 14ft 7in
PANTRY
DINING ROOM 12ft x 14ft 6 | KITCHEN 11ft2 x 16ft8
PARLOR 11ft x 14ft | MUSIC R. 8ft6x16ft6
HALL 6ft wide

CHAMBER 10ft x 14ft | CHAMBER 13ft4 x 10ft6
HALL | BATH ROOM
CHAMBER 14ft6 x 12ft 8in | CHAMBER 14ft x 10ft
CHAMBER 12ft x 14ft | CHAMBER 10ft x 10ft
CHAMBER 11ft x 14ft6 | CHAMBER 8ft6x13ft6
HALL | BATH R.
DRESS. R.

—876—

GRAYDON RESIDENCE.—Design 1924M; cost $2,682 to $2,890; plans $25. Double house. See page 65.

MT. CARROLL RESIDENCE.—Design 6025-O; in frame, $2,490 to $2,680; plans, $20; width, 30 ft. 10 in.; width over all, 40 ft.; story heights, 10 ft.; special features: Good for corner lot.

Mt. Carroll Residence No. 2, Schaeffler design, same as above, with 9 ft. octagon tower; with 3 ft. bay to dining-room; with wide porch extending to bath-room, with door at rear hall; with 9 ft. 6 in. and 8 ft. 8 in. story heights. See page 65.

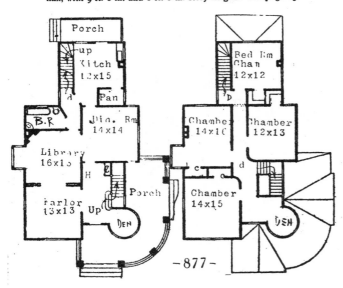

-877-

CINCINNATI RESIDENCE.—Design 9298M; in brick, $3,200 to $3,500; in frame, $2,000 to $2,200; plans, $35 in brick, $25 in frame; width, 29 ft. 4 in. by 37 ft. 6 in.; width over all 32 ft; story heights, 10 ft. Special features: Attractive library back of reception room; similar room above.

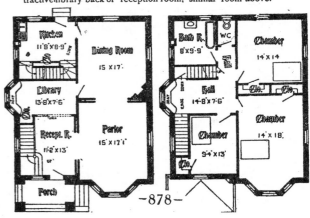

-878-

story heights 10 and 9 ft.
Plans $20.

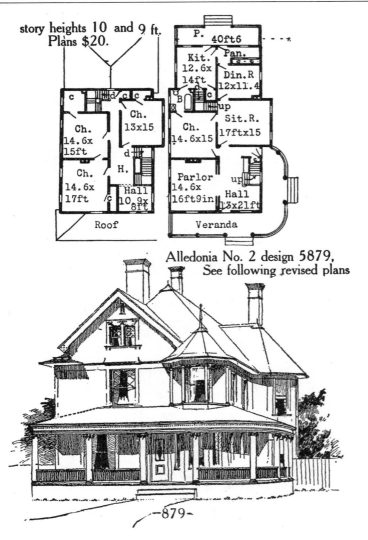

Alledonia No. 2 design 5879,
See following revised plans

-879-

Estella plan No. 4, Clark design
See page 65. See plans on page

Estella No. 8 design 5880-A, see exterior page 887, story heights 10 and 9-ft 4. Plans $20.

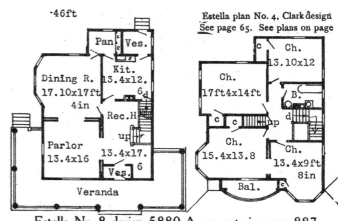

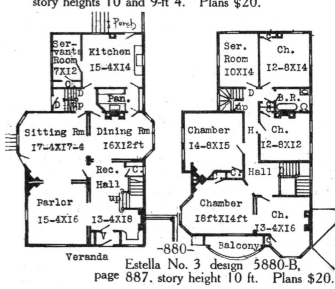

-880-

Estella No. 3 design 5880-B,
page 887, story height 10 ft. Plans $20.

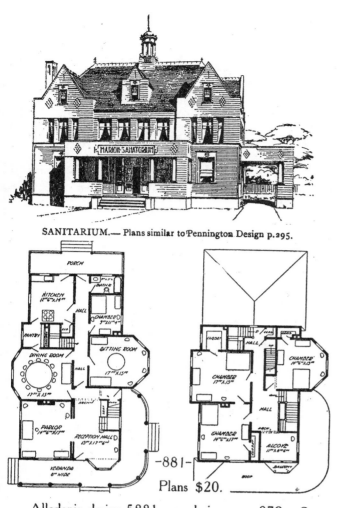

SANITARIUM.— Plans similar to Pennington Design p. 295.

Alledonia design 5881, see design page 879. See following similar plans. Story heights 10 and 9 ft.

—881—

Plans $20.

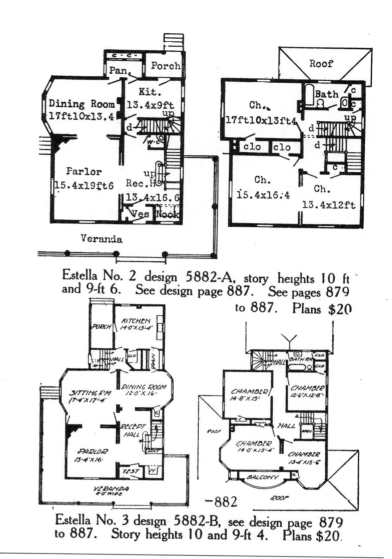

Estella No. 2 design 5882-A, story heights 10 ft and 9-ft 6. See design page 887. See pages 879 to 887. Plans $20

—882—

Estella No. 3 design 5882-B, see design page 879 to 887. Story heights 10 and 9-ft 4. Plans $20.

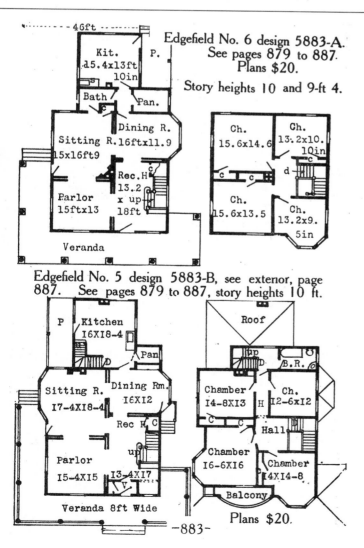

Edgefield No. 6 design 5883-A. See pages 879 to 887. Plans $20.

Story heights 10 and 9-ft 4.

Edgefield No. 5 design 5883-B, see exterior, page 887. See pages 879 to 887, story heights 10 ft.

—883—

Plans $20.

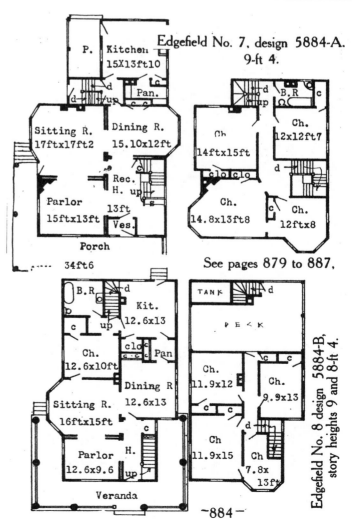

Edgefield No. 7. design 5884-A. 9-ft 4.

See pages 879 to 887.

Edgefield No. 8 design 5884-B, story heights 9 and 8-ft 4.

—884—

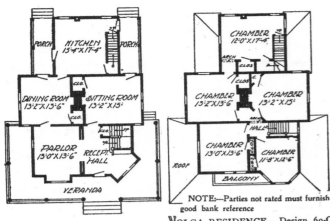

NOTE:—Parties not rated must furnish good bank reference

VOLGA RESIDENCE.—Design 69-O; cost, $2,390; plans $20; similar exterior to Edgefield residence on page

—ORDER BLANK—

HERBERT C. CHIVERS, Architect,
St. Louis, Mo. Date..................

Please make preliminary drawings (for approval) complete working drawings, details and legally worded specifications, for which I agree to pay you $.... upon delivery.
Respectfully,

Street.................. Name..........

City.......... State..........

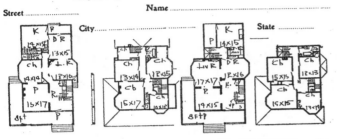

OHARA RESIDENCE. — Design 36-O; cost, $2,700 to $2,900; size 29 ft. 8 in. by 34 ft. 5 in.; story heights, 10 ft. and 9 ft. 4 in. Special features: Porte-cochere lavatory under stairs and side entrance. Plans $20. See design on page. See page 65.

LANCELL RESIDENCE. — Design 37-O; cost $2 344 to $2 598; size 29 ft. 8 in. by 52 ft.; story heights, 10 ft. and 9 ft. 4 in.; plans $20. See design of Edgefield Cottage on page See page 65.

—885—

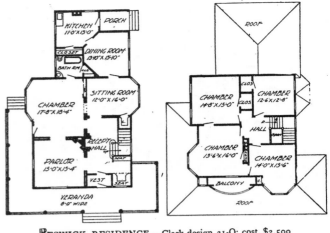

BESWICK RESIDENCE.—Clark design 31-O; cost, $2,500 to $2,700; size, 32 ft. by 55 ft. 6 in.; story heights, 9 ft. 6 in. and 9 ft.; plans, $10. See Edgefield design on page 605. See page 65. See plans on page 607.

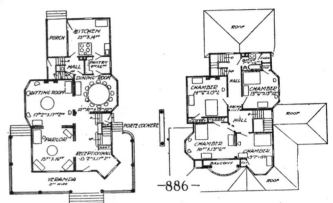

—886—

ALHAMBRA RESIDENCE.—Design 2252-O; cost in frame $2,590 to $2,682; plans $25. See Edgefield Res. for exterior

EDGEFIELD COTTAGE.—Design 190,199-O; in frame, $2,690 to $2,899; plans, $20; width, 30 ft. 4 in.; width over all, 45 ft.; story heights, 10 ft. and 9 ft. 4 in.; special features: Wide veranda; combination inside-and-outside cellar stairs, large bath-room and pantry; brick fire-place in reception hall. See index for Edgefield plans revised. See page 65.

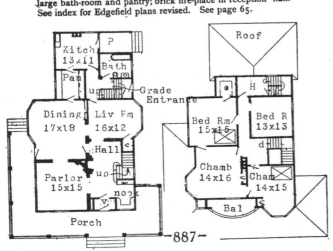

—887—

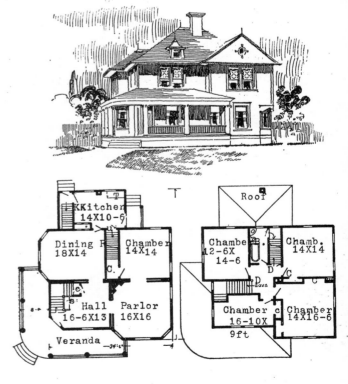

 OVANA RESIDENCE.—Design 1842-N; cost in frame. $2,390 to $2,498; plans $20; story heights, 9 ft. 6 in. and 8 ft. 6 in. Special features: Large rooms; neat, attractive design; good corner-lot design; attractive upper sash to second-story windows.

—888—

MONTEREY RESIDENCE.—Design 100,009M; cost, $2,806 to $3,886; size, 43 x 36 ft. Special features: Large brick fire-place in hall; large pantry; well-ventilated front

I cannot afford to have my clients in any way dissatisfied. I want your future business and that of your friends. I am interested in bettering your locality architecturally and when you hear of anyone who has intentions to build, please do not fail to mention my name and at the same time drop me a line.

HERBERT C. CHIVERS,

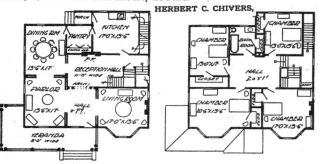

—889—

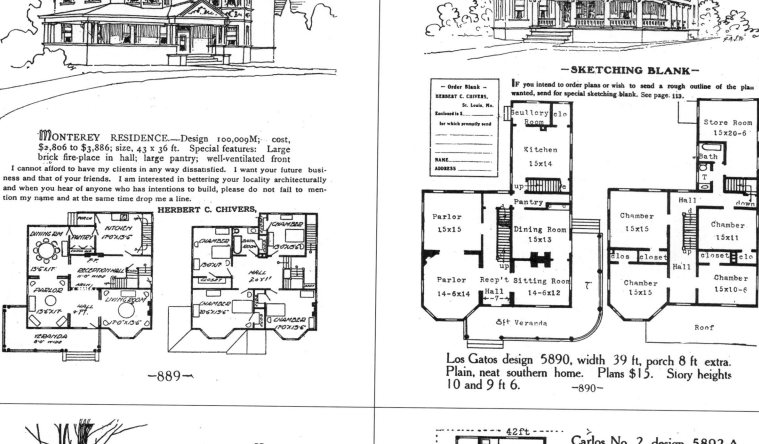

Los Gatos design 5890, width 39 ft, porch 8 ft extra. Plain, neat southern home. Plans $15. Story heights 10 and 9 ft 6.

—890—

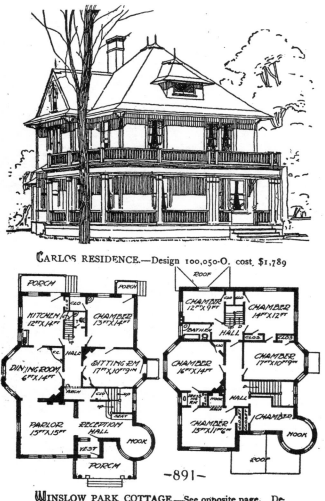

CARLOS RESIDENCE.—Design 100,050-O. cost $1,789

—891—

WINSLOW PARK COTTAGE.—See opposite page. Design 2469-M; cost in brick, $7,000 to $7,500. Plans, $55.

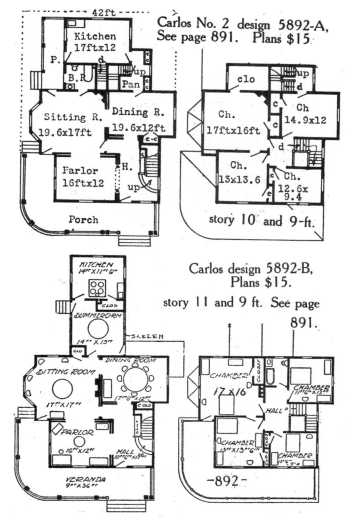

Carlos No. 2 design 5892-A, See page 891. Plans $15.

story 10 and 9-ft.

Carlos design 5892-B, Plans $15.

story 11 and 9 ft. See page 891.

—892—

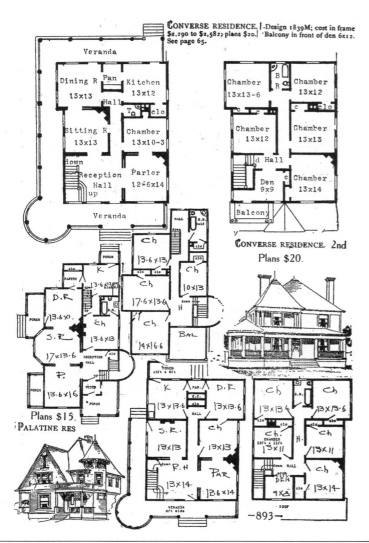

CONVERSE RESIDENCE.—Design 1839M; cost in frame $2,290 to $2,582; plans $20. Balcony in front of den 6x12. See page 65.

Veranda

Dining R 13x13 | Pan | Kitchen 13x12

Hall

Sitting R 13x13 | Chamber 13x10-3

down | Reception Hall | up | Parlor 12-6x14

Veranda

Chamber 13x13-6 | B R | Chamber 13x12

clo

Chamber 13x12 | Chamber 13x13

clo

d Hall

Den 9x9 | Chamber 13x14

Balcony

CONVERSE RESIDENCE. 2nd
Plans $20.

Plans $15.
PALATINE RES

Ch 13-6x13

Ch 10x13

Ch 17-6x13-6

BAL

Ch 14x16-6

D.R 13-6x1

S.R 17x13-6

Ch 13-6x13

P. 13-6x16

K 13-6x13-6

K 13x13-6 | D.R 13x13-6 | Ch 13x13-6 | Ch 13x13-6

S.R 13x13 | Ch 13x13 | Ch 13x11 | Ch 13x11

R.H 13x14 | PAR 12-6x14 | DEN 9x8 | Ch 13x14

—893—

ERDA RESIDENCE.—Design 100,045-O; size, 34.6x33 ft. 6 in.; cost, $1,588 to $1,792; plans, $15; story heights, 1st 9 ft. 6 in., 2d 9 ft., cellar 7 ft. A plain, practical house. See page 65.

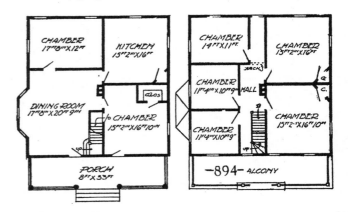

CHAMBER 17'8"X12'' | KITCHEN 15'2"X16'' | CHAMBER 14'X11' | CHAMBER 13'2"X16''

DINING ROOM 17'8"X20'9'' | CHAMBER 11'4"X10'9' | HALL | CHAMBER 15'2"X16'10'' | CHAMBER 11'4"X10'9' | CHAMBER 13'2"X16'10''

PORCH 8'7"X33'' | —894— BALCONY

ROBERTS RESIDENCE.—Design 9289-O; in frame, $2,190 to $2,389; plans, $25; width, 34 ft. by 44 ft.; story heights, 9 ft. 4 in. and 9 ft. (full story); special features: Large reception hall, with bay; octagon parlor, well ventilated; conveniently arranged stairs; four rooms with front view. Modifications: By eliminating closet to down-stairs chamber, grade entrance to cellar can be had. See page 65.

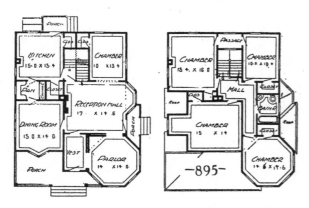

KITCHEN 15-0 X 13-4 | CHAMBER 10 X 13-4

RECEPTION HALL 17 X 14-5

DINING ROOM 13-0 X 14-0

PARLOR 14 X 14

CHAMBER 13-4 X 16-0 | CHAMBER 10-3 X 10

HALL

CHAMBER 15 X 14

CHAMBER 14-6 X 14-6

—895—

VICKSBURG RESIDENCE.—Design 1870M; in frame, $1589 to $1798; plans, $25; story heights, 9 ft. 6 in. and 8 ft. 6 in.; full story. Special features: Designed for stained shingle effect. See page 65.

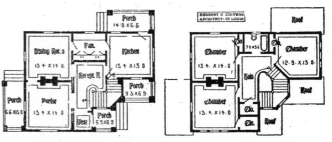

PORCH 14-0 X 6-6

DINING ROOM 13-4 X 14-0 | Fam. | KITCHEN 13-4 X 13-0

RECEPT. R.

PARLOR 13-4 X 13-0

PORCH 6-6 X 5-0 | PORCH 5-9 X 6-9

Chamber 13-4 X 14-0 | Chamber 12-9 X 13-6

Hall

Chamber 13-4 X 14-0

Roof | Roof | Roof

The plans which you furnished me for my house were all right in every way and were entirely satisfactory. I can heartily recommend the plans drawn by you to any person intending to build.—Wm. H. Gilmartin, Bloomington, Ill.

—896—

TILDEN RESIDENCE.—Design 1558M; in frame, $2,500 to $2,890; plans, $25; width over all, 43 ft. 6 in.; story heights 10 ft. Special features: Large, wide veranda; large rooms. See page 65.

Boston, Mass., June 30, 19

Mr Herbert C. Chivers,
St. Louis, Mo.
Dear Sir:—

The plans and specifications received from you are very complete and you have carried out my ideas very clearly. I think it is going to make just the house I want. I am really getting more for my money, than I thought I would.

The plans have been favorably commented on by our local architects. They say that you understand how to carry out the details of colonial work correctly.

Yours respectfully,

(Jeweler)   HENRY F. GUILD.

—897—

ANITA RESIDENCE.—Design 100,038-O; plans, $25. width 50.6,; story heights, 1st 12 ft., 2d 11 ft.; cost $2,498 to $2,699 See page 65.

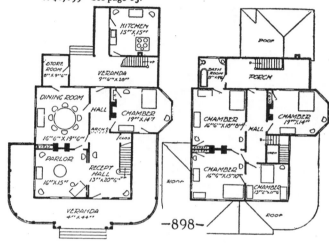

—898—

MONTEER RESIDENCE.—Design 100,037-O; cost $2,298 to $2,497; plans, $20; story heights, 1st 9 ft. 2d 8 ft. cellar 7 ft; width 42 ft. Special features: Large rooms; parlor is 14.10x19.6. See page 65.

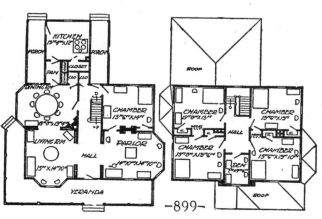

—899—

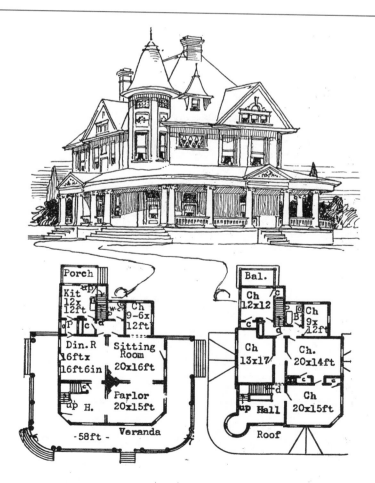

Mariposa design 5900, large rooms, imposing corner-lot house, well lighted front rooms. Story heights 10 ft. Plans $25.

—900—

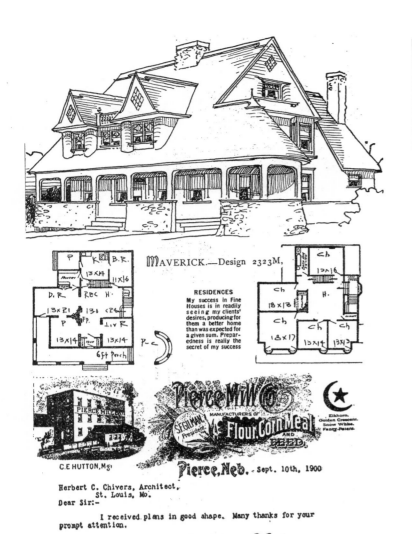

MAVERICK.—Design 2323M,

RESIDENCES

My success in Fine Houses is in readily seeing my clients' desires, producing for them a better home than was expected for a given sum. Preparedness is really the secret of my success

P—c

Pierce Mill Co.
MANUFACTURERS OF
Va. Flour, Corn Meal AND FEED

S. F. GILMAN, President

Elkhorn. Golden Crescent. Snow White. Fancy Patent.

C. E. HUTTON, Mgr

Pierce, Neb.—Sept. 10th, 1900

Herbert C. Chivers, Architect,
St. Louis, Mo.
Dear Sir:—

I received plans in good shape. Many thanks for your prompt attention.

—901—   Very truly, C. E. Hutton

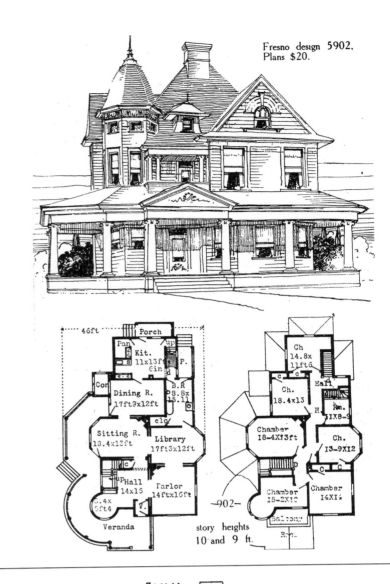

Fresno design 5902.
Plans $20.

—902—   story heights 10 and 9 ft.

Berendo design 5903, story heights 9 ft 6 and 9. Suitable for lot with double front, or overlooking body of water. Plans $50.

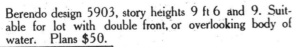

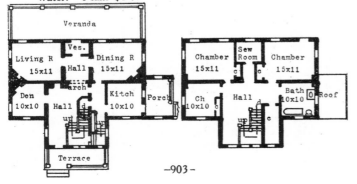

—903—

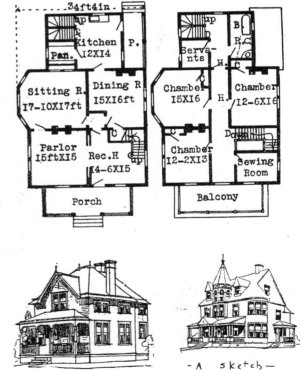

—A sketch—

GOODLAND RESEIDENCE. — Design 9686-O; in frame, $1,280 to $1,360; plans, $10; story heights, 9 ft. 6 in. and 8 ft. 6 in. (cut down by roof to 5 ft.) See page 6s

Sugar Grove, Ohio, Aug. 6, 190
Herbert C. Chivers, Esq.,
St. Louis, Mo.
Dear Sir:—
Under separate cover I mail you photograph of my house and will say that I built same according to plans furnished by you and am highly pleased. I think I have the best arranged and most artistic-looking house in our town.
Very respectfully,
I. N. MATHENY.

—904—

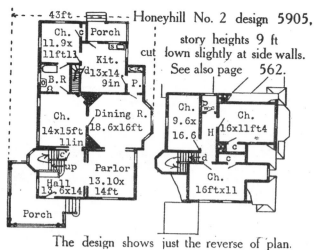

Honeyhill No. 2 design 5905,
story heights 9 ft
cut down slightly at side walls.
See also page 562.

43ft

Ch. c Porch
11.9x
11ft11

Kit.
d13x14
9in

B.R

P.

Ch.
14x15ft
11in

Dining R.
18.6x16ft

up

Hall
13.6x14

Porch

Ch.
9.6x
16.6

w.c.
H

Ch.
16x11ft4

c

d

Ch.
16ftx11

The design shows just the reverse of plan.

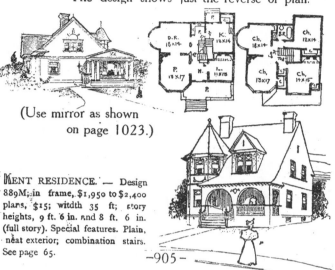

(Use mirror as shown
on page 1023.)

D.R.
15x14

K.
12x14

P.
13x17

H.
11x15

Ch.
18x14

Ch.
12x14

Ch.
13x17

Ch.
14x15

KENT RESIDENCE. — Design
889M; in frame, $1,950 to $2,400
plans, $15; width 35 ft; story
heights, 9 ft. 6 in. and 8 ft. 6 in.
(full story). Special features. Plain,
neat exterior; combination stairs.
See page 65.

—905—

SALEM RESIDENCE.—Design 1878M; in frame, $1599 to
$1898; plans, $20; width, 28 ft. 2 in. x 31 ft.; width over all,
36 ft.; story heights, 9 ft. 6 in. and 9 ft. Special features:
Simple tower effect; combination inside-and-outside cellar entrance, with door at grade; compact plan; the working plans
show a more attractive design than the sketch given, with
ornamental gable end. See page 65.

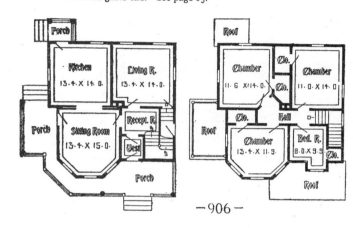

Porch

Kitchen
13.4 X 14.0

Living R.
13.4 X 14.0

Porch

Sitting Room
13.4 X 15.0

Recept. R.

Vest.

Roof

Chamber
11.6 X14.0

Clo.

Clo.

Chamber
11.0 X 14.0

Clo.

Roof

Hall

Clo.

Chamber
13.4 X 11.9

Bed. R.
8.0 X 9.5

Clo.

Porch

Roof

—906—

SELMA DESIGN 5907
HEIGHTS 9-6 & 9'

Plans $10

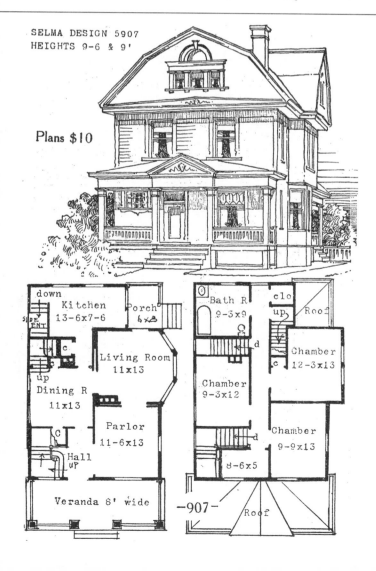

down

Kitchen
13-6x7-6

Porch
4x8

SIDE
ENT

c

up

Living Room
11x13

Dining R
11x13

c

Parlor
11-6x13

Hall
up

Veranda 8' wide

Bath R
9-3x9

clo
up

Roof

d

Chamber
12-3x13

c

Chamber
9-3x12

d

Chamber
9-9x13

8-6x5

—907—

Roof

WILMOT RESIDENCE.—Design 1935M; cost in frame,
$2,590 to $2,780; plans $25; cost in brick $4,580 to $5,690;
plans $65.

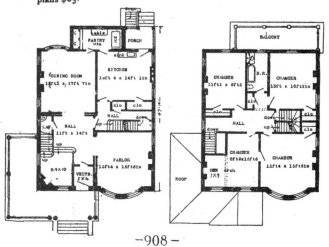

c

PANTRY
11x6

ICE

table

PORCH

sink

KITCHEN

DINING ROOM
18ft3 x 17ft 7in

16ft 4 x 14ft 1in

clo

clo

LAV.
11ft x 14ft

HALL

down

up

PARLOR
15ft4 x 15ft6in

8-9X10

VESTB.
7x6

BALCONY

CHAMBER
11ft1 x 6ft2

B.R.

CHAMBER
13ft x 16ft2in

clo

HALL

down

up

clo

ROOF

CHAMBER
6ft6x18ft6

DEN
7X9

CHAMBER
15ft x 15ft2in

—908—

LENARVEE COTTAGE.—Design 2351-N; cost in frame, $1,292 to $1,399; plans, $15. Economical stair arrangement.

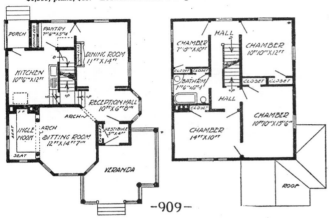

—909—

KENSICO RESIDENCE.—Design 2060M; cost in frame $1,680 to $1,792; plans $15. See page 65.

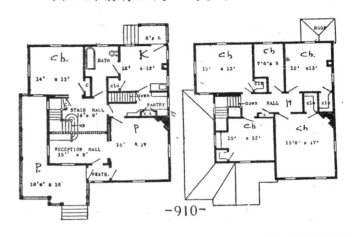

—910—

 JULIETTA RESIDENCE.—Design 2387-N; cost in frame, $2,592 to $2,780; plans, $25. Special features: Down stairs chamber and bath; large veranda; door from dining-room out onto side porch; combination cellar entrance.

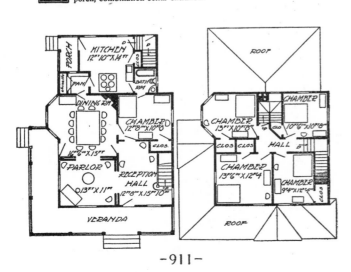

—911—

 OLANDUS COTTAGE.—Design 2354-N; cost, $2,450 to $2,700; plans, $15; story heights, 10 ft. and 9 ft. 6 in. Special features: Large veranda; pleasant outlook from front rooms; front of house is not cut up by stairs. A wide, imposing front.

Secure an Architect who can combine style and dignity in DESIGN with practicability and economy in construction.

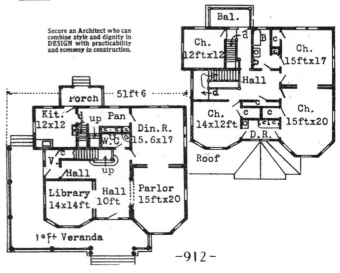

—912—

A STATELY HOME.

OSGOOD RESIDENCE.—Design 100,025M; size, 45 x 48.6: special features; large rooms, Southern plan. wide varanda, good ventilation Plans. $60. See page 65.

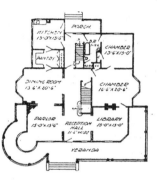
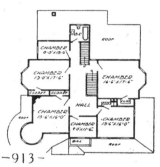

—913—

MILLSDALE RES.—Design 2270M; cost in frame $1,692 to $1,789; plans, $25. See page 65.

—914—

MINOOKA RESIDENCE.—Design 2273M; cost in frame, $3,500 to $4,690; plans, $75. See page 65.

Los Banos design 5915, story heights 9 ft 6 and 9. Plain, neat exterior. Plans $15.

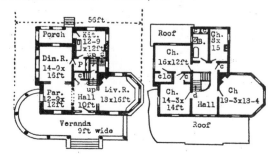

South St. Joseph, June 6, 1904.
H. C. Chivers, Esq.,
St. Louis, Mo
Dear Sir:—
I am pleased with the plans which you prepered for two houses for me and will send you photographs of them at the earliest opportunity.
Yours truly,
V. W. EMMERT.

—915—

Esmeralda 5916, story heights 11 and 10. Plans $12.

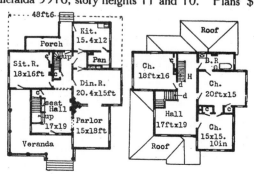

I desire to state that the house in question, as built from your plans, is highly satisfactory to all concerned.—Frank C. Patten, Sycamore, Ill.

—916—

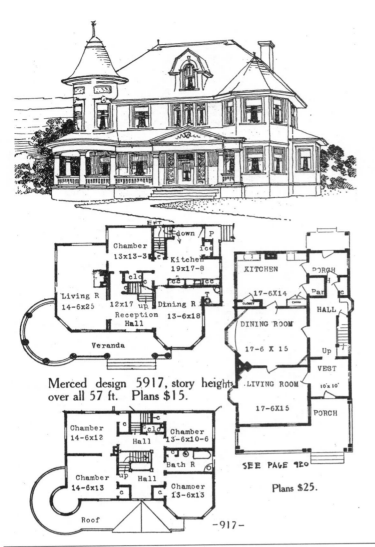

Merced design 5917, story heights
over all 57 ft. Plans $15.

Plans $25.

-917-

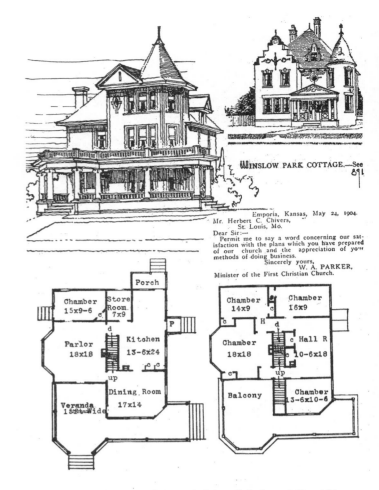

WINSLOW PARK COTTAGE.—See 891

Shasta design 5918, story heights 9-ft 6 and 9, width
over all 46 ft. Plans $10.

-918-

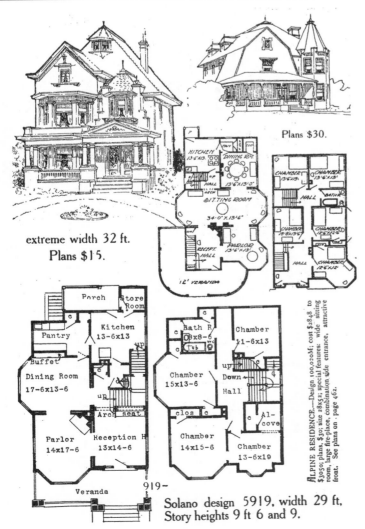

Plans $30.

extreme width 32 ft.
Plans $15.

ALPINE RESIDENCE.—Design 100,020M; cost $2,888 to
$3050; plans, $30; size 28x34; special features: wide sitting
room, large fire-place, combination side entrance, attractive
front. See plans on page 461.

Solano design 5919, width 29 ft,
Story heights 9 ft 6 and 9.

919-

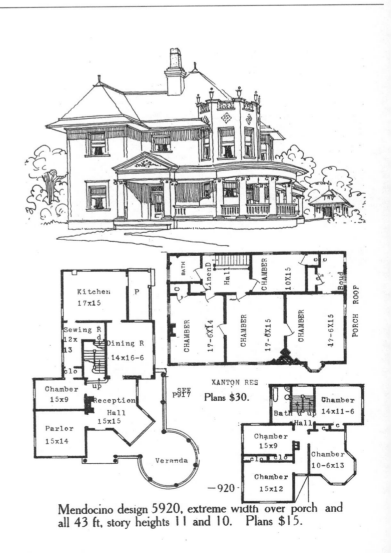

XANTON RES   Plans $30.

SEE
P917

-920-

Mendocino design 5920, extreme width over porch and
all 43 ft, story heights 11 and 10. Plans $15.

YUMA RESIDENCE.—Design 2381-O; cost in frame, $2,299 to $2,498; plans, $20. See page 65.

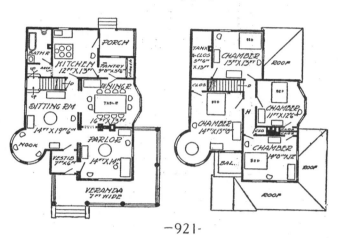

-921-

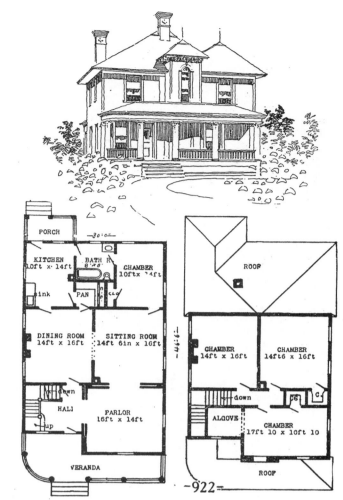

MARILLA RESIDENCE.—Design 2003-N; cost, 2,192 to $2,380; plans, $20.

-922-

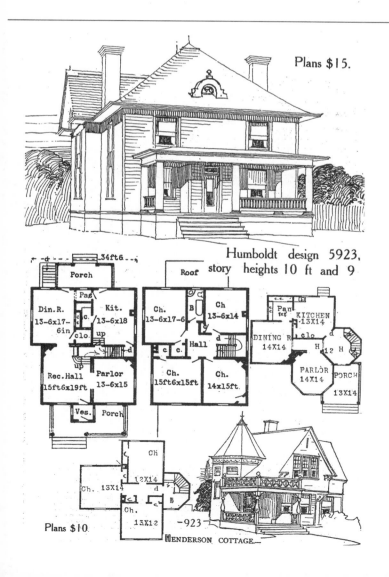

Plans $15.

Humboldt design 5923, story heights 10 ft and 9

Plans $10.

HENDERSON COTTAGE.

-923-

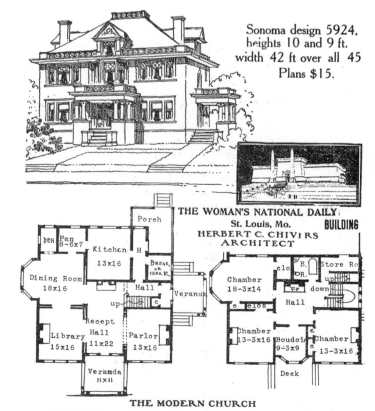

Sonoma design 5924. heights 10 and 9 ft. width 42 ft over all 45 Plans $15.

THE WOMAN'S NATIONAL DAILY BUILDING
St. Louis, Mo.
HERBERT C. CHIVERS ARCHITECT

THE MODERN CHURCH

HE modern church is not a mere meeting house nor is it exclusively a place of worship. It is an institution where many interests center. Architects who follow the old models and attempt to add on the library, the committee room, the reception room, the parlors and the kitchen and to include the various Sunday School rooms and the pastor's study produce patch work. The exterior is incongruous and the interior inconvenient. The design for any structure should be based, not on convention but on requirements. A medieval Gothic Cathedral or parish church met the demands of the time but would be hopelessly inadequate to meet the needs of the present, that is in a moderate-cost structure. When I am given an order for a church I inform myself thoroughly as to the purposes for which it is to be used, the meetings, other than the regular religious services, to be held, and then, according to the amount appropriated for the building. I plan the arrangement of the auditorium and the various apartments with a view not only to securing perfect accommodation but to insuring the noblest architectural effect in the entire structure. Trustees, committees and pastors having in charge the securing of designs for a new church building will do well to communicate with me as I have made a special study of ecclesiastical architecture of all periods, and I have devoted myself especially to the adaptation to modern needs of the various styles associated with religious uses.—Herbert C. Chivers.

-924-

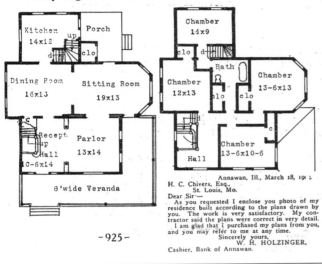

Siskiyou design 5925 width 25 ft, extreme width 36-ft 6, story heights 9 and 8 ft 6.   Plans $15.

Annawan, Ill., March 18, 190 .
H. C. Chivers, Esq.,
                St. Louis, Mo.
Dear Sir—
   As you requested I enclose you photo of my
residence built according to the plans drawn by
you. The work is very satisfactory. My con-
tractor said the plans were correct in very detail.
   I am glad that I purchased my plans from you,
and you may refer to me at any time.
                Sincerely yours,
                        W. H. HOLZINGER,
Cashier, Bank of Annawan.

-925-

Del Norte design 5926, story heights 11 and 10.   Attractive reception hall.   Plans $15.

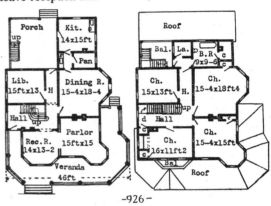

-926-

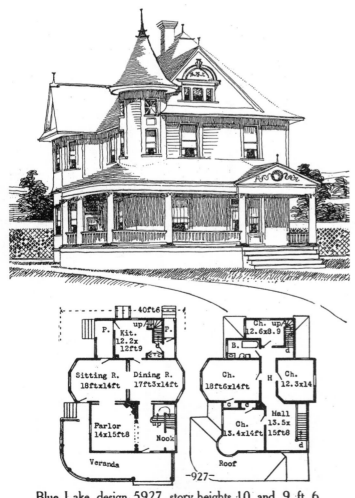

Blue Lake design 5927, story heights 10 and 9 ft 6.
Plans $25.

-927-

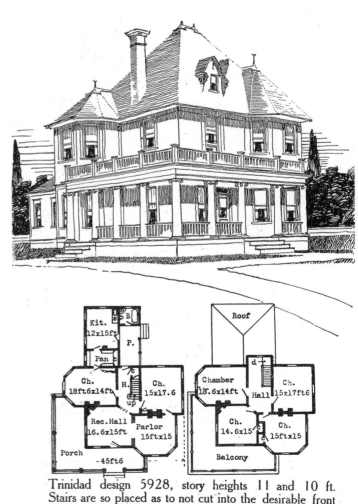

Trinidad design 5928, story heights 11 and 10 ft.
Stairs are so placed as to not cut into the desirable front
portion. Plans $15. -928-

Ferndale design 5929, good front room arrangement. Toilet under stairs.　Plans $12.　Story heights 10 and 9 ft.

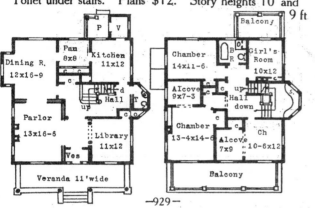

Dining R. 12x16-9	Pan 8x8	Kitchen 11x12
Parlor 13x16-6		d Hall up
	Library 11x12	Ves

P V

Veranda 11'wide

Balcony

Chamber 14x11-6	B R	Girl's Room 10x12
Alcove 9x7-3		up Hall down
Chamber 13-4x14-6	Alcove 7x9	Ch 10-6x12

Balcony

—929—

Sausalito design 5930, story heights 10 and 9-ft 6. Plans $15.　A very striking, yet economical exterior.

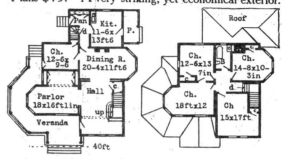

Roof

Ch. 12-6x 9-6	Pan d	Kit. 11-6x 13ft6	P.
Parlor 18x16ft1in	Dining R. 20-4x11ft6	
Veranda	Hall	up

40ft

| Ch. 12-6x13 7in | B | Ch. 14-8x10-3in |
| Ch. 18ftx12 | | Ch 15x17ft. |

Your plans were very satisfactory.—C. I. Cobb, Attleboro, Mass.

-930-

Utah design 5931. Plans $25.

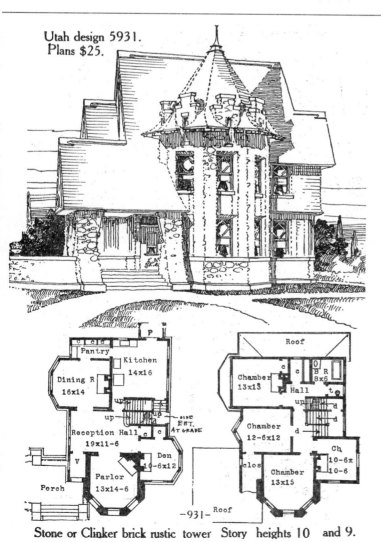

Pantry	P
	Kitchen 14x16
Dining R 16x14	
up	SIDE ENT. AT GRADE
Reception Hall 19x11-6	
	Den 10-6x12
Porch V	Parlor 13x14-6

Roof

Chamber 13x13	B R 8x6
	Hall up
Chamber 12-6x12	d
clos	Ch. 10-6x 10-6
Chamber 13x15	

—931— Roof

Stone or Clinker brick rustic tower　Story heights 10　and 9.

Diablo design 5932, 9 ft 6 story heights, depth 29 ft 6. Very compact plan.　Large chambers.　Plans $10.

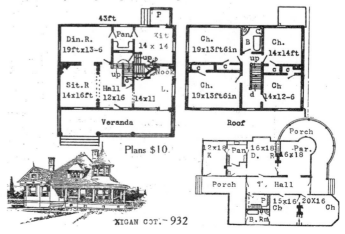

43ft

Din. R. 19ftx13-6	Pan	Kit 14 x 14
	up	Nook
Sit. R. 14x16ft	Hall 12x16 14x11	L.

Veranda

Ch. 19x13ft6in	B	Ch. 14x14ft
	up	
Ch. 19x13ft6in	d	Ch. 14x12-6

Roof

Plans $10.

Porch

12x18 K	Pan	16x18 D. R.	Par. 16x18
Porch		I', Hall	
P	15x16 Ch	20X16 Ch
B. Rm		

XIGAN COT.— 932

MANSTON RESIDENCE.—Design 4511-N; in frame, $2,990 to $3,198; plans, $20; width, 31 ft. 6 in. by 43 ft. 7 in.; width over all, 36 ft. 10 in.; story heights, 10 ft. and 9 ft. 6 in. Manston Residence No. 2, Campbell design, same as above, with porte-cochere on right hand side, with 6 ft. porch in its place extending from front porch to servant's room; bay with hall extending to rear porch; balcony above.

—933—

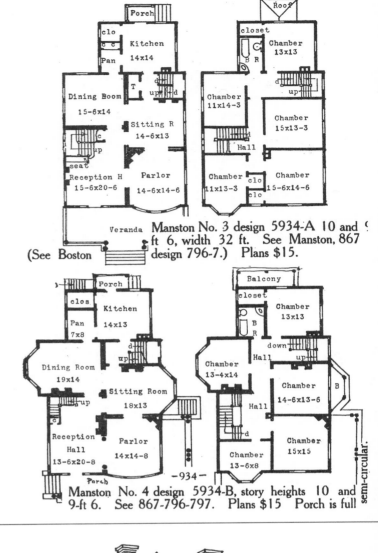

Veranda   Manston No. 3 design 5934-A 10 and 9
ft 6, width 32 ft.   See Manston, 867
(See Boston   design 796-7.)   Plans $15.

—934—

Manston No. 4 design 5934-B, story heights 10 and
9-ft 6.   See 867-796-797.   Plans $15   Porch is full

BURGIN RESIDENCE.—Design 2388-N; cost in frame, $2,990 to $3,290; plans, $30; story heights, 10 ft. and 9 ft. 6 in.; two rooms in attic, 14x17 ft. and 19x13 ft.; large storage room. Special features: Large veranda; combination inside and outside cellar stairs.

A reliable and well-to-do builder will always recommend that you go to an architect and formulate your ideas in a practical way, and to then have regular working plans made, including legally worded specifications, and above all, details of construction, giving box-frames, porches, cornices, etc.

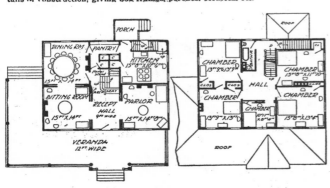

—935—

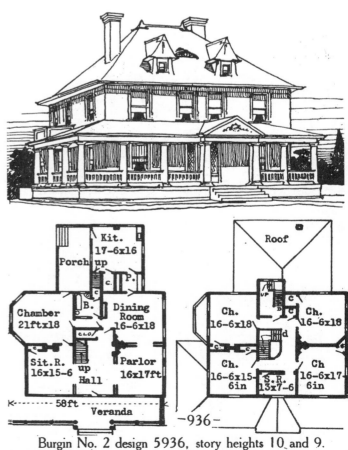

—936—

Burgin No. 2 design 5936, story heights 10 and 9.
See similar design on opposite page.   Large rooms.
Fire-place in hall.   Plans $18.   8-ft side porch.

A building difficulty is perhaps the worst and longest remembered difficulty that a person ever gets into. A builder when he is inclined to be dishonest can cause you more worry and anxiety than most any other entanglement, and his defective work is always before you.

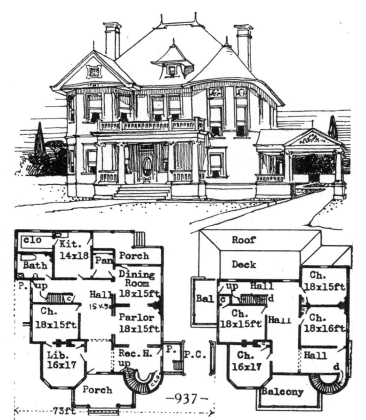

Albuquerque design 5937, large rooms. Story heights 10 and 9-ft 8. Bath on first floor. Suitable for a southern home. A well-proportioned exterior effect. Plans $18.

You can judge the cost of house for a given locality by other houses already built, and the number of rooms they contain. Of course a nearly square house is more economical to build and by improved methods of construction it is safe to figure 10 to 20 per cent less for building from our plans.

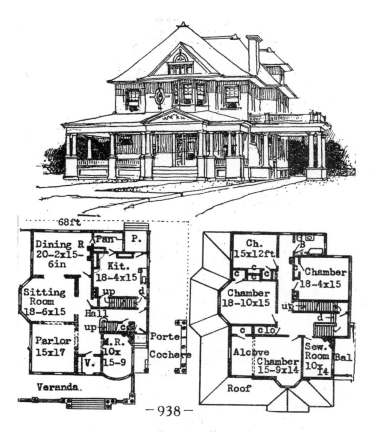

Silver City design 5938, story heights 10 ft each. 8-ft porch along left hand side full length of house. Large rooms. Plans $18.

SUPERINTENDENCE.

My plans are so drawn that any competent builder can follow them. I am very particular about the construction and ornamental details, which save the builder so much time in figuring and laying out his work, and these details are sent in blue print form.

-938-

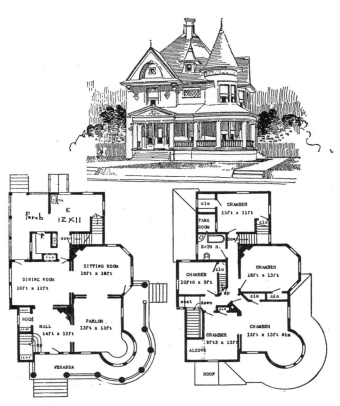

Y ALMER RESIDENCE.—Design 1925-N; cost in frame, $2,280 to $2,340; plans, $15. Yalmer Design No. 2, same as above, with corner closet in place of fire-place in hall; kitchen placed where porch is with direct entrance to dining-room, with window facing front and no serving-pantry. Yalmer Design No. 3, same as above, with octagon porch and tower. Yalmer No. 4, same as above with lavatory off of rear hall; with fire-place in sitting-room only.

-939-

Yalmer design No. 2 5940, in brick. Story heights 9-ft 6 and 9. See design page 939. Plans $15.

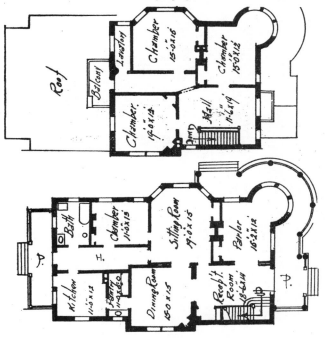

THE FREE SKETCH IDEA.

The profession of architecture has been cheapened somewhat by the practice some architects have made of sending out free sketches. When an architect has come to this in order to secure work, it is reasonably certain that he will take the easiest way to please you, inasmuch as he will not make any effort to improve upon your ideas. When you go to an architect, a lawyer, or a doctor, you do not always care for him to coincide exactly with your ideas. You want advanced ideas, suggestions and conscientious advise. Now with the "free sketch architect," he is after an early adoption of plan, usually an anti-dated stock plan at that, or a poor original made by cheap help. We would rather sell special plans as we like to improve on every job turned out and even on our past work. It stands to reason that no reputable architect can improve his work when he copies one job after another.

-940-

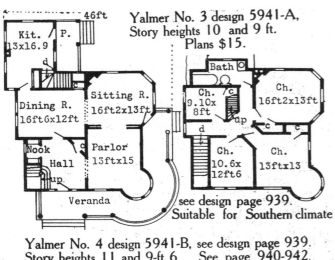

Yalmer No. 3 design 5941-A,
Story heights 10 and 9 ft.
Plans $15.

Kit.
13x16.9   P.

Dining R.
16ft6x12ft

Sitting R.
16ft2x13ft

Nook
Hall   Parlor
up.   13ftx15

Veranda

Bath

Ch.
9.10x
8ft

Ch.
16ft2x13ft

Ch.
10.6x
12ft6

Ch.
13ftx13

see design page 939.
Suitable for Southern climate

Yalmer No. 4 design 5941-B, see design page 939.
Story heights 11 and 9-ft 6.   See page 940-942.

42ft

Kit. up
15ftx11   Porch

Pan.

Dining R.
16ftx13ft

Sitting R.
16.3x13.9

Rec.H
14.3x
13ft6   Parlor
              13x15ft9

Veranda

Ch.
15x11ft

B.R.

Ch.
12.3x9ft

Hall

Ch.
14.3x12.4

Ch.
16.3x13rt9

Ch.
13ftx14

Roof

Plans $15
—941—

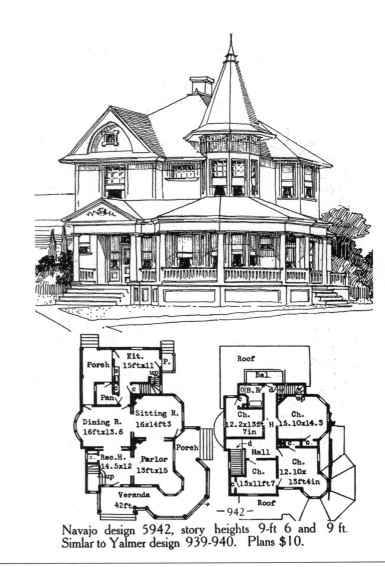

Porch   Kit.
          15ftx11   P.

Pan.

Dining R.
16ftx13.6

Sitting R.
16x14ft3

Rec.H.
14.5x12   Parlor
            13ftx15   Porch

Veranda
42ft

Roof

Bal.

B.R.

Ch.
12.2x13ft
7in

Ch.
15.10x14.3

Hall
Ch.

Ch.
13x11ft7

Ch.
12.10x
13ft4in

Roof

—942—

Navajo design 5942, story heights 9-ft 6 and 9 ft.
Simlar to Yalmer design 939-940.   Plans $10.

SHABBONA RESIDENCE.—Design 2385-N; cost in frame, $2,690 to $2,782; plans, $35. Special features: A very attractive summer house design. The exterior walls are made up of a combination of rough stone and shingles.

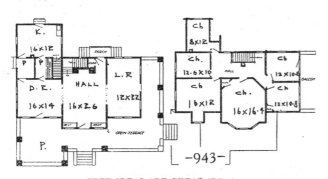

K.
16x12

D.R.
16x14

HALL
16x26

L.R
12x22

PORCH

OPEN TERRACE

P.

ch
8x12

ch
12.6x10

ch
16x12

HALL

ch

ch

cb

16x16.4

12x10.8

cb
12x10.8

BALCONY

—943—

FREE IDEAS ARE CHEAP IDEAS.
It is unreasonable to expect sketches of an architect of his ideas until an order is placed. My ideas are what I charge for and if I offered these free, they would be of little value, I believe.

HUDSON RIVER RESIDENCE.—Design 4222-N; in frame, $3,000 to $3,500; plans, 25; story height, 10 ft. Special features: Attractive stained shingle exterior; castelated design; would appear well on high ground or on an island, with the terraces.

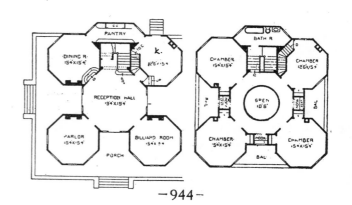

PANTRY

DINING R.
15'4x15'4   K.
                 16'x15'4

RECEPTION HALL
15'4x19'4

PARLOR
15'4x15'4

BILLIARD ROOM
15'4x15'4

PORCH

BATH R

CHAMBER
15'4x15'4

CHAMBER
12x15'4

OPEN
10'8

CHAMBER
15'4x15'4

CHAMBER
15'4x15'4

BAL.

—944—

Jerseyville No. 2 design 5945. See design opposite
page 946. Story heights 9-ft 4 and 9. Plans $30.

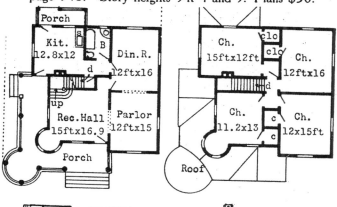

Porch

Kit.
12.8x12   B   Din. R.
                12ftx16
          d
up
Rec. Hall   Parlor
15ftx16.9   12ftx15
        Porch

Ch.   clo
15ftx12ft   clo   Ch.
                    12ftx16
              d
Ch.   Ch.
11.2x13 c   12x15ft
         c
             Roof

–945–

JERSEYVILLE RESIDENCE.—Design 60170; in frame,
$2500 to $3200; plans, $30. See page 65.

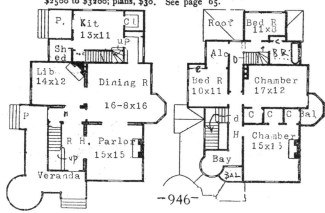

P.   Kit   Cl   Roof   Bed R
     13x11   uP   11x8
Sh   B R
ed
Lib   Alo d
14x12   Dining R   Bed R   Chamber
         16-8x16   10x11   17x12
P   M   c   d C C C Bal
     R H. Parlor   Bay H Chamber
     15x15   15x15
uP
Veranda   Bay   Bal

–946–

PENSYVANIA RESIDENCE.—Design 874M; in frame and
stone, $4,509 to $5,500: plans, $65; story heights, 10 ft. Spec-
ial features; Large varanda: attractive entrance. See page 65.

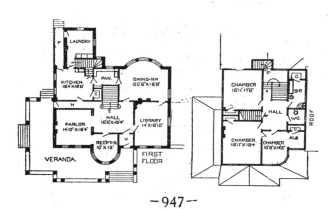

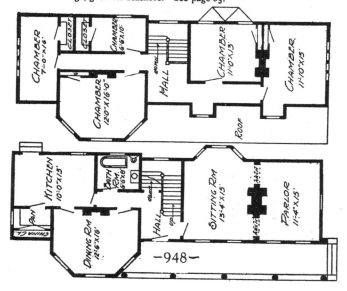

LAKESIDE RESIDENCE.—Design 2998 M; in frame,
$2,090 to $2,198; plans, $25; story heights, 9 ft, 6 in. and
8 ft. 6 in. (full story). Special features: Wide imposing
frontage; good for seashore. See page 65.

–947–

–948–

NEW IDEAS.

This is not all there is to be considered. You want a house with all modern improvements. There are constantly coming out new methods of construction, new building materials, new plumbing and other fixtures, and as a leader in my profession these new features are brought to my early attention.

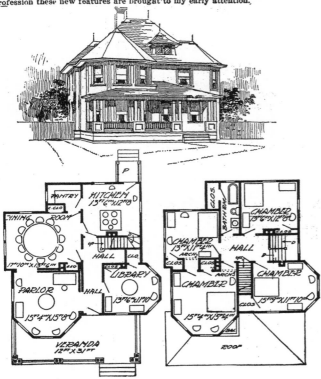

 AKELEE RESIDENCE.—Design 1928-N; cost in frame, $2,380 to $2,490; plans, $25. Central stair arrangement; bay-shaped parlor and library; deep veranda; simple, clean-cut dignified design.

OGDEN RESIDENCE.—Design 865M; in frame, $2290 to $2598; plans, $20; width, 30 ft. 4 in.; width over all, 33 ft. Special features: Large reception hall, 15 ft. 6 in. x 13 ft.; nook in hall; bays in front; vestibule entrance, plain, simple roof treatment. See page 65.

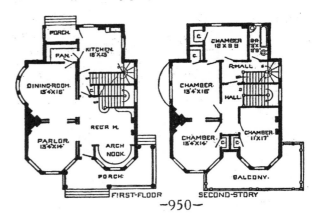

FROSTON RESIDENCE—Design 100,093-O; cost $1,998 to $2,190; story heights, 10 ft. and 9 ft. 6 in, cut down to 6 ft. walls above; plans $15. See page 65.

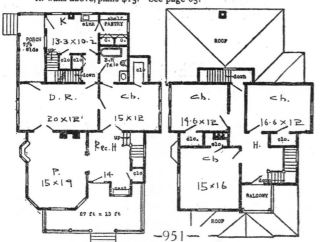

Mural Decoration

AMONG savage nations, so the Ethnologists tell us, decoration precedes dress. Primitive people paint their bodies before they think of clothing them. There seems to be among all races an instinctive love of color and form. In dress, among the most highly civilized human beings, this display is principally confined to the women. The conventional male costume being limited to dull shades and not being especially graceful in outline. But the man who creates a home has an opportunity to exhibit his taste in decoration. No matter how critical his judgment or how delicate his appreciation of values he is almost certain to disappoint himself and all beholders unless he consults his architect and obtains professional advice on this important subject. The painting of the exterior of a wooden house from porch to roof, coloring is not a matter to be lightly considered. The color scheme must be harmonious and few indeed are they who, not having given the subject serious and profound consideration, are capable of producing the proper effects.

The interior requires still subtler thought. The shape of the room, the size of the room, the lighting of the room, the purposes for which the room is to be used must all receive the most careful attention.

In consulting with my clients on this subject I endeavor to embody their ideas, when they are not too incongruous, and to convince them that certain modifications will greatly improve the result. This I seldom have difficulty in doing as my experience in interior and exterior house decoration in stone, brick, tiling, wood-carving and color has been so extensive and so effective that I am able to please the most fastidious and especially to gratify the ever increasing number of house and church builders who desire something original, something different from anything they have ever seen.

C. A. MOSELEY, Vice President.

The Bloomfield Bank

Bloomfield, Mo., 11/12/16

R. C. Chivers, Esq.,
St. Louis, Mo.

Dear Sir:-

The plans of bank and masonic hall were satisfactory to us. The building is practical in all respects. We shall not build the hotel, for which you prepared plans until Spring.

Thanking you, I remain,

Very truly,

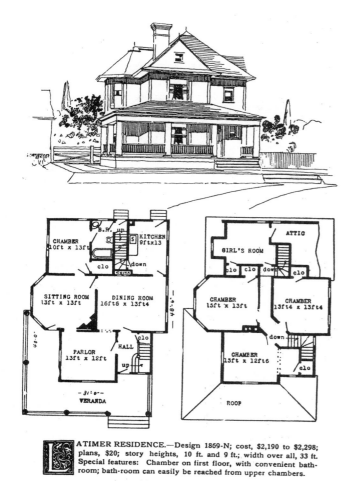

LATIMER RESIDENCE.—Design 1869-N; cost, $2,190 to $2,298; plans, $20; story heights, 10 ft. and 9 ft.; width over all, 33 ft. Special features: Chamber on first floor, with convenient bath-room; bath-room can easily be reached from upper chambers.

See page 953.

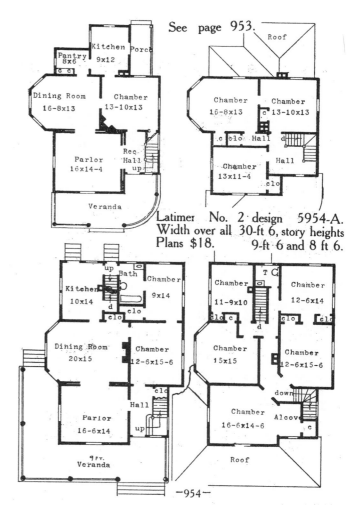

Latimer No. 2 design 5954-A. Width over all 30-ft 6, story heights 9-ft 6 and 8 ft 6. Plans $18.

Latimer No. 2 design 5954-B. See page 953. Width over all 31-ft 6, story heights 10 ft. Plans $20.

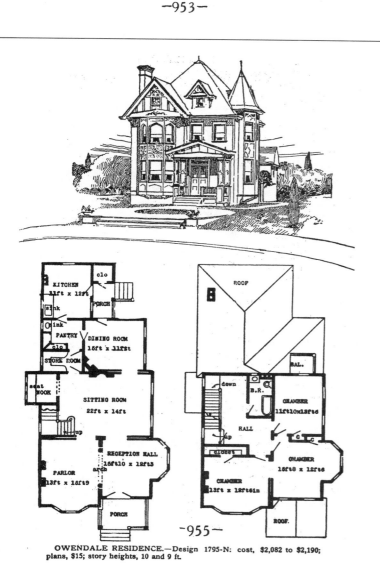

OWENDALE RESIDENCE.—Design 1795-N; cost, $2,082 to $2,190; plans, $15; story heights, 10 and 9 ft.

MORGAN RESIDENCE.—Design 891-O; in frame, $5,500; in brick, $6,000; plans, $55; width over all, 42 ft.; story heights, 10 ft. Special features: Dignified colonial design; large pantry and grocery closet; looks well in buff brick and light green slate.

Morgan Plan No. 2, James design, same as above, with 12.6x11 ft. 2 in. office back of main stairs; with stoop at side; suitable for a physician.

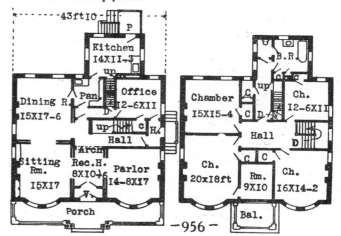

Buenos Ayres design 5957, width 35ft, width over all
50 ft. Story heights 10 and 9 ft. Plans $18.

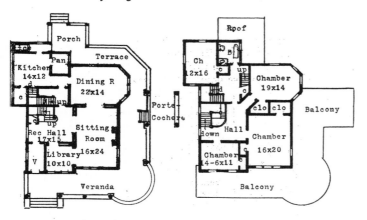

As far as plan is concerned I am very well pleased with it and also the
specifications and think they will be well worth the money.—W. E. Bartsch,
Corning, Cal.

Peacove No. 2 design 5958 in brick, story heights 10
and 9 ft, width 41 ft, width over all 52 ft. See pages
959-960. Plans $40.
(See Peacove design No. 2, page 958.)

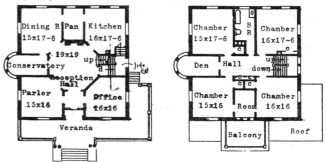

The drawings which you sent were in every way satisfactory.
WILSON & KENNEDY CO., (Lumber), Townson, Md.

BARDOLPH RESIDENCE.—Design 2386M; cost in frame,
$2,498 to $2,792; plans, $25. Special features: Large at-
tractive reception hall 19x19 ft, suitable for a physician; with
plate glass window at conservatory. See page 65.

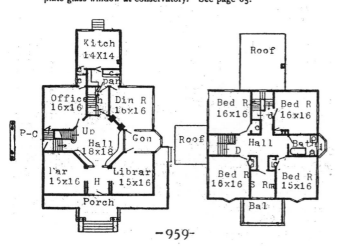

PEACOVE RESIDENCE.—Design 2022-O; cost in frame,
$2,786 to $2,990; plans, $40. Cost in brick, $4,500 to
$5,000; plans, 3 1-2 per cent. on cost.

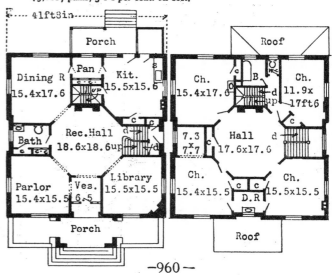

OSBORN RESIDENCE.—Design 32-O; plans $20; cost $2,140 to $2,390; size 31 ft. by 53 ft.; story heights 9 ft. 6 in. and 8 ft. See page 6c.

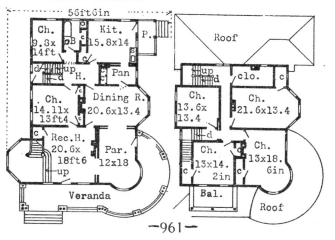

56ft6in

Ch. 9.8x 14ft
Kit. 15.8x14
P.
Roof
Ch. 14.11x 13ft4
Dining R. 20.6x13.4
Ch. 13.6x 13.4
Ch. 21.6x13.4
Rec.H. 20.6x 18ft6
Par. 12x18
Ch. 13x14. 2in
Ch. 13x18. 6in
Veranda
Bal.
Roof
H.
Pan

—961—

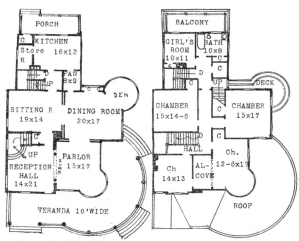

PORCH
KITCHEN 16x12
Store R
PAN 8x9
DEN
SITTING R 19x14
DINING ROOM 20x17
RECEPTION HALL 14x21
PARLOR 15x17
VERANDA 10'WIDE

BALCONY
GIRL'S ROOM 10x11
BATH 10x8
CHAMBER 15x14-6
CHAMBER 15x17
HALL
Ch. 14x13
AL-COVE
Ch. 12-6x17
DECK
ROOF

Longview No. 3 design 5963-A. See opporite page, also general effect in design on page 961. See plans on page 962-963. Story heights 9-ft 6 and 9. Plans $30.

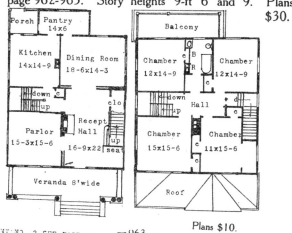

Porch
Pantry 14x6
Kitchen 14x14-9
Dining Room 18-6x14-3
Parlor 15-3x15-6
Recept Hall 16-9x22 seat
clo
Balcony
Chamber 12x14-9
Chamber 12x14-9
Hall
Chamber 15x15-6
Chamber 11x15-6
Veranda 8'wide
Roof

Plans $10.

WILMONT NO. 2 SEE PAGE 203
STORY HEIGHTS 10 & 9-6

—963—

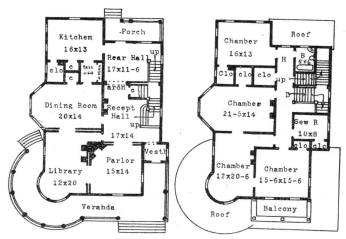

Porch
Kitchen 16x13
clo
Rear Hall 17x11-6
Porch
arch
Dining Room 20x14
Recept Hall 17x14
up
Library 12x20
Parlor 15x14
Vest
Verahda

Roof
Chamber 16x13
Clo clo clo
B
up
Chamber 21-5x14
Sew R 10x8
clo clo
Chamber 12x20-6
Chamber 15-6x15-6
Balcony
Roof

Osborn No. 2 design 5962-A. See page 964, also opposite page and page 963, story heights 11-ft 6 and 10-ft 6. Plans $20.

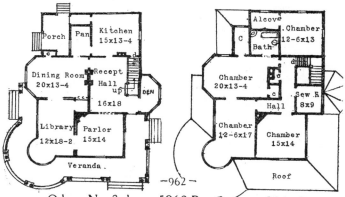

Porch
Pan
Kitchen 15x13-4
Dining Room 20x13-4
Recept Hall up 16x18
DEN
Library 12x18-2
Parlor 15x14
Veranda

Alcove
Chamber 12-6x13
Bath
Chamber 20x13-4
Hall
Sew R 8x9
Chamber 12-6x17
Chamber 15x14
Roof

—962—

Osborn No. 3 design 5962-B. See page 964, also opposite page and page 963, story heights 9-ft 6 and 8-ft 6. Plans $20.

LONGVIEW RESIDENCE.—Design 6-N; cost, $3,000 to $3,890; size, 33 ft. 6 in. by 54 ft. 6 in.; story heights, 11 ft. and 9 ft. 6 in.; plans, $30. Special features: Front of house not cut up by stairs; large attractive balcony. A very attractive design.

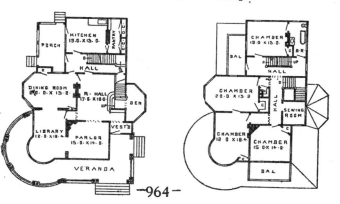

Porch
Kitchen 15-0 X 13-0
Pantry
Dining Room 20-0 X 13-2
R. Hall 17-6 X 18-0
Hall
Den
Library 12-0 X 18-0
Parlor 15-0 X 14-0
Vest
Veranda

Chamber 15-0 X 13-0
Bal
Hall
Chamber 20-0 X 13-2
Sewing Room
Chamber 12-0 X 18-0
Chamber 15-0 X 14-0
Bal

—964—

TIPPECANOE RESIDENCE.—Design 1829-N; cost in frame, $2,980 to $3,590; plans, $25. Special features: Large rooms.

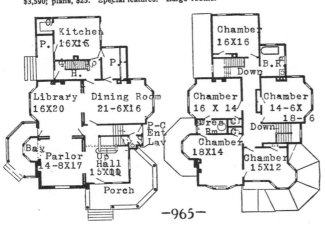

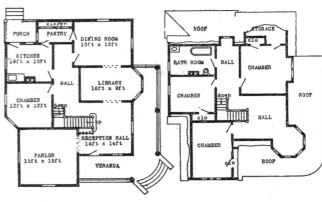

ROCKTOWN RESIDENCE. — Design 2263M; cost in frame, $1,892 to $1,990; plans, $10. See page 65

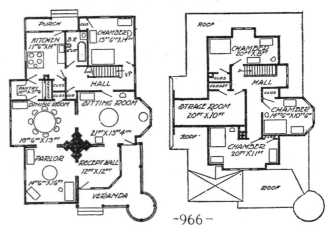

RIFTON RESIDENCE.—Design 2264M; cost in frame, $1,692 to $1,780; plans, $10.

VALLEY FALLS RESIDENCE.—Design 980M; in frame, $2,190 to $2,260; plans, $20. See page 65.

Valley Falls No. 2, Turner design, same as above, with more attractive appearance, with 15x15 parlor; with 15x15 sitting-room; with 8x11 chamber; with closet in place of bath; with combination cellar entrance; with triple fireplace where flues are shown; with bath-room over present location and rear room omitted. See page 65.

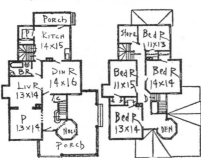

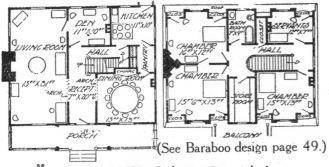

(See Baraboo design page 49.)

HOWELL RESIDENCE.—Design 2252M; cost in frame, $1,192 to $1,240; plans $10; story heights 10 and 9 ft. 6 in. See Brandon Residence for exterior. See page 65.

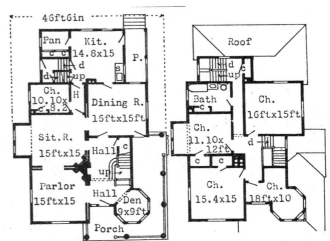

Valley Falls No. 2 design 5968-A. See opposite page 967. Story heights 9-ft 6 and 9. Plans $20.

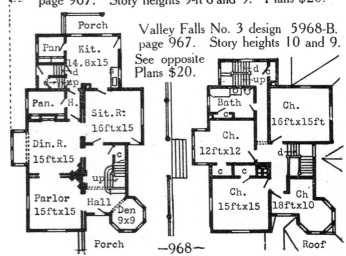

Valley Falls No. 3 design 5968-B. page 967. Story heights 10 and 9. See opposite Plans $20.

Many send plans to my office of a building and I often show them where 10 to 20 per cent can readily be saved, and at the same time secure a more attractive house than at first contemplated. This is where competent advise is of practical value.

Steel and Reinforced Concrete Construction

HERBERT C. CHIVERS, ARCHITECT
—ST. LOUIS—
16TH FLOOR CALL BLDG.
SAN FRANCISCO

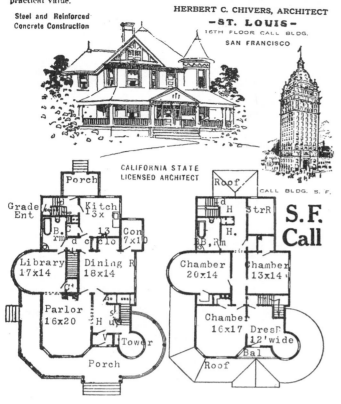

CALIFORNIA STATE LICENSED ARCHITECT

S.F. Call

CALL BLDG. S. F.

GUION RESIDENCE.—Design 2012M; cost in frame $2 890 to $2,990; plans $25. See page 65.

HIGH-CLASS ARCHITECTURAL WORK

HERBERT C. CHIVERS · ARCHITECT

GREENTOWN RESIDENCE.—Design 1833M; cost in frame $2,780 to $2,940; plans $25. Good large rooms; plenty of closets. See page 65.

TO BUILD SATISFACTORILY

In all of my work, I have made it a policy to build as economically and with as little annoyance to the owner as possible.

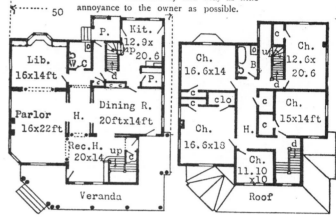

—ARTISTIC HOMES—
IT CONTAINS NO ADVERTISEMENTS

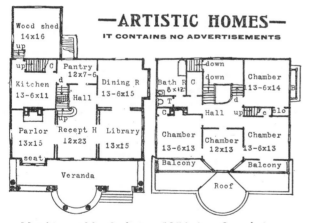

Hutchinson No. 2 design 5971-A. See design page 972. Width 41 ft, story heights 10 and 9. Plans $30.

Selecting an architect, like that of a lawyer or physician, is often a matter of casual acquaintance rather than real qualification

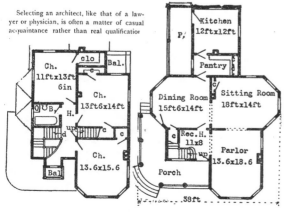

Marleboro No. 16 design 5971. See page 501. Story heights 11 and 9 ft. Plans $10.

HUTCHINSON Residence.—Design 8999-O; in frame, $3,500 to $4,500; plans, $30; width, 44 ft. 4 in. by 40 ft. 2 in.; story heights, 10 ft. and 9 ft. 6 in. Special features: Wide imposing frontage; flower terrace in front; large reception hall; fine arch effect in hall and parlor. Modifications: See index for Hutchinson plan reversed. See page 65.

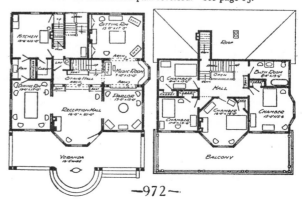

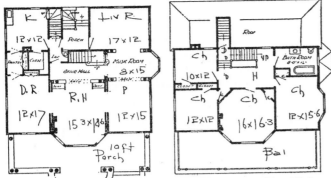

Hutchinson No. 3 design 5973-A, width 42 ft.
See design page 972. See page 971-974. Story
heights 10 and 9-ft 6. Plans $30.

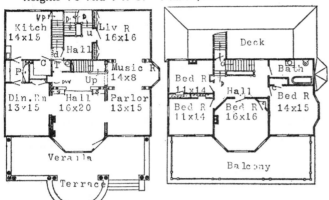

Hutchinson No. 4 design 5973-B, see design page
972. Story heights 10 ft, width 45 ft. See pages
971-974-975-976. Plans $30

PERSONAL CRITICISMS.

Many parties who have plans made elsewhere send their plans to me for
criticism before undertaking the personal responsibility of building, and for
such criticism I make a charge ordinarily of $3, and in all cases will give a fair,
unprejudiced and impartial decision.

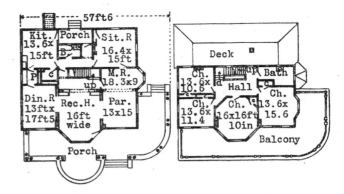

Hutchinson No. 5 design 5974-A. See design 972.
See pages 971-974-975-976. Story heights 10 ft
each. Plans $30.

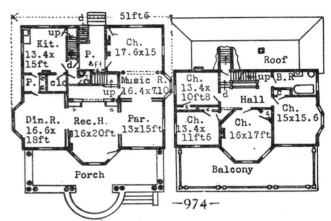

Hutchinson No. 6 design 5974-B, see design 972.
Story heights 10 ft. Lavatory under main stairs.
See design 971-964-975-976 Plans $30.

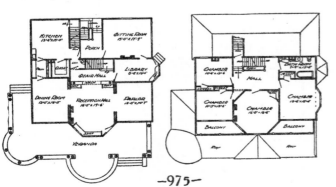

MONTPELIER RESIDENCE.—Bailey design 1827-N; cost, $2,890
to $3,500; plans, $25. Modification No. 2, Barnett design, with
fire-place to sitting-room only; with flues to all rooms; with bath
on first floor, back of main stairs, in place of rear stairs; with
hall between main stairs and bath; with door out onto rear porch
and to sitting-room and kitchen; with front porch extending to library;
with rounded corner; story heights, 10 ft. and 10 ft.

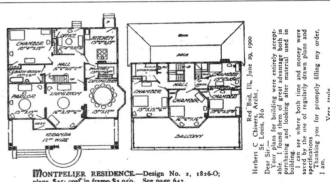

MONTPELIER RESIDENCE.—Design No. 2, 1826-O;
plans $25; cost in frame $3,050. See page 647.

Herbert C. Chivers, St. Louis, Mo.

Red Bud, Ill., June 29, 1900

Dear Sir—Your plans for building were entirely acceptable. I found them of great advantage both in
purchasing and looking after material used in
building.

I can see where both time and money were
saved by the use of regularly drawn plans and
specifications instead of the ordinary method.

Thanking you for promptly filling my order,
I am,

Very truly,
ALFRED D RIESS
(Attorney)

CONFUSING THE CLIENT.

THERE is in every profession, art and trade certain terms more or less clearly understood by
the practitioner, but frequently confusing to the client. Architects are not entirely free from
the failing of trying to impress their patrons by employing technical expressions meaning-
less to the average person about to build. They rattle on glibly about "Early Norman," "Middle English," "Tudor Gothic," "Elizabethan" and "Georgian." They introduce the French
and Italian Renaissance and medieval German, in a way which makes the listener's head swim. They
discourse at length upon the fine points of difference between "New England, New York and Virginia
Colonial." If a church is under consideration the committee is bewildered by the rapid swim and
specifications of Grecian, Roman, Byzantine and the various styles of Gothic architecture. Now all this is reprehensible
nonsense confusing a client with such architectural technic. I have made it a rule to be sure that my
client will understand the meaning of the terms I employ in talking to them. I illustrate every example
cited and when they place the order for the design they know which to expect, except of course,
where the matter is left entirely in my hands and then it is unnecessary to bother their heads about
that which does not interest them. It is results that they want not words.—Herbert C. Chivers.

Hutchinson No. 7 design 5976-A. See design page
972. Width over all 49 ft. Story heights 10 ft 4 and
10. See pages 971 to 975. Plans $30.

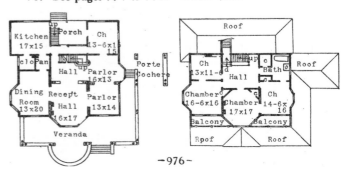

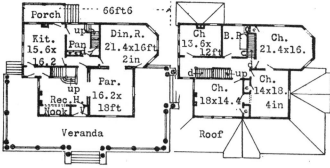

Castorville design 5978-A.
Plans $25.

THE NECESSITY OF PLANS.

It is very necessary that you have complete working drawings, and above all, legally worded specifications. It excites competition among the builders, and then since you know that all builders are figuring on the same basis, you can very readily see how the price of plans and specifications may be saved many times over.

Story heights 10 ft and 9-ft 6,

—977—

THIS volume presents a number of illustrations of exteriors, interiors, and plans of Suburban houses of various design and arrangement. It is for the use of people intending to build, that they may possible find among the many designs and plans, suggestions that will enable them to intelligently describe to the Architect, their wants, tastes, and preferences in the matter of building a house. Any of these designs or plans we are ready to modify to suit individual tastes, or the peculiarities of a building site

CASTORVILLE RESIDENCE.—Design 43-O; cost in brick $5,000 to $5,500; size 47 ft. 6 in. by 51 ft.; story heights 10 ft. and 9 ft. 6 in.; plans $55. Very neat colonial design. SEE 977.

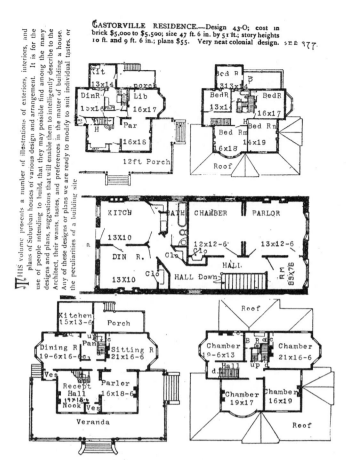

Castorville No. 3 design 5978-B. See design page 977. Story heights 11 ft and 9 ft, width over steps and all 60 ft. Plans $25.

—978—

KALAMAZOO RESIDENCE.—Design 6031M; in frame, $2390 to $2899; plans, $10; width, 33 ft. 4 in., width over all; 36 ft. 4 in.; story heights, 20 ft. and 9 ft. Special features: Large parlor, toilet room, on first floor, side entrance, large pantry; Swiss design. See page 65

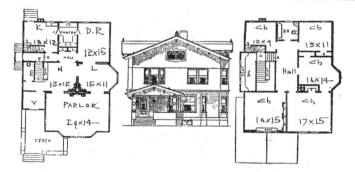

FERRYSBURG COTTAGE.—Design 1934M; cost in frame $1,892 to $1,920; plans $20. See page 65.

—979—

PENFIELD COTTAGE.—Design 1051-O; in frame, $2,480 to $2,650; plans; $25; width over all, 38 ft. 10 in.; story heights, 10 ft. Special features: Stairs reversed, with attractive nook at second landing; grade entrance to cellar; working plans show a porte-cochere adjoining side porch. See page 65.

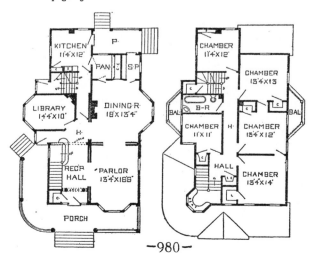

—980—

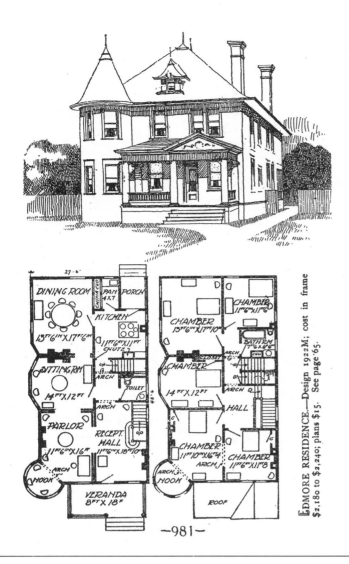

VANLOON RESIDENCE.—Design 1828M; cost in frame $2,980 to $3,240; plans $25. Special features: Large central reception hall. See page 65.

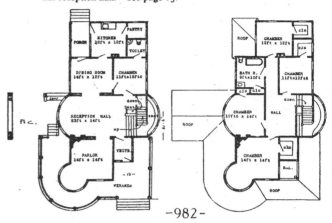

EDMORE RESIDENCE.—Design 1922M; cost in frame $2,180 to $2,240; plans $15. See page 65.

—981—

—982—

Wickenburg design 5983, story heights 9-ft. 6. We have this in either frame or brick. Plans $15.

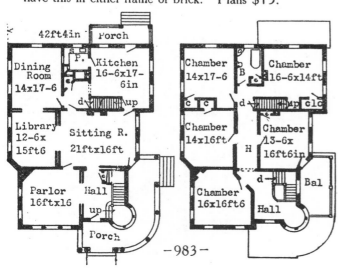

—983—

PENNINGTON RESIDENCE.—Design 1935-O; cost in frame $3,292 to $3,580; plans $40. See revised design page 294. See page 65.

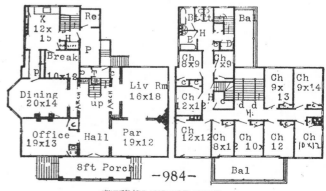

—984—

AFTER PLANS ARE MADE.
After order is placed and plans are made and during construction you may ask as many questions as you choose, and so long as they are put in rotation on separate sheet (with space to write answer) they will be promptly answered, and if you will send photos of house during its construction, we can tell you at a glance if the general design and proportions are being carried out properly.

MELVIN RESIDENCE.—Design 2010M; cost in frame $2,790 to $2,850; plans $35. See page 65.

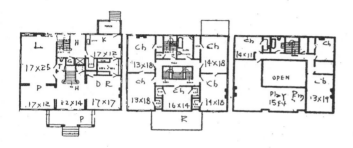

I have not as yet decided to build. However I ought to be satisfied with your work.—Dwight Nutter, Richfield, Utah.
Am pleased with results.—Fred Enfield, Lyons, Neb.

PALEROMA RESIDENCE.—Design 100.047-O; width, 42ft.; cost, $3.598 to $3,989; plans, $40; story heights, 1st 10 ft.; 2d 9 ft. 6 in.; cellar. See page 65.

EFFNER RESIDENCE.—Design 2009M; cost in frame $2,892 to $2,940; plans $35. See page 65.

Oliver Springs, Tenn., July 16, 190-.
Mr Herbert C. Chivers,
St. Louis, Mo.
Dear Sir—
We are well pleased with our home, the plans of which were furnished by you, and every one who calls has only the highest praise for it. It is situated on the railroad and every one passing remarks about is beauty. It IS a thing of beauty and we think we have the prettiest cottage in our end of the state.
Respectfully,
D. C. RICHARDS,
Secretary, Oliver Coal Co

GLOUSTER RESIDENCE.—Design 100,039-O; plans, $15; width 43 ft.; cost $2,499 to $2,987; story heights, 1st 10 ft., 2d 10 ft.

Seattle, Wash., Jan. 3, 190-
Herbert C. Chivers, Architect,
St. Louis, Mo.
Dear Sir:—
A few days ago I sent you several views of the house designed by you. It is one of the representative residences in one of the most desirable locations of the city, and is greatly admired by all who see it. Will send you some interiors if you desire them.
Yours very truly,
(Real Estate) ALBERT M. ROBINSON

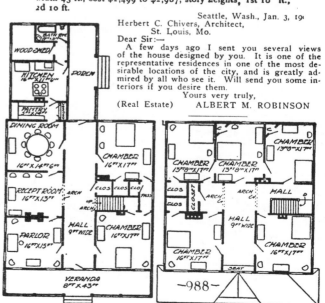

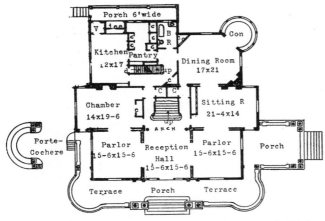

Jolon design 5969, width 49 ft 6, width over all 75 ft, story heights 11 and 10 ft. The building Edition of the Scientific American of October 1904 contains a full-page photograph and plan of this residence as planned by this office.

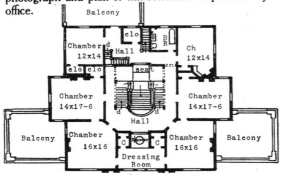

Jolon residence on page 990 is similar, except this design has about twice the width, by reason of porch and porte-cochere at side. Plans 3 1-2 per cent on actual cost.

JOLON RESIDENCE.— Design 100,053-N; plans, 3 1-2 per cent on actual cost; size, 49x48; story heights, 1st, 11 ft., second, 10 ft. Special features: Commodious arrangement; pure colonial design. We have this in a more compact arrangement and two less rooms.

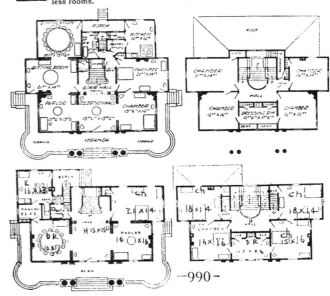

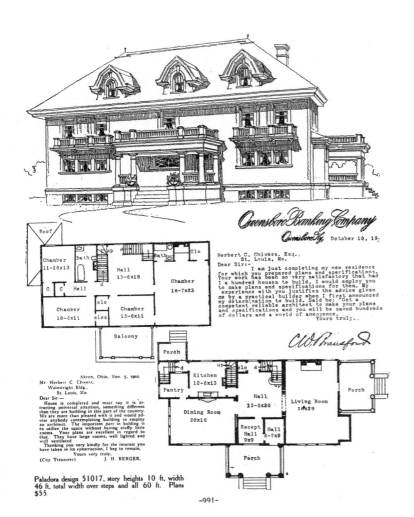

Qwensboro Banking Company

Qwensboro Ky., October 10, 19;

Herbert C. Chivers, Esq.,
St. Louis, Mo.
Dear Sir:—
I am just completing my new residence for which you prepared plans and specifications. Your work has been so very satisfactory that had I a hundred houses to build, I would employ you to make plans and specifications for them. My experience with you justifies the advice given me by a practical builder when I first announced my determination to build. Said he: "Get a competent reliable architect to make your plans and specifications and you will be saved hundreds of dollars and a world of annoyance.
Yours truly,.
C.W. Bransford

Akron, Ohio, Nov. 5, 1902.
Mr. Herbert C. Chivers,
Wainwright Bldg.,
St. Louis, Mo.
Dear Sir:—
House is completed and must say it is attracting universal attention, something different than they are building in this part of the country. We are more than pleased with it and would advise anybody contemplating building to employ an architect. The important part in building is to utilize the space without having studly little rooms. Your plans are excellent in regard to that. They have large rooms, well lighted and well ventilated.
Thanking you very kindly for the interest you have taken in its construction, I beg to remain,
Yours very truly,
(City Treasurer)   J. H. BERGER.

Paladora design 51017, story heights 10 ft, width 46 ft, total width over steps and all 60 ft. Plans $55.

ENDELL RESIDENCE.—Design 100,044M; size, 35 x 45; cost, $3,315; story heights, 1st. 10 ft, 2d 10 ft. Plans, $30. A good Southern house of plain, neat exterior. See page 65.

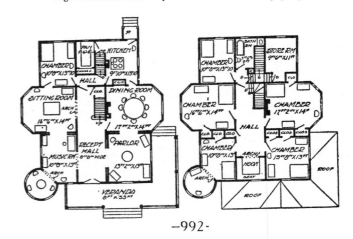

IRA COTTAGE.—Design 1037M; cost in frame, $3,490 to $3,999, (with stone arch and tower $200 extra). Plans, $40: width, 57.4 x 29. Width over all, 67 ft., story heights, 9.4 and 9 ft. in the clear. Special features Bath room on first floor, large convenient rooms; a striking design for a country estate. See page 65.

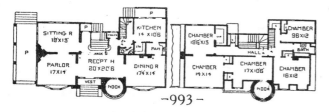

—993—

WHEN ADVICE IS OF VALUE.

When one contemplates building, it is in the early stages of the enterprise that the architect should be selected. The advice and experience of a trustworthy architect should be secured by all means. Do not expect an architect to put his best ideas on paper for you, unless you have a positive understanding with him that he is to do the work. Parties who struggle along themselves with all the preliminary work and later on, employ the architect do not secure full services. The most valuable portion of a plan, and often its most vital points are rendered during its embryotic period.

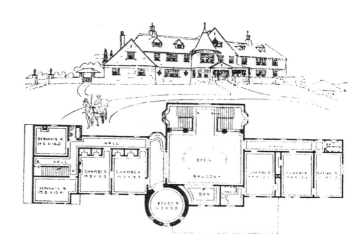

DOUTY.—Design 50M; English country home; cost, $4,590 to $5,680. Plans; $100, with any changes.

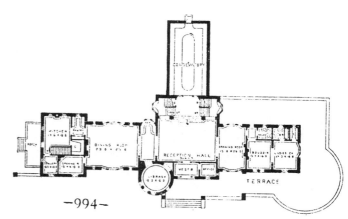

—994—

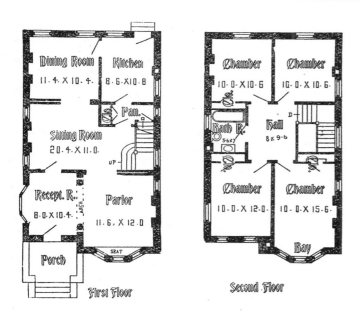

First Floor   Second Floor

DETROIT RESIDENCE.—Design 8258-O; in frame, $1,

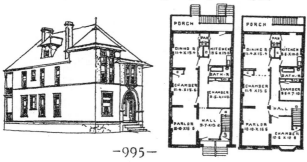

—995—

MILTENBERGER—Design 9066-O; in brick, cost $3,200 to $3,450. Plans $25.

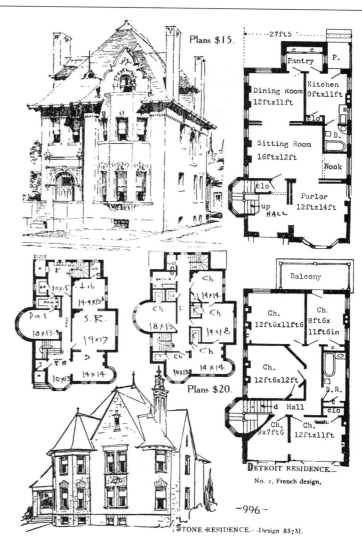

Plans $15.

Plans $20.

DETROIT RESIDENCE.
No. 2, French design,

—996—

STONE RESIDENCE.—Design 887M;

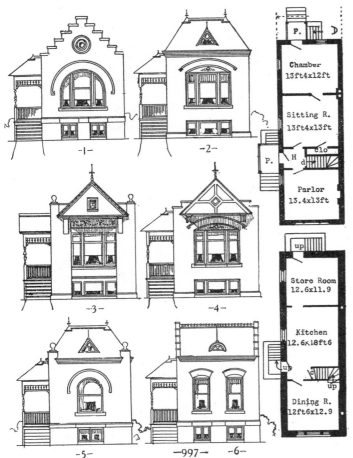

Bricktown design 5998 in brick, width 16 ft, story 10 ft. Basement 8 ft. We can furnish either one of the six exteriors as shown, design No. 1, design No. 2, design No. 3, design No. 4, design No. 5, design No. 6. Plans $5.

(Floor plan labels, design 997:)
- P. D
- Chamber 13ft4x12ft
- Sitting R. 13ft4x13ft
- clo
- P. H up
- Parlor 13.4x13ft
- up
- Store Room 12.6x11.9
- Kitchen 12.6x18ft6
- up
- Dining R. 12ft6x12.9

—1— —2— —3— —4— —5— —997— —6—

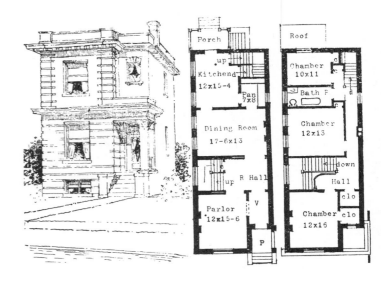

Manzano design 5998-A in brick, width 19 ft, story heights 9 ft 6. Composition or tin roof. Plans $10.

(Floor plan labels:)
- Porch — Roof
- up
- Kitchend 12x15-4
- Pan 7x8
- Chamber 10x11
- Bath R
- Dining Room 17-6x13
- Chamber 12x13
- down
- up R Hall
- Hall
- Parlor 12x15-6
- V
- clo
- Chamber clo 12x16
- P

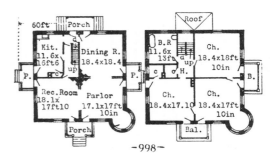

Elrito design 5998-B. Plain brick tower-like house. Story heights 11 and 9 ft. Plans $10.

(Floor plan labels, design 998:)
- 60ft Porch — Roof
- Kit. 11.6x16ft6
- Dining R. 18.4x18.4
- B.R 11.6x13ft
- Ch. 18.4x18ft 10in
- P.
- Rec.Room 18.1x17ft10
- Parlor 17.1x17ft 10in
- Ch. 18.4x17.10 10in
- Ch. 18.4x17ft 10in
- Porch
- Bal.

—998—

998-

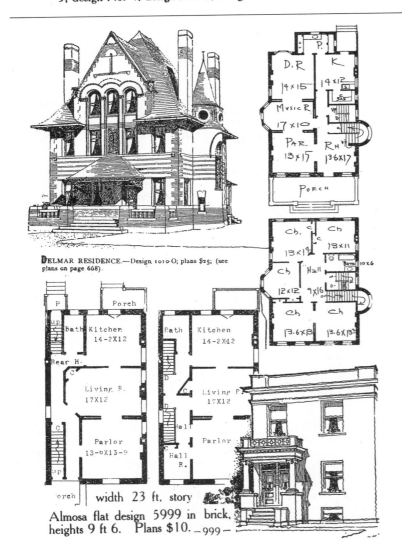

DELMAR RESIDENCE.—Design 1010-O; plans $25; (see plans on page 668).

(Floor plan labels:)
- P.
- D. R. 14x15
- K. 14x12
- Music R. 17x10
- PAR. 13x15
- R H 13.6x17
- PORCH
- Cb. 13x19
- Ch 13x11
- Ch 12x12
- Hall 9x16
- Bath 10x6
- Ch 13.6x13
- Ch 13.6x13

(Lower plan:)
- P
- Porch
- Bath Kitchen 14-2X12
- Bath Kitchen 14-2X12
- Rear H.
- Living R. 17X12
- Living R. 17X12
- Parlor 13-0X13-9
- Parlor
- Hall R.
- Porch

Almosa flat design 5999 in brick, width 23 ft, story heights 9 ft 6. Plans $10.

—999—

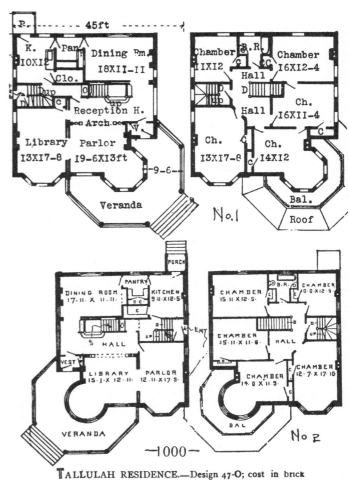

(Floor plan No. 1 labels:)
- P. — 45ft —
- K. 10X12
- Pan
- Dining Rm. 18X11-11
- Chamber 11X12
- B. R.
- Chamber 16X12-4
- Clo.
- Hall
- up
- Reception H.
- Ch. 16XII-4
- Arch
- Hall
- V
- Library 13X17-8
- Parlor 19-6X13ft
- Ch. 13X17-8
- Ch. 14X12
- 9-6
- Veranda
- No.1
- Bal.
- Roof

(Floor plan No. 2 labels:)
- Porch
- Dining Room 17-11 X 11-11
- Pantry
- Kitchen 9-11 X12-5
- Chamber 15-11 X12-5
- B. R.
- Chamber 10-0 X12-5
- Hall
- Ent
- Chamber 15-11 X 11-8
- Hall
- up
- Vest
- Library 15-1 X 12-11
- Parlor 12-11 X17-9
- Chamber 14-0 X 11-9
- Chamber 12-7 X 17-10
- Veranda
- Bal.
- No 2

—1000—

TALLULAH RESIDENCE.—Design 47-O; cost in brick $4,500 to $5,000; plans $40.
TALLULAH RESIDENCE No. 2.—Anthony design with octagon tower with five windows; with fire-place in parlor; with entire plan reversed.

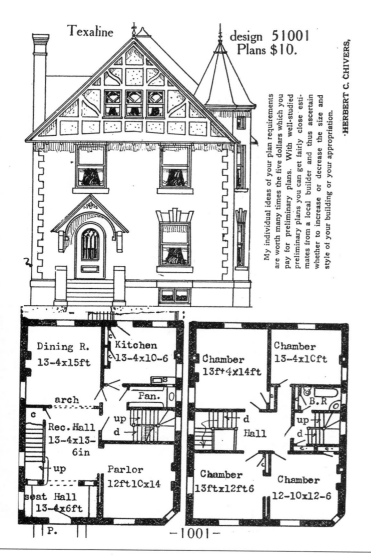

Texaline
design 51001
Plans $10.

—HERBERT C. CHIVERS,

My individual ideas of your plan requirements are worth many times the five dollars which you pay for preliminary plans. With well-studied preliminary plans you can get fairly close estimates from a local builder and thus ascertain whether to increase or decrease the size and style of your building or your appropriation.

Dining R. 13-4x15ft
Kitchen 13-4x10-6
Chamber 13f+4x14ft
Chamber 13-4x1Cft
arch
Pan.
B.R.
c
Rec. Hall 13-4x13-6in
up
d
Hall
up
d
seat Hall 13-4x6ft
Parlor 12ft1Cx14
Chamber 13ftx12ft6
Chamber 12-10x12-6
P.

—1001—

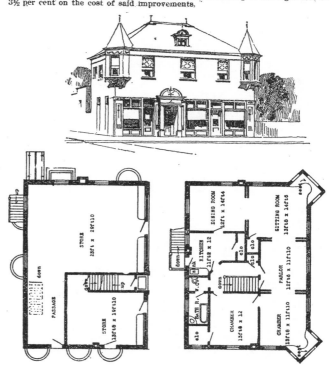

STORE AND FLAT NO. 15.—Cost in brick, $3,250 to $4,000; plans, $50.

—1002—

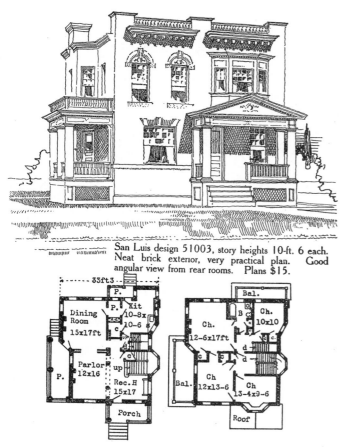

San Luis design 51003, story heights 10-ft. 6 each. Neat brick exterior, very practical plan. Good angular view from rear rooms. Plans $15.

33ft3
Dining Room 15x17ft
P.
Kit 10-8x 10-6
c
Bal.
Ch. 10x10
B
Ch. 12-6x17ft
Parlor 12x16
P.
up
c
Rec.H 15x17
Bal.
Ch 12x13-6
Ch 13-4x9-6
Porch
Roof

—1003—

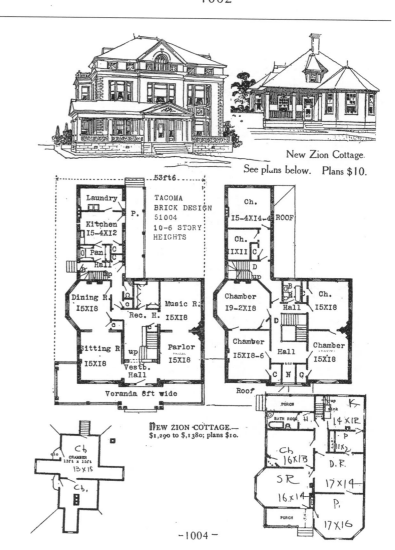

New Zion Cottage.
See plans below. Plans $10.

53ft6
Laundry
P.
Kitchen 15-4x12
TACOMA BRICK DESIGN 51004 10-6 STORY HEIGHTS
Ch. 15-4x14-4
ROOF
Pan.
c
Hall
Ch. 1IX11
c
D
Dining R. 15X18
c
Music R. 15X18
Rec. H. 15X18
Chamber 19-2X18
B R
Hall
Ch. 15X18
D
Sitting R 15X18
up
Parlor 15X18
Vestb. Hall
Chamber 15X18-6
Hall
Chamber 15X18
C N C
Veranda 8ft wide
Roof

NEW ZION COTTAGE.—$1,290 to $1,380; plans $10.

Ch CHAMBER 13ft x 15ft
13 X 15
Ch.

PORCH
up
K
BATH ROOM
H
14 X 12
Ch 16X13
P
D. R.
SR 17X14
16X14
P
PORCH
17X16

—1004—

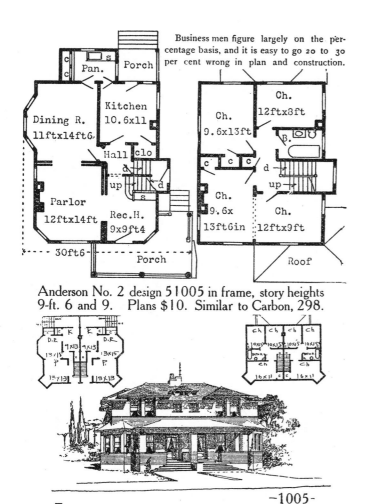

Business men figure largely on the percentage basis, and it is easy to go 20 to 30 per cent wrong in plan and construction.

Anderson No. 2 design 51005 in frame, story heights 9-ft. 6 and 9. Plans $10. Similar to Carbon, 298.

-1005-

THOMAS RESIDENCE.—Design 5000M; cost in frame, $2,600 to $3,000; width over all, 23 ft. 6 in., parlor, 12.6x13 ft.; dining room, 13x13 ft.; kitchen, 9x13 ft. See page 65.

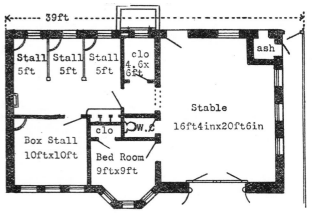

Brick Stable design 51006.

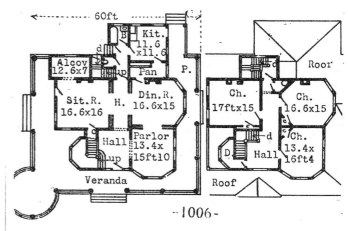

-1006-

Lambsville No. 3 design 51006-B, story heights 10 ft. See 415.

HINTON RESIDENCE.—Design 640-O; in frame, $1490 to $1880; in brick, $1920 to $2440; plans, 25; width, 30 ft. 6 in. x 32 ft. in brick; width over all, 38-ft. Special features; Compact plan, combination stairs, a good corner-lot design.

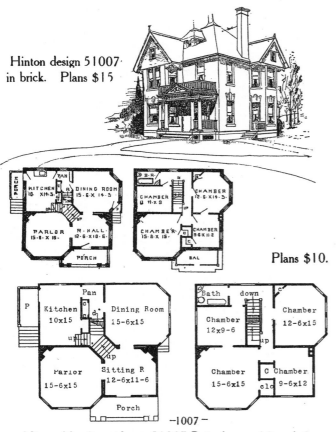

Hinton design 51007 in brick. Plans $15

Plans $10.

-1007-

Hinton No. 2, residence 51007-B in frame, 10 and 9 ft story. Very compact. 29 ft 6 wide, 36 ft over all.

HOLCOMB RESIDENCE. Design 100,024-O; cost $4406 to $4,846; plans, $40; size, 48x61; width over all, 61 ft.; special features: Convenient reception hall; well-ventilated parlor; suitable for a physician's home. See page 65.

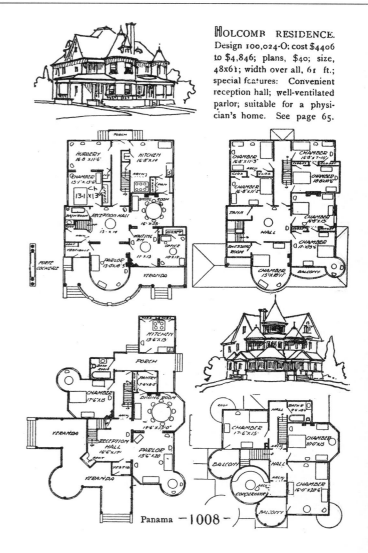

Panama -1008-

My success in planning stylish houses is in readily seeing my clients' desires, producing for them a better home than was expected for a given sum. Preparedness is really the secret of my success

MELROSE RESIDENCE.—Design 100,0030; cost $2862 to $3598; plans, $35; size 26 ft. 6 in. x 45 ft extreme width 23 ft.; special features: large dining room; cozy reception hall; a good corner-lot design, with stained shingle gables. See plans on page 462.

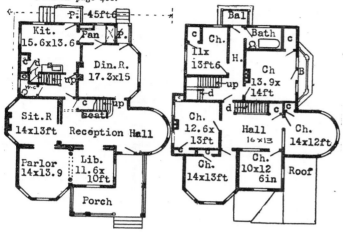

Many send plans to my office of a building and I often show them where 10 to 20 per cent can readily be saved, and at the same time secure a more attractive house than at first contemplated. This is where competent advise is of practical value.

MASCAUTHA RESIDENCE.—Design 2325M; Cost $3,200 to $3590; plans, $59; a neat, simple, modified; Colonial effect. See page 65.

Bes Line Construction Company.

Paid-up Capital, $600,000.00.

General Office, St. Louis Mo.

Perkham,
General Manager

Blackwell, Oklahoma, Nov. 3, 1902

Mr. Herbert C. Chivers,
Wainwright Bldg.,
St. Louis, Mo.

Dear Sir:—

Replying to yours of the 20th will state I have never had any photographs of any of my houses taken. Otherwise, I should be glad to send you one. Will state, however, that the plans you sent me worked out to my entire satisfaction.

Yours truly,

Ed L Perkham
General Manager.

[INDEX]